UNITED NATIONS CONFERENCE ON TRADE AND DEVELOPMENT

UNCTAD

GW00762840

REVIEW
OF MARITIME TRANSPORT

2011

**REPORT BY
THE UNCTAD SECRETARIAT**

UNITED NATIONS
New York and Geneva, 2011

NOTE

The *Review of Maritime Transport* is a recurrent publication prepared by the UNCTAD secretariat since 1968 with the aim of fostering the transparency of maritime markets and analysing relevant developments. Any factual or editorial corrections that may prove necessary, based on comments made by Governments, will be reflected in a corrigendum to be issued subsequently.

*

* *

Symbols of United Nations documents are composed of capital letters combined with figures. Use of such a symbol indicates a reference to a United Nations document.

*

* *

The designations employed and the presentation of the material in this publication do not imply the expression of any opinion whatsoever on the part of the Secretariat of the United Nations concerning the legal status of any country, territory, city or area, or of its authorities, or concerning the delimitation of its frontiers or boundaries.

*

* *

Material in this publication may be freely quoted or reprinted, but acknowledgement is requested, with reference to the document number (see below). A copy of the publication containing the quotation or reprint should be sent to the UNCTAD secretariat at the following address: Palais des Nations, CH-1211 Geneva 10, Switzerland.

UNCTAD/RMT/2011

UNITED NATIONS PUBLICATION

Sales No. E.11.II.D.4

ISBN 978-92-1-112841-3

ISSN 0566-7682

ACKNOWLEDGEMENTS

The *Review of Maritime Transport 2011* was prepared by the Trade Logistics Branch of the Division on Technology and Logistics, UNCTAD, under the coordination of Jan Hoffmann, the supervision of José María Rubiato, and the overall guidance of Anne Miroux. The authors were Regina Asariotis, Hassiba Benamara, Hannes Finkenbrink, Jan Hoffmann, Jennifer Lavelle, Maria Misovicova, Vincent Valentine and Frida Youssef.

Administrative support and the desktop publishing were undertaken by Florence Hudry. Additional desktop publishing was carried out by Wendy Juan. Graphic support was provided by Philippe Terrigeol, and the publication was edited by Daniel Sanderson, Mike Gibson and Lucy Délèze-Black.

This publication was externally reviewed by the following persons:

Chapter 1:	Socrates Leptos-Bourgi, Michael Tamvakis, Liliana Annovazzi-Jakab, Melissa Dawn Newhook.
Chapter 2:	Daniel S.H. Moon, Thomas Pawlik, Tengfei Wang.
Chapter 3:	Herman de Meester, Aleksandra Pieczek.
Chapter 4:	Sharmila Chavaly, Patrick Donner, Ki-Soon Hwang, Peter Marlow, Arvind Mayaram.
Chapter 5:	Mahin Faghfouri, Mia Mikic, André Stochniol.
Chapter 6:	Tilmann Boehme, Kevin Cullinane, Peter Faust, Maximilian Mrotzek, Hong-Oanh (Owen) Nguyen.
Annexes:	Desislava Oblakova.

In addition, the publication was internally reviewed in full by Vladislav Chouvalov.

CONTENTS

Annexes

LIST OF TABLES, FIGURES AND BOXES

Tables   Page

Figures

Boxes

ABBREVIATIONS AND EXPLANATORY NOTES

AEO	Authorized Economic Operator
AfDB	African Development Bank
AGF	United Nations Secretary-General's High-level Advisory Group on Climate Change Financing
AIS	Automatic Identification System
ASEAN	Association of Southeast Asian Nations
ATA	actual time of arrival
ATD	actual time of departure
ATL	actual total loss
BAF	bunker adjustment factor
bcm	billion cubic metres
BDI	Baltic Exchange Dry Index
BIMCO	Baltic and International Maritime Council
BIWTA	Bangladesh Inland Water Transport Authority
BLO	build-lease-own
BMP	best management practice
BOOT	build-own-operate-transfer
BOT	build-operate-transfer
BRIC	Brazil, Russian Federation, India and China
CBDR	Common but Differentiated Responsibilities and Respective Capabilities
CAC	CRCC Africa Construction
cbm	cubic metre
CO2	carbon dioxide
COMESA	Common Market for Eastern and Southern Africa
CMR	Convention on the Contract for the International Carriage of Goods by Road
CRCC	China Railway Construction Corporation
CSAV	Compañía Sudamericana de Vapores
CSR	corporate social responsibility
CTL	constructive total loss
DBO	design-build-operate
DHS	United States Department of Homeland Security
DIS	Danish International Ship Register
DP World	Dubai Ports World
dwt	deadweight ton

ECA	emission control area
ECDIS	electronic chart display and information
ECE	United Nations Economic Commission for Europe
ECLAC	United Nations Economic Commission for Latin America and the Caribbean
EIA	United States Energy Information Administration
EEDI	Energy Efficiency Design Index
EEOI	Energy Efficiency Operational Indicator
EFTA	European Free Trade Association
EORI	Economic Operator Registration and Identification
ESCAP	United Nations Economic and Social Commission for Asia and the Pacific
ETS	emissions trading scheme
EU	European Union
FEU	40-foot equivalent unit
FTK	freight ton-kilometre
GATT	General Agreement on Tariffs and Trade
GDP	gross domestic product
GHG	greenhouse gas
GISIS	Global Integrated Shipping Information System
HPH	Hutchison Port Holdings
HRS	high-risk ship
HSBC	Hongkong and Shanghai Banking Corporation
IACS	International Association of Classification Societies
ICA	Infrastructure Consortium for Africa
ICC	International Chamber of Commerce
ICT	information and communications technology
IEA	International Energy Agency
IGP&I	International Group of P&I Clubs
ILO	International Labour Organization
IMB	International Maritime Bureau
IMO	International Maritime Organization
IRS	Indian Register of Shipping
ISO	International Organization for Standardization
ISPS	International Ship and Port Facilities Security
ISSC	International Ship Security Certificate
IT	information technology
km	kilometre

LDC	least developed country
LLDC	landlocked developing country
LNG	liquefied natural gas
LPG	liquefied petroleum gas
LRS	low-risk ship
LSCI	Liner Shipping Connectivity Index
MARPOL	International Convention for the Prevention of Pollution from Ships
MBM	market-based measure
mbpd	million barrels per day
MDG	Millennium Development Goal
MEPC	Marine Environment Protection Committee
MFN	most favoured nation
MLC	Maritime Labour Convention
MLM	Maritime Liens and Mortgages
MoU	Memorandum of Understanding
MSC	IMO Maritime Safety Committee
MSM	Maritime Security Manual
MSWG	Working Group on Maritime Security
n.a.	not available
NEPAD	New Partnership for Africa's Development
NIS	Norwegian International Ship Register
NYPE	New York Produce Exchange
OECD	Organization for Economic Cooperation and Development
OECS	Organization of Eastern Caribbean States
OPEC	Organization of the Petroleum Exporting Countries
P&I	protection and indemnity
PFSP	Port Facility Security Plan
PFSO	Port Facility Security Officer
PIDA	Programme for Infrastructure Development in Africa
PPP	public–private partnership
PSA	Port of Singapore Authority
RAKIA	Ras Al Khaimah Investment Authority
ro-ro	roll-on roll-off
RSO	Recognized Security Organization
RTA	regional trade agreement
SACU	Southern African Customs Union

SADC	Southern African Development Community
SAFE	Framework of Standards to Secure and Facilitate Global Trade
SAR	Special Administrative Region
SEEMP	Ship Energy Efficiency Management Plan
SIDS	small island developing State
SIN	ship identification number
SMEs	small and medium-sized enterprises
SoCPF	Statement of Compliance of the Port Facility
SOLAS	International Convention for the Safety of Life at Sea
SRS	standard-risk ship
SSA	Ship Security Assessment
SSAS	Ship Security Alert System
SSI	Sustainable Shipping Initiative
SSO	Ship Security Officer
SSP	Ship Security Plan
STCW	International Convention on Standards of Training, Certification and Watchkeeping for Seafarers
SVS–IP	Small Vessel Security Implementation Plan
SVSS	Small Vessel Security Strategy
TEU	20-foot equivalent unit
THC	terminal handling charge
ULCC	ultra-large crude carrier
UNCITRAL	United Nations Commission on International Trade Law
UNCLOS	United Nations Convention on the Law of the Sea
UNDOALOS	United Nations Division for Ocean Affairs and the Law of the Sea
UNFCCC	United Nations Framework Convention on Climate Change
UN-OHRLLS	United Nations Office of the High Representative for the Least Developed Countries, Landlocked Developing Countries and Small Island Developing States
VES	Vessel Efficiency System
VHSS	Hamburg Shipbrokers' Association
VIMSAS	Voluntary IMO Member State Audit Scheme
VLCC	very large crude carrier
VLOC	very large ore carrier
WCO	World Customs Organization
WS	Worldscale
WTO	World Trade Organization

* * *

Explanatory notes

- The Review of Maritime Transport 2011 covers data and events from January 2010 until June 2011. Where possible, every effort has been made to reflect more recent developments.

- All references to dollars ($) are to United States dollars, unless otherwise stated.

- Unless otherwise stated, "ton" means metric ton (1,000 kg) and "mile" means nautical mile.

- Because of rounding, details and percentages presented in tables do not necessarily add up to the totals.

- Two dots (..) indicate that data are not available or are not separately reported.

- A hyphen (-) signifies that the amount is nil or less than half the unit used.

- In the tables and the text, the terms *countries* and *economies* refer to countries, territories or areas.

- Since 2007, the presentation of countries in the *Review of Maritime Transport* has been different from that in previous editions. Since 2007, the new classification is that used by the Statistics Division, United Nations Department of Economic and Social Affairs, and by UNCTAD in its Handbook of Statistics. For the purpose of statistical analysis, countries and territories are grouped by economic criteria into three categories, which are further divided into geographical regions. The main categories are developed economies, developing economies, and transition economies. See annex I for a detailed breakdown of the new groupings. Any comparison with data in pre-2007 editions of the *Review of Maritime Transport* should therefore be handled with care.

Vessel groupings used in the *Review of Maritime Transport*

As in the previous year's Review, five vessel groupings have been used throughout most shipping tables in this year's edition. The cut-off point for all tables, based on data from Lloyd's Register – Fairplay, is 100 gross tons (GT), except those tables dealing with ownership, where the cut-off level is 1,000 GT. The groups aggregate 20 principal types of vessel category, as noted below.

Review group	Constituent ship types
Oil tankers	Oil tankers
Bulk carriers	Ore and bulk carriers, ore/bulk/oil carriers
General cargo	Refrigerated cargo, specialized cargo, roll on-roll off (ro-ro) cargo, general cargo (single- and multi-deck), general cargo/passenger
Container ships	Fully cellular
Other ships	Oil/chemical tankers, chemical tankers, other tankers, liquefied gas carriers, passenger ro-ro, passenger, tank barges, general cargo barges, fishing, offshore supply, and all other types
Total all ships	Includes all the above-mentioned vessel types

Approximate vessel size groups referred to in the *Review of Maritime Transport*, according to generally used shipping terminology

Crude oil tankers

ULCC, double-hull	350,000 dwt plus
ULCC, single hull	320,000 dwt plus
VLCC, double-hull	200,000–349,999 dwt
VLCC, single hull	200,000–319,999 dwt
Suezmax crude tanker	125,000–199,999 dwt
Aframax crude tanker	80,000– 124,999 dwt; moulded breadth > 32.31m
Panamax crude tanker	50,000– 79,999 dwt; moulded breadth < 32.31m

Dry bulk and ore carriers

Large capesize bulk carrier	150,000 dwt plus
Small capesize bulk carrier	80,000–149,999 dwt; moulded breadth > 32.31 m
Panamax bulk carrier	55,000–84,999 dwt; moulded breadth < 32.31 m
Handymax bulk carrier	35,000–54,999 dwt
Handysize bulk carrier	10,000–34,999 dwt

Ore/oil Carrier

VLOO	200,000 dwt

Container ships

Post-Panamax container ship	moulded breadth > 32.31 m
Panamax container ship	moulded breadth < 32.31 m

Source: IHS Fairplay.

EXECUTIVE SUMMARY

Developments in international seaborne trade

The world economic situation has brightened in 2010. However, multiple risks threaten to undermine the prospects of a sustained recovery and a stable world economy – including sovereign debt problems in many developed regions, and fiscal austerity. These risks are further magnified by the extraordinary shocks that have occurred in 2011, which have included natural disasters and political unrest, as well as rising and volatile energy and commodity prices. Given that for shipping, all stands and falls with worldwide macroeconomic conditions, the developments in world seaborne trade mirrored the performance of the wider economy. After contracting in 2009, international shipping experienced an upswing in demand in 2010, and recorded a positive turnaround in seaborne trade volumes especially in the dry bulk and container trade segments. However, the outlook remains fragile, as seaborne trade is subject to the same uncertainties and shocks that face the world economy.

Structure, ownership and registration of the world fleet

The year 2010 saw record deliveries of new tonnage, 28 per cent higher than in 2009, resulting in an 8.6 per cent growth in the world fleet. Deliveries amounted to 11.7 per cent of the existing fleet; the previous peak had been in 1974, when deliveries amounted to approximately 11 per cent of the existing fleet.

The world merchant fleet reached almost 1.4 billion deadweight tons in January 2011, an increase of 120 million dwt over 2010. New deliveries stood at 150 million dwt, against demolitions and other withdrawals from the market of approximately 30 million dwt. Since 2005, the dry bulk fleet has almost doubled, and the containership fleet has nearly tripled. The share of foreign-flagged tonnage reached an estimated 68 per cent in January 2011.

The surge in vessel supply is the result of orders placed before the economic crisis. This, combined with lower-than-expected demand, has led to a situation where there is an excess supply of shipping capacity. In the dry bulk and container sectors especially, analysts forecast an oversupply of tonnage in coming years. In both sectors, recent and upcoming record-sized newbuildings pose a further challenge to owners, who will need to find cargo to fill their ships.

Price of vessels and freight rates

The price of newbuildings was lower for all vessels types in 2010, reflecting market views that the capacity of the world fleet is sufficient to meet world trade in the short-term. In the second-hand market, the results were mixed. The larger oil tankers held their value, while smaller tankers and specialized product tankers declined in value. In the dry bulk sector, the price of medium-sized Panamax vessels decreased, while the price of smaller and larger vessels increased. The price for all sizes of second-hand container ships also rose in value during 2010 as trade volumes recovered.

Freight rates in the tanker sector performed better than the previous year, rising between 30 and 50 per cent by the end of 2010. Every month for all vessel types was better than the corresponding month for the previous year. However, tanker freight rates in general still remained depressed, compared with the years immediately preceding the 2008 peak. Freight rates in the dry bulk sector performed well for the first half of the year, but the Baltic Exchange Dry Index (BDI) lost more than half its value from the end of May 2010 to mid-July 2010. A partial rally occurred in August 2010 before the Index continued its downward trajectory. Between May 2010 and May 2011, the BDI declined by about two thirds. Container freight rates in 2010 witnessed a major transformation brought about by a boost in exports and measures introduced by shipowners to limit vessel oversupply. The result can be seen in the New ConTex Index, which tripled in value from early 2010 to mid-2011.

Port and multimodal transport developments

World container port throughput increased by an estimated 13.3 per cent to 531.4 million TEUs in 2010 after stumbling briefly in 2009. Chinese mainland ports continued to increase their share of total world container port throughput to 24.2 per cent. The

UNCTAD Liner Shipping Connectivity Index (LSCI) reveals that China continues its lead as the single most connected country, followed by Hong Kong SAR, Singapore and Germany. In 2011, 91 countries increased their LSCI ranking over 2010, 6 saw no change, and 65 recorded a decrease. In 2010, the rail freight sector grew by 7.2 per cent to reach 9,843 billion freight ton kilometres (FTKs). The road freight sector grew by 7.8 per cent in 2010 over the previous year with volumes reaching 9,721 billion FTKs.

Legal issues and regulatory developments

Important legal issues and recent regulatory developments in the fileds of transport and trade facilitation included the entry into force on 14 September 2011 of the International Convention on Arrest of Ships, which had been adopted at a joint United Nations/International Maritime Organization (IMO) Diplomatic Conference held in 1999 under the auspices of UNCTAD. Moreover, during 2010 and the first half of 2011, important discussions continued at IMO regarding the scope and content of a possible international regime to control greenhouse gas (GHG) emissions from international shipping. Finally, there were a number of regulatory developments in relation to maritime security and safety, as well as in respect of trade facilitation agreements at both the multilateral and the regional levels.

Developing countries' participation in Maritime Businesses

Developing countries are expanding their participation in a range of different maritime businesses. They already hold strong positions in ship scrapping, ship registration, and the supply of seafarers, and they have growing market shares in more capital-intensive or technologically advanced maritime sectors such as ship construction and shipowning. China and the Republic of Korea between them built 72.4 per cent of world ship capacity (dwt) in 2010, and 9 of the 20 largest countries in shipowning are developing countries. Ship financing, insurance services and vessel classification are among the few maritime sectors that have so far been dominated by the more advanced economies. However, here, too, developing countries have recently demonstrated their potential to become major market players. India, for instance, joined the International Association of Classification Societies; through this it gains easier access to the global ship classification market. China now has two of the world's largest banks in ship financing.

DEVELOPMENTS IN INTERNATIONAL SEABORNE TRADE

CHAPTER 1

The world economic situation has brightened in 2010. However, multiple risks threaten to undermine the prospects of a sustained recovery and a stable world economy – including sovereign debt problems in many developed regions, and fiscal austerity. These risks are further magnified by the extraordinary shocks that have occurred in 2011, which have included natural disasters and political unrest, as well as rising and volatile energy and commodity prices. Given that for shipping, all stands and falls with worldwide macroeconomic conditions, the developments in world seaborne trade mirrored the performance of the wider economy. After contracting in 2009, international shipping experienced an upswing in demand in 2010, and recorded a positive turnaround in seaborne trade volumes especially in the dry bulk and container trade segments. However, the outlook remains fragile, as seaborne trade is subject to the same uncertainties and shocks that face the world economy.

This chapter covers developments from January 2010 to June 2011. Section A reviews the overall performance of the global economy and world merchandise trade. Section B considers developments in world seaborne trade volumes and looks at trends unfolding in the economic sectors and activities that generate demand for shipping services, including oil and gas, mining, agriculture and steel production. Section C highlights some developments that are currently affecting maritime transport and have the potential to deeply reshape the landscape of international shipping and seaborne trade.

A. WORLD ECONOMIC SITUATION AND PROSPECTS[1]

1. World economic growth[2]

In 2010, the world economy embarked on a recovery path with gross domestic product (GDP) growing at 3.9 per cent over the previous year (table 1.1). The stimulus measures taken by governments at the onset of the crisis helped jump-start growth. However, the effect of these measures started to fade away as governments initiated a shift towards fiscal consolidation. The end of the inventory cycle, the downside risks in developed economies and the dampening effect on GDP growth of rising energy prices, with Brent crude oil prices averaging $80 per barrel in 2010 against $62 per barrel in 2009,[3] have combined to also slow down growth in the second half of the year.

In 2010, developed economies recorded positive growth, with their GDP expanding by 2.5 per cent. The United States and Japan performed better than the European Union, growing respectively by 2.9 per cent, 4.0 per cent and 1.8 per cent. Developing economies and economies in transition continued to drive the global recovery with the rebound being led by large emerging economies, in particular China (10.3 per cent), India (8.6 per cent) and Brazil (7.5 per cent). Almost unburdened by the financial crisis and consequent economic downturn, China, India and other developing countries resumed their expansion by generating their own growth instead of relying on exports to developed economies' markets. While the Unites States remains the main source of import demand for Asia, China has evolved into an independent engine of regional growth and a larger source of final demand for a number of emerging developing economies, including the Philippines, the Republic of Korea and Taiwan, Province of China.[4]

The lead taken by developing countries in powering global growth reflects a shake-up in the world's economic order which has taken decades to unfold. UNCTAD data show that the share of developing countries in the global economic output rose from about 17 per cent in 1980 to over 28 per cent in 2010, raising the influence of these countries in the world's economic performance. In 2010, China overtook Japan as the world's second biggest economy (in nominal terms) and is leading the transformation together with some of the world's fastest-growing economies such as India and Indonesia. An important economic milestone in 2010 was Brazil's ranking as the world's seventh largest economy after surpassing Italy.[5] Goldman Sachs is now predicting that the BRIC countries (Brazil, Russian Federation, India and China) will overtake the G–7 countries in size of their economies by 2018, i.e. much sooner than its original prediction of 2040 made a decade ago.[6]

The overall strong performance of developing countries as a group conceals differences between countries and groupings. For example, GDP growth in South Africa (2.8 per cent) was much lower than the rates recorded by China, India and Brazil. Similarly, the recovery in many of the least developed countries (LDCs) remained below their potential with GDP growth (4.8 per cent) not returning to its pre-crisis levels.

The economic downturn and consequent increase in unemployment, together with the drop in social spending, can cause a serious setback to social equity and poverty alleviation. Although some ground has been gained, between 2007 and the end of 2009, at least 30 million jobs are estimated to have been lost worldwide as a result of the global financial crisis.[7] The global economy still needs to create at least another 22 million jobs to return to the pre-crisis level of global employment.[8] It is further estimated that 47 million to 84 million more people are falling into or staying in extreme poverty because of the global crisis.[9] While these considerations are not specific to the LDCs, they are nevertheless more detrimental for these countries in view of their inherent vulnerability to any erosion in economic and development gains achieved as part of efforts to attain the Millennium Development Goals (MDGs).

Trends in world industrial production – a leading indicator of demand for maritime transport services – mirrored the developments in world GDP. The industrial production index published by the Organization for Economic Cooperation and Development (OECD) shows that the index for OECD countries, with 1990 as the base year, fell in 2009, before rebounding in 2010 for both OECD and non-OECD countries. The pace-setters were the Republic of Korea and China, with their 2010 industrial production expanding by 17.2 per cent and 15.7 per cent, respectively.[10]

The strong correlation between industrial activity, GDP growth, merchandise and seaborne trade continues unabated, as shown in figure 1.1. The deep contraction of 2009 is followed by a V-shaped recovery

Table 1.1. World economic growth, 2007–2011[a] *(annual percentage change)*

Region/country	1991–2004 Average	2007	2008	2009	2010[b]	2011[c]
WORLD	2.9	4.0	1.7	-2.1	3.9	3.1
Developed economies	2.6	2.6	0.3	-3.6	2.5	1.8
of which:						
United States	3.4	2.1	0.4	-2.6	2.9	2.3
Japan	1.0	2.4	-1.2	-6.3	4.0	-0.4
European Union (27)	2.3	3.0	0.5	-4.2	1.8	1.9
of which:						
Germany	1.6	2.7	1.0	-4.7	3.6	3.0
France	2.1	2.4	0.2	-2.6	1.5	2.1
Italy	1.5	1.5	-1.3	-5.0	1	0.9
United Kingdom	2.9	2.7	-0.1	-4.9	1.3	1.3
Developing economies	4.7	8.0	5.4	2.5	7.4	6.3
of which:						
China	9.9	14.2	9.6	9.1	10.3	9.4
India	5.9	9.6	5.1	7.0	8.6	8.1
Brazil	2.6	6.1	5.2	-0.6	7.5	4.0
South Africa	2.5	5.5	3.7	-1.8	2.8	4.0
Least Developed Countries (LDCs)	4.6	8.5	6.7	4.5	4.8	5.2
Transition economies	-1.0	8.6	5.4	-6.7	4.1	4.4
of which:						
Russian Federation	-1.0	8.5	5.6	-7.9	4.0	4.4

Sources: UNCTAD secretariat calculations, based on United Nations Department of Economic and Social Affairs (UN–DESA), National Accounts Main Aggregates database, and World Economic Situation and Prospects (WESP) 2011: Mid-year Update; Economic Commission for Latin America and the Caribbean (ECLAC), 2011; OECD. Stat database; and national sources.

[a]   Calculations for country aggregates are based on GDP at constant 2005 dollars.

[b]   Preliminary estimates.

[c]   Forecasts.

in all indicators with signs of some stabilization in 2011. Interestingly, some decoupling between GDP growth and the industrial production, reflecting partly the growing contribution of services to GDP, can be observed. Equally, seaborne trade grows faster than both the industrial production and GDP, also reflecting, in particular the rapid expansion in container trade which carries semi-finished and manufactured goods (consumer goods and durables).

The world recovery is set to continue, albeit at a slower pace, with world GDP projected to grow by 3.1 per cent in 2011. While GDP growth in all economies is expected to decelerate, the recovery continues to be driven by emerging developing markets. However, these projections are subject to many downside risks which can derail growth. These include renewed stresses in the euro area, sovereign risks, high unemployment in advanced economies, rising food and commodity prices, the risk of a rise in trade protectionism, inflationary pressures in emerging markets, and the end of the stimulus funding impact as all countries, with the exception of the United States, proceed with fiscal consolidation. In addition, the world economy is facing new problems stemming

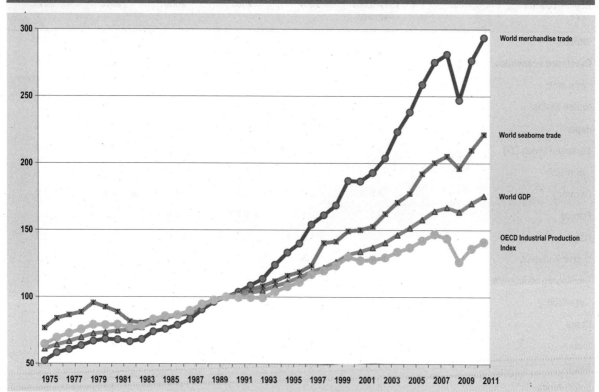

Figure 1.1. Indices for world GDP, the OECD Industrial Production Index, world merchandise trade and world seaborne trade *(1975–2011) (1990=100)*

Source: UNCTAD secretariat, on the basis of OECD Main Economic Indicators, May 2011; UNCTAD's *The Trade and Development Report 2011*; UNCTAD's *Review of Maritime Transport,* various issues; WTO's *International Trade Statistics 2010*, Table A1a; and the World Trade Organization (WTO) press release issued in March 2011, "World trade 2010, prospects for 2011". WTO merchandise trade data (volumes) are derived from customs values deflated by standard unit values and adjusted price index for electronic goods. The 2011 index for seaborne trade is calculated on the basis of the growth rate forecast by Clarkson Research Services.

from a number of exceptional events. These include (a) some of the worst natural disasters in history, such as the floods and cyclones hitting Australia and the triple disaster of earthquake, a tsunami and nuclear crisis in Japan; (b) political unrest in Western Asia and North Africa; and (c) a continued trend of higher oil prices and global energy insecurity. Oil prices (Brent) edging up in April to $125 per barrel could act as a drag on economic growth. Already, in 2011, a softening in household consumption demand and rising inflation is being observed in many economies.[11] These factors are combining to erode the gains from the rapid yet fragile recovery of 2010 and are undermining the prospects of more sustainable future economic growth.

With Japan representing the world's third largest economy and a key player in industrial networks, the ripple effects of the disaster in Japan are being felt globally due to the disrupted production networks and reduced business confidence. Japan's retail

sales are estimated to have dropped by 8 per cent and household spending by 2 per cent.[12] Preliminary estimates indicate that the value of damage to building and infrastructure is nearing 25 trillion Yen or about $300 billion.[13] Another estimate by the World Bank puts the cost of the damage caused by the earthquake and tsunami to Japan's economy at $122 billion–$235 billion.[14] These figures are equivalent to 2.5 per cent to 4 per cent of the country's GDP in 2010. Some data confirmed the severity of the impact of the earthquake in Japan and its economy, with industrial production falling by 15 per cent (annualized rate) in March 2011, the sharpest monthly drop on record.[15] UNCTAD revised downward projections for Japan's GDP growth, although reconstruction and investment activity are likely to revive the economy.

In sum, while the overall economic situation in 2010 has brightened and expectations for 2011 remain positive, multiple risks are currently clouding the prospects of a sustained recovery and a stable world economy. These risks are magnified by extraordinary shocks and events, including natural disasters and political unrest as well as rising and volatile energy and other commodity prices.

2.   World merchandise trade[16]

Overcoming the slump of 2009 (–13.6 per cent) and in tandem with the recovery in the world economy, the volume of merchandise trade (i.e. trade in real terms, adjusted for changes in prices and exchange rates), bounced back, and is estimated by UNCTAD to have grown at a robust rate of 16.2 per cent in 2010 (table 1.2). During the same year, the value of world merchandise exports increased by 22 per cent, owing in particular to the price effect of rising commodity prices.

According to WTO, the surge in the volume of world exports registered the largest annual growth recorded in a data series dating back to 1950. The recovery was robust from mid-2009 to mid-2010, when trade volumes expanded at an annualized rate of nearly 20 per cent.[17] The rapid rise in volumes can also be explained by the same factors that had precipitated the slump in 2009. These include the transmission channels offered by the spread of global supply chains and the product composition of trade compared to GDP. However, trade growth lost momentum during the second half of 2010 in line with the deceleration of world economic growth. Although global trade is estimated to have returned by the end of 2010 to its 2008 peak level, the recovery remains below-trend.[18]

An uneven economic recovery has led to an equally uneven merchandise trade performance, with the speed of the recovery varying across regions and country groupings (table 1.2). Just as the global economic recovery was anchored by developing regions, so was the rebound of world merchandise trade. Robust growth in large emerging economies such as China and India, combined with their deeper economic integration and intensified intraregional trade, have powered the expansion in world merchandise trade. The share of developing countries in global trade increased from about one third to more than 40 per cent between 2008 and 2010.[19]

The deepening of economic ties between developing regions is best illustrated by the fast–evolving relationship between China and large emerging economies such as Brazil. In early 2009, when China overtook the United States as Brazil's main trading partner,[20] it also became the main investor in Brazil in 2010 with $17 billion in capital being injected.[21] China is also involved in Africa, with 1,600 Chinese companies investing in African agriculture and mining as well as in manufacturing, infrastructure and commerce.[22]

Driven, in particular, by the fast growth of import demand in Eastern Asia and Latin America, export volumes of developed economies have also recovered, growing by 16.5 per cent in 2010. This growth is set against the low levels of 2009, when their export volumes contracted by 22.4 per cent. Export volumes in Africa and Latin America also recovered, although at rates slower than the world average. As shown in table 1.2, Asia recorded the largest increase in export volumes led by China (28.3 per cent) and Japan (27.9 per cent). However, growth in Japan is to be measured against the low levels of 2009 when, unlike China, Japan's export volumes contracted by 24.9 per cent. The United States and the European Union saw their export volumes grow by 15.3 per cent and 18.2 per cent, respectively. Exports of transition economies also recovered and expanded by 12 per cent.

World imports grew at a slightly slower pace than exports (15.2 per cent). Imports into developing countries expanded at a faster rate (18.7 per cent) than exports (16.6 per cent) driven in particular by growth in import volumes of developing Asia. Transition economies have also recorded growth in import volumes (17.8 per cent), a rate faster than the rate of exports. Positive growth was recorded in imports volumes of developed countries (16.5 per cent), led by the positive performances of the United States, the European Union and Japan. Considering the disaster in Japan, WTO expects Japan's export volumes to drop by 0.5–0.6 per cent and its imports to increase by 0.4–1.3 per cent. Beyond the direct impact on ports and related services resulting in their inability to berth ships and to handle trade (e.g. ships unable to load perishable goods in Japan due to lack of refrigeration), the disaster in Japan has implications for global supply chains and manufacturing. For example, there have been reports about a shortage in the supply of parts needed in the production of computers, automobiles and mobile phones, including in Germany and the United States.[23] The disruption to business revealed that certain industries tend to rely heavily on few suppliers. That being said, the impact on the global manufacturing industry – and therefore trade – is expected to be limited by the fact that many industries have sufficient supplies for production purposes despite the "just-in-time" inventory management.

Table 1.2. Growth in the volume[a] of merchandise trade, by geographical region, 2008–2010 (annual percentage change)

Exports			Countries/regions	Imports		
2008	2009	2010		2008	2009	2010
2.6	-13.6	16.2	**WORLD**	2.9	-13.6	15.2
11.3	-22.4	16.5	**Developed countries**	11.6	-24.9	16.5
			of which:			
2.3	-24.9	27.9	Japan	-0.6	-12.4	10.3
5.5	-14.9	15.3	United States	-3.7	-16.4	14.7
2.9	-14.7	18.2	European Union	1.4	-14.8	14.1
0.4	-13.8	12.0	**Transition economies**	18.2	-28.8	17.8
3.2	-10.6	16.6	**Developing countries**	6.7	-10.0	18.7
			of which:			
-2.0	-11.2	8.6	Africa	10.3	-2.7	1.4
3.0	-15.7	13.7	Latin America and the Caribbean	-2.8	-16.2	13.8
7.2	-10.5	23.5	**East Asia**	0.4	-5.3	23.1
10.5	-13.6	28.3	of which: China	2.3	-1.7	27.1
7.7	-6.2	15.3	South Asia	20.5	-3.0	12.0
16.8	-6.6	22.4	of which: India	29.7	-0.8	11.5
1.5	-10.7	18.3	**South-East Asia**	8.2	-16.6	22.0
4.0	-6.0	6.5	**West Asia**	13.4	-14.2	10.1

Source: UNCTAD (2011). Table 1.2. *The Trade and Development Report 2011.*

a Data on trade volumes are derived from international merchandise trade values deflated by UNCTAD unit value indices.

Also, alternative sources of supply chains are likely to emerge as substitutes are obtained from other locations. It is anticipated that structural changes such as relocating production sites and redesigning supply networks are likely to be marginal, as such decisions have to weigh the costs and benefits that may arise.

According to WTO, including the potential impact of Japan's earthquake, world trade is expected to grow at a slower rate of 6.5 per cent in 2011 with growth in developing economies' trade (9.5 per cent) outstripping that of advanced economies (4.5 per cent). Growth in world merchandise trade will continue, but is anticipated to moderate in 2011. A global survey by HSBC across 21 countries and involving 6,390 small and medium-sized shippers reveals that traders globally remain positive, with 9 out of 10 expecting trade volumes to increase or hold at current levels in the next six months.[24] Strengthened intraregional trade and greater connectivity with and within emerging markets constitute the main factor behind the positive sentiment.[25] However, the rebalancing toward domestic consumption and imports in large emerging economies such as China is expected to impact on global trade in the future. Signs are already apparent with China's net merchandise exports reported to have fallen from $40 billion in November 2008 to $17 billion in September 2010.[26] This will have a bearing on trade flows and volume balance.

This positive outlook notwithstanding, there remains the question of whether developing countries can retain their position as the engine behind the growth in GDP and trade. An added concern relates to the risk of a surge in protectionist measures. Despite the 2010 renewed pledges by the G-20 to refrain at least until the end of 2013 from increasing or imposing new barriers to investment or trade, the risk of greater protectionism is resurfacing due to the fragile and uneven economic and trade recovery.[27] While it is estimated that new import restrictions introduced between May and October 2010 applied to 0.2 per cent of total world imports against 0.8 per cent at the height of the crisis, non-tariff measures are being introduced under various headings, including protection of health and environment.[28] Despite the recovery, countries are continuing to introduce measures that have the potential to restrict trade.[29]

According to WTO, between November 2009 and May 2010, potentially restrictive measures surpassed those facilitating trade by a factor of 3:2. It is further estimated that the G–20 protectionist measures increased by 31 per cent over the same period and about 27 per cent are further expected.[30]

Counterbalancing to some extent the various downside risks, the proliferation of trade agreements is likely to boost trade and promote deeper economic integration. For example, Japan and India agreed on a free trade agreement that will eliminate import tariffs on over 90 per cent of bilateral trade by value within 10 years.[31] Also, a number of agreements came into force in 2010 and early 2011, including the regional trade agreement between China and the Association of Southeast Asian Nations (ASEAN), as well as ASEAN–Australia and New Zealand, Turkey–Chile, Turkey–Jordan, European Free Trade Association (EFTA)–Serbia, EFTA–Albania, and Hong Kong (China)–New Zealand. The United States is expected to speed up the implementation of its trade agreements with the Republic of Korea, Colombia and Panama before the 2012 election. The United Nations Economic and Social Commission for Asia and the Pacific (ESCAP) estimated that by the end of 2010, there were 170 preferential agreements involving at least one ESCAP member State. Of these 170 agreements, 125 are bilateral regional trade agreements.[32] Interestingly, these agreements are increasingly including provisions on trade facilitation (see chapter 5).

Thus, 2010 saw a swift but moderate recovery in the world economic activity and trade. While robust and sharp early on during the year, the recovery lost momentum in the second part of 2010 and into 2011. A number of uncertainties remain in view of the multiple downside risks and increase the likelihood of a much weaker than expected recovery.

B.　WORLD SEABORNE TRADE[33]

1.　General trends in seaborne trade

For shipping, all stands and falls with worldwide macroeconomic conditions. Developments in the world economy and merchandise trade are also driving developments in seaborne trade. Therefore, in line with the macroeconomic framework described in the previous section, world seaborne trade experienced similar evolution with an upswing in demand in 2010, and a positive turnaround in volumes, especially for dry bulk and container trade segments.

Preliminary data indicate that world seaborne trade in 2010 bounced back from the contraction of the previous year and grew by an estimated 7 per cent, taking the total of goods loaded to 8.4 billion tons, a level surpassing the pre-crisis level reached in 2008 (tables 1.3 and 1.4, and fig. 1.2). While the surge in seaborne trade volumes helped recover the lost

Table 1.3. Development of international seaborne trade, selected years *(millions of tons loaded)*				
Year	**Oil**	**Main bulks**[a]	**Other dry cargo**	**Total (all cargoes)**
1970	1 442	448	676	2 566
1980	1 871	796	1 037	3 704
1990	1 755	968	1 285	4 008
2000	2 163	1 288	2 533	5 984
2006	2 698	1 836	3 166	7 700
2007	2 747	1 957	3 330	8 034
2008	2 742	2 059	3 428	8 229
2009	2 642	2 094	3 122	7 858
2010[b]	2 752	2 333	3 323	8 408

Source:　Compiled by the UNCTAD secretariat on the basis of data supplied by reporting countries and as published on the relevant government and port industry websites, and by specialist sources. The data for 2006 onwards have been revised and updated to reflect improved reporting, including more recent figures and better information regarding the breakdown by cargo type. Figures for 2010 are estimated based on preliminary data or on the last year for which data were available.

[a]　Iron ore, grain, coal, bauxite/alumina and phosphate. The data for 2006 onwards are based on various issues of the *Dry Bulk Trade Outlook* produced by Clarkson Research Services Limited.

[b]　Preliminary estimates.

Table 1.4. World seaborne trade in 2006–2010, by type of cargo and country group

Country group	Year	Goods loaded				Goods unloaded			
		Total	Crude	Products	Dry cargo	Total	Crude	Products	Dry cargo
		Millions of tons							
World	2006	7 700.3	1 783.4	914.8	5 002.1	7 878.3	1 931.2	893.7	5 053.4
	2007	8 034.1	1 813.4	933.5	5 287.1	8 140.2	1 995.7	903.8	5 240.8
	2008	8 229.5	1 785.2	957.0	5 487.2	8 286.3	1 942.3	934.9	5 409.2
	2009	7 858.0	1 710.5	931.1	5 216.4	7 832.0	1 874.1	921.3	5 036.6
	2010	8,408.3	1 784.9	967.5	5 655.8	8 377.8	1 938.9	969.3	5 469.7
Developed economies	2006	2 460.5	132.9	336.4	1 991.3	4 164.7	1 282.0	535.5	2 347.2
	2007	2 608.9	135.1	363.0	2 110.8	3 990.5	1 246.0	524.0	2 220.5
	2008	2 715.4	129.0	405.3	2 181.1	4 007.9	1 251.1	523.8	2 233.0
	2009	2 554.3	115.0	383.8	2 055.5	3 374.4	1 125.3	529.9	1 719.2
	2010	2 832.5	125.7	418.5	2 288.2	3 592.1	1 158.5	545.1	1 888.5
Transition economies	2006	410.3	123.1	41.3	245.9	70.6	5.6	3.1	61.9
	2007	407.9	124.4	39.9	243.7	76.8	7.3	3.5	66.0
	2008	431.5	138.2	36.7	256.6	89.3	6.3	3.8	79.2
	2009	505.3	142.1	44.4	318.8	93.3	3.5	4.6	85.3
	2010	515.7	150.2	45.9	319.7	122.1	3.5	4.6	114.0
Developing economies	2006	4 829.5	1 527.5	537.1	2 765.0	3 642.9	643.6	355.1	2 644.3
	2007	5 020.8	1 553.9	530.7	2 932.6	4 073.0	742.4	376.3	2 954.3
	2008	5 082.6	1 518.0	515.1	3 049.6	4 189.1	684.9	407.2	3 097.0
	2009	4 798.4	1 453.5	502.9	2 842.0	4 364.2	745.3	386.9	3 232.1
	2010	5 060.1	1 509.0	503.1	3 047.9	4 663.7	776.9	419.6	3 467.1
Africa	2006	721.9	353.8	86.0	282.2	349.8	41.3	39.4	269.1
	2007	732.0	362.5	81.8	287.6	380.0	45.7	44.5	289.8
	2008	766.7	379.2	83.3	304.2	376.6	45.0	43.5	288.1
	2009	708.0	354.0	83.0	271.0	386.8	44.6	39.7	302.5
	2010	733.3	343.6	81.5	308.2	399.3	42.0	39.3	318.0
America	2006	1 030.7	251.3	93.9	685.5	373.4	49.6	60.1	263.7
	2007	1 067.1	252.3	90.7	724.2	415.9	76.0	64.0	275.9
	2008	1 108.2	234.6	93.0	780.6	436.8	74.2	69.9	292.7
	2009	1 029.8	225.7	74.0	730.1	371.9	64.4	73.6	234.0
	2010	1 129.6	231.0	73.2	825.4	407.5	69.3	76.6	261.6
Asia	2006	3 073.1	921.2	357.0	1 794.8	2 906.8	552.7	248.8	2 105.3
	2007	3 214.6	938.2	358.1	1 918.3	3 263.6	620.7	260.8	2 382.1
	2008	3 203.6	902.7	338.6	1 962.2	3 361.9	565.6	286.8	2 509.5
	2009	3 054.3	872.3	345.8	1 836.3	3 592.4	636.3	269.9	2 686.2
	2010	3 190.7	932.9	348.2	1 909.5	3 843.5	665.6	300.0	2 877.9
Oceania	2006	3.8	1.2	0.1	2.5	12.9	0.0	6.7	6.2
	2007	7.1	0.9	0.1	2.5	13.5	0.0	7.0	6.5
	2008	4.2	1.5	0.1	2.6	13.8	0.0	7.1	6.7
	2009	6.3	1.5	0.2	4.6	13.1	0.0	3.6	9.5
	2010	6.5	1.5	0.2	4.8	13.4	0.0	3.7	9.7

Table 1.4. World seaborne trade in 2006–2010, by type of cargo and country group *(concluded)*

Country group	Year	Goods loaded				Goods unloaded			
		Total	Crude	Products	Dry cargo	Total	Crude	Products	Dry cargo
		Percentage share							
World	2006	100.0	23.2	11.9	65.0	100.0	24.5	11.3	64.1
	2007	100.0	22.6	11.6	65.8	100.0	24.5	11.1	64.4
	2008	100.0	21.7	11.6	66.7	100.0	23.4	11.3	65.3
	2009	100.0	21.8	11.8	66.4	100.0	23.9	11.8	64.3
	2010	100.0	21.2	11.5	67.3	100.0	23.1	11.6	65.3
Developed economies	2006	32.0	7.4	36.8	39.8	52.9	66.4	59.9	46.4
	2007	32.5	7.5	38.9	39.9	49.0	62.4	58.0	42.4
	2008	33.0	7.2	42.3	39.7	48.4	64.4	56.0	41.3
	2009	32.5	6.7	41.2	39.4	43.1	60.0	57.5	34.1
	2010	33.7	7.0	43.3	40.5	42.9	59.7	56.2	34.5
Transition economies	2006	5.3	6.9	4.5	4.9	0.9	0.3	0.3	1.2
	2007	5.1	6.9	4.3	4.6	0.9	0.4	0.4	1.3
	2008	5.2	7.7	3.8	4.7	1.1	0.3	0.4	1.5
	2009	6.4	8.3	4.8	6.1	1.2	0.2	0.5	1.7
	2010	6.1	8.4	4.7	5.7	1.5	0.2	0.5	2.1
Developing economies	2006	62.7	85.6	58.7	55.3	46.2	33.3	39.7	52.3
	2007	62.5	85.7	56.9	55.5	50.0	37.2	41.6	56.4
	2008	61.8	85.0	53.8	55.6	50.6	35.3	43.6	57.3
	2009	61.1	85.0	54.0	54.5	55.7	39.8	42.0	64.2
	2010	60.2	84.5	52.0	53.9	55.7	40.1	43.3	63.4
Africa	2006	9.4	19.8	9.4	5.6	4.4	2.1	4.4	5.3
	2007	9.1	20.0	8.8	5.4	4.7	2.3	4.9	5.5
	2008	9.3	21.2	8.7	5.5	4.5	2.3	4.7	5.3
	2009	9.0	20.7	8.9	5.2	4.9	2.4	4.3	6.0
	2010	8.7	19.2	8.4	5.4	4.8	2.2	4.1	5.8
America	2006	13.4	14.1	10.3	13.7	4.7	2.6	6.7	5.2
	2007	13.3	13.9	9.7	13.7	5.1	3.8	7.1	5.3
	2008	13.5	13.1	9.7	14.2	5.3	3.8	7.5	5.4
	2009	13.1	13.2	7.9	14.0	4.7	3.4	8.0	4.6
	2010	13.4	12.9	7.6	14.6	4.9	3.6	7.9	4.8
Asia	2006	39.9	51.7	39.0	35.9	36.9	28.6	27.8	41.7
	2007	40.0	51.7	38.4	36.3	40.1	31.1	28.9	45.5
	2008	38.9	50.6	35.4	35.8	40.6	29.1	30.7	46.4
	2009	38.9	51.0	37.1	35.2	45.9	34.0	29.3	53.3
	2010	37.9	52.3	36.0	33.8	45.9	34.3	31.0	52.6
Oceania	2006	0.0	0.1	0.0	0.0	0.2	0.0	0.7	0.1
	2007	0.1	0.1	0.0	0.0	0.2	0.0	0.8	0.1
	2008	0.1	0.1	0.0	0.0	0.2	0.0	0.8	0.1
	2009	0.1	0.1	0.0	0.1	0.2	0.0	0.4	0.2
	2010	0.1	0.1	0.0	0.1	0.2	0.0	0.4	0.2

Source: Compiled by the UNCTAD secretariat on the basis of data supplied by reporting countries and as published on the relevant government and port industry websites, and by specialist sources. The data for 2006 onwards have been revised and updated to reflect improved reporting, including more recent figures and better information regarding the breakdown by cargo type. Figures for 2010 are estimated based on preliminary data or on the last year for which data were available.

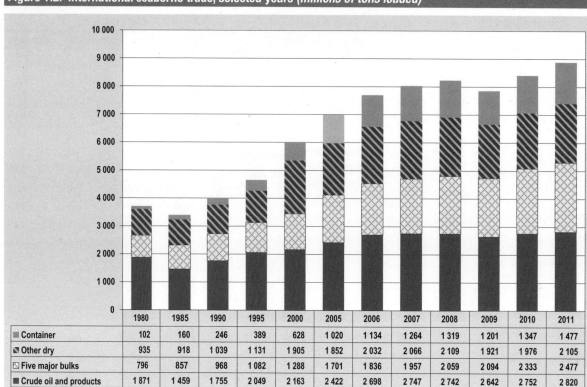

Figure 1.2. International seaborne trade, selected years *(millions of tons loaded)*

	1980	1985	1990	1995	2000	2005	2006	2007	2008	2009	2010	2011
■ Container	102	160	246	389	628	1 020	1 134	1 264	1 319	1 201	1 347	1 477
◨ Other dry	935	918	1 039	1 131	1 905	1 852	2 032	2 066	2 109	1 921	1 976	2 105
▧ Five major bulks	796	857	968	1 082	1 288	1 701	1 836	1 957	2 059	2 094	2 333	2 477
■ Crude oil and products	1 871	1 459	1 755	2 049	2 163	2 422	2 698	2 747	2 742	2 642	2 752	2 820

Source: *Review of Maritime Transport*, various issues. For 2006–2010, the breakdown by dry cargo type is based on Clarkson Research Services, *Shipping Review and Outlook*, various issues. Data for 2011 are based on a forecast by Clarkson Research in *Shipping Review and Outlook*, Spring 2011.

ground of 2009, growth in 2010 is to be measured, however, against a deep contraction of the previous year and set against a growing world fleet capacity.

As shown in table 1.4 and figure 1.2 container trade and major dry bulks are driving this expansion. In 2010, world seaborne trade continued to be dominated by raw materials, with tanker trade accounting for about one third of the total tonnage and other dry cargo including containerized accounting for about 40 per cent. The remainder (about 28 per cent) is made of the five major dry bulks, namely iron ore, coal, grain, bauxite and alumina and phosphate.

In 2010, dry cargo, including major dry bulks, minor dry bulks, general cargo and containerized trade bounced back and expanded by a firm 8.4 per cent over 2009. Growth reflected the continued effect of the stimulus spending which boosted investment and demand for raw materials. It was fuelled in particular by both industrial activity in emerging regions and inventory restocking. Oil trade volumes also recovered and grew by 4.2 per cent over 2009, driven in particular by growing energy demand in emerging regions of Asia.

Reflecting their rising position as the engine of growth, developing countries continued to account for the main loading and unloading areas, with their shares of total goods loaded and unloaded in 2010 amounting to 60 per cent and 56 per cent, respectively. Developed economies' shares of global goods loaded and unloaded were 34 per cent and 43 per cent, respectively. Transition economies accounted for 6 per cent of goods loaded, and 1 per cent of goods unloaded (fig. 1.3 (a)).

The contribution of various regions to world seaborne trade volumes underscores the dominance of large emerging developing economies and reflects the concentration of resources and raw materials, which make up the bulk of seaborne trade. Asia is by far the most important loading and unloading area, with a share of 40 per cent of total goods loaded and 55 per cent of goods unloaded. As shown in figure 1.3 (a), other loading areas ranked in descending order are the Americas (21 per cent), Europe (19 per cent), Oceania (11 per cent) and Africa (9 per cent). Europe unloaded more cargo tonnage (23 per cent) than the Americas (16 per cent), followed by Africa (5 per cent) and Oceania (1 per cent).

Figure 1.3. (a) World seaborne trade, by country group and region, 2010 *(percentage share in tonnage)*

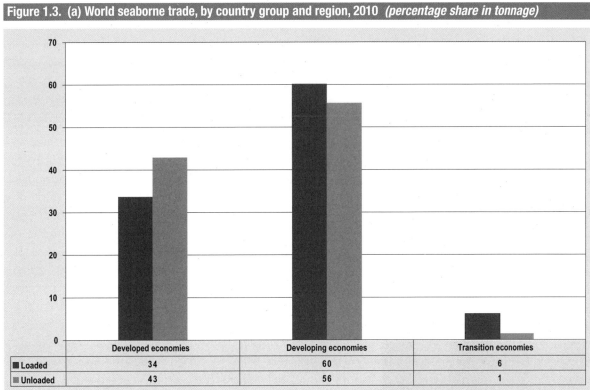

	Developed economies	Developing economies	Transition economies
■ Loaded	34	60	6
■ Unloaded	43	56	1

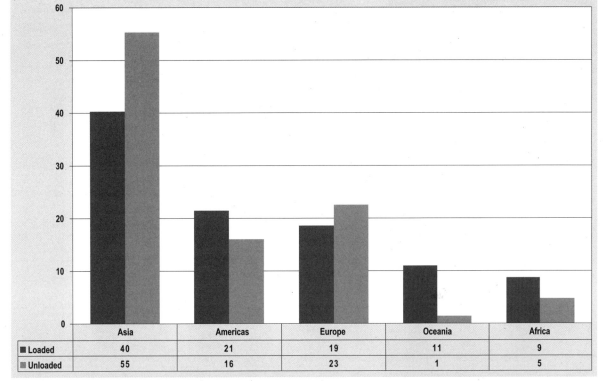

	Asia	Americas	Europe	Oceania	Africa
■ Loaded	40	21	19	11	9
■ Unloaded	55	16	23	1	5

Source: Compiled by the UNCTAD secretariat on the basis of data supplied by reporting countries and as published on the relevant government and port industry websites, and by specialist sources. Figures are estimated based on preliminary data or on the last year for which data were available.

Figure 1.3 (b) highlights the evolution of seaborne trade patterns of developing regions. Since 1970, and reflecting the structure of their trade and the predominance of high volume and low value bulk cargoes such as raw materials and natural resources, developing economies had a surplus in terms of cargo tonnage, since they have consistently loaded (exports) more than unloaded (imports) cargoes. Another distinct trend observed in figure 1.3 (b) is that the volume of cargo unloaded (imports) in developing regions has grown steadily over the same period and has reached near parity with the percentage volume of goods loaded (exports) in 2010.

Growing import and export volumes of developing regions reflect their greater participation in world trade and globalized production. As argued in sections A and B above, the relative weight of developing economies has been increasing due in particular to their role as a catalyst of growth, which helped weather the 2009 downturn and propel the economic recovery in 2010. The rising prices of energy and raw materials, and new resource discoveries have helped promote increases in exports of mineral fuels and chemicals from resource–rich countries in Asia, Latin America and Africa. Additionally, many developing countries followed export-led economic growth policies, effectively increasing their relative share of manufactured goods exports over the years.

The growth in the proportion of goods unloaded also reflects the emergence of developing countries as a major source of import demand, largely attributable to a fast–growing middle class and increased requirements for more sophisticated consumption goods and diversified imports. The expansion of South–South trade, enabled by more South–South investments, has also helped boost the import demand of developing countries as new markets that offer goods at more competitive prices become accessible (e.g. growth in container trade from China to West Africa to the detriment of Europe). This trend is likely to continue and vary with shifting patterns of comparative advantages (e.g. higher labour costs in China as compared with other emerging economies in Asia and Africa).

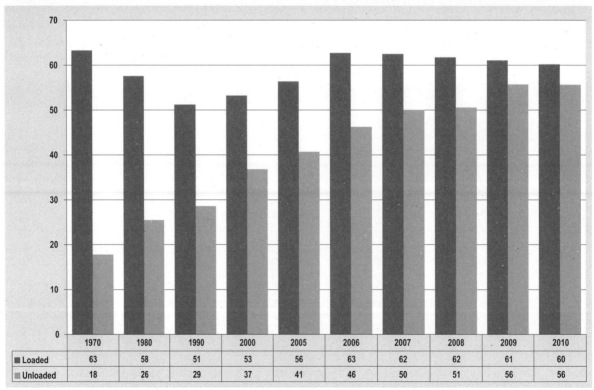

Figure 1.3. (b) Participation of developing countries in world seaborne trade, selected years (percentage share in world tonnage)

	1970	1980	1990	2000	2005	2006	2007	2008	2009	2010
Loaded	63	58	51	53	56	63	62	62	61	60
Unloaded	18	26	29	37	41	46	50	51	56	56

Source: *Review of Maritime Transport,* various issues.

2. Seaborne trade by cargo type

Tanker trade

Crude oil production and consumption

Oil is a commodity of key strategic importance, accounting for over 34 per cent of the world's primary energy consumption in 2010. Crude oil production and reserves are heavily concentrated among a handful of major producers and regions, in particular in Western Asia. Major players in the oil business – including producers, consumers, importers and exporters – are featured in table 1.5. In 2010, about 1.8 billion tons of crude, equivalent to 45 per cent of world crude oil production, were loaded on tankers and carried through fixed maritime routes.

The pace of world oil trade and the dependence on longer haul supply have increased over the last several years, with China and India emerging as major importers, and West Africa and more recently Brazil with its latest offshore oil finds, as growing major exporters. With more recent oil discoveries and the depletion of some oil fields in Europe and Western Asia, some shifts in global oil supply and demand networks are likely to emerge (e.g. exports from Brazil to Asia). Reflecting its ever–growing energy demand and increasing dependence on imports for meeting this demand, China's oil companies have, over recent years, boosted their investments in overseas oil-related extraction and production activities through strategic partnerships and acquisition deals. Pursuing its diversified geographical approach to securing its supply, China has developed an impressive global network with investments in neighboring Kazakhstan and the Russian Federation, and has stretched this network to Australia, West Africa, Sudan and the Americas. These developments are already altering the patterns of shipping globally, and trends in oil trade are shifting, as illustrated by growth in tanker ton-mile demand. They are anticipated to intensify as China looks at both existing and new regions from which to secure its supply. In 2010, tanker demand measured in ton-miles was estimated to have grown by 2.2 per cent after declining by 1.9 per cent in 2009.[34]

In 2010, oil demand followed trends in the global economic growth, namely growing along two tracks and at uneven pace. After a decline in 2009, oil demand is estimated to have grown by 3.1 per cent to reach 87.4 million barrels per day (mbpd) in 2010. Demand from the OECD countries, which make up 52.5 per cent of the world total, increased by 0.9

per cent. Oil consumption in advanced economies is expected to remain flat in the coming years due to policies that encourage, among others, fuel efficiency, increased use of ethanol and biofuels, as well as measures taken to reduce dependency on fossil fuels and cut carbon emissions.

In contrast, non-OECD countries saw their oil demand jump by a strong 5.6 per cent in 2010. China recorded world's fastest growth with its oil demand expanding by an impressive 10.4 per cent in 2010. It imported 54 per cent of crude requirements in 2010, exceeding its initial target of not importing more than 50 per cent of its crude requirements. China's reliance on imports is projected to intensify further, reaching 66 per cent in 2015 and 70 per cent in 2020.[35]

For 2011, world consumption growth is expected to remain relatively robust, but moderate due partly to the fact that the 2010 levels were relatively high and to the dampening effect of higher oil prices and tighter monetary policies in many developing countries.

Global crude oil production is estimated to have risen by 2.2 per cent in 2010 to reach 82.1 mbpd. Production in countries of the Organization of the Petroleum Exporting Countries (OPEC) increased by 2.5 per cent, given the slippage in compliance with the production ceiling. Non-OPEC production grew by 1.9 per cent, driven by growth in Brazil, China and transition economies of Asia. The importance of OPEC producers is expected to grow with their share of global production, projected to rise from 40 per cent in 2010 to 46 per cent in 2030, a level not reached since 1977.[36]

Globally, a number of geopolitical risks are also weighing on the supply forecast. These include the spread of the political unrest to other countries of North Africa and Western Asia and the possible disruption in crude oil supply. Other concerns are equally ever–present and include the risk of lower production in the Niger Delta region, tensions relating to the Islamic Republic of Iran's nuclear programme and resumed security problems in Iraq. These uncertainties – together with other concerns over the state of the world economy, fiscal sustainability and China's efforts to slow the rapid growth of its economy – are exerting further pressure on oil prices.

In 2010, oil prices rebounded from their 2009 levels, which had fallen off drastically from the surge in 2008. With growing positive sentiment about the prospects of the world economy and the events in North Africa and Western Asia, oil prices (Bent) soared to well over $120 per barrel in April 2011.[37] The projected

Table 1.5. Oil and natural gas: major producers and consumers, 2010 *(world market share in percentage)*

World oil production		World oil consumption	
Western Asia	31	Asia Pacific	31
Transition Economies	17	North America	25
North America	13	Europe	17
Africa	12	Latin America	9
Latin America	12	Western Asia	9
Asia Pacific	10	Transition Economies	5
Europe	5	Africa	4

World natural gas production		World natural gas consumption	
North America	24	North America	25
Transition Economies	24	Europe	19
Western Asia	14	Asia	17
Asia	14	Transition Economies	15
Europe	9	Western Asia	13
Latin America	7	Latin America	7
Africa	7	Africa	3
Other	2	Other	1

Source: UNCTAD secretariat on the basis of data published in British Petroleum (BP) *Statistical Review of World Energy 2011* (June 2011).

Note: Oil includes crude oil, shale oil, oil sands and natural gas liquids (NGLs, the liquid content of natural gas where this is recovered separately). Excludes liquid fuels from other sources as biomass and coal derivatives.

growth in oil demand, coupled with uncertainties over supply, will continue to support oil prices at current or increased levels in 2011. Most forecasters have settled in the $100–$125 per barrel range with differences in projections showing that it is difficult to predict oil prices when an element of speculation is also at play.

Crude oil shipments

Demand for crude oil tankers is closely correlated with the global oil demand. In 2010, seaborne shipments of crude oil recovered and returned to pre-crisis levels. Crude oil loaded in 2010 amounted to about 1.8 billion tons, a 4.3 per cent increase over 2009. Western Asia remained the largest loading area, followed by the economies in transition, Africa and developing America (see tables 1.4 and 1.5). The major unloading areas were North America, developing Asia, Europe and Japan. Growing energy demand of Asian developing economies, specifically China and India, as well as stronger demand in Western Asia are positioning these regions as importing players. This is reflected, as previously noted, in China's increased involvement in the energy and mining sectors of resource-rich

countries through growing partnerships. Companies based in China or Hong Kong, China, participated in a total of $13 billion of outbound mining acquisitions and investments in 2009.[38] Major oil importers in advanced economies are losing their relative importance as a source of import demand, given the relatively high stocks of crude oil in developed economies and their subdued demand for oil, with the exception of the United States.

Looking ahead, growth in crude oil trade is expected to slow down in 2011. Uncertainties such as the political turmoil in oil–exporting regions or natural disasters such as the earthquake and tsunami in Japan could have unforeseen consequences for crude tanker trade.[39] The disruption in oil supply in the Libyan Arab Jamahiriya could lead to increased demand for tanker ton-miles as importing countries look for alternative sources of crude to compensate the reduced output. For example, ton-mile demand for Suezmax could increase due to the European refineries buying more West African crude since West Africa's crude oil is of similar grade to crude oil from the Libyan Arab Jamahiriya.

Refinery developments and shipments of petroleum products

Global refinery throughputs averaged 74.8 mbpd, an increase of 2.4 per cent over 2009. A cold winter in the United States and Europe and the economic recovery boosted oil demand and caused a rebound in OECD output. Refineries in non-OECD countries, namely China and India, as well as the Russian Federation, also recorded high outputs. Normal temperatures in the United States and Europe and a slowdown in global economic growth are expected to moderate oil demand growth, and consequently throughput growth, compared with recent high levels. Also, the earthquake in Japan could lead to reduced crude oil demand as refineries damaged by the earthquake continue to be out of operation.

The refining sector has moved from an era of booming demand between 2004 and mid-2008 to difficult times, when demand is constrained and capacity is in surplus, especially in OECD regions. Capacity continues to grow with the largest capacity growth expected to take place in Asia–Pacific followed by Western Asia. During 2009, five new refineries were brought on line in Western Asia and the Far East.

In this context, while 2010 may have been a positive year, some uncertainty remains as regards the prospects of petroleum products shipments. Reflecting developments in the world economy and the influence of weather patterns of 2010, world shipments of petroleum products increased by 3.7 per cent in 2010, taking the total to 967.5 million tons (see table 1.4). The outlook for 2011 remains overall positive but subject to the same downside risks facing the global economy and oil demand: considerations such as an expansion in product tanker fleet capacity, a surplus in the global refining capacity, and a geographical shift of global refining centres to the East in tandem with the shift of the main source of consumption demand. These factors are likely to alter the structure, patterns, ton-mile demand and the overall geography of petroleum product trade.

In a separate development and with its position as the third–largest oil importer, an important issue emerging in 2011 is the impact of the disaster in Japan on tanker shipping. The shortfall in refinery output in Japan could raise the demand for petroleum product to make up for the reduced gasoline and fuel oil. However, lower refinery throughput is likely to diminish crude oil tanker demand as crude oil for feedstock declines. As refineries return to full operation, crude oil tanker demand would then benefit from a surge in demand. That being said, it should be noted that Japan held 590 mbpd of crude and products in December 2010, an amount equivalent to 169 days of net import. This means that any potential effect on tanker trade will not be felt in the short term.

Natural gas supply and demand

Natural gas makes up about 24 per cent of the world energy consumption, after oil and coal. Considered to be a much cleaner fossil fuel source in view of its lower carbon content, natural gas is increasingly emerging as an attractive fuel source. Liquefied natural gas (LNG) has more recently emerged as a viable alternative to nuclear energy.

In 2010, world production of natural gas rebounded by 7.3 per cent to reach 3,193.3 billion cubic metres (bcm). Together, Europe and the transition economies combined accounted for 32.6 per cent of the global production, followed by North America. Other producers included the Asia–Pacific region, with a share of 15.4 per cent (table 1.5). The production is boosted by a strong recovery in the output of the Russian Federation, rising United States production and a surge of output from Qatar. Global LNG production also expanded in 2010 with the largest LNG producer, Qatar, being responsible for the bulk of the additional supply. With rising production in Qatar, Western Asia is expected to overtake the Asia–Pacific region as the world's third largest producing region in 2012. Train 7 of the Qatar Gas 4 project initially contracted to supply the United States, China and Dubai, has been recently completed. However, some of the cargo is likely to be diverted away from the United States market towards Asia, particularly Japan. Expected growth in Japan's LNG demand, the world's largest LNG consumer, and higher Asian LNG prices are contributing to shifting LNG exports towards Asia.

While growing from a low base, world consumption of natural gas rebounded by 7.4 per cent to reach 3,169 bcm in 2010, owing to lower prices and stronger industrial production in both the OECD countries and emerging economies. Demand increased in all regions, with the fastest regional growth being recorded in Europe, Asia and the Pacific region. Demand for natural gas is projected to grow at a stronger rate after 2011, driven mainly by higher oil prices, efforts to reduce carbon emissions and the surge in Asia's demand for LNG. Again, growth in demand is expected to be propelled by non-OECD countries, particularly China and India, as well as the Islamic Republic of Iran and Saudi Arabia. Demand in advanced economies is also expected to rise, driven by policies aimed at reducing dependency on higher carbon content energy sources such as oil. Japan is expected to increase its consumption of LNG as a result of the damage sustained by its nuclear power facilities.

Liquefied natural gas shipments

In 2010, world LNG shipments increased by over 22 per cent to reach 297.6 bcm, driven by over 50 per cent growth in Qatar's output. In October 2010, there were 56 export terminal projects in operation in 18 countries, with a number of projects under construction or planned, including in Australia, the Islamic Republic of Iran and Papua New Guinea.[40] Canada and Brazil might also emerge as potential LNG exporters as plans for developing liquefaction facilities are being drawn. Qatar remains the main LNG exporter, followed by Malaysia, Indonesia, Algeria and Nigeria. Several new exporters are emerging and include Angola, Australia, Peru, Saudi Arabia and Yemen.

As of October 2010, there were 90 import terminals in 20 countries with several others reported to be under construction or envisaged (e.g. in Germany, Croatia, Romania and Singapore).[41] China has six import terminal projects set for completion in 2013 while the Netherlands, Thailand and Sweden expect their import terminals currently under construction to start operations in 2011. Overall, the number and the size of storage tanks are increasing together with growing average size of gas carriers.[42]

Reflecting a stronger industrial demand, the largest Asian LNG markets – Japan, the Republic of Korea and Taiwan, Province of China – experienced a rapid growth in imports in 2010. Also, with the advent of the United States gas boom, large volumes of LNG are being diverted and shipped to areas of stronger demand, mainly in Asia. Capitalizing on the strong demand, the Russian Federation and China are expected to sign an export agreement for gas delivery by mid-2011, while an agreement between China and Turkmenistan is expected to be signed later in 2011. South America is also growing into an important LNG importer, with the start–up of import terminals in Chile, Brazil and Argentina in recent years. As regards Japan, the reconstruction-related demand is likely to benefit LNG trade through the potential transition away from coal and nuclear during

the rebuild of powering plants. The diversification of sources of supply and the geographical shift in LNG trade brought about new discoveries and the emergence of new import players could lead to increased ton miles.

Dry cargo shipments: major and minor dry bulks and other dry cargo

The year 2010 was positive for dry cargo as total volumes bounced back and grew by 8.4 per cent to nearly 5.7 billion tons. Dry bulk cargo (major and minor bulks) amounted to about 3.3 billion tons of this total, up by a firm 11 per cent over 2009. The strong comeback is due in particular to the recovery in world steel production and the associated growth in import demand for iron ore and coking coal. Growing demand for steam coal fuelled by, among other things, growing urbanization in large emerging developing countries such as China and India, also had a role to play. Income growth in emerging economies has also supported growth in grain shipments used as feedstock, with the evolving consumption needs of these economies and their shifting towards the consumption of more diversified foods, including meat and related products. While these developments are encouraging, the low base effect should also be taken into account given the sharp drop in dry cargo volumes recorded in 2009.

Major dry bulks: iron ore, coal, grain, bauxite/alumina and phosphate rock

The share of major dry bulks has been expanding over the past four decades, while that of oil trade has been losing its relative weight over the same period. Major dry bulks accounted for 17.4 per cent of total goods loaded in 1970, 24.4 per cent in 1990 and 21.5 per cent in 2000, and ranged between 25 per cent and 28 per cent between 2008 and 2010. Within the major dry bulk commodities, coal accounted for 28 per cent of the total loaded in 1984, 33.3 per cent in 1990, 31.8 per cent in 2000 and 38.6 per cent in 2010. The share of iron ore stood at 36.3 per cent of total major dry bulks loaded in 1984, and fluctuated between 35.8 per cent in 1990, 34.7 per cent in 2000, and 42.3 per cent in 2010. Over the 1984–2010 period, coal and iron ore volumes moved in tandem, both growing at an average annual rate of over 5 per cent (figure 1.4). The share of bauxite and alumina has been decreasing, from 5.5 per cent in 1984 to 3.4 per cent in 2010, owing partly to producers preferring to refine bauxite on site which results in less shipments of bauxite.

This growing share of dry bulk cargo reflects in particular the fast–growing demand for raw materials such as coal and iron ore used as inputs in steel–making and industrial activity, especially in large developing regions such as China, India, and increasingly in oil–rich Western Asian countries, where important investments are poured into their infrastructure development.

Coal production, consumption and shipments

Growth in global coal demand outpaces overall energy demand growth, largely because of coal's increasing share in the energy mix of emerging countries. World coal consumption grew by 7.6 per cent in 2010, reflecting the requirements of the economic recovery and a higher demand from the steel industry. Growth in China's consumption remained robust, as did India's. However, consumption in China is expected to grow at a slower rate over 2011–2012 in tandem with developments in the wider economy,[43] lower demand from the steel industry, and heightened efforts to curb carbon emissions (table 1.6).

Global coal production rebounded strongly in 2010, growing by 6.3 per cent, owing to the recovery in demand and the favourable prices, and led by Indonesia (19.4 per cent), New Zealand (16.8 per cent)

and China (9 per cent). The outlook for 2011 remains positive, with the global coal production expected to growth, albeit at a more moderate rate than in 2010, reflecting in particular the expected weaker demand in China and the relatively high production levels recorded in 2010.

In 2010, the volume of coal shipments (thermal and coking) totalled 904 million tons, up by 14.4 per cent year on year. Thermal coal exports, where Indonesia holds a present market share of 43.9 per cent, increased by 12.4 per cent in 2010 to reach 663 million tons. In 2010, Australia and Indonesia together accounted for 65.2 per cent of the world's total thermal coal shipments. Other major thermal coal exporters included Columbia, the Russian Federation, South Africa China and the Bolivarian Republic of Venezuela. A strong demand in China and India has boosted import levels of thermal coal while the return to strong economic growth in Japan and the Republic of Korea offered further support. Thermal coal exports to the Pacific have more than outweighed the downturn in import demand in Europe and the United States, which dropped in 2010 due to a combination of stringent environmental measures and comparatively low gas prices.

Figure 1.4. Growth in five major dry bulks, 1982–2010 *(indices, 1990 = 100)*

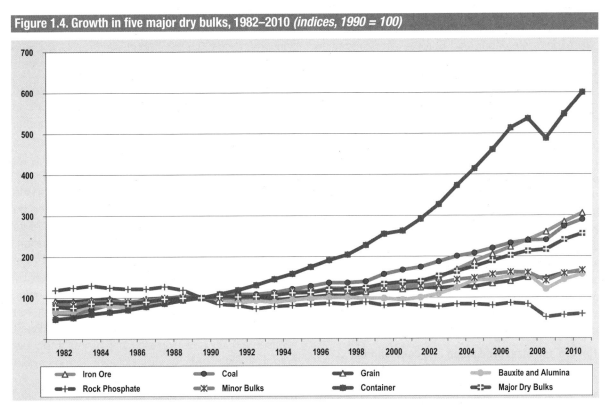

Source: UNCTAD secretariat based on *Review of Maritime Transport,* various issues; and on Clarkson Research Services; *Shipping Review and Outlook,* Spring 2011.

As coking coal is used in steelmaking, its trade patterns follow closely developments in the world economy as well as those in steel demand and production and the associated iron ore trade. Dominated by Australia, with a market share of 66 per cent, shipments of coking coal also increased even at a much faster rate (20 per cent) than thermal coal taking the total to 241 million tons in 2010.

Over recent years, coal exporters such as Colombia, South Africa, the United States and Canada are increasingly directing their exports towards Asia. In 2010, Colombia shipped cargo to India, a change reported to have been encouraged by weaker demand in Europe and the United States, relatively better prices in Asia and lower shipping costs. South Africa is also eyeing the Asian market with India becoming its largest single market in Asia, a diversion from its traditional European and United States markets. The problems facing Australia may have contributed to this trend as Australia's exports have been affected by heavy rains in 2010 and a cyclone in early 2011, as well as persistent infrastructure bottlenecks. Australia estimated the lost coal and agricultural exports at $2.97 billion[44] while the Queensland Resources Council notes that coking coal output will be 10–20 per cent lower year on year in the second quarter of 2011.[45]

The main destinations of both thermal and coking coal exports are Japan and Europe, which together account for 38.4 per cent of global imports in 2010 (table 1.6). In 2009, China became a net importer of coal for the first time and an increasing proportion of China's demand will be met by imports. Its demand, however, may fluctuate depending on the level of its domestic stocks and international prices. However, India was the foremost driver of growth in seaborne coking coal trade in 2010. It overtook China as the second largest importer due to the emergence of Mongolia as a major supplier (some 30 per cent in 2010). India is expected to overtake China as a major driver of growth in steam coal trade. China's concerns about its economy overheating, large coal reserves, uncompetitive prices and India's greater dependence on imports explain the shift in China's import demand and the emergence of India as an increasingly large importer.

Iron ore and steel production and consumption

Iron ore trade is correlated with growth in world steel production. In 2010, global steel production increased by 15 per cent, taking the total output to 1.4 billion tons. Crude steel production in China totalled 626.7

million tons, accounting for 44.3 per cent of the world total. In 2010, the world's apparent steel consumption grew by 13.2 per cent in 2010 and is projected to further increase by 5.9 per cent in 2011 to reach 1,339 million tons. While steel consumption is projected to expand in all regions in both 2011 and 2012, world steel demand is nevertheless expected to be affected by the introduction of tighter monetary policy aimed to slow down the Chinese economy and its steel-intensive construction sector. Preliminary estimates for Japan point to a 15 per cent disruption to supply of the steelmaking industry. In the short term, Japanese demand is forecast to fall by 10 per cent in 2011. However, given the reconstruction requirements, a complete recovery is likely by 2012.

A recovery in global crude steel production supported growth in global iron ore shipments which expanded by 9.0 per cent in 2010, taking the total to 982 million tons. Major iron ore exporters included Australia, Brazil, Canada, India, and South Africa (table 1.6). Key iron ore mining companies remain Vale (Brazil), BHP Billiton (Australia) and Rio Tinto (Australia/United Kingdom). In 2010, Australia and Brazil, which together control nearly three quarters of the market, saw their export volume rise by 10.9 per cent and 17.0 per cent respectively. With the exception of India and Mauritania, growth in volumes of other exporters such as Canada, Sweden, South Africa and Peru have also picked up speed.

Strong imports into Japan, the Republic of Korea and the European Union more than offset the decline in China's imports (–2 per cent). China's iron ore imports totalled 602.6 million tons, or around 61.4 per cent of the world total. China's consumption patterns may be currently changing in line with changes in its economy, growth model and steelmaking sector. Iron ore imports by China, which saw an unparalleled growth over the past few years, are likely to change by efforts of its Government to slow down rapid economic expansion. China's dominant role as a key player cannot be overemphasized, as illustrated by actions taken by iron ore mining companies and exporting countries to ensure that they are able to meet the strong iron ore demand from China. In February 2011, Brazil released a national mining plan which aims to double output of key mineral groups including iron ore, gold and copper between 2010 and 2030. With a $270 billion investment in mining research and processing, Brazil's iron ore output is set to increase by 58 per cent between 2010 and 2015.[46]

Table 1.6. Major dry bulks and steel: major producers, users, exporters and importers, 2010
(market shares in percentages)

Major steel producers		Major steel users	
China	44	China	45
Japan	8	EU 27	11
United States	6	North America	9
Russian Federation	5	CIS	4
India	5	Middle East	4
Republic of Korea	4	South America	4
Germany	3	Africa	2
Ukraine	2	Other	22
Brazil	2		
Turkey	2		
Others	19		
Major iron ore exporters		**Iron ore importers**	
Australia	40	China	61
Brazil	31	Japan	14
India	10	EU 15	11
South Africa	5	Republic of Korea	6
Canada	3	Middle East	2
Sweden	2	Other	6
Other	9		
Major coal exporters		**Major coal importers**	
Australia	33	Japan	22
Indonesia	32	Europe	17
Colombia	8	China	14
South Africa	7	India	13
Russian Federation	7	Republic of Korea	13
United States	5	Taiwan, Province of China	7
Canada	3	United States	2
China	2	Thailand	2
Others	3	Malaysia	2
		Brazil	1
		Other	10
Major grain exporters		**Major grain importers**	
United States	33	Asia	31
EU	10	Latin America	22
Canada	9	Africa	22
Argentina	8	Middle East	18
Australia	8	Europe	5
Others	33	CIS	2

Source: UNCTAD secretariat on the basis of data from the World Steel Association (2011); Clarkson Research Services, published in the May 2011 issue of *Dry bulk Trade Outlook;* and World Grain Council (WGC), 2011.

A new trend to observe with respect to iron ore trade is the evolution of purpose-built very large ore carriers (VLOCs). To capitalize on the important iron ore demand from China and to ensure high market share on this trade, Vale, the Brazilian mining giant ordered a giant fleet of 80 VLOCs by 2015.[47] Of these, 36 ships will be of 400,000 deadweight tons (DWT), which is roughly twice as large as existing Capesize ships. Business with China alone is contributing one third of Vale's operating revenue.[48]

Looking ahead, the outlook for iron trade is positive, with iron ore shipments expected to grow by a firm 6 per cent to hit the 1 billion mark for the first time in 2011. Nevertheless, it remains subject to developments in the wider economy and the steelmaking sector, and more importantly, to the exact effect of China's policies aimed at moderating its economic expansion including its steel making sector.

Grain shipments

Grain shipments are to a large extent determined by weather conditions in producing and exporting countries. However, other factors are increasingly influencing the volume, structure and patterns of grain shipments and include (a) the shift in demand and usage (e.g. industrial purposes vs. feed); (b) environmental and energy policies that promote the use of alternative energy sources such as biofuels; (c) the evolution in consumption and demand patterns (e.g. higher meat consumption in emerging developing countries lead to more grain shipments for feedstock); and (d) trade measures aimed at promoting or restricting trade flows.

Total grain production in 2009/2010 fell by 4.4 per cent to 1,794 million tons while consumption increased by 2 per cent to reach 1,761 million tons. As in recent years, growth remains strongest in feed and industrial sectors with direct human food consumption rising at a comparatively slower pace. In mid-2010, drought and fires in the Russian Federation, Ukraine and, to a lesser extent, North America affected the harvests and led to an increase in grain import volumes of many regions. The increased demand was met largely by the United States and Argentina, and entails positive implications for grain trade ton-mile, especially the supramaxes engaged on long-haul transatlantic routes. For 2010/2011 global grain production is expected to decline by 3.6 per cent while consumption is set to grow (1.7 per cent).

World grain shipments totalled 343 million tons in the calendar year 2010, up by 8.2 per cent over 2009. Wheat and coarse grain accounted for 72.6 per cent of the total grain shipments. For the crop year 2010/11, volumes of wheat exports are expected to fall by 4 per cent due to a 49 per cent drop in exports from countries other than the five largest exporters (Argentina, Australia, Canada, the European Union and the United States) whose exports, as a group, are expected to grow by a solid 19 per cent (see table 1.6 for major grain exporters and importers). Wheat exports from Argentina and the United States, in particular, are expected to rise by a robust 47 per cent and 45 per cent respectively, reflecting improved harvests and demand in areas which recorded less positive crop years or are experiencing strong growth in demand.

For the crop year 2010/11, grain imports (table 1.6) are expected to expand at a strong rate in the European Union (68 per cent), the Russian Federation (500 per cent), China (41 per cent), Ecuador (20 per cent), and Morocco (43 per cent). The additional import requirements of these countries are offset by reduced demand in Japan (–5 per cent), Bangladesh (–13 per cent) and the Islamic Republic of Iran (–49 per cent). It is estimated that if demand were to remain constant at the 2010 level, global wheat consumption could increase by 40 per cent by 2050, a growth rate that would mirror expansion in the world population by that time.[49] Based on projections by the United States Wheat Associates, domestic production of North Africa, Western Asia, Sub-Saharan Africa, Indonesia, the Philippines, Brazil, Mexico, India and China will increase by 23 per cent while their consumption is expected to grow by 49 per cent between 2010 and 2050.[50] It is likely that with changes in political regimes in North African and Western Asian countries there would see changes in policies affecting grain shipments. New leaders of these countries may be pursuing food policies along different path which will impact on the global grain business. For example, they could follow the Saudi Arabia's approach to enhancing its food security by adding sufficient storage space to boost stocks and acquiring cropland in other countries.[51]

An important development with a bearing on grain markets and trade is the rise in food prices recorded in 2010 and early 2011. In February 2011, food prices have increased by more than 30 per cent year-on-year, owing in particular to production shortfalls resulting from adverse weather, falling stocks and the strong demand supported by a recovery of many emerging economies. It has been estimated that if a 30 per cent increase in global food prices persists throughout 2011, GDP growth for some food-importing countries in Asia, for example, could decline by 0.6 percentage points.[52] Combined with a 30 per cent increase in world oil prices, the reduction in GDP growth could reach 1.5 percentage points compared with a situation with no hikes in food and oil prices.[53] Clearly, there is a need to improve productivity, increase agricultural investment, and adopt all measures necessary to enhance food security especially for the more vulnerable populations.

Bauxite/alumina and phosphate rock

In 2010, world trade in bauxite and alumina rebounded by a strong 22.7 per cent, and totalled 81 million tons. With Europe, North America and Japan being the main importers, the strong recovery reflects the improved situation in industrial activity in these economies and the continued investment expenditure in emerging developing economies supported by the stimulus funding and the rapid pace of industrialization. The major loading areas for bauxite included Africa, the Americas, Asia and Australia. Australia was also a major exporter of alumina, accounting for about half of world exports, while Jamaica contributed a growing share.

Rock phosphate volumes bounced back at a firm rate of 21 per cent, to 23 million tons, reflecting the improved economic situation in main importing countries such as the United States. Increased grain production encouraged by higher prices and growing demand, especially from Asia, helped boost demand for fertilizers. Some easing of the credit conditions may have also helped in relation to the sale of farm inputs such as fertilizers. Phosphate rock volumes are expected to remain steady in 2011, partly reflecting further consolidation in the economic recovery and demand for grains. Plans are still under way for the expansion of existing operations, for example in Brazil, China, Egypt, Finland, Morocco, the Russian Federation and Tunisia. Once operational, supply and demand and the underlying shipping patterns will likely be affected, especially as regards demand for handysize capacity and deployment.

Dry cargo: minor bulks

In 2010, minor bulks trade also recovered from the 2009 dip and expanded by 11 per cent, taking the total volume of minor bulk shipments to 954 million tons. Overall, trade in minor bulks fared well, although imports remained around 3 per cent below the pre-

downturn levels. Steel and forest product trades account for the largest growth in terms of volumes while in terms of growth rate, coke (78.7 per cent) and potash (59.7 per cent) trades recorded the most significant year-on-year expansion. With the bouncing back of the world steel production, scrap volumes increased by 10 per cent to reach 98.8 million in 2010, a level almost equivalent to the 2008 level and above the 2007 level. Strong demand and favourable weather conditions supported growth in sugar and rice shipments, which increased respectively by 10.4 per cent and 7.8 per cent in 2010. Trade in the majority of fertilizers rebounded strongly (16.9 per cent), whilst imports of metals and minerals such as manganese ore and cement all increased in tandem with the resurgence of the global steel production and construction industries. Minor dry bulk trades are projected to grow by 5 per cent in 2011, driven in particular by strong growth in agribulks, metals and minerals and manufactures.

Other dry cargo: containerized cargo

The balance of 2.4 billion tons of dry cargoes is made up of containerized (56 per cent) and general cargoes. Driven largely by the increasing international division of labour and productivity gains within the sector, container trade, the fastest-growing cargo segment expanded at an average rate of 8.2 per cent between 1990 and 2010 (tables 1.7 and 1.8 and figures 1.5 and 1.6).

Container trade volumes experienced an unexpected robust recovery fuelled by a surge in demand across nearly all trade lanes. In 2010, global container trade volumes bounced back at 12.9 per cent over 2009, among the strongest growth rates in the history of containerization (figure 1.5). Table 1.7 features container trade volumes on the three major East–West container routes from 1995 to 2009. Over this period, the continuing expansion in container trade volume is compelling, as is the drastic drop in volumes recorded in 2009. According to Clarkson Research Services data, container trade volumes reached 140 million 20-foot equivalent unit (TEUs) in 2010, or over 1.3 billion tons.

Growth in container trade volumes was propelled by the double-digit rates involving Asia, namely Far East–North America and Asia–Europe (table 1.8). Volumes on these two largest East–West trade lanes are expected to exceed 2008 levels. However, volumes on the transatlantic lane, which experienced a drop of 19 per cent in 2009, are expected to remain below the pre-downturn levels. While the transatlantic lane is gradually diminishing in global importance, Western Asia' s trade with developing economies in the Indian Subcontinent and southern hemisphere is expanding rapidly. It should be noted that, although conditions have improved, slow steaming continues to be implemented by container operators as a way of cutting costs of fuel and absorbing capacity as well as a move to fulfill other strategic objectives such as energy efficiency and environmental sustainability, including cutting carbon emissions (see section C and chapter 2).

Growth in 2010 is estimated to have been more robust on North–South (14.1 per cent) and non-main lane East–West trades (18.7 per cent). This has been illustrated by the Europe to South/Central America trade, which grew by 20.1 per cent in the first quarter of 2011 and Europe to sub-Saharan Africa trade, which grew by 27.5 per cent year-on-year over the same period. Meanwhile, intraregional trade grew by an estimated 11.6 per cent in 2010, propelled by intra-Asian trade, which continues to be fuelled by growth in developing economies such as China.

Along with fast-growing intraregional trade, these emerging lanes provided a market for the deployment of cascaded ships.

With trade growing at a faster-than-expected rate, the container sector was caught by surprise and created a shortage of container equipment in particular empty boxes. The shortage of containers observed in 2009 resulted from the large-scale scrapping of old boxes during the downturn, low production levels and financially strapped carriers, and their attempts to cut costs, including that of repositioning empty boxes. Equipment and ship capacity shortages that were experienced following a rebound in demand in the fourth quarter of 2009 and early 2010 have led to a fact-finding investigation by the Federal Maritime Commission into the availability or non-availability of supply capacity on the transpacific trade during that same period.[54] While it was concluded that no clear evidence was found as regards unlawful practices by carriers, ocean liners were nevertheless urged to ensure that capacity shortages are prevented in the future. Also, Global Alliances (Grand, Green and New

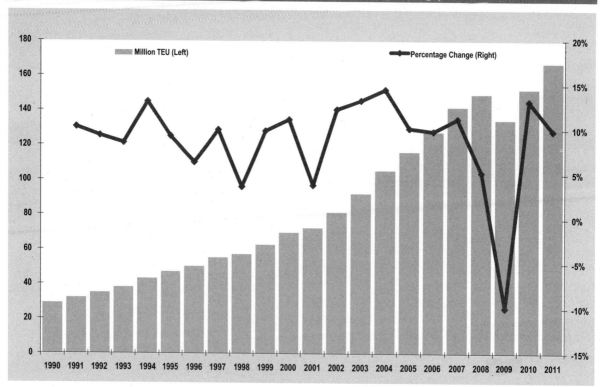

Figure 1.5. Global container trade, 1990–2011 *(TEUs and annual percentage change)*

Source: Drewry Shipping Consultants, *Container Market Review and Forecast* 2008/09; and Clarkson Research Services, *Container Intelligence Monthly,* May 2011.

Note: The data for 2011 were obtained by applying growth rates forecasted by Clarkson Research Services in *Container Intelligence Monthly,* May 2011.

Table 1.7. Estimated cargo flows on major East–West container trade routes, 1995–2009 *(TEUs)*

	Transpacific		Europe Asia		Transatlantic	
	Far East - North America	Far East - North America	Far East - Europe	Europe - Far East	Europe - North Amerrica	North America - Europe
1995	3 974 425	3 535 987	2 400 969	2 021 712	1 678 568	1 691 510
1996	3 989 883	3 649 871	2 607 106	2 206 730	1 705 173	1 603 221
1997	4 564 690	3 454 598	2 959 388	2 323 256	2 055 017	1 719 398
1998	5 386 786	2 857 440	3 577 468	2 097 209	2 348 393	1 662 908
1999	6 108 613	2 922 739	3 898 005	2 341 763	2 423 198	1 502 996
2000	7 308 906	3 525 749	4 650 835	2 461 840	2 694 908	1 707 050
2001	7 428 887	3 396 470	4 707 700	2 465 431	2 577 412	1 553 558
2002	8 353 789	3 369 647	5 104 887	2 638 843	2 633 842	1 431 648
2003	8 997 873	3 607 982	6 869 337	3 763 237	3 028 691	1 635 703
2004	10 579 566	4 086 148	8 166 652	4 301 884	3 525 417	1 883 402
2005	11 893 872	4 479 117	9 326 103	4 417 349	3 719 518	1 986 296
2006	13 164 051	4 708 322	11 214 582	4 457 183	3 735 139	2 053 710
2007	13 540 168	5 300 220	12 982 677	4 969 433	3 510 123	2 414 288
2008	12 896 623	6 375 417	13 311 677	5 234 850	3 393 751	2 618 246
2009	10 621 000	6 116 697	11 361 971	5 458 530	2 738 054	2 046 653

Source: Based on Global Insight Database as published in the "International Maritime transport in Latin America and the Caribbean in 2009 and projections for 2010". *Bulletin FAL*, Issue No. 288 – Number 8/2010, ECLAC.

Figure 1.6. Indices for global container, tanker, and major dry bulk volumes, 1990–2011 *(1990 = 100)*

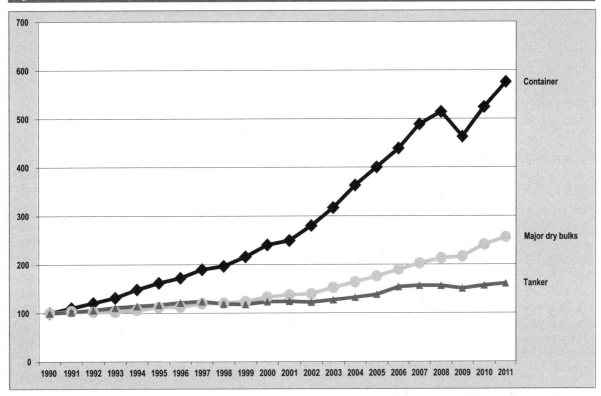

Source: UNCTAD secretariat, based on *Review of Maritime Transport*, various issues; and on Clarkson Research Services, *Shipping Review and Outlook*, Spring 2011.

Table 1.8. Estimated cargo flows on major East–West container trade routes, 2008 –2010
(millions of TEUs and percentage change)

	Transpacific		Europe Asia		Transatlantic	
	Far East – North America	North America – Far East	Asia – Europe	Europe – Asia	Europe – North America	North America– Europe
2008	13.4	6.9	13.5	5.2	3.3	3.3
2009	12.0	7.0	11.5	5.5	2.8	2.5
2010	14.3	8.6	13.5	5.6	3.2	2.8
% change 2009–2010	19%	23%	18%	2%	13%	10%

Source: Container Trade Statistics (CTS), May 2011, and *Containerisation International*, May 2011.

World), the Transpacific Stabilization Agreement and the Westbound Transpacific Stabilization Agreement are now subject to special monitoring requirements and greater oversight. According to the new rules, the groupings have to report changes in overall capacity at a monthly instead of at a quarterly basis, as well as disclose copies of minutes of meetings held by the member lines.

A related development on the regulatory front was the growing pressure to reform the anti-trust legislation governing liner shipping in the United States.[55] Capacity constraints noted above, and their impact on rates, have led shippers to seek the abolition of the antitrust immunity of ocean carriers. Motivated by concerns over some container carrier practices, including abrupt enactment of surcharges, rolling scheduled cargo from ships, and refusing to carry containers on ships from other carriers, a bill was introduced in the United States Congress in 2010 proposing the removal of the antitrust immunity given to the liner shipping industry engaged in United States trade. While the bill died on the order, pressure, including from shippers to amend the existing legislation, is expected to continue. Elsewhere and in a separate and yet related development, Singapore decided to extend by five years until 31 December 2015 its block exemption for liner shipping antitrust immunity.[56]

Empty boxes and their repositioning result from the notorious trade flow imbalances inherent to container shipping. Empty container repositioning is a challenge for the industry since it raises costs and complicates the operational environment. Drewry estimates that there were 50 million TEUs of empty container movement in 2009. Assuming a nominal cost of $400 per TEU for each empty movement (covering terminals, box hire, damage, storage, etc.) carriers imbalance costs are estimated at $20 billion in 2009. If the cost of land-side repositioning of empty containers is added, the total cost in 2009 would reach $30.1 billion or 19 per cent of global industry income in 2009.

According to Clarkson Research Services, global container trade is projected to grow by 9.7 per cent in 2011 to reach 154 million TEUs, outpacing supply growth by 1.7 percentage points. The realization of the outlook, however, depends on continued and sustained growth in demand as well as a good management of growth in ship supply capacity. Aside from the downside risks associated with a potential overcapacity, other uncertainties include the strength of the recovery in Europe and the United States, the evolution in the financial situation in Europe, and the unemployment rate. In addition, container shipping is increasingly facing new challenges that entail potentially some cost implications as well as changes to the structure and operations of the industry.

Relevant emerging challenges include the rise of environmental awareness resulting in more stringent environmental regulation, capacity bottlenecks at ports and hinterland connections, rising fuel prices and rising protectionist bias. The triple disaster, including the nuclear crisis, affecting Japan since March 2011, had direct (e.g. infrastructural damage) and indirect impacts (e.g. broader implications for container trade) on some container ports. For example, concerns over radiation have the potential to affect the level of service and capacity deployment. It has been reported that, after the unfolding of the nuclear crisis, many ships did not call at Japan's ports over concerns of contamination. Container shipping could also be impacted by lack of exports from Japanese factories, causing liner companies to skip Japan's ports on their transpacific trading lanes. More importantly, disruption to the supply chains and the manufacturing business and the potential related consequences, including a structural shift in the global manufacturing industry, are likely to affect container trade.

While the challenges facing the container industry may be significant, a number of opportunities are also emerging and could pave the way for further growth and open new markets. As argued throughout this chapter, the global economy is increasingly being driven by emerging economies, not just BRICs (Brazil, Russian Federation, India and China) but also other emerging economies such as Argentina, Chile, Indonesia, Nigeria, Oman, Qatar, Saudi Arabia, South Africa, Thailand and Viet Nam. New arteries of growth are opening up and more value added services are being packed into containers. The potential is important and many industry players are aware of it as well as the need to be prepared to capitalize on related commercial opportunities. This seems to be already the case, as evidenced by the evolving strategies of some ocean carriers and logistics services such as Maersk Line, CMA CGM, Hamburg Sud, Damco, and Kuehne and Nagel. Over recent years, these companies appear to be preparing to take full advantage of the rising opportunities in emerging markets and sectors including through equipment procurement, personnel designation and changes to organizational structures.

C. SELECTED EMERGING TRENDS AFFECTING INTERNATIONAL SHIPPING

The latest economic downturn and the subsequent recovery have highlighted new trends that are reshaping the landscape of international maritime transport and trade. While not an exhaustive list, the key issues set out below are emerging as very important. These include, in particular, (a) a global new design; (b) energy security, oil prices and transport costs; (c) cutting carbon emissions from international shipping and adapting to climate change impacts; (d) environmental sustainability and Corporate Social Responsibility; and (e) maritime piracy and related costs.

1. A Global new design

With large emerging economies such as the BRICs being the main engine of growth and trade expansion, the relative weight of advanced economies such as the European Union and the United States appears

to be diminishing. The downturn has reinforced a shift of the economic influence from the North and the West to the South and East. This, clearly, is altering the shipping industry's operating context and can be expected to evolve further as cargoes, markets and trade patterns also change in response to the new global design. One recent study finds that China will overtake the United States and dominate global trade in 2030; China will feature in 17 of the top 25 bilateral sea and air freight trade routes.[57] The study also concludes that four key areas could potentially present significant opportunities for transport and logistics firms, including (a) increased intra–Asia–Pacific trade, developed–developing region trade (e.g. China and Germany); (b) intra-emerging economies trade (e.g. China–Latin America); and (c) China–Africa trade. Together, these developments are expected to cause a shift in global trade away from advanced economies toward emerging developing countries as these continue on their urbanization path, growing consumer demand, and a relocation of lower value manufacturing toward new locations (e.g. from China to Indonesia). These developments are likely to affect market segments differently and result in shifts in international transport patterns, with transport growing faster on some routes than others. This also raises the opportunity of opening new markets. In this respect, one study assessing the routing flexibility of container shipping finds that the Cape of Good Hope route has the potential to emerge as a viable alternative to the Suez Canal route for 11 South–South trade lanes, including West Africa–Oceania, West Africa–East Africa, East Coast South America–Oceania and East Coast South America–East Africa.[58] From the perspective of shipping, however, these trends raise crucial questions and uncertainties. For example, there remain questions with respect to the future and the shape of globalization in view of (a) a potential growth in regionalization;[59] (b) the Doha Round of multilateral trade negotiations; (c) the proliferating trade agreements; (d) the possible growth of trade protectionism; (e) efforts of balancing global economic growth and trade flows; and (f) the complex nexus between energy security, oil prices, transport costs, climate change and generally environmental sustainability. These issues need to be better understood and their implications duly considered and assessed, and to the extent possible, incorporated into the decision-making process involving shipping (e.g. planning, investment, ship design, expansion, market locations, etc.).[60]

2.   Energy security, oil prices and transport costs

The rapid growth in global trade recorded over the past few decades was powered by easily available and affordable oil. Shipping, which handles over 80 per cent of the volume of world trade, is heavily reliant on oil for propulsion and is not yet in a position to adopt alternative energy sources.[61] However, as evidenced by the recent surges in oil prices and as highlighted by many observers, the era of easy and cheap oil is drawing to an end with the prospect of a looming peak in global oil production. It should be noted, however, that there could be some mitigating facts such as high oil prices and carbon emissions concerns that push the industry to consider alternatives such as natural gas and renewable energy sources.

Supply and demand fundamentals are the major driver of oil price hikes. According to the International Energy Agency (IEA), worldwide oil demand is outstripping growth in new supplies by 1 million barrels per year. China is leading the growth in demand and nearly 20 million vehicles will be added to roads in 2011. The IEA estimates that some $60 billion must be invested in global oil production capacity every year in order to meet global demand.[62] Higher oil prices can impact on shipping and trade through both their dampening effect on growth – as it is estimated that $10 per barrel rise in the price of oil, if sustained for a year, can cut about 0.2 percentage points from GDP growth[63] – and the upward pressure on the cost of fuel used to propel ships – as higher oil prices drive up ship bunker fuel prices. As fuel costs can account for as much as 60 per cent of a ship's operating costs, a rise in oil prices will undoubtedly increase the transport cost bill for the shippers and therefore potentially undermine trade.[64] A recent study by UNCTAD has shown that a 10 per cent increase in oil prices would raise the cost of shipping a container by around 1.9 per cent to 3.6 per cent, while a similar increase in oil prices would raise the cost of shipping one ton of iron ore and one ton of crude oil would increase by up to 10.5 per cent and 2.8 per cent, respectively.[65] The study concludes that "the results of the investigation confirm that oil prices do have an effect on maritime freight rates in the container trade as well as in the bulk trade with estimated elasticities varying, depending on the market segment and the specification. Moreover, the results for container trade suggest the presence of a structural break, whereby the effect of oil prices on container freight rates is larger in periods of sharply rising and more volatile oil prices, compared to

periods of low and stable oil prices".[66] Bearing in mind the perspective of developing countries, another recent study estimated the impact of higher bunker prices on freight rates, as well as the impact of higher freight rates on consumers and producers.[67] The analysis, which was conducted for several markets – including grain, iron ore, and the container and tanker trades – finds that in the longer term, a change in fuel costs may alter patterns of trade, as the competitiveness of producers in different locations changes as a result of increased transport costs. In line with results of UNCTAD's own investigation, the elasticity of freight rates to bunker prices was found to differ across shipping routes and trades. "The costs pass-through of increased freight rates into product prices also varied across product and market from nearly zero to over 100 per cent: this meant that in some cases the increased costs were effectively paid for by the consumer, and in other cases by the producer." In this context, a good understanding of the interplay between transport costs, energy security and oil price levels is fundamental, especially for the trade of developing countries.

Apart from the impact on transport costs, sustained high oil prices raise a number of questions for international shipping. These include, for example, how to deal with related implications for capital–intensive newly built ships of any changes in fuel type and fuel technology requirements; and the potential for a modal shift when feasible from other modes of transport in favour of shipping, given the relative energy efficiency of ships as compared with other modes of transport. Another issue arising as important for shipping is regulatory-driven and relates to the transition to low sulphur fuel.[68] Tighter sulphur limits for marine fuels were introduced through amendments to the International Convention on the Prevention of Pollution from Ships, known as MARPOL 73/78. The MARPOL Convention includes Annex VI titled "Regulations for the Prevention of Air Pollution from Ships" and which sets limits on NOx and SOx emissions from ship exhausts, and prohibits deliberate emissions of ozone depleting substances.[69] The limits set out in Annex VI can have far-reaching implications for the shipping and oil industry as they affect bunker fuel costs and quality,[70] the future of residual fuel, oil refineries, as well as technologies such as exhaust cleaning systems and alternative fuels. Sulfur limits under MARPOL Annex VI will become effective for emission control areas (ECAs) such as the Baltic Sea, the North Sea, the United States and Canada in 2015. The limits will apply globally from 2020 or 2025.[71]

3. Cutting carbon emissions from international shipping and adapting to climate change impacts

The discussion on energy security and sustainability is closely tied to the current debate on addressing the climate change challenge, since energy can be viewed as both the root cause of the problem and the potential solution. Carbon emissions from international shipping result from the burning of heavy oil in ships' bunkers. Consequently, addressing the issue of bunker fuel through, for example, technology or operational solutions and economic instruments or other measures that provide incentives and/or deterrents can help cut emissions and therefore solve the carbon emissions problem. However, recent estimates by the IEA indicate that greenhouse gas (GHG) emissions increased by a record amount in 2009, to the highest carbon output in history, jeopardising the likelihood of reaching manageable carbon concentration levels.[72] The IEA estimates that if the world is to mitigate the worst impacts of climate change, annual energy-related emissions should not exceed 32Gt by 2020. If the 2010 emissions level is sustained, the 32Gt limit will be exceeded a full nine years ahead of schedule.[73]

Like other economic sectors, international shipping is facing a dual challenge in relation to climate change. International shipping relies heavily on oil for propulsion and generates at least 3 per cent of global carbon emissions and these emissions are projected by the International Maritime Organization (IMO) to treble by 2050. Iinternational shipping is now the subject of negotiations under the auspices of the IMO and the United Nations Framework Convention on Climate Change (UNFCCC). Current discussions are guided by a number of proposals that aim to introduce a variety of measures that could help curb carbon emissions from international shipping. Relevant measures being considered include operational and technological as well as market-based instruments, such as emissions trading scheme and a levy on ships' bunker fuel (see chapter 5 for detail on the IMO/UNFCCC negotiations). However, international shipping and more broadly maritime transport is also facing the challenge of adapting to the current and potential impacts of climate change.

Little attention has been paid so far to the impact of climate change factors such as sea-level rise and extreme weather events on maritime transport, especially ports – the crucial nodes of the global chains linking together buyers and sellers, importers and exporters, and producers and consumers.[74] While mitigation action in international shipping is crucial to curb carbon emissions, building the resilience of the maritime transport systems and strengthening their ability to cope with climatic factors are equally important. Adaptation in transport involves enhancing the resilience of infrastructure and operations through, inter alia, changes in operations, management practices, planning activities and design specifications and standards. The extended timescale of climate change impacts and the long service life of maritime infrastructure, together with sustainable development objectives, imply that effective adaptation is likely to require rethinking freight transport networks and facilities. This may involve integrating climate change considerations into investment and planning decisions, as well as into broader transport design and development plans.[75]

One recent study has estimated that, assuming a sea level rise of 0.5 m by 2050, the value of exposed assets in 136 port mega-cities will be as high as $28 trillion.[76] The challenge is thus significant, and raising awareness and improving understanding of the impacts of climate change on maritime transport and the associated adaptation requirements, including funding needs, are fundamental. Accurate information on the likely vulnerabilities and a good understanding of relevant climatic impacts – including their type, range and distribution across different regions and industries – are required for the design of an effective strategy for adequate adaptation measures in transport. Mobilizing requisite resources to finance adaptation action in maritime transport is important, particularly for developing regions. Yet, so far, resources generally allocated to adaptation remain inadequate, especially when compared with the significant adaptation costs estimated in various reports and studies.[77] It is against this background that the High-level Advisory Group on Climate Change Financing (AGF) – established by the Secretary-General of the United Nations in February 2010 to consider, among other things, the potential sources of revenue that will enable achievement of the level of climate change financing that was promised during the UNFCCC in Copenhagen in December 2009 – recommended imposing a price on carbon emissions from international transport as a potential source for important funding for climate action.[78]

To help fill the prevalent information gap, raise awareness and contribute to shaping effective adaptation action in transport, UNCTAD is increasingly devoting attention to dealing with "the climate change challenge on maritime transport". Earlier related work by the UNCTAD secretariat includes the Multi-year Expert Meeting on Transport and Trade Facilitation, held 16–18 February 2009, whose theme was "Maritime Transport and the Climate Change Challenge". The meeting, held in Geneva, brought together around 180 delegates from 60 countries, including representatives from 20 international organizations, as well as the international shipping and port industries. The three-day meeting was the first of its kind to deal with the multiple challenges of climate change for the maritime transport sector in an integrated manner, focusing both on mitigation and adaptation, as well as on related issues, such as energy, technology and finance.[79] Experts at the meeting highlighted the urgent need to reach agreement in the ongoing negotiations on a regulatory regime for GHG emissions from international shipping.[80] They noted then with great concern that so far, insufficient attention had been paid to the potential impacts and implications of climate change for transportation systems, and in particular for ports, which are key nodes in the supply chain and vital for global trade. The central role of technology and finance was highlighted, as was the need for international cooperation among scientists and engineers, industry, international organizations and policymakers in relation to the preparation and design of adequate adaptation measures.[81]

More recently, and drawing on its mandate and this work, UNCTAD and the United Nations Economic Commission for Europe (ECE) jointly convened a one day workshop on 8 September 2010 with a focus on "Climate Change Impacts on International Transport Networks".[82] The workshop aimed in particular to help raise awareness of the various issues at stake, with a view to assisting policymakers and industry stakeholders, including transport planners, operators, managers and investors, in making informed adaptation decisions. The workshop provided a useful platform for considered discussions and set the pace for future work on how best to bridge the knowledge gap relating to climate change impacts on transport networks and effective adaptation responses for both developed and developing countries. Work on these important considerations continues with the establishment in March 2011 of an international group of experts under the auspices of the ECE to help advance understanding of climate change impacts on international transport networks and related adaptation requirements.[83] The first meeting of the international Expert Group was held on 5 September 2011. It approved the work plan of the Expert Group and its key deliverables, which will include

a substantive report on relevant issues as well as an international conference to disseminate the results of its findings.

Following up on the abovementioned work, UNCTAD organized on 29-30 September 2011 an Ad Hoc Expert Meeting on "Climate Change Impacts and Adaptation: A Challenge for Global Ports". The meeting aimed to provide policymakers, key public and private sector stakeholders, international organizations as well as scientists and engineers with a platform for discussion and an opportunity to share best practices relating to climate change impacts on ports and associated adaptation requirements.[84]

4.   Environmental sustainability and corporate social responsibility

Greater public awareness is driving demand for industries to adopt the principles of corporate social responsibility (CSR) including environmental sustainability.[85] This pressure about the socio-economic as well as environmental sustainability is being felt among the shipping community from both individuals and corporate customers, and there is an increasing call for the shipping industry to adopt as part of its strategic planning, business and operations increased levels of CSR, especially as it applies to environmental sustainability.[86] In adhering to these principles, the shipping community is expected to achieve efficiency, effectiveness and quality of service, while at the same time taking into account the cost generated by any potential negative externalities generated by their activities, including environmental and social. This is particularly illustrated by the growing demand for greater transparency which means that customers and business throughout the supply chains, whether internal or external to the shipping industry, are demanding that social and environmental targets be set and fulfilled to ensure better performances. New technology enables real-time monitoring and assessment of the degree to which shipping is demonstrating leadership in terms of complying with environmental and social targets. The shipping industry can be expected to demonstrate the quality of its performance by allowing customers, regulators and other potentially interested parties to review their performance records. The shipping industry – through the Case for Action paper, which looks ahead to 2040 – recognizes this emerging trend and is considering ways in which it can best respond to these shifting demands.[87] The Case for Action Paper was released under the Sustainable Shipping Initiative (SSI) which brings together leading companies from across the industry and around the world. The goal of the SSI is to transform the global shipping industry and the wider maritime sector by establishing a new, sustainable approach as the norm.

This is illustrated by the liner operators who are increasingly adapting their market strategies to emphasize the ecological and social dimensions as factors of competitiveness business. An example is the ordering by Maersk Line of the triple E-class 18,000 TEUs ships. The design of the 18,000 TEU ships is named triple E-class, reflecting three principles: economy of scale, energy efficiency and environmental improvement.[88] The ships are expected to be deployed on the Asia–Europe route. This trend is likely to step up competition as few other carriers could potentially be in a position to also order larger ships with a view to enhancing economic and resource-use efficiency, environmental sustainability as well as safeguarding market shares. For instance, CMA CGM announced in May 2011 that three of its 13,830 TEU ships on order are to be increased in size to a super-post-Panamax 16,000 TEU class, i.e. potentially the largest ships afloat if received before Maersk's 18,000 TEU ships.[89] Germanischer Lloyd, a leading classification society for large vessels, maintains that the technology is available for the building of 18,000 TEU ships, although the port infrastructure required for the handling of such ships may be lacking. As these ships are expected to be delivered in 2014, it can be expected that ports will be modified to adapt to the new ship sizes. However, ports that rely on tides may be facing more challenges in handling these super-post-Panamax ships.[90]

5.   Maritime piracy and related costs[91]

Despite international efforts to address the problem of maritime piracy, IMO reports that a total of 489 actual or attempted acts of piracy and armed robbery against ships occurred in 2010. This represents an increase of 20.4 per cent over the 2009. Consequently, 2010 is marked by the IMO as the fourth successive year that the number of reported incidents increased. The scale of the attacks and the size of the vessels targeted are raising further concerns in the international community. This threatens to undermine one of the world's busiest shipping routes (Asia–Europe) and chokepoint (the Suez Canal).[92]

While shipping has in many cases avoided the piracy affected area in the Gulf of Aden and off the coast of Somalia by rerouting via the Cape of Good Hope, this alternative is not without costs. These costs are likely to be passed on to shippers in the form of higher freight rates and surcharges. Piracy activities raise insurance fees and ship operating costs, and generate additional costs through rerouting of ships. It is argued that if piracy attacks increased 10 times, it would lead to a reduction of 30 per cent in total traffic along the Far East–Europe trade lane, and that only 18 per cent of the total traffic would sail through the Cape of Good Hope. Existing studies provide a wide range of cost estimates depending on the methodology and the cost items considered. One recent study has estimated the total cost of maritime piracy in 2010 at $7 billion–$12 billion per year, including the ransoms, insurance premiums, rerouting ships, security equipment, naval forces, prosecutions, piracy deterrent organizations and the cost to regional economies.[93] Re-routing ships, insurance premiums, naval forces and security equipment account for the bulk of the costs.

It is estimated that a rerouting through the Cape of Good Hope results in a diversion which lengthens the voyages, and generates costs in addition to the opportunity cost of being unable to make more voyages in a given time period. Additionally, in view of the geographical concentration of recent piracy activity, Africa is likely to be directly affected. In 2010, the macroeconomic costs for four selected African countries and Yemen amounted to $1.25 billion, with Egypt incurring largest loss per year ($642 million) followed by Kenya ($414 million), Yemen ($150 million), Nigeria ($42 million) and Seychelles ($6 million).[94] In Kenya, for example, the costs of imports are estimated to increase by $23.9 million per month and the costs of its exports by $9.8 million per month due to the impact of piracy on the supply chains.[95] However, another report shows that – based on a case study of a 10,000 TEU ship sailing from Rotterdam to Singapore – insurance risk premiums and the Suez Canal transit fees offset to a great extent the additional fuel and opportunity costs of going through the Cape of Good Hope.[96] Thus, in addition to the security risk involved in sailing through piracy ridden areas and related direct costs (e.g. loss of life, injury, loss of ship or cargo, etc.), transiting through the Suez Canal or rerouting via the Cape of Good Hope both entail other significant costs (e.g. delays, higher insurance premiums, opportunity costs, fuel costs, revenue loss for the Suez Canal Authority/Egypt, etc.) which pose a burden to the shipping industry and will ultimately be borne by global trade.[97]

ENDNOTES

1   Data and information used in Section A are based on various sources including in particular: United Nations Department of Economic and Social Affairs. (2011). *World Economic Situation and Prospects 2011*. United Nations publication. New York; United Nations Department of Economic and Social Affairs. *The World Economic and Social Survey*. (2010): Retooling Global Development. New York; International Monetary Fund (2011). *World Economic Outlook*: *Tensions from the Two-Speed Recovery: Unemployment, Commodities, and Capital Flows*. April; Podan P.C, Organization for Economic Cooperation and Development (OECD). (2011). *What is the Economic Outlook for OECD Countries? An Interim Assessment*. April. Paris; Economic Commission for Africa. and African Union. (2011). *Economic Report on Africa: Governing Development in Africa-The Role of the State in Economic Transformation*; World Trade Organization (WTO). (2011). *World Trade 2010, Prospects for 2011*. Press Release. 7 April; and Economist Intelligence Unit (EIU). (2011). *Country Forecast. Global Outlook*. May.

2   For a more comprehensive overview of world economic developments, see UNCTAD's Trade and Development Report, 2011, available at www.unctad.org.

3   United States Energy Information Administration data available at www.eia.gov (data accessed on 25 May 2011).

4   Economist Intelligence Unit (EIU). (2011). *Country Forecast. Global Outlook*. May.

5   Based on data by the UNCTAD secretariat.

6   Foroohar, R. (2011). Rise of the Rest – Developing Economies See Rising Wealth. *Time*. Economy Briefing. 4 April.

7   United Nations Department of Economic and Social Affairs. (2011). *World Economic Situation and Prospects 2011*. United Nations publication. New York.

8   Ibid.

9   Ibid.

10   Clarkson Research Services. (2011). Dry Bulk Trade Outlook. May.

11   Ibid.

12   United Nations Department of Economic and Social Affairs. (2011). *World Economic Situation and Prospects*. Monthly Briefing No 31. May.

13   Shipping and Finance. (2011). 23 May. p. 24.

14   Mathews S (2011). Disaster Could Cost Japan $235 Billion. *Lloyd's List*. 23 March.

15   United Nations Department of Economic and Social Affairs (2011). *World Economic Situation and Prospects*. Monthly Briefing No 31. May.

16   Based, in particular, on the *UNCTAD Handbook of Statistics* and on information published by the World Trade Organization (2011) in "World trade 2010, prospects for 2011". Press release. April. Available at www.wto.org .

17   United Nations Department of Economic and Social Affairs (2011). *World Economic Situation and Prospects 2011*. United Nations publication. New York.

18   Ibid.

19   Ibid.

20   *Containerisation International*. (2011). Building BRICs. 1 March. (http://www.ci-online.co.uk/).

21   Ibid.

22   Economist Intelligence Unit (EIU). (2011). *Country Forecast. Global Outlook*. May.

23   United Nations Department of Economic and Social Affairs. (2011). *World Economic Situation and Prospects 2011*. New York. United Nations. Also reported in various press clippings from *Containerisation International* and *IHS Fairplay*.

24   Shipping and Finance. (2011). *Bright Prospects of World Trade*. p.26.

25   Ibid.

26   Price Waterhouse Coopers (PWHC). (2011). *Economic Views: Future of World Trade: Top 25 Sea and Air Freight Routes in 2030*. 2011.

27   United Nations Department of Economic and Social Affairs. (2011). *World Economic Situation and Prospects 2011*. United Nations publication. New York.

28   OECD-WTO-UNCTAD. (2010). *Report on G20 Trade and Investment Measures (September 2009 to February 2010)*. 8 March.

29   Economist Intelligence Unit (EIU). (2011). *Country Forecast. Global Outlook*. May.

30   Ibid.

31   Masaki H (2011). "Japan, India to Sign Free Trade Agreement". *The Journal of Commerce Online*. 15 February.

32   United Nations Economic and Social Commission for Asia and the Pacific (ESCAP). (2011), *Economic and Social Survey of Asia and the Pacific- Regional Connectivity and Economic Integration*. Bangkok: United Nations.

33   Data and information in Section B are based on UNCTAD's statistics and reports as well as on various specialized sources, including: (a) British Petorleum (BP) (2011). *Statistical Review of World Energy 2011*. June; (b) International Energy Agency (IEA) (2010). *World Energy Outlook 2010*; (c) British Petroleum (BP) (2011). *Energy Outlook 2030*. January. London. (d) International Energy Agency (IEA). *Oil Market Report*. Various issues; (e) International Energy Agency (IEA) (2010). *Medium-Term Oil Market Report*. June; (f) United States Energy Information Administration (EIA) (2011). *Short-Term Energy Outlook*. June; (g) Organization of the Petroleum Exporting Countries (OPEC) (2011). *Monthly Oil Market Report*. June; (h) Organization of the Petroleum Exporting Countries (OPEC) (2010). World Oil Outlook; (i) Economist Intelligence Unit (EIU) (2011). *World Commodity Forecasts: Industrial Raw Materials*. May; (j) Economist Intelligence Unit (EIU) (2011). *World Commodity Forecasts: Food, Feedstuffs and Beverages*. May; (k) World Steel Association (2011). *World Steel Short Range Outlook*. April; (l) International Grains Council (IGC) (2011). *Grain Market Report*. April; (m) Clarkson Research Services Limited (2011). *Shipping Review and Outlook*. Spring issue; (n) Clarkson Research Services Limited (2011). *Container Intelligence Monthly*. Various issues; (o) Clarkson Research Services Limited. (2011). *Dry Bulk Trade Outlook*. Various issues; (p) Lloyd's Shipping Economist (LSE). Various issues; (q) *Drewry Shipping Consultants* (2010). *Container Forecasters – Quarterly Forecast of the Container Market*. September; (r) Drewry Shipping Consultants. *Drewry Shipping Insight*. Monthly Analysis of the Shipping Markets. Various issues; (s) Institute of Shipping Economics and Logistics (ISL). *Shipping Statistics and Market Review*. Various issues; (t) Dynamar. *DynaLiners*. Various issues; (u) *IHS Fairplay*. Various press articles; (v) *BIMCO Bulletins*, various issues; (w) *ICS/ISF Annual Review 2011*; (x) United States Geological Survey. (2011). Mineral Commodity Summaries; and (y) International Transport Forum (ITF) (2011). *Transport Outlook: Meeting the Needs of 9 Billion People.*

34   Schmidt JM (2010). "Ton-mile Demand for VLCCs to Rise by 2.4% Reversing Last Year's -2.95". *Shipping and Finance*. September. p.4.

35   Baird Maritime (2011). "Focus on China: Thirst for Oil". 18 May.

36   British Petroleum (2011). *Energy Outlook 2030*. January. London.

37   United States Energy Information Administration (EIA). Accessed on 25 May 2011.

38   Deloitte Global Service Ltd. (2011). *Energy Predictions 2011*. The "China Effect" No Signs of Slowing Down.

39   See for example, Sand P (2011). "Tsunami and Earthquake in Japan also Affects Shipping". BIMCO. 3 March; "Shipping Prepares to Meet Japan's Post-quake Demand", 24 March 2011. *IHS Fairplay*.

40   Wang S and Notteboom T (2011). "World LNG Shipping: Dynamics in Markets, Ships and Terminal Projects" in *Current Issues in Shipping, Ports and Logistics*. PortEconomics. Uitgeverij UPA University Press Antwerp, Brussels.

41   Ibid.

42   Ibid.

43   Economist Intelligence Unit (EIU). (2011). *World Commodity Forecasts: Industrial Raw Materials*. May.

44   *IHS Fairplay*. (2011). "Australia Reveals Cost of Flood Damage to Exports". 27 January.

45   See also Leander, T. (2011). Floods Expose Hazards in Global Coal Supply. *Lloyd's List*. 11 January.

46   Shipping and Finance. (2011). "Brazil to Double Output of Key Minerals". May. p.12.

47   See Vale Looms Over China. (2011). *Seatrade*. Issue 1. February.

48   Clarskon Research Sercices. (2011). *Dry Bulk Market Outlook*. March.

49   Donley A (2011). Wheat Trade to Double by 2050. *World Grain*. April.

50   Ibid.

51   See for example Sosland M (2011). "Arab Revolution of Great Importance for Wheat". World-Grain.com. 10 March.

52   Asian Development Bank (ADB). (2011). *Global Food Price Inflation and Developing Asia*. March. Philippines.

53   Ibid.

54   *Dynamar B.V. (2011). Dynaliners 05/2011, 04 February; Dynamar B.V (2011). Dynaliners 02/2011, 14 January; and Dynamar B.V (2010). Dynaliners 50/2010, 17 December.*

55   See for example, *IHS Fairplay* (2010). *Anti-competitive Laws Close in on US Carriers*. 14 October (www.fairplay.co.uk); Lloyd's Shipping Economist (2010). "Liner Conferences Battle Goes on". November.

56   *IHS Fairplay* (2010). *Shippers in Singapore Denounce Liner Protection*. 14 October.

57   Price Waterhouse Coopers (PWHC). (2011). *Economic Views: Future of World Trade: Top 25 Sea and Air Freight Routes in 2030.*

58   Notteboom T (2011). "In search of Routing Flexibility in Container Shipping: the Cape Route as an Alternative to the Suez Canal" in *Current Issues in Shipping, Ports and Logistics*. PortEconomics. Uitgeverij UPA University Press Antwerp, Brussels.

59   Forum for the Future – Action for a Sustainable World. (2011). Sustainable Shipping Initiative. The Case of Action.

60   ESKEA (2011). *Deliverable D2.1.1.1.: Maritime Transport Market*. 15 May.

61　　See for example, Chapter 1 of UNCTAD *Review of Maritime Transport 2009 and 2010*. See in particular, UNCTAD. (2010). *Oil Prices and Maritime Freight Rates: An Empirical Investigation Technical report by the UNCTAD secretariat.* UNCTAD/DTL/TLB/2009/2. 1 April.

62　　Blair D (2011). "Price Rises Wipe Out Bids to Cut Fuel Subsidies". *Financial Times.* 12 May and Hargreaves H (2011). "Oil Price Spike: Speculators Aren't to Blame". *CNN Money.* 29 April.

63　　Economist Intelligence Unit (EIU). (2011). *Country Forecast. Global Outlook.*, May; International Monetary Fund (2011). *World Economic Outlook: Tensions from the Two-Speed Recovery: Unemployment, Commodities, and Capital Flows.* April and Te Velde, D.W. (2011). *Oil Prices, Poor Countries and Policy Responses.* Overseas Development Institute (ODI). 16 March.

64　　See for example, Chapter 1 of UNCTAD *Review of Maritime Transport 2009 and 2010*. See in particular, UNCTAD (2010). *Oil Prices and Maritime Freight Rates: An Empirical Investigation Technical report by the UNCTAD secretariat.* UNCTAD/DTL/TLB/2009/2. 1 April.

65　　UNCTAD (2010). *Oil Prices and Maritime Freight Rates: An Empirical Investigation Technical report by the UNCTAD secretariat.* UNCTAD/DTL/TLB/2009/2. 1 April.

66　　Ibid.: 32.

67　　Vivideconomics (2010.) *Assessment of the Economic Impact of Market-based Measures.* Prepared for the Expert Group on Market-based Measures, International Maritime Organization. Final Report. August.

68　　See for example, Einemo, U. (2011). "Fuelling Up". *IHS Fairplay.* 6 January.

69　　For additional information see www.imo.org.

70　　Annex VI (Regulations for the Prevention of Air Pollution from Ships) was added to the International Convention for the Prevention of Pollution from Ships (MARPOL) in 1997, with a view to minimizing airborne emissions from ships (SOx, NOx, ODS, VOC) and their contribution to global air pollution and environmental problems. The Annex VI entered into force on 19 May 2005 and was amended in October 2008. Two sets of emission and fuel quality requirements are defined by Annex VI: (a) global requirements, and (b) more stringent requirements applicable to ships in Emission Control Areas (ECA). An Emission Control Area (ECA) can be designated for SOx and PM, or NOx, or all three types of emissions from ships, subject to a proposal from a Party to Annex VI. Existing Emission Control Areas include: the Baltic Sea; the North Sea; the North American ECA, including most of United States and Canadian coast (NOx & SOx, 2010/2012).

71　　See www.imo.org. See also, ICS/ISF Annual Review 2011; Shipping and the Environment: an insightful look at the environmental issues that are affecting the shipping industry (2011). Issue 02/ Spring. *Lloyd's Register.* London.

72　　Harvery F (2011). "Worst Ever Carbon Emissions Leave Climate on the Brink". *The Guardian.* 29 May. www.guardian.co.uk.

73　　Blair D (2011). "Price Rises Wipe Out Bids to Cut Fuel Subsidies". *Financial Times.* 12 May and Hargreaves H (2011). "Oil Price Spike: Speculators Aren't to Blame". *CNN Money.* 29 April.

74　　See for example International Finance Corporation (IFC). (2011). "Climate Risk and Business Ports: Terminal Marítimo Muelles el Bosque, Cartagena, Colombia".

75　　See for example UNCTAD (2009). *Report of the Multi-year Expert Meeting on Transport and Trade Facilitation on its first session.* TD/B/C.I/MEM.1/3. 23 March. See also ECE and UNCTAD (2010). *Climate Change Impacts on International Transport Networks: Note by the United Nations Economic Commission for Europe and United Nations Conference on Trade and Development secretariats* (ECE/TRANS/WP.5/2010/3). 29 June. Additional information about UNCTAD's work on maritime transport and the climate change challenge, including Joint UNECE-UNCTAD Workshop "Climate Change Impacts on International Transport Networks" available at www.unctad.org/ttl/legal.

76　　Lenton T, Footitt A, Dlugolecki A (2009). *Major Tipping Points in the Earth's Climate System and Consequences for the Insurance Sector.* World Wide Fund For Nature(WWF) and Allianz. Germany.

77　　See for example UNCTAD (2008). *Maritime Transport and the Climate Change Challenge. Note by the UNCTAD secretariat.* TD/B/C.I/MEM.1/2. 9 December. See also, UNCTAD (2009). *Multi-Year Expert Meeting on Transport and Trade Facilitation: Maritime Transport and the Climate Change Challenge. Summary of Proceedings.* UNCTAD/DTL/TLB/2009/1. 1 December.

78　　United Nations (2010). *Report of the Secretary-General's High-Level Advisory Group on Climate Change Financing.* 5 November. United Nations. New York: United Nations. www.un.org/climatechange/agf.

79　　UNCTAD (2009). Report of the Multi-year Expert Meeting on Transport and Trade Facilitation on its first session. TD/B/C.I/MEM.1/3. 23 March.

80　　Ibid.

81　　A summary of the proceedings of the meeting was published in December 2009 (publication No. UNCTAD/DTL/TLB/2009/1) and submitted to the United Nations Framework Convention on Climate Change (UNFCCC) secretariat ahead of the Copenhagen Conference to provide reference material, including a substantive background note prepared by the UNCTAD secretariat.

82   Additional information about the workshop including a joint UNECE-UNCTAD background note and other relevant meeting documentation are available at http://www.unctad.org/Templates/meeting.asp?intItemID=2068&lang=1 &m=20101.

83   For additional information visit www.unctad.org/ttl/legal or http://live.unece.org/trans/main/wp5/wp5_workshop4. html. The Terms of Reference of the expert group are available at http://live.unece.org/fileadmin/DAM/trans/doc/2010/ wp5/ECE-TRANS-WP5-48e.pdf.

84   Additional information about the Ad Hoc Expert Meeting, including related documentation, presentations and the report of the meeting are available at www.unctad.org/ttl/legal under "Meetings and Events".

85   See, for example, "Global Shipping Leaders Call for Sustainable Industry". (2011). Press Release. 17 May; Meade R (2011). "Sustainable Shipping Gets More Industry Clout". Lloyd's List. 23 May.

86   See. for example. Lloyds Register. Shipping and the Environment. Issue 02. Spring 2011. See also Matthews M (2011). "Stopford Calls for Rethink on Economics and Environment". *Lloyd's List*. 30 March.

87   The Case for Action paper can be downloaded from http://www.forumforthefuture.org/project/sustainable-shipping-initiative/more/ssi-case-action.

88   *IHS Fairplay* (2011). "Maersk's Big Ship Order Leaves Competition Training". 10 March.

89   Wackett M (2011). CMA CGM's leviathans to pip Maersk to the post? *Containerisation International*. 26 May.

90   Beddow M (2010). Maersk examining super-super post Panamax vessels. *Containerisation International. Containerisation International*. 26 November.

91   De Coster P, Notteboom T (2011). "Piracy off the Horn of Africa: Impact on Regional Container Services on the Middle East-Africa Trade" in *Current Issues in Shipping, Ports and Logistics*. See also Bowden, A. Hurlburt K, Aloyo, E, Marts, C and Lee, A. (2010). *The Economic Cost of Maritime Piracy*. One Earth Future Working Paper.

92   See, for example, Sand P (2011). *Need for Rethinking When to Sail Around the Cape of Good Hope to Avoid Piracy?* – Update 3. BIMCO. 3 March and Roussanoglou, N. (2011). Hellenic Shipping News Worldwide. 11 March.

93   Bowden A, Hurlburt K, Aloyo E, Marts C and Lee A (2010). *The Economic Cost of Maritime Piracy*. One Earth Future Working Paper.

94   Ibid.

95   Tsolakis K (2011). "African Trade Pays the Price for Piracy". *IHS Fairplay*. 27 January.

96   Bendall HB (2009). *Cost of Piracy: a Comparative Voyage Approach*. IAME. Copenhagen.

97   On the issue of maritime commerce and security in the Indian Ocean see for example Pandya AA, Herbert-Burns H and Kobayashi J (2011). *Maritime Commerce and Security: the Indian Ocean*. The Henry L. Stimson Center. February.

2

STRUCTURE, OWNERSHIP AND REGISTRATION OF THE WORLD FLEET

The year 2010 saw record deliveries of new tonnage, 28 per cent higher than in 2009, resulting in an 8.6 per cent growth in the world fleet. The world merchant fleet reached almost 1.4 billion deadweight tons in January 2011, an increase of 120 million dwt over 2010. New deliveries stood at 150 million dwt, against demolitions and other withdrawals from the market of approximately 30 million dwt. Since 2005, the dry bulk fleet has almost doubled, and the containership fleet has nearly tripled. The share of foreign-flagged tonnage reached an estimated 68 per cent in January 2011.

This chapter presents the supply-side dynamics of the world maritime industry. It covers the structure, age profile, ownership and registration of the world fleet. The chapter also reviews deliveries, demolitions, and tonnage on order.

A.   STRUCTURE OF THE WORLD FLEET

1.   World fleet growth and principal vessel types

Long-term trends in vessel types

The composition of the world fleet reflects the demands for seaborne trade of different commodities, including dry and liquid bulk and manufactured goods (see chapter 1). As manufactured goods are increasingly containerized, the containership fleet has increased its share from 1.6 per cent of the world fleet in 1980 to over 13 per cent in 2011. This has happened mostly at the expense of general cargo vessels, whose share has dropped from 17 to 7.8 per cent during the same period. Refrigerated cargo is also increasingly containerized, and very few new specialized reefer ships are being built. It is estimated that in 2010, only 35 per cent of seaborne perishable reefer cargo was transported by specialized reefer vessels, while 65 per cent was already containerized – a share which is forecast to grow to 85 per cent by 2015.[1] Most of the exporters of refrigerated cargo such as bananas, other fruit, beef and fish are developing countries, which need to adapt their supply chain to this trend of further containerization.

The share of dry bulk tonnage has gone up from 27 per cent to 38 per cent since 1980, while the share of oil tankers has decreased from almost 50 per cent to 34 per cent.

The world fleet in 2011

In January 2011, there were 103,392 seagoing commercial ships in service, with a combined tonnage of 1,396 million dwt. Oil tankers accounted for 475 million dwt and dry bulk carriers for 532 million dwt – an annual increase of 5.5 and 16.5 per cent respectively. Container ships reached 184 million dwt in January 2011, an increase of 8.7 per cent over 2010. The general cargo fleet remained stable, standing at 109 million dwt in January 2011.

Among other vessel types, tonnage of liquefied gas carriers continued to grow, reaching 43 million dwt by January 2011 – an increase of 6.6 per cent over the previous year (fig. 2.1 and table 2.1). Early 2011 saw growing interest in liquefied gas carriers, given that demand for LNG cargo is expected to grow as part of the search for alternative sources of energy.

Among oil tankers, it is estimated that about 26 million dwt of single-hulled ships are still active, although they were scheduled to be phased out by the end of 2010 to reduce the risk of oil spills. They are largely

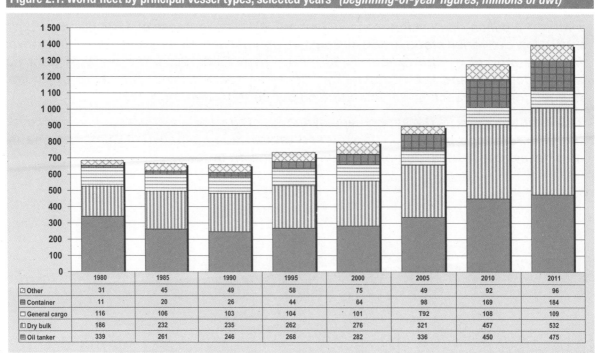

Figure 2.1. World fleet by principal vessel types, selected years[a] *(beginning-of-year figures, millions of dwt)*

	1980	1985	1990	1995	2000	2005	2010	2011
Other	31	45	49	58	75	49	92	96
Container	11	20	26	44	64	98	169	184
General cargo	116	106	103	104	101	T92	108	109
Dry bulk	186	232	235	262	276	321	457	532
Oil tanker	339	261	246	268	282	336	450	475

Source: Compiled by the UNCTAD secretariat on the basis of data supplied by IHS Fairplay.

[a]   Seagoing propelled merchant ships of 100 gross tons and above.

Table 2.1. World fleet size by principal types of vessel, 2010–2011[a] (beginning-of-year figures, thousands of dwt; market share in italics)			
Principal types	2010	2011	Percentage change 2011/2010
Oil tankers	450 053	474 846	5.5
	35.3	*34.0*	*-1.2*
Bulk carriers	456 623	532 039	16.5
	35.8	*38.1*	*2.3*
General cargo ships	108 232	108 971	0.7
	8.5	*7.8*	*-0.7*
Container ships	169 158	183 859	8.7
	13.3	*13.2*	*-0.1*
Other types of ship	92 072	96 028	4.3
	7.2	*6.9*	*-0.3*
Liquefied gas carriers	40 664	43 339	6.6
	3.2	*3.1*	*-0.1*
Chemical tankers	7 354	5 849	-20.5
	0.6	*0.4*	*-0.2*
Offshore supply	24 673	33 227	34.7
	1.9	*2.4*	*0.4*
Ferries and passenger ships	6 152	6 164	0.2
	0.5	*0.4*	*0.0*
Other/n.a.	13 229	7 450	-43.7
	1.0	*0.5*	*-0.5*
World total	1 276 137	1 395 743	9.4
	100.0	*100.0*	

Source: Compiled by the UNCTAD secretariat, on the basis of data supplied by IHS Fairplay.

[a] Seagoing propelled merchant ships of 100 gross tons and above. Percentage shares are shown in italics.

deployed in developing countries, including intra-Indonesian traffic, and for exports from Saudi Arabia to India and Egypt.[2] Under exceptions permitted by IMO, single-hulled tankers are allowed to trade until 2015, so long as they are under 25 years old and are able to pass a condition assessment survey.

Enhancing fuel efficiency

Shipowners are confronted with the long-term prospect of higher fuel prices and stricter emission requirements. Nuclear-fuelled vessels are being considered, which, however, may not find public acceptance in view of recent discussions concerning nuclear energy. Increased attention is being paid to natural gas as a potential fuel for commercial shipping; in 2010, two European companies presented an 8,700 TEU containership concept that uses gas fuel and reportedly cuts CO_2 emissions by as much as one third.[3]

In a similar vein, a shipyard in the Republic of Korea has announced that it has built a ship with lower operating costs, making use of an electronic ship area network.[4] In the medium term, analysts expect more technological advances – including concepts with modified hull forms; the use of air bubble lubrication, air cavity systems and new types of surface materials; and, possibly, ballast-free ships.[5]

New maximum vessel sizes

A classic approach to enhancing fuel efficiency is to increase vessel sizes in order to achieve economies of scale – assuming that the ships will be full. As the industry was recovering from the economic crisis, early 2011 saw orders and deliveries of ships of record-breaking size, in various dry cargo vessel categories.

At the beginning of 2011, the Danish shipping line Maersk announced that it had ordered twenty 18,000 TEU ships, which is a new record for containership size.[6] The cost per ship is reported to be $190 million. The size has been announced as being 400m long and 59m wide, with a draught of 14.5m and tonnage of 165,000 dwt. The new "Triple-E Class" ships will be the longest vessels in existence, as the oil tankers that previously held the record have been scrapped. Delivery of the first vessels is scheduled to take place in 2013. According to the carrier, Triple-E Class ships' CO_2 emissions per transported container are 50 per cent below the current industry average on the Asia–Europe route. Instead of the traditional single propeller, the ships use two engines driving two propellers, with an estimated energy saving of 4 per cent. The Triple-E Class ships have a maximum service speed of 23 knots, which is 2 knots slower than the largest Maersk ships currently in use.

Also with a view to achieving economies of scale, the French carrier CMA CGM and the German owner Offen are reported to be in joint negotiation with shipyards in the Republic of Korea about enlarging five ships from their original specification of 12,800 TEUs to a new specification of 16,000 TEUs. In common with the Maersk E-class vessels, these ships are to be deployed on the Asia–Europe route.

A new vessel of record-breaking size has been launched in the roll-on roll-off (ro-ro) market. In early 2011, the Wilhelm Wilhelmsen company took delivery of the first in a series of four 265-metre-long ships built in Japan by Mitsubishi Heavy Industries.

Containerized reefer capacity has increased too. Hamburg Süd took delivery of a 7,100 TEU container ship in December 2010 which has 1,600 slots for reefer containers – this is among the highest reefer capacity on the container ships that are currently available.

The year 2011 also saw delivery of a dry bulk carrier of record-breaking size, built in the Republic of Korea for the Brazilian conglomerate Vale. The Vale Brasil is 365m long, 66m wide, and has a draught of 23m. It has a capacity of 400,000 dwt – almost 10 per cent larger than the previous record holder. The Vale Brasil is the first in a series of ships called "chinamax" or also "valemax", planned to be deployed by Vale on the Brazil–China route, for iron ore. There are currently 30 chinamax dry bulk carriers on the order books. They are being built by STX and Daewoo Shipbuilding in the Republic of Korea and by Rongsheng in China.[7]

Are these record vessel sizes in various dry cargo shipping markets economically justified? In the 1970s, shipowners that had invested in record-size oil tankers able to carry 3 million barrels of oil lost most of their investment. As fuel prices unexpectedly fell, energy efficiency became less relevant and traders "preferred the 2m barrel parcel".[8] Could the same happen to those that now invest in huge new container ships, ro-ro vessels or dry bulkers? While it is impossible to foresee future downturns in demand, fuel efficiency will certainly remain on the agenda, and economies of scale will be achieved by, for example, reducing construction and labour costs per TEU. As regards the question of shippers' preferences for "parcel" sizes, container ships are different from tankers. Each voyage carries the cargo of thousands of traders who use the containerized liner shipping services. Unlike in oil or dry bulk shipping, no single trader would move an 18,000 TEU "parcel" on his own. It is thus unlikely that containership operators would be confronted by a lack of clients as oil tanker owners were in the 1970s.

In the case of Vale's large dry bulk carriers, the owner of the cargo and the owner of the ship are one and the same company. Again, it appears unlikely that the 1970s oil tanker story of insufficient demand will be repeated, as there is no risk of not finding a "client".

There are, however, other challenges that arise with ever-increasing vessel sizes. Ports and access channels may need to be dredged, cargo handling equipment needs to be able to cope with ever-higher volumes and the wider beam, and arrangements need to be in place to move cargo onwards by road, rail, barge, or feeder ships. If the unloading of a container ship takes several days, a consignee may not know if his box will be the first to be delivered or the last. Other vessels are likely to be pushed onto routes that may not yet be able to cater for larger ships, which include ports in many developing countries. There is also the issue of insurability, as "underwriters are worried about the accumulated level of exposures for mega vessels".[9]

As the first chinamax dry bulk vessels are being delivered to Vale from Brazil, they are confronted with the challenge of finding ports of call. In early 2011, China had not yet authorized them to enter Chinese ports fully loaded, and an iron ore distribution centre at the Chinese port of Qingdao had reportedly not yet been approved. Vale is considering calling in ports in Malaysia and then transshipping the iron ore from there to China, or entering Qingdao not fully loaded.[10]

The need to generate enough cargo for ever-larger ships may lead to further consolidation among shipping lines. Recent years have seen relative stability, but the new wave of large container ships entering service may force carriers to either strengthen their operational alliances or to pursue further growth through mergers and acquisitions.

Will container ships get much bigger than 18,000 TEUs? The possible plateau of 18,000 TEUs was already mentioned more than a decade ago, under the name of "malaccamax", as presented in the year 2000 by Professor Niko Wijnolst of Delft University of Technology. The dimensions of the malaccamax were different, as it had a draught of 21m. This would have required the dredging of the Suez Canal, and is the maximum draught to pass the Malacca Strait. In 2000, an article in Lloyd's List asked "what could happen if mad shipping companies decide to go down this road" of 18,000 TEU ships "in pursuance of lowest possible costs for the sea leg, with all the present ports furiously dredging to stay connected".[11] With a draught of 14.5m, the Triple-E class vessels will not face restrictions passing the Malacca Strait. Some shipyards in the Republic of Korea have presented designs for ships of up to 22,000 TEUs, which would be longer, but not significantly wider or deeper.[12] Although designs exist for malaccamax container ships of up to 35,000 TEUs, the depth and crane outreach in today's major container ports can only handle ships with a maximum capacity of between

18,000 and 22,000 TEUs. Any further significant growth in vessel sizes would require massive port investments. Probably a plateau has been reached.

Container ships

The sizes of newly delivered container ships continued to grow in 2010, leading to an increase in the average container-carrying capacity per ship of 5.5 per cent between early 2010 and early 2011. Of the container ships delivered in 2010, twenty-nine units were larger than 10,000 TEUs, including seven 14,000 TEU ships operated by the Swiss carriers MSC, and owned by the German company Offen. The average container-carrying capacity of the 293 new fully cellular container ships delivered in 2010 was 4,810 TEUs – an increase of 20 per cent over 2009. The total container-carrying capacity of the fully cellular containership fleet reached more than 14 million TEUs (table 2.2).

Most new container ships are gearless. In 2010, only 4.4 per cent of TEU capacity on new vessels was geared – a further decrease from the 7.5 per cent share in 2009 (table 2.3). The share of geared ships is highest in the 2,000 to 2,499 TEU size range, where 63 per cent of the existing fleet is geared. Among the smallest ships, of 100 to 499 TEUs, the geared share is 31 per cent, whereas for ships larger than 4,000 TEUs, the share is practically zero.[13] Even

smaller container ports in developing countries need to cater more and more for gearless vessels, leaving them with no choice but to invest in container cranes.

Containers

The importance of containerization for global trade is mirrored by the growth in the fleet of containers themselves. In early 1991, there were slightly under 7 million TEUs of containers in use for transporting seaborne trade; by January 2011, this figure had grown more than fourfold, to 29 million TEUs.

While the box fleet is growing, so is the efficiency of its deployment. In 1990, each container was loaded or unloaded approximately 14 times during the year. Thanks to more transshipment, faster ships, and improved port handling and customs clearance, this figure had gone up to about 19 port moves per container by 2010. A similar trend is observed when the box fleet is compared with the total slot capacity on container ships; the rate decreased from three to two boxes per slot between January 1991 and January 2011. This, however, is not only a reflection of the improved productivity of the containership fleet; it is also, to some extent, a result of the current oversupply of containership capacity against a shortage of empty containers.[14]

Generally, the production of containers reacts relatively quickly to shifts in demand. Unlike ship construction,

Table 2.2. Long-term trends in the cellular container ship fleet[a]

World total	1987	1997	2007	2008	2009	2010	2011	Growth 2011/2010 (per cent)
Number of vessels	1 052	1 954	3 904	4 276	4 638	4 677	4 868	4.08
TEU capacity	1 215 215	3 089 682	9 436 377	10 760 173	12 142 444	12 824 648	14 081 957	9.80
Average vessel size (TEU)	1 155	1 581	2 417	2 516	2 618	2 742	2 893	5.50

Source: Compiled by the UNCTAD secretariat, on the basis of data supplied by IHS Fairplay.

[a]   Fully cellular container ships of 100 gross tons and above. Beginning-of-year figures (except those from 1987, which are mid-year figures).

Table 2.3. Geared and gearless fully cellular container ships built in 2009 and 2010

	Geared			Gearless			Total		
	2009	2010	Change %	2009	2010	Change %	2009	2010	Change %
Ships	45	30	-33.3	235	263	11.9	280	293	4.6
Percentage of ships	16.1	10.2		83.9	89.8		100.0	104.6	
TEU	84 436	61 694	-26.9	1 040 119	1 347 515	29.6	1 124 555	1 409 209	25.3
Percentage of TEU	7.5	4.4		92.5	95.6		100.0	125.3	
Average vessel size (TEU)	1 876	2 056	9.6	4 426	5 124	15.8	4 016	4 810	19.8

Source: Compiled by the UNCTAD secretariat on the basis of data on the existing containership fleet from Containerisation International Online, May 2010 (2009 data) and May 2011 (2010 data).

where order books usually deal with periods lasting several years, and construction easily takes a year (depending on the vessel type), container factories can increase or decrease production relatively easily, and the period between ordering a new standard container and its delivery can be just three months. Nevertheless, in early 2011, some carriers were expressing concerns about a shortage of containers, after production in 2009 practically came to a standstill, while today's demand has surged in line with new box ship deliveries and continued slow steaming. The latter further adds to the demand, because containers (empty and full) spend more time at sea. The March 2011 tsunami in Japan reportedly resulted in the loss of as many as 1 million TEUs.[15] Carriers have reacted by extending the life of older boxes and by deploying entire ships just to reposition empties. Maersk Line reportedly started manufacturing new containers on its own account, and lines may again impose "peak season surcharges" on shippers.[16]

In 2009, following the economic crisis, lessors of containers had to adjust to a dramatic standstill in demand, as shipping lines returned their leased containers to them. When demand resumed, lessors reacted first by ordering new boxes. During 2010, lessors increased their fleet by 23 per cent, and now own 43.4 per cent of the global TEU capacity (fig. 2.2). As regards specialized reefer boxes, which account

for about 6.4 per cent of the container fleet, lessors in 2010 took delivery of 55 per cent of new reefer containers, up from just 30 per cent in 2008.

2. Age distribution of the world merchant fleet

Container ships continue to be the youngest vessel type, with an average age per ship of 10.7 years, followed by bulk carriers (15.3 years), oil tankers (16.4 years), general cargo ships (24.2 years) and other types (25.1 years) (table 2.4). The average age of the world fleet continued to decrease during 2010, as a result of record deliveries of new tonnage. In particular, the age per deadweight ton decreased (compared to the age per ship), as the new ships tend to be larger than most of those in the existing fleet. Vessels built during the last four years are, on average, 6.5 times larger than those built 20 years earlier.

With regard to flags of registration, the open registry fleet is, on average, the youngest among the country groups depicted in table 2.4, with an average age per ship of 14.8 years and with 27 per cent of ships younger than five years. Among the ten major open registries, the Marshall Islands has the youngest fleet (with an average age per ship of 8.8 years), followed by the Isle of Man (10.4), Liberia (10.9) and Antigua and Barbuda (11.3). The oldest ships are those registered in Saint Vincent and the Grenadines (24.5

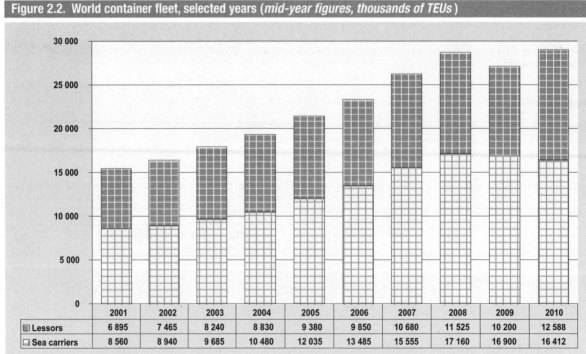

Figure 2.2. World container fleet, selected years (*mid-year figures, thousands of TEUs*)

	2001	2002	2003	2004	2005	2006	2007	2008	2009	2010
Lessors	6 895	7 465	8 240	8 830	9 380	9 850	10 680	11 525	10 200	12 588
Sea carriers	8 560	8 940	9 685	10 480	12 035	13 485	15 555	17 160	16 900	16 412

Source: Compiled by the UNCTAD secretariat on the basis of data supplied by *Containerisation International*.

years), among which general cargo vessels have the highest average age (29.1 years) (fig. 2.3).

Different registries specialize in different vessel types (see also below chapter 2.C). Accordingly, some registries focus on new general cargo ships, others on new bulk carriers, and yet others on new container ships. Antigua and Barbuda, for example, has the youngest fleet of general cargo ships (12.1 years), while the Marshall Islands has the youngest liquid and dry bulk vessels (7.0 and 8.5 years respectively). Liberia and Cyprus have the youngest fleets of container ships (8.2 years). For all four major vessel types, Saint Vincent and the Grenadines has the oldest ships.

B. OWNERSHIP AND OPERATION OF THE WORLD FLEET

1. Shipowning countries

As at early 2011, owners from Greece controlled an estimated 16.2 per cent of the world's deadweight tonnage – a record amount, equating to more than 202 million dwt. Next were Japan (15.8 per cent), Germany (9.2 per cent) and China (8.6 per cent) (table 2.5).[17] In terms of vessel numbers, owners from Germany, Japan and China have more ships than Greek owners. In terms of nationally flagged and nationally owned tonnage, the Greek fleet continues to be by far the world's largest, accounting for 65 million dwt, followed by the Chinese-

Table 2.4. Age distribution of the world merchant fleet, by vessel type, as at 1 January 2011 (percentage of total ships and dwt)

Country grouping Types of vessel		0–4 years	5–9 years	10–14 years	15–19 years	20 years and +	Average age (years) 2010	Average age (years) 2009	Change 2011/2010
WORLD									
Bulk carriers	Ships	25.1	14.6	13.2	11.6	35.5	15.29	16.58	-1.28
	dwt	32.0	17.4	14.0	13.1	23.5	12.49	13.77	-1.28
average vessel size (dwt)		75 607	70 918	63 151	67 114	39 294			
Container ships	Ships	28.2	24.4	19.7	14.8	12.9	10.70	10.56	0.15
	dwt	35.6	28.8	17.2	10.4	7.9	8.84	8.72	0.12
average vessel size (dwt)		47 516	44 240	32 751	26 509	23 117			
General cargo	Ships	10.4	9.0	8.4	11.0	61.1	24.15	24.63	-0.47
	dwt	18.9	11.4	12.6	9.6	47.6	20.27	21.40	-1.13
average vessel size (dwt)		9 221	6 399	7 601	4 453	3 962			
Oil tankers	Ships	25.1	18.5	10.1	11.7	34.6	16.37	17.03	-0.67
	dwt	33.6	29.2	16.4	11.6	9.1	9.74	10.13	-0.39
average vessel size (dwt)		57 414	67 739	69 451	42 595	11 322			
Other types	Ships	10.0	9.4	9.2	8.4	63.1	25.19	25.33	-0.14
	dwt	29.0	15.5	10.7	8.1	36.7	17.11	17.47	-0.37
average vessel size (dwt)		4 891	2 789	1 957	1 633	979			
All ships	Ships	13.9	11.4	10.0	9.9	54.8	22.49	22.93	-0.44
	dwt	31.8	22.3	14.9	11.6	19.3	12.59	13.35	-0.76
average vessel size (dwt)		30 935	26 356	20 161	15 927	4 760			
DEVELOPING ECONOMIES									
Bulk carriers	Ships	26.0	14.9	12.3	11.1	35.7	14.99	16.35	-1.36
	dwt	31.6	16.9	12.6	13.4	25.6	12.77	14.04	-1.26
average vessel size (dwt)		74 932	70 111	63 365	74 904	44 247			
Container ships	Ships	29.6	22.8	18.0	15.4	14.1	10.83	10.74	0.09
	dwt	38.3	27.6	14.9	10.9	8.3	8.71	8.59	0.12
average vessel size (dwt)		46 371	43 329	29 602	25 431	21 115			
General cargo	Ships	10.7	9.8	7.5	8.9	63.1	24.07	24.73	-0.66
	dwt	19.7	10.6	10.8	9.2	49.6	20.39	21.75	-1.36
average vessel size (dwt)		10 013	5 892	7 870	5 597	4 271			
Oil tankers	Ships	24.8	15.2	9.6	11.1	39.3	17.15	18.18	-1.03
	dwt	34.2	26.4	14.2	13.7	11.5	10.33	11.02	-0.70
average vessel size (dwt)		58 677	73 757	62 818	52 400	12 441			
Other types	Ships	12.8	10.0	7.6	8.3	61.2	24.33	24.66	-0.33
	dwt	25.2	13.0	9.6	8.7	43.5	19.06	19.16	-0.10
average vessel size (dwt)		3 777	2 503	2 432	2 025	1 368			
All ships	Ships	16.1	11.8	9.0	9.5	53.5	21.61	22.31	-0.70
	dwt	31.9	20.5	13.1	12.6	21.9	13.11	14.01	-0.90
average vessel size (dwt)		31 657	27 741	23 394	21 117	6 535			

Table 2.4. Age distribution of the world merchant fleet, by vessel type, as at 1 January 2011 *(% of total ships and dwt)*

Country grouping Types of vessel		0–4 years	5–9 years	10–14 years	15–19 years	20 years and +	Average age (years) 2010	Average age (years) 2009	Change 2011/2010
DEVELOPED ECONOMIES									
Bulk carriers	Ships	16.9	11.8	15.3	17.1	38.9	18.13	19.18	-1.06
	dwt	30.5	18.8	19.0	14.4	17.3	12.06	13.42	-1.36
average vessel size (dwt)		94 405	83 519	65 207	44 002	23 204			
Container ships	Ships	21.3	32.1	25.0	13.5	8.1	10.28	9.91	0.37
	dwt	26.3	35.2	23.6	9.1	5.9	9.12	8.68	0.44
average vessel size (dwt)		60 730	54 058	46 475	33 221	35 477			
General cargo	Ships	15.3	11.6	15.2	21.3	36.6	19.66	20.84	-1.18
	dwt	25.6	17.1	20.6	11.8	25.0	15.19	16.68	-1.50
average vessel size (dwt)		7 032	6 152	5 684	2 318	2 864			
Oil tankers	Ships	22.8	27.9	12.8	18.6	17.9	13.67	13.82	-0.15
	dwt	29.6	38.6	21.3	8.0	2.6	8.18	7.87	0.30
average vessel size (dwt)		54 561	58 280	70 009	18 061	6 061			
Other types	Ships	7.9	10.4	12.9	9.2	59.6	24.91	25.29	-0.38
	dwt	23.3	21.9	17.4	10.2	27.3	15.49	16.36	-0.87
average vessel size (dwt)		3 013	2 168	1 381	1 136	469			
All ships	Ships	10.8	12.6	13.6	11.9	51.1	22.66	23.15	-0.49
	dwt	28.3	29.9	20.7	10.3	10.7	10.78	11.02	-0.24
average vessel size (dwt)		20 949	18 961	12 106	6 846	1 675			
COUNTRIES WITH ECONOMIES IN TRANSITION									
Bulk carriers	Ships	27.0	5.5	5.8	13.3	48.4	17.99	20.83	-2.83
	dwt	24.8	7.3	8.5	16.6	42.7	17.33	19.35	-2.03
average vessel size (dwt)		33 165	47 672	53 274	45 041	31 842			
Container ships	Ships	13.2	18.0	9.6	25.2	34.0	15.95	15.85	0.10
	dwt	24.6	29.7	3.9	17.5	24.3	12.35	12.23	0.12
average vessel size (dwt)		49 182	43 476	10 694	18 333	18 821			
General cargo	Ships	6.4	10.8	4.5	9.3	68.9	24.68	24.54	0.15
	dwt	6.9	7.9	4.5	6.4	74.2	25.68	25.59	0.09
average vessel size (dwt)		3 838	2 611	3 589	2 460	3 852			
Oil tankers	Ships	15.0	12.7	4.1	9.3	58.9	22.19	23.50	-1.32
	dwt	37.3	26.2	6.3	13.7	16.5	10.97	13.06	-2.08
average vessel size (dwt)		39 610	32 848	24 281	23 488	4 470			
Other types	Ships	6.5	5.7	3.5	8.6	75.7	25.71	25.76	-0.05
	dwt	36.4	25.3	6.8	11.3	20.2	11.55	13.93	-2.38
average vessel size (dwt)		25 024	19 799	8 588	5 854	1 189			
All ships	Ships	9.6	8.9	4.3	9.9	67.3	23.90	24.37	-0.47
	dwt	26.6	16.3	6.8	13.5	36.8	16.24	18.09	-1.85
average vessel size (dwt)		25 088	16 586	14 003	12 346	4 931			
TEN MAJOR OPEN AND INTERNATIONAL REGISTRIES									
Bulk carriers	Ships	30.0	17.1	13.8	10.3	28.8	13.08	14.33	-1.25
	dwt	34.9	18.4	13.1	11.8	21.8	11.49	12.65	-1.17
average vessel size (dwt)		80 152	74 256	65 540	78 864	52 092			
Container ships	Ships	32.0	25.2	19.3	14.0	9.5	9.61	9.61	0.00
	dwt	39.0	28.4	15.7	9.9	7.1	8.28	8.30	-0.02
average vessel size (dwt)		46 510	42 977	31 031	27 028	28 512			
General cargo	Ships	17.9	11.0	13.4	11.7	45.9	18.58	19.81	-1.22
	dwt	24.3	13.7	15.1	9.6	37.4	16.21	17.77	-1.56
average vessel size (dwt)		13 041	11 950	10 807	7 839	7 862			
Oil tankers	Ships	37.1	27.0	13.5	8.6	13.8	9.81	10.70	-0.89
	dwt	32.7	30.3	17.5	12.1	7.4	9.14	9.48	-0.34
average vessel size (dwt)		67 760	86 077	100 017	107 455	41 024			
Other types	Ships	21.6	11.5	11.1	6.9	49.0	20.49	21.23	-0.74
	dwt	35.3	14.5	9.5	5.7	35.0	15.84	15.88	-0.04
average vessel size (dwt)		19 604	15 188	10 297	9 890	8 565			
All ships	Ships	27.0	17.4	13.9	10.2	31.5	14.79	15.89	-1.09
	dwt	34.1	23.2	14.8	11.2	16.6	11.10	11.83	-0.73
average vessel size (dwt)		51 393	54 248	43 583	44 719	21 480			

Source: Compiled by the UNCTAD secretariat, on the basis of data supplied by IHS Fairplay.
[a] Seagoing propelled merchant ships of 100 gross tons and above.

Figure 2.3. Average age per ship, by vessel type, 10 major open registries *(beginning of 2011, in years)*

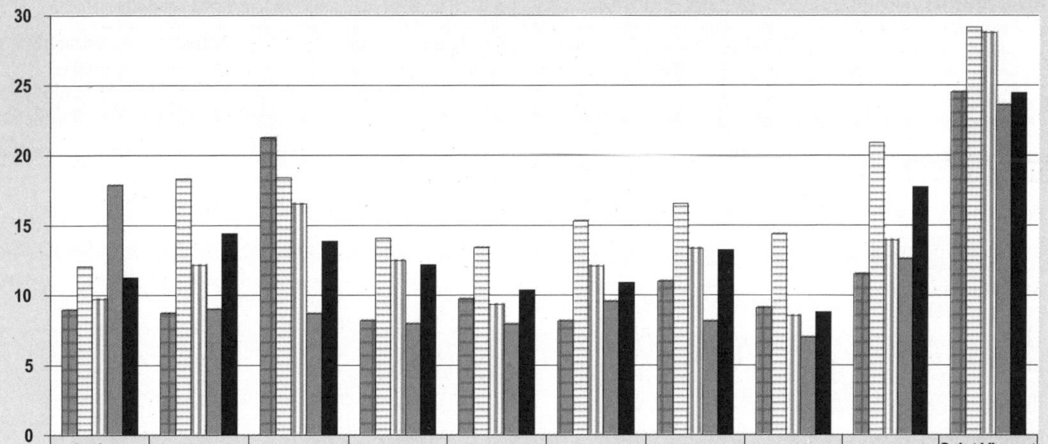

	Antigua and Barbuda	Bahamas	Bermuda	Cyprus	Isle of Man	Liberia	Malta	Marshall Islands	Panama	Saint Vincent and the Grenadines
Container	8.9	8.7	21.3	8.2	9.7	8.2	11.0	9.1	11.5	24.5
General cargo	12.1	18.3	18.4	14.1	13.4	15.3	16.5	14.4	20.9	29.1
Dry bulk	9.7	12.2	16.5	12.5	9.3	12.1	13.3	8.5	13.9	28.7
Oil tanker	17.9	9.0	8.7	8.0	7.9	9.5	8.1	7.0	12.6	23.6
All ships	11.3	14.4	13.9	12.2	10.4	10.9	13.2	8.8	17.7	24.5

Source: Compiled and calculated by the UNCTAD secretariat on the basis of data supplied by IHS Fairplay.

Table 2.5. The 35 countries and territories with the largest owned fleets (dwt), as at 1 January 2011[a]

Country or territory of ownership [b]	Number of vessels			Deadweight tonnage				
	National flag[c]	Foreign flag	Total	National flag[c]	Foreign flag	Total	Foreign flag as a percentage of total	Total as a percentage of world total, 1 Jan. 2011
Greece	758	2 455	3 213	64 659 201	137 728 951	202 388 152	68.05	16.17
Japan	724	3 071	3 795	18 942 573	178 287 143	197 229 716	90.40	15.76
Germany	442	3 356	3 798	17 149 221	97 623 425	114 772 646	85.06	9.17
China	2 044	1 607	3 651	46 207 468	61 762 042	107 969 510	57.20	8.63
Republic of Korea	736	453	1 189	18 135 391	29 317 780	47 453 171	61.78	3.79
United States	971	1 001	1 972	24 363 690	22 011 225	46 374 915	47.46	3.71
Norway	818	1 166	1 984	14 850 693	28 127 239	42 977 932	65.45	3.43
China, Hong Kong SAR	399	313	712	24 102 438	13 080 401	37 182 839	35.18	2.97
Denmark	383	592	975	13 998 073	21 113 253	35 111 326	60.13	2.81
China, Taiwan Province of	97	565	662	4 096 790	28 863 160	32 959 950	87.57	2.63
Singapore	659	362	1 021	18 693 547	12 939 490	31 633 037	40.90	2.53
Bermuda	17	268	285	2 297 441	28 252 207	30 549 648	92.48	2.44
Italy	616	220	836	16 556 782	6 774 107	23 330 889	29.03	1.86
United Kingdom	366	412	778	8 927 892	13 395 899	22 323 791	60.01	1.78
Turkey	551	648	1 199	7 869 898	11 914 688	19 784 586	60.22	1.58
Russian Federation	1 406	485	1 891	5 548 938	13 952 473	19 501 411	71.55	1.56
Canada	210	226	436	2 474 401	16 654 836	19 129 237	87.06	1.53
India	460	74	534	14 679 913	3 445 887	18 125 800	19.01	1.45

Table 2.5. The 35 countries and territories with the largest owned fleets (dwt), as at 1 January 2011ᵃ (concluded)

Country or territory of ownership ᵇ	Number of vessels			Deadweight tonnage				
	National flagᶜ	Foreign flag	Total	National flagᶜ	Foreign flag	Total	Foreign flag as a percentage of total	Total as a percentage of world total, 1 Jan. 2011
Malaysia	421	105	526	9 323 448	4 743 829	14 067 277	33.72	1.12
Belgium	91	158	249	6 119 923	6 835 060	12 954 983	52.76	1.04
Iran (Islamic Republic of)	62	80	142	628 381	12 024 439	12 652 820	95.03	1.01
Saudi Arabia	70	105	175	1 745 029	10 675 882	12 420 911	85.95	0.99
Brazil	128	44	172	2 227 804	8 400 258	10 628 062	79.04	0.85
Indonesia	868	85	953	8 203 079	1 757 088	9 960 167	17.64	0.80
Cyprus	129	158	287	4 016 022	5 462 113	9 478 135	57.63	0.76
Netherlands	522	320	842	4 357 102	5 076 376	9 433 478	53.81	0.75
United Arab Emirates	69	354	423	655 296	8 705 135	9 360 431	93.00	0.75
France	177	274	451	3 179 832	5 888 255	9 068 087	64.93	0.72
Viet Nam	476	86	562	4 723 669	2 249 774	6 973 443	32.26	0.56
Sweden	115	186	301	1 161 602	4 481 787	5 643 389	79.42	0.45
Kuwait	35	45	80	2 986 997	2 636 129	5 623 126	46.88	0.45
Isle of Man	-	33	33	-	5 456 847	5 456 847	100.00	0.44
Spain	163	226	389	1 508 173	3 482 572	4 990 745	69.78	0.40
Thailand	285	53	338	3 475 509	1 014 469	4 489 978	22.59	0.36
Qatar	46	32	78	878 634	3 315 599	4 194 233	79.05	0.34
Total top 35 countries	15 314	19 618	34 932	378 744 850	817 449 818	1 196 194 668	68.34	95.57
Other owners	2 077	1 838	3 915	20 509 703	34 945 087	55 454 790	63.02	4.43
Total of known country of ownership	17 391	21 456	38 847	399 254 553	852 394 905	1 251 649 458	68.10	100.00
Others, unknown country of ownership			6 815			126 581 435		
World total			45 662			1 378 230 893		

Source: Compiled by the UNCTAD secretariat on the basis of data supplied by IHS Fairplay.
ᵃ Vessels of 1,000 GT and above, ranked by deadweight tonnage; excluding the United States Reserve Fleet and the United States and Canadian Great Lakes fleets (which have a combined tonnage of 5.4 million dwt).
ᵇ The country of ownership indicates where the true controlling interest (i.e. parent company) of the fleet is located. In several cases, determining this has required making certain judgements. Thus, for instance, Greece is shown as the country of ownership for vessels owned by a Greek national whose company has representative offices in New York, London and Piraeus, although the owner may be domiciled in the United States.
ᶜ Includes vessels flying the national flag but registered in territorial dependencies or associated self-governing territories such as Gibraltar, Guernsey, Isle of Man or Jersey (United Kingdom), and in second registries such as DIS (Denmark), NIS (Norway) or FIS (France). For the United Kingdom, British-flagged vessels are included under the national flag, except for Bermuda.

owned and -flagged fleet which accounts for 46 million dwt. Eight of the top ten shipowning countries use foreign flags for more than half of their tonnage. The exceptions are the United States, which uses the national flag for 53 per cent of its nationally owned fleet, and owners from Hong Kong (China), who use the flag of Hong Kong (China) for 75 per cent of their tonnage. Together, the top 35 shipowning countries have an estimated market share of 95.6 per cent of the world

tonnage. About a third of this tonnage is controlled by developing-country owners, about 66 per cent by developed-country owners, and 1.56 per cent by Russian Federation owners.[18] Of the top 35 shipowning countries and territories, 17 are developed, 17 are developing, and one is a transition economy. With regard to regional distribution, 17 countries or territories are in Asia, 14 are in Europe, and 4 are in the Americas, while none are in Africa or Oceania.

As regards flags of registration, 68.3 per cent of the world's tonnage is foreign-flagged. One of the motivations for shipowners to use a foreign flag is the possibility of employing foreign seafarers. This is of particular interest to companies based in countries with high wage levels – which is more likely to be the case in developed than in developing countries. It is, hence, not surprising that the percentage of foreign registration is higher for developed countries (where approximately 74 per cent of the nationally owned tonnage is foreign-flagged) than it is for developing countries (where about 65 per cent is foreign-flagged) (see also chapter 6 for a more detailed discussion on the participation of developing countries in different shipping businesses). The tonnage of owners from the Russian Federation grew by

23 per cent between 2005 and 2010. The Russian Federation increasingly uses foreign flags, and as a result, the nationally flagged Russian fleet effectively decreased by 20 per cent over the same period.[19]

2. Container shipping operators

Container shipping is an increasingly concentrated sector. The market share of the top 20 liner shipping companies continued to grow in 2010, reaching almost 70 per cent of TEU capacity in January 2011 (table 2.6). The highest year-on-year growth was recorded by Chilean carrier CSAV (see also chapter 6), followed by PIL from Singapore, and Israel's Zim.

Table 2.6. The 20 leading service operators of container ships, 1 January 2011 (number of ships and total shipboard capacity deployed (TEUs))

Ranking	Operator	Country/territory	Number of vessels	Average vessel size	TEU	Share of world total, TEU	Cumulated share, TEU	Percentage of growth in TEU over 2010
1	Maersk Line	Denmark	414	4 398	1 820 816	11.2%	11.2%	4.2%
2	MSC	Switzerland	422	4 176	1 762 169	10.8%	22.0%	16.9%
3	CMA CGM Group	France	288	3 715	1 069 847	6.6%	28.6%	13.2%
4	Evergreen Line	China, Taiwan Province of	162	3 666	593 829	3.7%	32.3%	0.2%
5	APL	Singapore	141	4 197	591 736	3.6%	35.9%	12.8%
6	COSCON	China	147	3 848	565 728	3.5%	39.4%	14.1%
7	Hapag-Lloyd Group	Germany	126	4 446	560 197	3.4%	42.8%	19.1%
8	CSCL	China	120	3 841	460 906	2.8%	45.7%	0.8%
9	Hanjin	Republic of Korea	98	4 565	447 332	2.8%	48.4%	11.8%
10	CSAV	Chile	119	3 217	382 786	2.4%	50.8%	95.4%
11	OOCL	China, Hong Kong SAR	85	4 408	374 714	2.3%	53.1%	29.1%
12	MOL	Japan	91	3 989	362 998	2.2%	55.3%	4.2%
13	NYK	Japan	85	4 152	352 915	2.2%	57.5%	-1.9%
14	K Line	Japan	84	4 143	347 989	2.1%	59.6%	7.0%
15	Hamburg Sud	Germany	98	3 423	335 449	2.1%	61.7%	18.2%
16	Yang Ming	China, Taiwan Province of	78	4 137	322 723	2.0%	63.7%	1.7%
17	HMM	Republic of Korea	60	4 753	285 183	1.8%	65.4%	9.7%
18	Zim	Israel	73	3 857	281 532	1.7%	67.2%	30.5%
19	PIL	Singapore	111	2 146	238 241	1.5%	68.6%	36.9%
20	UASC	Kuwait	47	3 800	178 599	1.1%	69.7%	1.1%
Total top 20 carriers			2 849	3 979	11 335 689	69.7%	69.7%	12.4%
Others			6 839	719	4 918 299	30.3%	30.3%	1.1%
World containership fleet			9 688	1 678	16 253 988	100.0%	100.0%	8.7%

Source: UNCTAD secretariat, based on Containerisation International Online, Fleet Statistics. Available at www.ci-online.co.uk.

Note: Includes all container-carrying ships. Not fully comparable to tables 2.2. and 2.3 above, which only cover the specialized fully cellular container ships.

Maersk Line from Denmark continues to occupy the top position, although the second and third carriers, MSC and CMA CGM, grew three to four times faster during the year, narrowing the gap. In terms of vessel numbers, the Geneva-based carrier MSC was effectively ahead of Maersk.

The top 20 liner companies have remained unchanged, for a second consecutive year since 2009. Asian economies dominate the list, with 14 companies from that region. One of the top 20 carriers is from Latin America, five are from Europe, and none are from Oceania or North America.

C.   REGISTRATION OF SHIPS

1.   Flags of registration

In 2011, more than 68 per cent of the world's tonnage is registered under a foreign flag (fig. 2.4). Most of the major flags of registration are not host to any significant national shipowning interests, but mainly provide their flag to vessels owned by nationals of other countries. This is the case for the three largest flags of registration, notably Panama, with 306 million dwt (21.9 per cent of the world fleet), Liberia (11.9 per cent) and the Marshall Islands (7.1 per cent).

In January 2011, the 35 largest flags of registration together accounted for 93.8 per cent of the world fleet, a further increase from the 93.2 per cent share of one year earlier (table 2.7).[20] The top five registries together accounted for 52.6 per cent of the world's dwt, and the top ten registries accounted for 72.7 per cent – both figures again showing increases over the previous year.

As regards the number of ships, the largest fleets are flagged in Panama (7,986 seagoing propelled merchant ships of 100 gross tons and above), the United States (6,371), Japan (6,150), Indonesia (5,763), China (4,080) and the Russian Federation (3,485). Except for Panama, these fleets include a large number of general cargo and work vessels that are employed in coastal, inter-island and waterway cabotage services.

Among the major open registries, the Marshall Islands recorded the highest year-on-year growth (+27 per cent), especially among Greek-owned tonnage (+35 per cent). Among the national flags that cater mostly for national owners, Thailand has made significant progress since 2009; its nationally registered tonnage grew by 22 per cent in 2010.

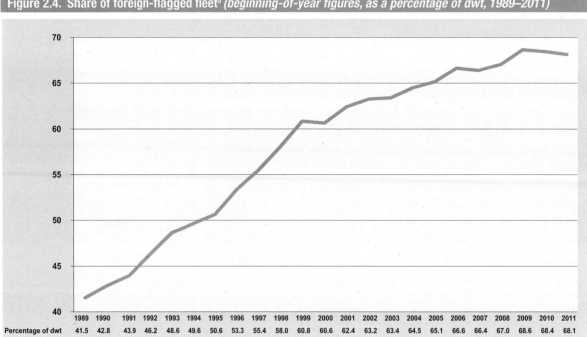

Figure 2.4. Share of foreign-flagged fleet[a] *(beginning-of-year figures, as a percentage of dwt, 1989–2011)*

	1989	1990	1991	1992	1993	1994	1995	1996	1997	1998	1999	2000	2001	2002	2003	2004	2005	2006	2007	2008	2009	2010	2011
Percentage of dwt	41.5	42.8	43.9	46.2	48.6	49.6	50.6	53.3	55.4	58.0	60.8	60.6	62.4	63.2	63.4	64.5	65.1	66.6	66.4	67.0	68.6	68.4	68.1

Source: Compiled by the UNCTAD secretariat on the basis of data supplied by IHS Fairplay.

[a]   Estimate based on available information of commercial seagoing vessels of 1,000 gross tons and above.

Table 2.7. The 35 flags of registration with the largest registered deadweight tonnage, as at 1 January 2011[a]

Flag of registration	Number of vessels	Share of world total, vessels	Deadweight tonnage, 1 000 dwt	Share of world total, dwt	Cumulated share, dwt	Average vessel size, dwt	Dwt growth 2011/2010 as %
Panama	7 986	7.72	306 032	21.93	21.93	38 321	5.98
Liberia	2 726	2.64	166 246	11.91	33.84	60 985	16.97
Marshall Islands	1 622	1.57	98 757	7.08	40.91	60 886	26.89
China, Hong Kong SAR	1 736	1.68	91 733	6.57	47.48	52 841	23.11
Greece	1 433	1.39	71 420	5.12	52.60	49 840	5.61
Bahamas	1 384	1.34	67 465	4.83	57.44	48 747	5.24
Singapore	2 667	2.58	67 287	4.82	62.26	25 230	9.13
Malta	1 724	1.67	61 294	4.39	66.65	35 553	9.15
China	4 080	3.95	52 741	3.78	70.43	12 927	16.79
Cyprus	1 014	0.98	32 321	2.32	72.74	31 875	3.25
Japan	6 150	5.95	22 201	1.59	74.33	3 610	25.38
Republic of Korea	2 913	2.82	20 155	1.44	75.78	6 919	-3.19
Italy	1 649	1.59	19 440	1.39	77.17	11 789	12.53
Isle of Man	385	0.37	19 422	1.39	78.56	50 447	16.22
Norway (NIS)	521	0.50	18 065	1.29	79.86	34 674	-3.12
Germany	931	0.90	17 566	1.26	81.11	18 867	-0.03
United Kingdom	1 638	1.58	16 999	1.22	82.33	10 378	-4.27
India	1 404	1.36	15 278	1.09	83.43	10 882	2.06
Denmark (DIS)	524	0.51	14 304	1.02	84.45	27 297	5.95
Antigua and Barbuda	1 293	1.25	13 892	1.00	85.45	10 744	6.59
United States	6 371	6.16	12 662	0.91	86.35	1 987	-1.02
Indonesia	5 763	5.57	12 105	0.87	87.22	2 100	15.61
Bermuda	158	0.15	10 860	0.78	88.00	68 732	7.45
Malaysia	1 391	1.35	10 725	0.77	88.77	7 710	4.89
Turkey	1 334	1.29	8 745	0.63	89.39	6 556	11.01
France (FIS)	160	0.15	7 880	0.56	89.96	49 253	-5.40
Russian Federation	3 485	3.37	7 400	0.53	90.49	2 123	1.61
Netherlands	1 302	1.26	7 036	0.50	90.99	5 404	-2.98
Philippines	1 946	1.88	6 946	0.50	91.49	3 570	-1.23
Belgium	245	0.24	6 800	0.49	91.98	27 755	3.42
Saint Vincent and the Grenadines	942	0.91	6 701	0.48	92.46	7 114	-8.57
Viet Nam	1 451	1.40	5 899	0.42	92.88	4 065	8.93
Thailand	888	0.86	4 564	0.33	93.21	5 139	21.80
China, Taiwan Province of	677	0.65	4 310	0.31	93.52	6 366	9.28
Cayman Islands	158	0.15	3 688	0.26	93.78	23 344	-6.87
Total: top 35 flags of registration[b]	70 051	67.75	1 308 939	93.78	93.78	18 686	10.02
World total	103 392	100.00	1 395 743	100.00	100.00	13 500	9.37

Source: Compiled by the UNCTAD secretariat, on the basis of data supplied by IHS Fairplay.

[a] Seagoing propelled merchant ships of 100 gross tons and above, ranked by deadweight tonnage.

During 2010, the 10 major open and international registries further increased their combined market share, reaching 56.1 per cent of dwt in January 2011. Their highest market share is among dry bulk carriers (61 per cent), followed by oil tankers (56 per cent).

Among the remaining registries, the share of developed countries decreased by a further 0.94 per cent, while developing countries increased slightly (by 0.27 per cent), now accounting for 25.5 per cent of the world's tonnage. Developed countries' fleets have their highest shares among container ships (24 per cent), while developing countries provide their flag above

all to general cargo vessels (35 per cent of the world fleet in this vessel category). Among the developing countries, Asia has by far the largest share, with 23 per cent of the world fleet (table 2.8).

Different registries specialize in different market segments as regards vessel types, sizes, country of ownership and age (for age of vessels, see also fig. 2.3). As different vessel types and countries of ownership require different services and certificates, registries tend to adjust their pricing and service structure accordingly. Among the top 10 open registries, Antigua and Barbuda has the highest

Table 2.8. Distribution of dwt capacity of vessel types, by country group of registration, 2011[a] (percentage change 2011/2010 in italics)

	Total fleet	Oil tankers	Bulk carriers	General cargo	Container ships	Other types
World total	100.00	100.00	100.00	100.00	100.00	100.00
Developed countries	16.96	19.42	10.95	17.68	23.98	23.81
	-0.94	*-0.81*	*-0.05*	*-0.16*	*-2.36*	*-1.36*
Countries with economies						
in transition	0.93	0.81	0.41	4.53	0.09	1.96
	-0.07	*-0.03*	*-0.03*	*-0.02*	*-0.01*	*-0.10*
Developing countries	25.50	23.50	27.17	35.04	20.61	24.67
	0.27	*0.27*	*0.17*	*-0.53*	*0.80*	*0.62*
of which:						
Africa	0.68	0.72	0.35	2.09	0.11	1.78
	0.00	*-0.01*	*0.05*	*0.21*	*-0.01*	*-0.13*
America	*1.64*	*1.83*	*1.06*	*4.18*	*0.37*	*3.49*
	-0.11	*-0.04*	*-0.18*	*-0.04*	*0.10*	*-0.08*
Asia	*22.80*	*20.78*	*25.30*	*27.97*	*20.11*	*18.26*
	0.44	*0.46*	*0.39*	*-0.71*	*0.71*	*0.61*
Oceania	*0.38*	*0.18*	*0.45*	*0.80*	*0.02*	*1.14*
	-0.06	*-0.14*	*-0.09*	*0.02*	*0.00*	*0.22*
Other, unallocated	*0.51*	*0.24*	*0.30*	*2.61*	*0.13*	*1.33*
	0.07	*0.02*	*0.03*	*0.52*	*0.02*	*0.34*
10 major open and						
international registries[b]	56.10	56.03	61.17	40.14	55.18	48.24
	0.66	*0.55*	*-0.12*	*0.19*	*1.55*	*0.50*

Source: Compiled by the UNCTAD secretariat on the basis of data supplied by IHS Fairplay.

[a]   Seagoing propelled merchant ships of 100 gross tons and above.

[b]   No clear definition exists of "open and international registries". UNCTAD has grouped the 10 major open and international registries to include the 10 largest fleets with more than 90 per cent foreign-controlled tonnage. See annex III or figure 2.5 for the list of registries.

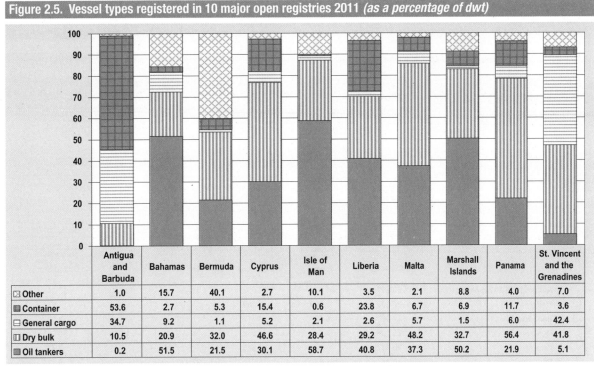

Figure 2.5. Vessel types registered in 10 major open registries 2011 *(as a percentage of dwt)*

	Antigua and Barbuda	Bahamas	Bermuda	Cyprus	Isle of Man	Liberia	Malta	Marshall Islands	Panama	St. Vincent and the Grenadines
Other	1.0	15.7	40.1	2.7	10.1	3.5	2.1	8.8	4.0	7.0
Container	53.6	2.7	5.3	15.4	0.6	23.8	6.7	6.9	11.7	3.6
General cargo	34.7	9.2	1.1	5.2	2.1	2.6	5.7	1.5	6.0	42.4
Dry bulk	10.5	20.9	32.0	46.6	28.4	29.2	48.2	32.7	56.4	41.8
Oil tankers	0.2	51.5	21.5	30.1	58.7	40.8	37.3	50.2	21.9	5.1

Source: Compiled by the UNCTAD secretariat on the basis of data supplied by IHS Fairplay.

share in container ships; the Bahamas, the Isle of Man and the Marshall Islands have more than half of their tonnage in oil tankers; Bermuda caters largely for "other" vessels, including passenger ships such as ferries and cruise ships; Panama provides its flag above all to dry bulk carriers; and Saint Vincent and the Grenadines has the largest share in general cargo vessels (fig. 2.5).

2. Nationality of controlling interests

Figures 2.6 and 2.7 and annex IV combine data on the top 35 shipowning countries (table 2.5) with information on the top 20 flags of registration (table 2.7). This allows us to identify in more detail (a) which flags cater mostly for national owners; and (b) which open and international registries specialize in which countries of ownership.

Among the top 20 registries, seven* are "national" registries, catering mostly for owners from the same country. These are the flags of China, Germany, Greece, India, Italy, Japan and the Republic of Korea. Some of the national registries also provide their national flag to foreign owners. Within the European Union especially, it is increasingly common for owners from partner countries to register their ships under other members' flags. In the case of Italy, the Lloyd

Triestino company is effectively owned by Evergreen Line from Taiwan Province of China, and it deploys ships owned by Greek as well as Taiwanese interests; indeed, 4.7 per cent of the tonnage registered in Italy belongs to Greek and Taiwanese owners (annex IV).

Two of the top 20 flags can be called "international registries" – notably DIS (the Danish International Ship Register) and NIS (the Norwegian International Ship Register). These international registries cater mostly for owners from their respective countries, albeit under conditions that are more favorable than those of the more classic national registries, which, for example, place stricter limitations on the employment of foreign seafarers. Danish owners account for 98.8 per cent of the tonnage under the DIS registry, whereas in the case of NIS, 25 per cent of the owners are from other countries. These foreign owners include Bermuda-based companies, whose shareholders, in turn, include Norwegian nationals.

Eight of the top 20 flags of registration are major "open registries", catering almost entirely for foreign owners. These are Antigua and Barbuda, the Bahamas, Cyprus, the Isle of Man, Liberia, Malta, the Marshall Islands and Panama. German owners account for more than 90 per cent of the tonnage registered in Antigua and Barbuda. Cyprus has a much broader portfolio of owners among its clients, including

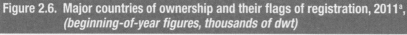

Figure 2.6. Major countries of ownership and their flags of registration, 2011ᵃ, (beginning-of-year figures, thousands of dwt)

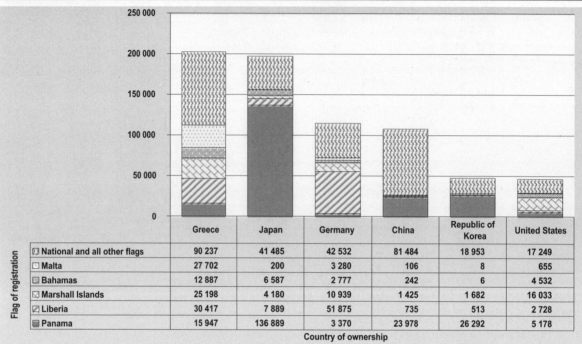

Flag of registration	Greece	Japan	Germany	China	Republic of Korea	United States
National and all other flags	90 237	41 485	42 532	81 484	18 953	17 249
Malta	27 702	200	3 280	106	8	655
Bahamas	12 887	6 587	2 777	242	6	4 532
Marshall Islands	25 198	4 180	10 939	1 425	1 682	16 033
Liberia	30 417	7 889	51 875	735	513	2 728
Panama	15 947	136 889	3 370	23 978	26 292	5 178

Country of ownership

Source: Compiled by the UNCTAD secretariat on the basis of data supplied by IHS Fairplay.

ᵃ Seagoing propelled merchant ships of 1000 gross tons and above.

Figure 2.7. Major open and international registries and the countries of ownership, 2011ᵃ (beginning-of-year figures, thousands of dwt)

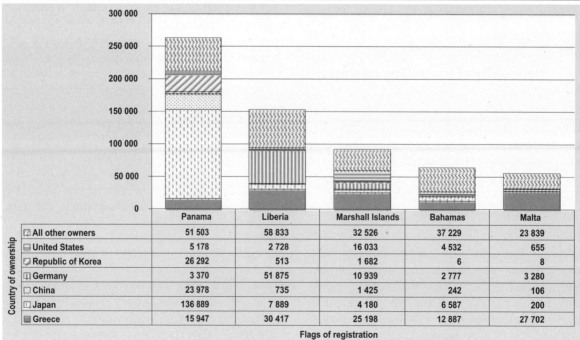

Country of ownership	Panama	Liberia	Marshall Islands	Bahamas	Malta
All other owners	51 503	58 833	32 526	37 229	23 839
United States	5 178	2 728	16 033	4 532	655
Republic of Korea	26 292	513	1 682	6	8
Germany	3 370	51 875	10 939	2 777	3 280
China	23 978	735	1 425	242	106
Japan	136 889	7 889	4 180	6 587	200
Greece	15 947	30 417	25 198	12 887	27 702

Flags of registration

Source: Compiled by the UNCTAD secretariat on the basis of data supplied by IHS Fairplay.

ᵃ Cargo-carrying vessels of 1,000 gross tons and above.

more than 4 million dwt of tonnage registered by Cypriot nationals. The single largest flag/ownership combination in the world fleet is the 137 million dwt of Japanese-owned tonnage registered in Panama; Japanese owners account for 45 per cent of the fleet of the world's largest registry.

Some registries have historical or other special relations with the countries where the shipowning companies are domiciled. The Marshall Islands, for example, has an agreement with the United States that the United States Coast Guard also acts as coast guard for the Marshall Islands. Liberia has a double tax agreement with Germany, which makes the registry more attractive for an owner who wants to employ German officers. European registries such as Cyprus, the Isle of Man and Malta benefit from the European common market, which allows European-flagged ships to provide certain cabotage services in EU member countries.

Finally, there are three registries among the top 20 flags that include both national owners and a significant share of owners from other countries or territories. These are Hong Kong (China), Singapore, and the United Kingdom. Owners from China and from Hong Kong (China) together account for about three fifths of the tonnage registered in Hong Kong (China), the remainder belonging mostly to owners from Canada, Japan, Norway and the United States. About 28 per cent of Singapore's nationally registered fleet belongs to owners from Singapore, with the largest foreign fleets owned by nationals of Denmark and Japan. The flag of the United Kingdom (not including the registries of Gibraltar, Guernsey, the Isle of Man and Jersey) is used mostly by owners from other European countries – especially Denmark, France and Germany.

D. SHIPBUILDING, DEMOLITION, AND OUTLOOK ON VESSEL SUPPLY

1. Deliveries of newbuildings

The year 2010 set a new record in the history of shipbuilding, which was the result of vessel orders that had been placed before the 2008 economic crisis. The deliveries recorded amounted to 3,748 ships, with a total gross tonnage of 96,433,000 GT (table 2.9). Although this is a historic record, it is lower than was expected in early 2010, because owners and shipyards continued to defer some deliveries. In the container sector especially, "non-deliveries" amounted to an estimated 39 per cent of the order book.[21]

In terms of gross tonnage, 45.2 per cent of the deliveries made in 2010 were of dry bulk carriers, and 27.7 per cent were of tankers. The latter included 467 chemical and products tankers, with a total tonnage of 7.8 million GT. New fully cellular container ships accounted for 15.2 per cent of the gross tonnage delivered in 2010.

Dry bulk carriers have continued to dominate deliveries in 2011, too. During the first quarter of the year, the dry bulk fleet grew by 2.7 per cent, resulting from the delivery of 222 new vessels and the demolition of only 67.[22] Containership deliveries in early 2011 included a large number of vessels of 10,000 TEUs and above; monthly deliveries amounted to more than 200,000 TEUs.[23]

The time lag between ordering a vessel and having it delivered is two to three years. After the peak in the vessel order book in 2008 (see fig. 2.10), 2010 marked a historic peak in vessel deliveries. In terms of deadweight tonnage, deliveries in 2010 amounted to 11.7 per cent of the existing fleet at the beginning of the same year. The previous historic peak was in 1974, when deliveries amounted to approximately 11 per cent of the existing fleet.

The peak in the mid-1970s was followed by a severe slump. Given the lessons from history, and awareness of the upcoming deliveries, it could perhaps be expected that such a slump will not be repeated. In fact, since 2010, the industry has seen resumed vessel ordering in all major markets, although there is no guarantee that this will suffice to cater for the upturn in demand. Already there are warnings that 2013 might see a shortage of oil tankers.[24] In the dry bulk and container sectors, however, the voices that are prevailing are those that expect an oversupply of tonnage in the coming years. In both dry sectors, the recent and upcoming record-sized newbuildings pose a further challenge to owners, who will need to find cargo to fill their ships.

For all vessel types, the expansion of yard capacities suggests that shipbuilding countries may build ships beyond the market's requirements, being more concerned about employment in shipbuilding. In practice, constructing more ships than required amounts to a subsidy on world trade, as this causes a fall in vessel prices, and consequently in freight costs too (see also chapter 3).

Table 2.9. Deliveries of newbuildings, different vessel types *(2010)*

	1 000 GT	Percentage	Units	1 000 TEU	1 000 dwt
Tankers					
Crude oil tanker	13 357	13.85	121	0	25 431
Chemical/products tanker	4 424	4.59	300	0	7 136
Products tanker	3 354	3.48	167	0	5 763
LNG tanker	2 790	2.89	26	0	2 263
Crude/oil products tanker	1 568	1.63	28	0	2 856
LPG tanker	869	0.90	61	0	991
Chemical tanker	96	0.10	21	0	154
Other tankers	296	0.31	19	0	435
Subtotal tankers	26 755	27.74	743	0	45 028
Bulk carriers					
Bulk carrier	40 276	41.77	949	1	73 424
Ore carrier	2 078	2.15	15	0	4 078
Ore/oil carrier	861	0.89	5	0	1 599
Woodchip carrier	239	0.25	5	0	302
Bulk carrier, self-discharging	48	0.05	3	0	73
Cement carrier	47	0.05	6	0	69
Aggregates carrier	1	0.00	2	0	2
Subtotal bulk carriers	43 549	45.16	985	1	79 547
Other dry cargo/passenger					
Container ship (fully cellular)	14 648	15.19	260	1 361	16 470
Vehicle carrier	3 088	3.20	64	2	998
General cargo ship	2 388	2.48	350	93	3 267
Passenger/cruise	1 245	1.29	17	0	102
Open hatch cargo ship	899	0.93	32	8	1 437
Ro-ro cargo ship	514	0.53	19	4	230
Passenger/ro-ro ship (vehicles)	461	0.48	46	0	111
Heavy load carrier, semi-submersible	89	0.09	4	2	80
Refrigerated cargo ship	54	0.06	6	2	55
Other dry cargo/passenger	182	0.19	76	2	203
Subtotal other dry cargo/passenger	23 568	24.44	874	1 474	22 952
Miscellaneous					
Tug	165	0.17	464	0	80
Trailing suction hopper dredger	150	0.16	14	0	208
Research survey vessel	113	0.12	22	0	51
Hopper, motor	28	0.03	10	0	41
Crane ship	26	0.03	2	0	0
Cutter suction dredger	23	0.02	3	0	8
Fishing vessels	43	0.04	66	0	31
Other miscellaneous	111	0.11	95	- 0	61
Subtotal miscellaneous	657	0.68	676	0	480

Table 2.9. Deliveries of newbuildings, different vessel types (2010) *(concluded)*					
	1 000 GT	Percentage	Units	1 000 TEU	1 000 dwt
Offshore					
Drilling ship	612	0.64	11	0	596
Anchor handling tug supply	538	0.56	235	0	441
Platform supply ship	223	0.23	92	0	265
Offshore support vessel	129	0.13	18	0	88
Pipe layer crane vessel	90	0.09	4	0	38
Offshore tug/supply ship	79	0.08	43	0	74
Diving support vessel	67	0.07	10	0	42
Crew/supply vessel	14	0.01	47	0	8
Other offshore	151	0.16	10	0	186
Subtotal offshore	1 904	1.97	470	0	1 739
Total deliveries in 2010	96 433	100.00	3 748	1 475	149 746

Source: Compiled by the UNCTAD secretariat on the basis of data from IHS Fairplay.

2.   Demolition of ships

Total ship-recycling activity in 2010 was similar to that in 2009, albeit with a change of vessel types. Demolitions of tankers more than doubled, whereas demolitions of container ships decreased by more than half. Tankers accounted for 41.5 per cent of the gross tonnage demolished in 2010, followed by container and other dry cargo and passenger ships (36 per cent) and dry bulk carriers (15 per cent) (table 2.10).

Figure 2.8 illustrates the age profile of the fleet demolished in 2010. Above all, the fleet demolished consisted of oil tankers built in the 1980s and early 1990s, dry bulk vessels built in the early 1980s, and general cargo ships built in the 1970s and 1980s. The trend in the average age of demolished tonnage by vessel type is illustrated in figure 2.9. While the average age went down between 2007 and 2009 during the economic crisis, in 2010 it remained mostly stable. The age differences between vessel types when demolished broadly reflect the age differences of the existing fleet (see also table 2.4).

If we compare cargo carrying capacity in terms of the number of deadweight tons delivered and demolished, there were 15 times more deliveries of dry bulk tonnage than demolitions. For the remainder of the fleet, the ratio was only 3:1.

3.   Tonnage on order

By the end of 2010, the world order book for new ships had been reduced by about 28 per cent since its peak before the 2008 economic crisis, and newbuildings now by far outnumber new vessel orders. Compared to the peak time, the reduction amounted to 45 per cent for container ships, 34 per cent for tankers, and 18 per cent for dry bulk carriers (table 2.11 and fig. 2.10).

As demand has picked up, new orders have resumed. The orders placed with Japanese shipyards as at January 2011 had more than tripled compared to one year earlier.[25] End-of-2010 data for China suggest that new orders in Chinese shipyards increased fourfold in the space of one year.[26] Many of the new orders are for container ships, with the value of the vessels ordered during the first three months of 2011 reportedly amounting to $7 billion – compared to orders worth $2.8 billion for dry bulk ships and just $0.5 billion for tankers.[27]

4.   Surplus tonnage

The combined idle tonnage of large tankers, dry bulk carriers and conventional general cargo ships at the end of 2010 stood at 14.1 million dwt, equivalent to 1.4 per cent of the world merchant fleet of these vessel types (table 2.12 and fig. 2.11). The overtonnage was

Table 2.10. Tonnage reported sold for demolition, different vessel types *(2010)*

	1 000 GT	Per cent	Units	1 000 TEU	1 000 dwt
Tankers					
Crude oil tanker	3 785	18.72	50	0	6 888
Crude/oil products tanker	1 454	7.19	38	0	2 555
Products tanker	975	4.82	62	0	1 577
Chemical/products tanker	927	4.58	79	0	1 528
LPG tanker	453	2.24	24	0	545
Chemical tanker	361	1.79	35	0	575
LNG tanker	72	0.36	1	0	51
Other tankers	355	1.76	28	0	599
Subtotal tankers	8 382	41.45	317	0	14 316
Bulk Carriers					
Bulk carrier	2 783	13.76	95	4	4 953
Cement carrier	67	0.33	9	0	106
Ore carrier	60	0.30	1	0	115
Aggregates carrier	0	0.00	1	0	1
Other bulk carriers	89	0.44	5	0	140
	2 999	14.83	111	4	5 315
Other Dry Cargo/ Passenger					
Container ship (fully cellular)	1 995	9.87	82	146	2 214
Vehicles carrier	1 694	8.37	45	2	662
General cargo ship	1 587	7.85	320	43	2 210
Ro-ro cargo ship	787	3.89	50	25	521
Passenger/ro-ro ship (vehicles)	408	2.02	44	2	107
Refrigerated cargo Ship	305	1.51	39	1	318
Heavy load carrier	75	0.37	3	0	107
Passenger/cruise	74	0.37	7	0	22
Open hatch cargo ship	21	0.10	1	1	32
Other dry cargo/passenger	305	1.51	29	10	307
Subtotal dry cargo/passenger	7 252	35.86	620	231	6 500
Miscellaneous					
Fishing vessel	106	0.52	120	0	70
Research survey vessel	24	0.12	8	0	10
Trailing suction hopper dredger	19	0.09	6	0	19
Tug	7	0.04	22	0	3
Other miscellaneous and vessel type not reported	747	3.17	88	6	1 060
Subtotal miscellaneous	903	3.94	244	6	1 162
Offshore					
Anchor handling tug supply	10	0.05	8	0	11
Pipe layer	8	0.04	1	0	5
Platform supply ship	5	0.02	6	0	5
Offshore tug/supply ship	4	0.02	6	0	5
Other offshore	659	3.26	11	0	1 318
Subtotal offshore	685	3.39	32	0	1 344
Total demolished in 2010	20 221	100.00	1 324	241	28 637

Source: Compiled by the UNCTAD secretariat on the basis of data from IHS Fairplay.

Figure 2.8. Tonnage reported sold for demolition in 2010, by year of built *(thousands of dwt)*

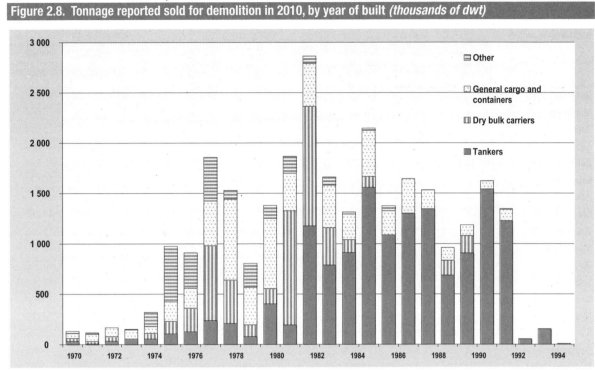

Source: Compiled by the UNCTAD secretariat on the basis of data from IHS Fairplay.

Figure 2.9. Average age of broken-up ships, by type, 1998 to 2010[a] *(years)*

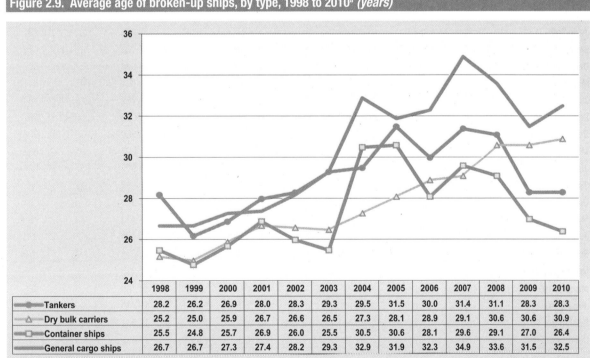

	1998	1999	2000	2001	2002	2003	2004	2005	2006	2007	2008	2009	2010
Tankers	28.2	26.2	26.9	28.0	28.3	29.3	29.5	31.5	30.0	31.4	31.1	28.3	28.3
Dry bulk carriers	25.2	25.0	25.9	26.7	26.6	26.5	27.3	28.1	28.9	29.1	30.6	30.6	30.9
Container ships	25.5	24.8	25.7	26.9	26.0	25.5	30.5	30.6	28.1	29.6	29.1	27.0	26.4
General cargo ships	26.7	26.7	27.3	27.4	28.2	29.3	32.9	31.9	32.3	34.9	33.6	31.5	32.5

Source: Compiled by the UNCTAD secretariat, on the basis of data from the Institute of Shipping Economics and Logistics
             presented in *Shipping Statistics and Market Review*, vol. 53, no. 1/2 – 2011, table 2.2.

[a]   Ships of 300 gross tons and over.

Table 2.11. World tonnage on order, 2000–2010[a] *(in millions of dwt)*

Beginning of month	Tankers			Bulk carriers			General cargo ships		
	1 000 dwt	Number of ships	Average vessel size, dwt	1 000 dwt	Number of ships	Average vessel size, dwt	1 000 dwt	Number of ships	Average vessel size, dwt
December 2000	40 328	284	142 001	31 208	486	64 214	3 966	446	8 892
March 2001	44 361	319	139 061	27 221	439	62 007	3 963	441	8 986
June 2001	45 123	339	133 105	26 103	400	65 258	4 154	419	9 914
September 2001	48 386	381	126 998	21 944	337	65 115	3 967	393	10 094
December 2001	51 894	399	130 060	22 184	353	62 845	3 826	372	10 286
March 2002	47 836	404	118 405	19 027	300	63 425	3 758	357	10 525
June 2002	49 564	425	116 622	18 132	283	64 069	3 932	353	11 139
September 2002	47 774	431	110 845	18 869	283	66 676	3 979	369	10 782
December 2002	47 591	488	97 523	28 641	391	73 251	2 832	257	11 018
March 2003	50 284	515	97 639	32 019	441	72 605	2 958	263	11 249
June 2003	55 771	540	103 279	33 408	455	73 425	2 592	250	10 368
September 2003	57 856	580	99 752	41 499	575	72 172	2 841	269	10 562
December 2003	61 123	631	96 867	46 732	640	73 019	3 068	295	10 400
March 2004	62 096	615	100 969	48 761	671	72 670	3 021	312	9 683
June 2004	66 652	649	102 699	50 545	696	72 623	2 838	317	8 954
September 2004	66 969	661	101 314	52 768	703	75 061	2 921	323	9 043
December 2004	71 563	701	102 087	62 051	796	77 953	3 306	370	8 935
March 2005	68 667	679	101 129	63 404	792	80 055	3 312	388	8 536
June 2005	70 520	686	102 799	65 326	801	81 556	4 079	456	8 945
September 2005	68 741	693	99 193	63 495	788	80 578	4 777	521	9 170
December 2005	70 847	724	97 855	66 614	805	82 750	5 088	584	8 712
March 2006	83 385	791	105 417	63 829	784	81 415	5 798	634	9 145
June 2006	93 277	887	105 160	69 055	859	80 390	7 370	683	10 791
September 2006	106 912	987	108 321	73 226	898	81 543	7 602	715	10 632
December 2006	118 008	1 078	109 470	79 364	988	80 328	8 004	737	10 860
March 2007	120 819	1 113	108 553	100 256	1 204	83 269	9 561	843	11 342
June 2007	122 429	1 107	110 595	143 795	1 657	86 781	10 782	885	12 184
September 2007	124 758	1 149	108 580	183 574	2 137	85 903	12 042	956	12 597
December 2007	124 845	1 134	110 093	221 808	2 573	86 206	13 360	1 035	12 908
March 2008	128 128	1 139	112 492	243 600	2 804	86 876	15 097	1 195	12 633
June 2008	142 333	1 202	118 413	262 452	3 009	87 222	15 911	1 255	12 678
September 2008	151 423	1 245	121 625	288 959	3 316	87 141	16 787	1 332	12 603
December 2008	140 504	1 154	121 754	292 837	3 347	87 492	17 849	1 374	12 991
March 2009	130 777	1 088	120 200	289 763	3 303	87 727	17 439	1 363	12 795
June 2009	119 709	986	121 409	280 102	3 194	87 696	16 684	1 296	12 874
September 2009	114 460	934	122 548	269 558	3 050	88 380	16 354	1 264	12 939
December 2009	109 310	884	123 654	258 343	2 918	88 534	15 018	1 179	12 738
March 2010	104 062	849	122 570	250 383	2 890	86 638	14 199	1 139	12 466
June 2010	103 245	824	125 297	257 229	2 951	87 167	13 480	1 095	12 311
September 2010	106 599	791	134 765	252 924	2 887	87 608	12 361	1 023	12 083
December 2010	100 442	741	135 549	239 898	2 823	84 980	13 487	989	13 637
Percentage of total, December 2010	23.8	9.5		56.9	36.1		3.2	12.6	

Table 2.11. World tonnage on order, 2000–2010[a] *(in millions of dwt) (concluded)*

Container vessels			Other ships			Total			Beginning of month
1 000 dwt	Number of Ships	Average vessel size, dwt	1 000 dwt	Number of Ships	Average vessel size, dwt	1 000 dwt	Number of Ships	Average vessel size, dwt	
16 140	394	40 964	8 870	1 087	8 160	100 513	2 697	37 268	**December 2000**
17 350	435	39 884	10 154	1 132	8 970	103 048	2 766	37 255	**March 2001**
18 393	441	41 708	11 790	1 138	10 360	105 563	2 737	38 569	**June 2001**
16 943	413	41 025	12 181	1 153	10 564	103 421	2 677	38 633	**September 2001**
16 550	393	42 111	13 501	1 201	11 242	107 955	2 718	39 719	**December 2001**
14 476	355	40 776	12 839	1 200	10 700	97 936	2 616	37 437	**March 2002**
14 793	362	40 865	15 415	1 324	11 643	101 836	2 747	37 072	**June 2002**
14 509	338	42 927	15 342	1 292	11 875	100 473	2 713	37 034	**September 2002**
13 000	296	43 919	16 174	1 386	11 669	108 238	2 818	38 409	**December 2002**
16 281	326	49 943	16 199	1 365	11 868	117 742	2 910	40 461	**March 2003**
18 296	367	49 853	17 085	1 367	12 498	127 152	2 979	42 683	**June 2003**
27 216	503	54 107	18 062	1 484	12 171	147 475	3 411	43 235	**September 2003**
30 974	580	53 403	19 277	1 492	12 920	161 174	3 638	44 303	**December 2003**
35 840	658	54 468	20 068	1 520	13 203	169 786	3 776	44 965	**March 2004**
38 566	724	53 268	22 833	1 682	13 575	181 434	4 068	44 600	**June 2004**
41 172	808	50 956	24 368	1 714	14 217	188 198	4 209	44 713	**September 2004**
43 904	880	49 891	27 361	1 898	14 416	208 185	4 645	44 819	**December 2004**
49 624	1 006	49 328	27 328	1 940	14 087	212 335	4 805	44 190	**March 2005**
53 605	1 101	48 688	29 884	2 002	14 927	223 414	5 046	44 275	**June 2005**
52 378	1 132	46 271	31 209	2 158	14 462	220 600	5 292	41 686	**September 2005**
50 856	1 124	45 245	33 147	2 285	14 506	226 551	5 522	41 027	**December 2005**
49 749	1 130	44 026	36 750	2 373	15 487	239 512	5 712	41 931	**March 2006**
53 876	1 185	45 465	39 768	2 522	15 768	263 347	6 136	42 918	**June 2006**
54 676	1 199	45 601	42 322	2 714	15 594	284 738	6 513	43 718	**September 2006**
51 717	1 143	45 247	45 612	2 962	15 399	302 706	6 908	43 820	**December 2006**
55 144	1 229	44 869	49 245	3 327	14 802	335 025	7 716	43 420	**March 2007**
63 063	1 305	48 324	52 382	3 562	14 706	392 451	8 516	46 084	**June 2007**
76 804	1 412	54 394	56 767	3 864	14 691	453 945	9 518	47 693	**September 2007**
78 348	1 435	54 598	56 947	3 876	14 692	495 309	10 053	49 270	**December 2007**
78 042	1 419	54 998	58 304	4 174	13 968	523 171	10 731	48 753	**March 2008**
76 388	1 352	56 500	57 574	4 302	13 383	554 657	11 120	49 879	**June 2008**
74 090	1 322	56 044	56 563	4 442	12 734	587 823	11 657	50 427	**September 2008**
69 593	1 209	57 563	52 088	4 256	12 239	572 871	11 340	50 518	**December 2008**
65 610	1 121	58 528	48 131	4 117	11 691	551 720	10 992	50 193	**March 2009**
63 064	1 028	61 346	43 989	3 796	11 588	523 548	10 300	50 830	**June 2009**
59 314	948	62 567	40 947	3 591	11 403	500 632	9 787	51 153	**September 2009**
53 903	813	66 301	37 434	3 428	10 920	474 008	9 222	51 400	**December 2009**
50 416	732	68 874	34 804	3 396	10 248	453 864	9 006	50 396	**March 2010**
44 071	628	70 176	30 135	3 137	9 606	448 160	8 635	51 900	**June 2010**
43 060	600	71 766	26 003	2 849	9 127	440 946	8 150	54 104	**September 2010**
43 180	566	76 289	24 888	2 702	9 211	421 895	7 821	53 944	**December 2010**
10.2	7.2		5.9	34.5		100.0	100.0		**Percentage of total, December 2010**

Source: Compiled by the UNCTAD secretariat on the basis of data supplied by IHS Fairplay.

[a] Seagoing propelled merchant ships of 100 gross tons and above.

Figure 2.10. World tonnage on order, 2000–2010[a] *(thousands of dwt)*

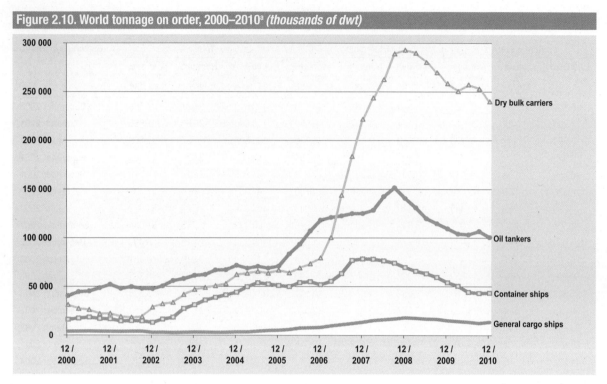

Source: Compiled by the UNCTAD secretariat on the basis of data supplied by IHS Fairplay.
[a]   Seagoing propelled merchant ships of 100 gross tons and above..

Table 2.12. Tonnage oversupply in the world merchant fleet, selected years *(end-of-year figures)*

	1990	2000	2005	2006	2007	2008	2009	2010
Millions of dwt								
Merchant fleet, three main vessel types[a]	558.5	586.4	697.9	773.9	830.7	876.2	930.3	1 023.3
Idle fleet[b]	62.4	18.4	7.2	10.1	12.1	19.0	12.0	14.1
Active fleet	496.1	568.0	690.7	763.7	818.6	857.2	918.3	1 009.1
Percentages								
Idle fleet as a percentage of merchant fleet	11.2	3.1	1.0	1.3	1.5	2.2	1.3	1.4

Source: Compiled by the UNCTAD secretariat on the basis of data supplied by *Lloyd's Shipping Economist*, various issues.
[a]   Tankers and dry bulk carriers of 10,000 dwt and above, and conventional general cargo vessels of 5,000 dwt and above.
[b]   Surplus tonnage is defined as tonnage that is not fully utilized because of slow steaming or lay-up status, or because it is lying idle for other reasons.

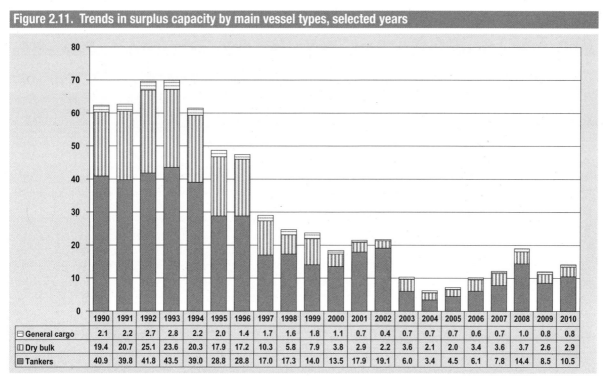

Figure 2.11. Trends in surplus capacity by main vessel types, selected years

	1990	1991	1992	1993	1994	1995	1996	1997	1998	1999	2000	2001	2002	2003	2004	2005	2006	2007	2008	2009	2010
General cargo	2.1	2.2	2.7	2.8	2.2	2.0	1.4	1.7	1.6	1.8	1.1	0.7	0.4	0.7	0.7	0.7	0.6	0.7	1.0	0.8	0.8
Dry bulk	19.4	20.7	25.1	23.6	20.3	17.9	17.2	10.3	5.8	7.9	3.8	2.9	2.2	3.6	2.1	2.0	3.4	3.6	3.7	2.6	2.9
Tankers	40.9	39.8	41.8	43.5	39.0	28.8	28.8	17.0	17.3	14.0	13.5	17.9	19.1	6.0	3.4	4.5	6.1	7.8	14.4	8.5	10.5

Source: Compiled by the UNCTAD secretariat on the basis of data from *Lloyd's Shipping Economist*, various issues.

highest for ro-ro vessels (3.21 per cent of the world fleet), followed by LNG carriers (2.99 per cent), oil tankers (2.34 per cent) and general cargo ships (1.47 per cent). It was lowest in the dry bulk sector, where idle tonnage accounted for only 0.55 per cent of the existing fleet (table 2.13).

The idle tonnage in the container market had been significantly reduced by early 2011. As a result of slow steaming, increased demand, and delays in new deliveries, only a few container ships remained idle by this time. By the same token, demand for LNG tankers had increased by early 2011, with very few vessels available for the spot market.[28]

With the aim of reducing fuel expenditure and vessel overcapacity, container lines in 2010 and 2011 continued to deploy ships at reduced operating speeds (i.e. "slow steaming"). Oil tankers, too, have been reported to reduce their speeds from as fast as 24 knots to under 12 knots on the empty return leg, achieving savings of up to $22,000 per day.[29]

In container shipping, the majority of Asia–Europe services run at only 17 to 19 knots (or nautical miles per hour, equivalent to 31.5–35 kilometres per hour), compared to the normal speeds of 21 to 25 knots. Depending on fuel prices, this is estimated to save the shipping line up to $100 per delivered TEU on major East–West routes. For the owner of the cargo, however, the additional inventory costs and requirements for safety stocks can far outweigh the savings made on the transport costs.[30]

In the longer term, it can be expected that demands from importers and exporters will put pressure on shipping lines to increase service speeds. While lines will be able to charge higher freights for faster services, the released containership capacity will put downward pressure on overall freight levels. From the perspective of the importer or exporter, this could be one more reason to insist on faster services.

Carriers may complain that there is an overcapacity of ships, however importers and exporters are happy about the resulting spare transport capacity to cater for the reviving international trade. In 2009 and 2010, shipyards delivered record levels of new tonnage – not only in absolute terms, but even in relative terms, as a percentage of the existing fleet. As has been shown in this chapter, throughout and after the economic crisis, the shipping industry has provided the supply of vessels that has been necessary to carry the growing demand from seaborne trade (see chapter 1). Matching supply with volatile demand will continue to be a challenge for the industry; this is dealt with in chapter 3.

Table 2.13. Analysis of tonnage surplus by main type of vessel, selected years[a] *(in millions of dwt or m³)*

(In millions of dwt or m³)	1990	2000	2005	2006	2007	2008	2009	2010
World tanker fleet (dwt)	266.2	279.4	312.9	367.4	393.5	414.04	435.25	447.64
Idle tanker fleet (dwt)	40.9	13.5	4.5	6.1	7.8	14.35	8.51	10.48
Share of idle fleet in tanker fleet (%)	15.4	4.8	1.4	1.7	2.0	3.47	1.96	2.34
World dry bulk fleet (dwt)	228.7	247.7	340.0	361.8	393.5	417.62	452.52	522.52
Idle dry bulk fleet (dwt)	19.4	3.8	2.0	3.4	3.6	3.68	2.64	2.86
Share of idle fleet in dry bulk fleet (%)	8.5	1.5	0.6	0.9	0.9	0.88	0.58	0.55
World conventional general cargo fleet (dwt)	63.6	59.3	45.0	44.7	43.8	44.54	42.53	53.10
Idle conventional general cargo fleet (dwt)	2.1	1.1	0.7	0.6	0.7	0.97	0.83	0.78
Share of idle fleet in general cargo fleet (%)	3.3	1.9	1.6	1.4	1.6	2.18	1.95	1.47
World ro-ro fleet (dwt)	n.a.	n.a.	n.a.	n.a.	n.a.	11.37	10.93	10.28
Idle ro-ro fleet (dwt)	n.a.	n.a.	n.a.	n.a.	n.a.	0.89	0.73	0.33
Share of idle fleet in ro-ro fleet (%)	n.a.	n.a.	n.a.	n.a.	n.a.	7.83	6.68	3.21
World vehicle carrier fleet (dwt)	n.a.	n.a.	n.a.	n.a.	n.a.	11.27	11.20	11.48
Idle vehicle carrier fleet (dwt)	n.a.	n.a.	n.a.	n.a.	n.a.	0.24	0.55	0.13
Share of idle fleet in vehicle carrier fleet (%)	n.a.	n.a.	n.a.	n.a.	n.a.	2.13	4.91	1.13
World LNG carrier fleet (m³)	n.a.	n.a.	n.a.	n.a.	n.a.	44.43	46.90	51.15
Idle LNG carrier fleet (m³)	n.a.	n.a.	n.a.	n.a.	n.a.	5.87	1.29	1.53
Share of idle fleet in LNG fleet (%)	n.a.	n.a.	n.a.	n.a.	n.a.	13.21	2.75	2.99
World LPG carrier fleet (m³)	n.a.	n.a.	n.a.	n.a.	n.a.	11.56	18.50	19.42
Idle LPG carrier fleet (m³)	n.a.	n.a.	n.a.	n.a.	n.a.	0.94	0.10	0.13
Share of idle fleet in LNG fleet (%)	n.a.	n.a.	n.a.	n.a.	n.a.	8.13	0.54	0.67

Source: Compiled by the UNCTAD secretariat on the basis of data from *Lloyd's Shipping Economist*, various issues.

[a] End-of-year figures, except for 1990 and 2000 which are annual averages. This table excludes tankers and dry bulk carriers of less than 10,000 dwt and conventional general cargo/unitized vessels of less than 5,000 dwt.

ENDNOTES

1   *Containerisation International* (2011), quoting Sextant Consultancy. April: 43.

2   Hellenic Shipping News (2011). 29 January. http://www.hellenicshippingnews.com. Also: *Lloyd's List* (2011). 18 March. http://www.lloydslist.com.

3   DNV and MAN Diesel and Turbo (2011). Quantum 9000 two-stroke LNG. Copenhagen.

4   Yonhap News (2011). 24 March. http://english.yonhapnews.co.kr.

5   DNV (2011). *Technology Outlook 2020*. http://www.dnv.com/news_events/news/2011/dnvpredictstechnology uptaketowards2020.asp. Oslo.

6   The nominal capacity may vary if empties are included. According to one estimate, the new Maersk ships could reach up to 20,000 TEUs. Source: The Motorship (2011), quoting Alphaliner. 25 January. http://www.motorship.com.

7   *Lloyd's List* (2011). 12 May. http://www.lloydslist.com.

8   Stopford M (2011). Super container ships to fall into the ULCC trap? In: Shipping and Finance. February.

9   Fairplay (2011). Size matters. London. 2 March.

10 *Lloyd's List* (2011). 21 January, 8 March and 9 May. http://www.lloydslist.com.

11 *Lloyd's List* (2000). 14 July. http://www.lloydslist.com.

12 *Seatrade* (2011). Issue 2. Colchester. April.

13 Clarkson Research Services (2011). *Container Intelligence Monthly*. London. April.

14 UNCTAD calculation based on data provided by Dynamar and Textainer.

15 *Cargo Systems* (2011). 19 May. http://www.cargosystems.net.

16 *Journal of Commerce* (2011). 8 March. http://www.joc.com.

17 Information in this section is based on data on commercial seagoing vessels of 1,000 GT and above.

18 Please refer to annex I for the classification of countries.

19 *Shipping and Finance* (2010). Athens. October.

20 Information in this section is based on data on vessels of 100 GT and above (see also annex III.(b), except where the country of vessel ownership is considered. In the latter case, the data are for vessels of 1,000 GT and above.

21 *Containerisation International*, www.ci-online.co.uk, 6 April 2011, quoting Trevor Crowe of Clarkson Research Services.

22 *Hellenic Shipping News*, www.hellenicshippingnews.com, 12 April 2011, quoting BIMCO.

23 *ifw*, www.ifw-net.com, May 2011, quoting Alphaliner.

24 *Fairplay*, www.fairplay.co.uk, 17 March 2011.

25 *Journal of Commerce* (2011). 21 February. http://www.joc.com.

26 *Bloomberg* (2011). 6 January. http://www.bloomberg.com.

27 *Lloyd's List* (2011). 26 April. http://www.lloydslist.com.

28 *Lloyd's List (*2011). 8 February. http://www.lloydslist.com.

29 *Lloyd's List* (2011). 22 February. http://www.lloydslist.com.

30 DNV (2010). Container Ship Update. No. 2. Oslo.

PRICE OF VESSELS AND FREIGHT RATES

This chapter covers the determinants of transport costs, the price of vessels and freight rates in the tanker market, the dry bulk cargo market and the liner shipping market. It concludes with an analysis of freight rates by region and fleet performance over the past few decades.

The price of newbuildings was lower for all vessels types in 2010, reflecting market views that the capacity of the world fleet is sufficient to meet world trade in the short-term. In the second-hand market, the results were mixed. The larger oil tankers held their value, while smaller tankers and specialized product tankers declined in value. In the dry bulk sector, the price of medium-sized Panamax vessels decreased, while the price of smaller and larger vessels increased. The price for all sizes of second-hand container ships also rose in value during 2010 as trade volumes recovered.

Freight rates in the tanker sector performed better than the previous year, rising between 30 and 50 per cent by the end of 2010. Every month for all vessel types was better than the corresponding month for the previous year. However, tanker freight rates in general still remained depressed, compared with the years immediately preceding the 2008 peak. Freight rates in the dry bulk sector performed well for the first half of the year, but the Baltic Exchange Dry Index (BDI) lost more than half its value from the end of May 2010 to mid-July 2010. A partial rally occurred in August 2010 before the Index continued its downward trajectory. Between May 2010 and May 2011, the BDI declined by about two thirds. Container freight rates in 2010 witnessed a major transformation brought about by a boost in exports and measures introduced by shipowners to limit vessel oversupply. The result can be seen in the New ConTex Index, which tripled in value from early 2010 to mid-2011.

A. OVERVIEW OF THE DETERMINANTS OF MARITIME TRANPORT COSTS AND THEIR IMPACT ON TRADE

Transport costs are key determinants of a country's trade competitiveness. Excessive shipping costs are considered a major barrier to trade, often surpassing the cost of customs duties. Several studies conclude that transport costs influence the volume, structure and patterns of trade, as well as the comparative advantage of a country.[1] A doubling of a country's transport costs can slow annual gross domestic product growth by slightly more than one half of one percentage point and lead to lower levels of foreign investment, less access to technology and knowledge, and reduced employment opportunities. Transport costs also influence modal choices, the commodity composition of trade and the organization of production.

Against this background, understanding the determinants of freight rates and transport costs and how such costs influence trade flows, volume, patterns and structure is crucial and can assist policymakers in decision-making. Relevant determinants of freight rates and transport costs include, inter alia, distance, competition in shipping and port services, economies of scale, trade imbalance, capital costs of infrastructure, and type and value of goods. This chapter provides a general overview of how vessel prices and maritime freight rates evolved in 2010 and early 2011.

B. THE PRICE OF VESSELS

The price of vessels is determined by construction costs and by market pressures derived from the demand for transport services and the supply of vessels, issues that are also discussed in detail in chapters 1 and 2.[2] Demand for newbuildings is a reflection of how shipowners perceive long-term demand, whereas demand for second-hand vessels may reflect short-term expectations.

Table 3.1 provides the newbuilding prices of all types of vessels that declined in 2010. Shipowners stopped placing new orders, cancelled existing orders and delayed taking delivery of vessels nearing construction; this is commonly referred to as "slippage". Shipyards reacted by lowering their prices to attract new orders, while ensuring that they had enough revenue to cover their operational expenditures. The largest percentage decline in vessel prices was for container vessels of 500 20-foot equivalent units (TEUs). In 2009, the price to build a new 500-TEU container ship cost on average $28,000 per TEU, whereas a 12,000-TEU vessel cost $9,500 per TEU: a 500-TEU vessel was almost 3 times more expensive per TEU than a 12,000-TEU

Table 3.1. Representative newbuilding prices, 2003–2010 *(millions of dollars, average prices)*									
Type and size of vessel	2003	2004	2005	2006	2007	2008	2009	2010	Percentage change 2010/2009
Oil tanker – Handy, 50 000 dwt	28	35	42	47	50	52	40	36	-10.0
Oil tanker – Suezmax, 160 000 dwt	47	60	73	76	85	94	70	66	-5.7
Oil tanker – VLCC, 300 000 dwt	67	91	119	125	136	153	116	103	-11.2
Chemical tanker – 12 000 dwt	12	16	18	21	33	34	33	28	-15.2
LPG carrier – 15 000 m³	28	36	45	49	51	52	46	41	-10.9
LNG carrier – 160 000 m³	153	173	205	217	237	222	226	208	-8.0
Dry bulk – Handysize, 30 000 dwt	16	19	21	22	33	38	29	25	-13.8
Dry bulk – Panamax, 75 000 dwt	23	32	35	36	47	54	39	35	-10.3
Dry bulk – Capesize, 170 000 dwt	38	55	62	62	84	97	69	58	-15.9
Container – geared, 500 TEUs	13	18	18	16	16	21	14	10	-28.6
Container – gearless, 6 500 TEUs	67	86	101	98	97	108	87	75	-13.8
Container – gearless, 12 000 TEUs	n.a.	n.a.	n.a.	n.a.	154	164	114	107	-6.1

Source: Compiled by the UNCTAD secretariat on the basis of data derived from *Drewry Shipping Insight.*

vessel. In 2010, the 500 TEU vessel price decreased significantly more (a 28.6 per cent decrease) than the price of a 12,000 TEU vessel which registered a 6.1 per cent decrease.

Table 3.2 reveals a mixed result of the prices of second-hand vessels, with some segments performing better than others. Chemical tankers experienced the greatest fall in price, at 35 per cent. Conversely, small container ships of 500 TEUs increased in price by 50 per cent. The 500-TEU container ships, which are proving unpopular as newbuildings, were in demand as second-hand tonnage.

C. FREIGHT RATES

The price that a carrier, that is, a shipowner or charterer, charges for transporting cargo is known as the freight rate. The freight rate depends on many factors, including the cost of operating the vessel (for example, crew wages, fuel, maintenance and insurance); the capital costs of buying the vessel, such as deposit, interest and depreciation; and the cost of the shore-side operation, which covers office personnel, rent and marketing.[3] Freight rates are not all-inclusive but a subject to numerous additions, for example, the bunker adjustment factor, the currency adjustment factor, terminal handling charges, war risk premiums, piracy surcharges,[4] container seal fees,[5] electronic release of cargo fees,[6] late fees or

equipment shortage fees.[7][8] Maersk Line, the largest liner shipping company, lists on its website 107 possible fees and surcharges.[9] Surcharges may also vary considerably among transport providers and do not necessarily reflect the cost of the service being rendered. For instance, currency adjustment factor rates applied by different carriers varied in June 2011 by as much as 6 percentage points, from 10.3 per cent to 16.7 per cent of the freight.[10]

In general, freight rates are affected by the demand for the goods being carried and the supply of available vessels to carry the goods. In addition to the fluctuations in supply and demand, the bargaining power of the service user (the shipper), the number of competitors and the availability of alternative transport modes also affect price.

Most manufactured goods are shipped in containers by container vessels. The rapid growth in containerization over the last 20 years is the result of a combination of factors that includes dedicated purpose-built container vessels, larger vessels capable of achieving increased economies of scale, improved handling facilities in ports, and the increasing amount of components parts being carried in containers. When there is little demand for containerized goods, these container ships cannot carry other cargo (e.g. general cargo, dry bulk cargoes or liquids in an uncontainerized form) because of the specialist nature of the vessel. Lower demand and lack of alternative cargo have led some

Table 3.2. Second-hand prices for five-year-old ships, 2003–2010 *(millions of dollars, end-of-year figures)*

Type and size of vessel	2003	2004	2005	2006	2007	2008	2009	2010	Percentage change 2010/2009
Oil tanker – Handy, 45 000 dwt, 5 years old	25	35	44	47	40	51	30	26	-13.3
Oil tanker – Suezmax, 150 000 dwt, 5 years old	43	60	72	76	87	95	59	62	5.1
Oil tanker – VLCC, 300 000 dwt, 5 years old	60	91	113	116	124	145	84	86	2.4
Chemical tanker – 12 000 dwt, 10 years old	9	11	12	14	23	23	20	13	-35.0
LPG carrier – 15 000 m³, 10 years old	21	23	30	39	40	39	30	25	-16.7
Dry bulk – Handysize, 28 000 dwt, 10 years old	10	15	20	20	28	31	17	20	17.6
Dry bulk – Panamax, 75 000 dwt, 5 years old	20	35	40	39	83	70	31	25	-19.4
Dry bulk – Capesize, 150 000 dwt, 5 years old	..	..	..	..	..	..	47	54	14.9
Dry bulk – Capesize, 150 000 dwt, 10 years old	23	41	32	44	75	82	32	..	n/a
Container – geared, 500 TEUs, 10 years old	5	7	11	10	9	13	4	6	50.0
Container – geared, 2 500 TEUs, 10 years old	20	29	39	41	24	36	18	23	27.8
Container – gearless, 12 000 TEUs	25	34	43	44	43	45	24	28	16.7

Source: Compiled by the UNCTAD secretariat on the basis of data from *Dewry Shipping Insight.*

liner operators to adopt measures to absorb capacity by reducing vessel speed and taking longer routes or laying up vessels. In 2010, these measures led to relatively stable liner freight rates, compared with other sectors. In the tanker market, ship operators decided to use very large crude carriers (VLCCs) and ultra-large crude carrier (ULCCs) as floating storage facilities. The advantage of laying up tanker vessels is that the cargo can be quickly put into storage by anchoring the vessel at a suitable place. However, as soon as the price of oil rises, the cargo owner sells the cargo, believes the price is near its maximum and the vessel is then returned to the spot market. The ship is unlikely to be used again as floating storage unless an opportunity arises to purchase oil cheaply and the buyer has faith in higher prices. Other markets, such as the liquefied natural gas (LNG) market, have no alternative other than laying up vessels when cargo demand falls.

Freight rates can be obtained through an agent or shipbroker. The shipbroker, whose role is to bring together cargo and vessel owners, may calculate, publish and maintain indices on historical data. The following section covers developments in approximately three quarters of the estimated 90 per cent of world cargo transported by sea.

1.   The tanker market

The tanker market is mainly concerned with the transportation of crude oil and petroleum products, which, taken together, represent approximately one third of world seaborne trade by volume. Tanker freight rates and the demand for world trade are inherently linked. Petroleum is a raw ingredient in some 70,000 manufactured products such as medicines, synthetic fabrics, fertilizers, paints and varnishes, acrylics, plastics and cosmetics, and falling demand or shortages in supply of these goods can cause tanker freight rates to fluctuate wildly and abruptly.[11] Tanker cargoes, that is, chemical products or crude oil, are often stored to help absorb sudden variations in price caused by stock depletion or renewal.

All tanker sectors

Freight rates for all tanker vessel sizes in 2010 performed better than the previous year, rising from 30 per cent to 50 per cent by the end of the year. This is not surprising, given that 2009 was a particularly bad year for tanker freight rates. However, freight rates in

general still remained depressed, compared with the years immediately preceding the peak of 2008 (see table 3.3 and figure 3.1). The best performing months of 2010 for freight rates were the first and last two months of the year, reflecting seasonal demands in the main energy consumption markets. In the first quarter of 2011, freight rates for all vessel types decreased by around 16 per cent, compared with the same period in 2010, although they remained around 23 per cent higher than the first quarter of 2009. During the course of 2010, 743 new tankers of various types were delivered, the largest numbers being chemical or product tankers (300), product tankers (167) and crude oil tankers (121). In 2011, the order book for new tankers to be delivered over the next three years stands at 611 vessels, totalling 105 million dwt and representing about 27.5 per cent of the existing fleet. Taking this high growth in potential supply into consideration, the outlook for 2011 does not augur well.

Table 3.4 illustrates average freight rates measured in Worldscale (WS), a unified measure for establishing spot rates on specific major tanker routes for various sizes of vessels. The table focuses on traditional benchmark routes, and is not intended to be exhaustive; for example, it does not cover the growing trade between many African countries and China. Trade between West Africa and China is expected to divert to the closer European market in 2011 because of disruptions to supply brought about by events in the Mediterranean, most notably in Libya. Another consequence of this is to push up freight rates on other routes servicing China, for example, from the Persian Gulf. The main loading areas indicated in the table are the Persian Gulf, West Africa, the Mediterranean, the Caribbean and Singapore, while the main unloading areas are East Asia, Southern Africa, North-West Europe, the Mediterranean, the Caribbean, and the East Coast of North America. The following sections describe developments by tanker types, in greater detail.

Very large and ultra-large crude carriers

Some of the world's largest ships are VLCCs and ULCCs, which offer the best economies of scale for the transportation of oil where pipelines are non-existent. VLCCs deliver vast quantities of crude oil that power manufacturing plants in many countries. VLCCs and ULCCs accounted for approximately 44 per cent of the world tanker fleet in dwt terms in 2010. Much of the world's oil exports that originate from the Persian

Table 3.3. Tanker freight indices, 2009–2011 *(monthly figures)*

| 2009 | Lloyd's Shipping Economist | | | | | Exchange Baltic Tanker | |
	>200	120–200	70–120	25–70	Clean	Dirty Index	Clean Index
October	41	62	76	96	89	557	515
November	47	78	81	100	94	588	439
December	53	77	111	121	124	671	528
Average	**47**	**72**	**89**	**106**	**102**	**605**	**494**
2010							
January	82	120	133	185	189	1 024	817
February	75	94	117	187	175	1 047	884
March	77	100	128	159	159	889	761
April	83	105	122	168	151	949	703
May	74	118	150	169	144	995	730
June	84	105	115	150	138	938	669
July	58	79	110	151	165	844	798
August	49	79	101	152	152	789	792
September	47	69	85	131	137	708	677
October	44	78	101	140	132	684	622
November	64	89	93	146	138	763	623
December	57	109	138	187	170	896	756
Average	**66**	**95**	**116**	**160**	**154**	**877**	**736**
2011							
January	52	67	88	154	134	842	635
February	59	76	99	123	136	660	642
March	63	106	135	188	175	965	749
April	48	89	109	178	170	927	836
May	49	84	102	150	177	822	882
June	52	70	98	141	148	750	706

Source: UNCTAD secretariat, based on information in *Lloyd's Shipping Economist* (a trade journal that specializes in maritime-related market data and reports), several issues; and in the Baltic Tanker, an index produced by the London Baltic Exchange, in which indices are reported for the first working day of the month.

Note: The numbers in the second row, columns 2–5, refer to vessel size expressed in thousands of dwt.

Gulf are destined for the world's largest economies, the United States of America, China, Germany and Japan. Needless to say, freight rates on these sea routes are important indicators for global supply and demand.

The beginning of 2010 marked a yearly high for VLCC freight rates. While they were consistently higher in 2010 when comparing month-on-month figures with 2009, they declined over the course of 2010, diminishing shipowners' hopes of a sustained recovery in freight rates. From December 2009 to December 2010, freight rates from the Persian Gulf to Japan increased by almost 9 per cent to WS 61. However, this figure masks a turbulent ride in freight rates. In December 2009, the freight rates were at WS 56 points and almost doubled in January 2010 to WS 104 points as a result of increased market sentiment and a high seasonal demand. In June 2010, rates on the same route stood at WS 95 points, but plummeted to 58 points the following month. Thereafter, freight rates continued to go down to a yearly low of WS 47 points in October 2010, before recovering at the end of the year. The falls were largely due to increases in supply of vessels brought about by new deliveries and less vessels ceasing to be used as offshore storage. The decrease in offshore storage occurred as traders seized the opportunity of a rise in oil prices to sell stock held in floating storage. Once they were sold,

Figure 3.1. Tanker freight market summary: various vessel sizes, 2003–2011

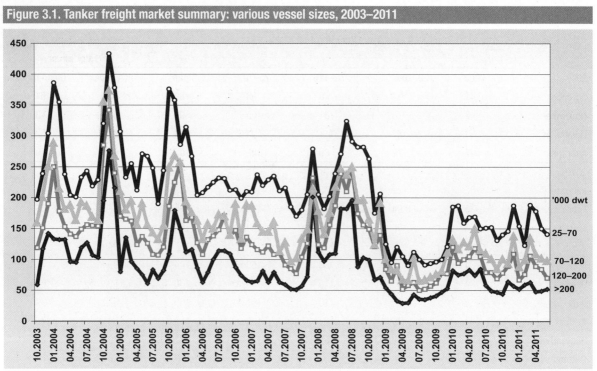

'000 dwt

25–70

70–120

120–200

>200

Source: UNCTAD secretariat, based on information from *Lloyd's Shipping Economist*, several issues.

Notes: (X = monthly figures; Y = indices)

The Baltic Exchange Tanker indices are reported for the first working day of the month. Ship sizes are expressed in deadweight capacity (in thousands of dwt).

the empty vessels were then returned to the spot market to seek new cargo, thus driving down tanker freight rates. The Persian Gulf–Europe route monthly WS rate increased by 67 per cent from December 2009 to December 2010, whereas that of the Persian Gulf–East Coast United States increased by just 3 per cent.

Average freight rates for VLCCs in 2010 were approximately $36,083 per day, down slightly from $38,533 per day in 2009 and significantly so from $74,663 per day during the highs of 2008. Preliminary figures for 2011 show that freight rates continued to decline to approximately $29,500 per day. Correspondingly, the price of a five-year-old VLCC in January 2011 declined to around $79 million, compared with average annual prices of $85.5 million in 2010 and $144.7 million in 2008. In addition to declining freight rates, rising fuel prices also put pressure on shipowners' profits. The average monthly price of 380 centistoke fuel oil in Fujairah increased from $444 per ton in September 2010 to $623 per ton in February 2011.[12] At this point, freight rates for VLCCs decreased to around $11,000 per day, forcing many owners to operate at a daily loss.

Suezmax tankers

Suezmax ships were named because they were the maximum-sized tankers that could transit the Suez Canal; their capacity ranges between 125,000 and 200,000 dwt.[13] There is a significant demand for Suezmax vessels on other routes that do not include the Suez Canal, for example from West Africa to North-West Europe, and to the Caribbean/East Coast of North America, as well as across the Mediterranean. Some 14 sea routes account for around three quarters of total demand for Suezmax cargoes.[14]

Freight rates for Suezmax tankers in 2010 fared relatively well from January to May and then declined until September before recovering most of their losses by year's end. The average Suezmax time charter rate was around $35,800 per day from 1997 to 2008.[15] In 2010, the average time charter earnings for a Suezmax vessel fell to $25,967 per day, down from $27,825 per day in 2009, which had already fallen from $46,917 in 2008. The one-year charter rates for a five-year old Suezmax vessel climbed by 1.7 per cent over the course of 2010 to reach around $24,000 per day in January 2011, thus faring better than the larger

Table 3.4. Tanker market summary: clean and dirty spot rates, 2009–2011 (Worldscale)

Vessel type	Route	2009 Dec	2010 Jan	Feb	Mar	Apr	May	Jun	Jul	Aug	Sep	Oct	Nov	Dec	% change 2009/2010	2011 Jan	Feb	Mar	Apr	May	Jun
VLCC/ULCC (200,000 dwt+)																					
	Persian Gulf–Japan	56	104	71	84	90	72	95	58	51	48	47	75	61	8.9	48	74	63	50	51	54
	Persian Gulf–Republic of Korea	53	88	76	76	91	68	81	55	50	46	56	67	56	5.7	50	55	50	49	49	54
	Persian Gulf–Europe	34	70	..	57	66	52	58	42	42	40	34	42	57	6.8	34	37	..	38	38	43
	Persian Gulf–Caribbean/East Coast of North America	35	65	52	56	58	53	63	48	39	35	30	44	36	2.9	32	37	42	38	37	39
	Persian Gulf–South Africa	..	..	..	89	..	80	..	..	..	..	..	66	..		52	..				..
Suezmax (100,000–160,000 dwt)																					
	West Africa–North-West Europe	77	127	100	104	114	125	110	85	78	64	80	95	118	53.2	63	75	107	83	84	..
	West Africa–Caribbean/East Coast of North America	73	114	97	98	112	118	103	73	74	65	78	81	103	41.1	60	72	101	79	81	66
	Mediterranean–Mediterranean	83	127	103	115	110	129	102	96	84	72	97	101	113	36.1	71	82	130	86	80	74
Aframax (70,000–100,000 dwt)																					
	North-West Europe–North-West Europe	115	137	113	126	116	141	100	108	107	90	103	94	162	40.9	88	97	122	95	99	94
	North-West Europe–Caribbean/East Coast of North America	100	135	117	110	..	153	104	103	115	..	..	85	120	20.0	131	90	135	85	90	84
	Caribbean–Caribbean/East Coast of North America	112	173	146	127	123	167	131	137	115	99	98	127	146	30.4	125	98	125	123	104	98
	Mediterranean–Mediterranean	117	124	95	135	114	160	110	108	107	87	112	92	138	17.9	75	97	122	95	99	94
	Mediterranean–North-West Europe	108	121	92	119	110	151	102	103	105	84	108	94	133	23.1	69	103	135	85	90	84
	Indonesia–East Asia	95	136	118	116	99	127	114	111	98	92	91	102	111	16.8	88	87	110	115	99	98
Handy size (less than 50,000 dwt)																					
	Mediterranean–Mediterranean	120	..	164	130	158	173	..	146	139	129	132	126	168	40.0	140	116	134	155	138	130
	Mediterranean–Caribbean/East Coast of North America	111	171	183	139	145	161	145	138	131	119	118	121	146	31.5	134	111	147	139	133	116
	Caribbean–East Coast of North America/Gulf of Mexico"	116	176	181	151	146	163	129	142	138	112	117	119	200	72.4	155	105	174	155	139	128
All clean tankers																					
70,000–80,000 dwt	Persian Gulf–Japan	111	140	123	118	106	124	112	124	144	130	101	99	125	12.6	107	98	105	123	129	111
50,000–60,000 dwt	Persian Gulf–Japan	121	151	139	124	126	143	123	128	161	141	110	120	128	5.8	119	111	122	142	145	124
35,000–50,000 dwt	Caribbean–East Coast of North America/Gulf of Mexico"	99	149	139	159	137	119	127	169	135	129	135	133	158	59.6	133	120	190	191	171	152
25,000–35,000 dwt	Singapore–East Asia	158	145	155	144	143	215	240	161	155	..	183	165	193	22.2	139	135	159	185	..	177

Source: UNCTAD secretariat, based on Dewry Shipping Insight, various issues.

Note: Two dots (..) means that no rate was reported. The classification of ship size in this table reflects the source used, and may vary when compared to other parts of this publicaion.

VLCCs. Average Suezmax freight rates on the West Africa and Caribbean/East Coast of North America route plunged from $36,000 per day in the first half of 2010 to $19,000 per day in the second half. This came at a time when the region's biggest oil exporter, Nigeria, began regaining lost ground. Nigeria's oil output, which peaked at 2.47 million barrels per day (mbpd) in early 2006, declined to 1.68 mbpd in July 2009 before increasing to 2.15 mbpd in the third quarter of 2010.[16] In early 2011, output began to fall back towards the 2 mbpd threshold. Around two thirds of Nigeria's oil exports is bound for the United States, with the remainder destined for Europe.

Despite the fluctuating fortunes of the Suezmax market during 2010, the price of a five-year-old Suezmax vessel rose by around 5 per cent over the course of the year to reach $62 million. This modest increase during a period of uncertainty reflects a positive market mood for the Suezmax segment. During previous economic downturns, Suezmax vessels have been able to reap benefits at the expense of the larger VLCCs, as importers typically demand smaller cargo volumes. Presently, the oversupply of Suezmax vessels is hampering a recovery in freight rates. However, the political turmoil in Libya has led importers to seek alternative sources from further afield, leading to the absorption of more capacity and pushing freight rates higher.

Aframax tankers

Aframax tankers offer a large carrying capacity with lower overheads than those of VLCCs or Suezmax vessels. The term is derived from the maximum-sized vessel (80,000–120,000 dwt) that is permitted under the average freight rate assessment procedure for adjusting long-term oil freight contract rates. They are often deployed for trading within and between the following regions: North-West Europe, the Caribbean, the East Coast of North America, the Mediterranean, Indonesia and East Asia.

In 2010, freight rates for all Aframax vessels generally fared well. From December 2009 to December 2010, all routes climbed between 16 and 40 per cent. The best performing region was Northern Europe. January 2010 was a particularly good month for all sectors and May represented a peak in all Aframax sectors. However, the following month witnessed significant falls as demand fell over mounting concerns about the Greek debt crisis and the dollar strengthened against the Euro. Pessimism over the United States recovery and the Chinese Government's efforts to curb rising

housing costs also added to concerns about the global economy. This pushed crude oil prices to a temporary two-year low before resuming their uphill climb. From $41.9 million in 2009, the annual average price of a five-year-old Aframax vessel rose 6 per cent in 2010 to $44.5 million. This increase reflected the preference for mid-sized tankers in an uncertain market. The one-year charter rates for a five-year-old 80,000 dwt tanker climbed by around 2.4 per cent in 2010 to reach around $16,800 per day in January 2011.

Handysize tankers

Handysize tankers are those of less than 50,000 dwt that have a draft of around 10 metres. These vessels are most suited for calling at destinations with depth and length constraints. Table 3.4 shows the freight rates for these types of ships deployed intra-Mediterranean and from the Mediterranean to the Caribbean and the East Coast of North America, plus trades from the Caribbean to the Gulf of Mexico and the East Coast of North America. Freight rates on all three routes increased between 31 and 72 per cent in 2010, after a particularly bad performance in 2009. Freight rates for Handymax vessels have remained depressed. The Caribbean–East Coast of North America–Gulf of Mexico route, the worst performing route for this segment in 2009, experienced a dramatic rise. A five-year-old 45,000 dwt Handysize vessel, which cost on average $30 million in 2009, declined by 13 per cent to $26 million in 2010.

All clean tankers

Product tankers are specialized cargo-carrying vessels that carry various chemicals, such as naphtha, clean condensate, jet fuel, kerosene, gasoline, gas oil, diesel, cycle oil and fuel oil. Unlike crude oil tanker markets, which primarily transport cargo from its origin to the point of refinery, this sector handles the processed cargo that leaves the refinery destined for consumption. The chemical tanker fleet is divided into three specifications established by the Internationl Martime Organization (IMO). The smallest market, accounting for less than 3 per cent of vessels, is the IMO 1 specification, which trades in the most hazardous cargoes such as chlorosulphonic acid that is used in detergents, pharmaceuticals, pesticides, and dyes, and trichlorobenzene, more commonly known as TCB, a solvent used in herbicides and pesticides.[17] The largest sector, with some two thirds of the fleet, trades primarily in pure chemical cargoes such as styrene, xylene and easychems, and is known as IMO 2. Around one third of chemical tankers are classified as IMO 3, or double-hull product tankers, trading only in chemicals and vegetable oils.

Freight rates on all four routes shown in table 3.4 increased between 6 per cent and 60 per cent in 2010, with the Caribbean–East Coast of North America/Gulf of Mexico route increasing the most. On the Persian Gulf–Japan route, freight rates oscillated between 100 and 150 WS throughout the year.

While 2009 was a low point for product tanker earnings, matters only slightly improved in 2010. May 2010 marked a bottom point for average time charter equivalent earnings on the Caribbean–East Coast of North America/Gulf of Mexico route at $7,300 per day. The one-year charter rates for a five-year old 30,000 dwt clean tanker climbed by around 21 per cent in 2010 to reach $12,800 per day in January 2011. The five-year-old 30,000 dwt clean tankers were the best performing type of tanker in 2010, reflecting a strong demand for small shipments of chemicals.

Liquefied natural gas tankers

Natural gas has many uses, such as generating electricity in large power plants, providing cooking and heating for domestic homes, fuelling vehicles (particularly in Pakistan, Argentina, Brazil, the Islamic Republic of Iran and India) and producing ammonia (with China as the main producer) for fertilizers. Cooling natural gas to minus 162°C turns it into a liquid, thereby making it easier to transport by vessel. A typical LNG tanker can carry around 160,000 cubic metres (cbm) of natural gas on a single voyage. The largest LNG tankers (Q-Max) have a capacity of 266,000 cubic metres, but their size limits which ports they can operate between. Because gasification and re-gasification are expensive, only a few countries are involved in this market. With approximately one quarter of the world's market share of LNG exports, Qatar is the single largest of 19 LNG-exporting countries. In 2010, Peru became the latest country to join this small group of specialized exporters. The number of countries importing LNG stands at 23, with Asia being the largest importing region. However, a lack of pipeline infrastructure linking LNG plants to domestic users limits the demand for gas.[18] The single largest LNG importer is Japan. The tragic nuclear accident at the Fukushima Daiichi nuclear power plant caused by the March 2011 earthquake and tsunami is likely to increase the county's need to import more LNG. Some analysts estimate that an additional 2 million cbm could be needed in order to compensate for the cessation in electricity output

from the affected nuclear power plants.[19] Previously, when the Kashiwazaki-Karima nuclear power plant shut down in 2007 because of another earthquake, LNG spot rates soared.[20]

The conversion of existing oil tankers into floating re-gasification vessels, at a fraction of the cost of building a dedicated gasification plant, is helping the number of LNG importers to grow. In 2010, Dubai commissioned its first floating re-gasification terminal at Jebel Ali. In Qatar, the RasGas Train-7, with a capacity of 7.8 million tons per year, became operational in February 2010. The BG Group announced that it was considering expanding its LNG facilities at Curtis Island in Queensland, Australia, to a maximum of five trains.

Because of the high investment requirement in building plants and vessels, LNG shipments tend to be negotiated on long-term contract of up to 20 years. For instance, in 2010 the BG Group signed a sales agreement with Tokyo Gas for the supply of 1.2 million tons of LNG a year for 20 years principally from its Queensland Curtis LNG facility, near Gladstone in Queensland, Australia. However, the number of LNG trades on the spot market or short-term contracts in 2010 increased to 727 from 491 in the previous year.[21] Freight rates for LNG vessels in 2010 remained low, with an average of around $35,000 per day, down from $50,000 per day in 2009. By the middle of 2011, the average one-year charter rates for LNG tankers increased to $100,000 per day. Prices for new LNG tankers fell by 8 per cent in 2010, bringing the price back to near 2005 levels. A limited supply of LNG vessels and an increase in demand is expected to keep freight rates firm for the short-term.

The Capital Link LNG/LPG Index, which tracks the market value of major United States-listed shipping companies (for example, Golar LNG, StealthGas Inc. and Teekay LNG) involved in the LNG/LPG sector increased by 50 per cent in 2010 from 2,088.39 points at the start of the year to 2,992.17 points in December. In April 2011, the index climbed further to 3,461.13 points, indicating a positive outlook for LNG among investors.

Summary of tanker freight rates

In sum, the tanker freight rates rebounded from the effects of the global financial crisis, albeit in most cases only slightly. Tanker freight rates, excluding LNG, remain depressed in comparison with their long-term average. Additions to the tanker fleet continue to have an effect on destabilizing prices, while demand remains uncertain. The immediate effects of the global economic crisis have been reflected in the falling price of newbuildings for all tanker vessel types. Because the tanker sector is providing the fuel to drive industrial centres, and is a key component of many manufactured goods, it is heavily dependent on the global economic outlook and the demand for those goods. While increasing vessel supply may hamper short-term growth, the future for this market segment looks more positive with the increased demand that will come from a growing global population enjoying a higher disposable income that will be used to consume more products and travel services.

2.   The main dry bulk shipping market

The main dry bulk shipping market consists primarily of five cargo types: iron ore, grain, coal, bauxite/alumina and phosphate. Many of the major cargo types are raw ingredients such as coal that are used either to generate power or to drive manufacturing activities. The main dry bulk sector accounts for just over one quarter of the total volume of cargo transported by sea. The demand for major dry bulk cargoes increased by around 11 per cent in 2010 but freight rates undulated.

Dry bulk freight rates

The dry bulk sector improved in 2010 over the previous year, with freight rates up 12 per cent on the tramp time and 16 per cent on the tramp trip. Dry cargo tramp time charter refers to vessels chartered for a period of time and dry cargo tramp trip charter refers to a charter for a specific voyage. Freight rates for dry bulk vessels were still down by around one third, compared with their 2007 and 2008 levels (see figure 3.2 and table 3.5). Freight rates for dry bulk vessels, which were buoyant during the first half of 2010, declined on average by a quarter for the second half of the year.

Freight rates for Capesize vessels chartered on the Far East–Europe route were $57,587 per day in January 2010 and declined to $17,358 per day in early 2011. In the opposite direction, from Europe to Asia, freight rates fell from $20,664 per day in January 2010 to minus $3,371 per day, as shipowners subsidized charterers' repositioning costs. Other factors have limited cargo availability, such as events in the world's number one iron ore exporting country, Australia (flooding in the coal-producing regions, followed by cyclones in the iron-ore exporting regions), and in the world's number three iron ore exporter, India, where Chhattisgarh and Orissa States have imposed a ban on ore exports.[22]

Figure 3.2. Dry cargo freight indices, 2004–2011

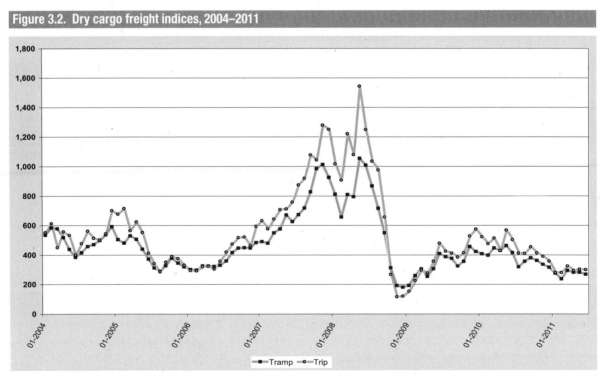

Source: UNCTAD secretariat, based on various issues of *Shipping Statistics* and *Market Review*, produced by the Institute of Shipping Economics and Logistics.

Table 3.5. Dry cargo freight indices, 2007–2011

Period	Dry cargo tramp time charter (1972 = 100)					Dry cargo tramp trip charter (1985 = 100)				
	2007	2008	2009	2010	2011	2007	2008	2009	2010	2011
January	491	812	193	408	276	632	1 018	154	523	281
February	480	657	259	398	237	577	908	227	476	280
March	550	810	305	447	294	644	1 221	296	514	325
April	576	795	254	430	282	707	1 080	277	430	294
May	671	1 055	306	463	282	712	1 544	358	568	303
June	626	1 009	410	415	269	759	1 250	479	503	300
July	673	868	388	319		875	1 036	426	413	
August	718	716	377	357		920	976	413	411	
September	828	550	325	381		1 078	657	385	455	
October	985	313	357	363		1 044	267	416	414	
November	1 013	192	457	336		1 280	117	529	391	
December	926	181	423	316		1 251	121	575	358	
Annual average	711	663	338	386	273	873	850	378	455	297

Source: UNCTAD secretariat, based on various issues of *Shipping Statistics and Market Review* produced by the Institute of Shipping Economics and Logistics.

Note: All indices have been rounded to the nearest whole number.

Chinese imports of iron ore represent around 63 per cent of the iron ore market transported by sea, which makes this market a major employer of Capesize vessels.[23] Iron ore freight rates from Brazil to China started 2010 at $29.83 per ton – more than double the January 2009 figure of $13.90 per ton – but still half the $64.05 per ton in 2008. In 2010, rates on this route declined by around 40 per cent. Also iron ore freight rates declined at a similar percentage on the Western Australia–China route rates. The falling freight rates for dry bulk carriers helped boost Chinese demand for foreign iron ore by 8 per cent per annum in 2010; demand in 2011 is estimated at 652.1 million tons.

The time charter earnings of a Capsize vessel in 2010 averaged $40,308 per day, up from $35,283 in 2009. By February 2011, the corresponding figure had fallen to $17,500 per day. During 2008, the average earning for a Capesize vessel was $116,175 per day and at one point, rates surpassed $300,000 per day. At a time of record profits for the biggest mining companies on the back of rising commodity prices, shipowners are experiencing some of the lowest freight rates since 2002.

Dry bulk time charter

In 2008, 45 per cent of charters were for short-term contracts of less than six months. This rose to 52 per cent in 2009 and 60 per cent in 2010. Whereas 18 per cent of charters were for long-term contracts of more than 24 months in 2008, this declined to between 8

and 9 per cent in 2009 and 2010. This may show that shipowners generally perceived the market as volatile, while expecting that rates would increase, or at least, remain higher than operating costs. Estimated rates for 12-month period charters (prompt delivery) were relatively stable for most of 2010, but in the last two months of 2010, rates began to slide. Capesize ships of 200,000 dwt aged five years fetched $39,700 per day at the start of 2010, compared with $19,700 per day for the same period in 2009; by the end of the year, the figure stood at $26,000 per day. By February 2011, the rate had fallen further to $18,000 per day. The best-performing sector was Handysize vessels of 28,000 dwt aged 10 years, which experienced a decrease of 14.8 per cent in rates between December 2009 and December 2010.[24]

Declining freight rates affected the price of vessels, but not dramatically. A five-year-old Capesize vessel which cost an average $123.2 million in 2008 and $47.3 million in 2009, rose 15 per cent to $54 million in 2010. By February 2011, the price had fallen back to 2009 levels, at $48 million. Given the high rate of delivery of newbuildings in 2011, the price is likely to slide further.

Dry cargo freight rates, which suffered a disastrous collapse in 2008, made a significant recovery by the end of 2009. However, it was short-lived and by June 2010, had petered out. To illustrate this, the BDI), which measures freight rates for dry bulk transported on selected maritime routes, started 2010 at 3,140 points and ended the year at 1,773 points (see figure 3.3).[25] From the end of May 2010 to the middle of July 2010, the BDI lost more than half its value as concern over the recovery of the global economy mounted. A partial rally occurred in August 2010 before the Index continued its downward trajectory. Between May 2010 and May 2011 the BDI declined by around two thirds. The most significant recent development in the dry bulk sector was the filing for bankruptcy protection in January 2011 of the second-largest shipping company in the Republic of Korea, Korea Line. With an owned fleet of 42 ships, over 100 vessels chartered in and three on order, the impact of the company's failure on other shipowners will be significant. Shipowners Eagle Bulk Shipping and Navios Maritime Partners were two companies whose chartering portfolios with Korea Line represented about 25 and 13 per cent of their business, respectively.

Freight rates for Capesize vessels on the major routes suffered a poor 2010, primarily because this sector is experiencing the strongest vessel oversupply of all the dry bulk sectors.[26] In 2011, an estimated 200 Capesize vessels, spanning some 35 miles end to end, will leave shipyards to join the existing 1,100-strong fleet.[27] As reported in chapter 2, the world's largest ore carrier, the 402,347 dwt Vale Brasil, was expected for delivery in 2011. Thus, not only are the numbers of ships increasing, but also their size.

Shipping companies are not the only ones to suffer. There is presently an oversupply of shipyards. If they are to survive, many of these shipyards need to diversify into higher-end production, for example, that of special-use vessels – multi-purpose vessels, cruise ships or specialized vessels carrying single cargoes such as LNG – or move into other manufacturing areas. However, there is no guarantee that diversification is the answer, since the higher-end shipyards in Odense, Denmark, and Mitsubishi Heavy Industries in Kobe, Japan, are both due to close in 2012.[28] [29] While the closure of a shipping company will result in the loss of jobs at the company's headquarters and in various other locations, including where it takes its seafarers (see chapter 6 for more details on which countries man the world's fleet), the closure of a shipyard will likely have a bigger impact on a single community, as shipyards tend to employ large workforces and buy local services. For example in Tuzla, Turkey, some 48 shipyards and various subcontracting firms employed around 30,000–35,000 workers in 2008; since then, the number has fallen to 8,000 workers (2011).[30] The number of shipyards in operation declined by 60 per cent from 2008 to 2011. Torgem Shipyard, for example, is reportedly operating at 20 per cent capacity owing to a series of cancelled orders, lowering employment levels at the shipyards from 270 to a mere 29.[31]

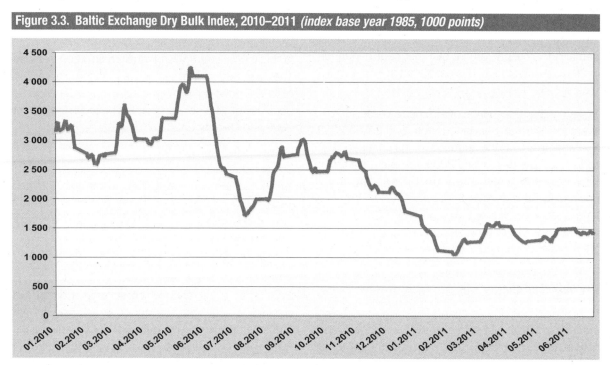

Figure 3.3. Baltic Exchange Dry Bulk Index, 2010–2011 *(index base year 1985, 1000 points)*

Source: UNCTAD, based on London Baltic Exchange data.

Despite the cancelled orders for newbuildings and dire predictions for shipyards in 2010, there was an average of 69 dry bulk vessels totalling 6.2 million dwt being delivered every month, compared with an average of 16 vessels of 1.6 million dwt over the decade beginning in 2000.[32] Surprisingly, orders for new vessels have not completely dried up, with around 55 new orders for dry bulk carriers being placed each month and 1,510 ships of 123 million dwt – approximately 23 per cent of the present fleet in dwt terms – expected to be delivered in 2011.

Reasons for the continued new orders could include renewed confidence in the world economy, lower vessels prices or attractive terms being offered by shipyards. Dry bulk vessels are one of the least complicated types to build, and new shipyards, which sprang up in the boom years of high commodity prices, entered this market and kept the prices of vessels low.

Summary of dry bulk freight rates

Demand for major dry bulk services rose about 11 per cent in 2010, with increased demand for raw materials from developing countries, most notably China. Further, in 2010 there was strong growth in steel, forest products, coke and potash. Fine weather also contributed to a good growing season for agricultural products, which also helped the sector. In particular, global imports of sugar increased 10 per cent, and rice, 6 per cent.[33] However, the carrying capacity of vessels servicing this market grew by 16 per cent, resulting in falling freight rates. The oversupply of vessels is the main cause of lower dry bulk freight rates, brought about by overordering during the boom years. The oversupply of shipyards is likely to continue to drive down the price of newbuildings and in particular, dry bulk vessels. Some shipowners will be attracted by the lower prices and will take the opportunity to modernize their fleet. However, unless their old vessels are sold for scrap, there will still be too many vessels, which will mean freight rates will continue to remain low.

3.   The liner shipping market

Liner shipping services operate vessels between fixed ports on a strict timetable. Liner services can be operated by one company or by a group of companies known as an alliance or a consortium.

Costs and revenues are shared in accordance with each company's contribution. Liner shipping companies primarily operate container ships, which carry containerized cargo. In 2010, total world containerized trade was estimated at 1.4 billion tons – an increase of around 17.6 per cent over the previous year. Container trade volumes amounted to an estimated 140 million TEUs in 2010, an increase of around 12.9 per cent from the 124 million TEUs recorded in 2009. Approximately 17 per cent of world seaborne trade in volume terms (tons) is transported in containers (see chapter 1 for more details). The following sections examine developments in the liner shipping market and freight rates.

The rapid growth in containerization over the last 20 years is due to a combination of factors such as dedicated purpose-built container vessels, larger vessels capable of achieving larger economies of scale, improved handling facilities in ports and increasing amounts of components parts being carried in containers. Although 39 per cent of newbuilding orders were not delivered, the world's fleet of container ships increased by 14.7 million dwt in 2010, or 8.7 per cent, to reach 184 million dwt, approximately 13.2 per cent of the total world fleet. In all likelihood, these vessels will be built, but delivery will be delayed. At the beginning of 2011, there were 4,868 container ships, with a total capacity of 14.1 million TEUs (see chapter 2 for more details on the container fleet).

Developments in the liner trade

In 2009, the top 30 liner carriers reported their worst financial performance ever, with an estimated collective loss of $19.4 billion from a reported $5 billion profit the year before.[34] In 2010, the same liners are estimated to have earned a combined $17 billion, whereas profits are forecast to be about $8 billion in 2011.[35] The turnaround is attributable to the following factors: methods adopted by the carriers, which absorbed capacity (for example, they removed some vessels by laying them up and added other vessels to existing routes with orders to sail at a lower speed); a fall in fuel prices, in some cases by as much as 30 per cent; and most importantly, an increase in demand from merchandise trade. Figure 3.4 illustrates trends in container shipping supply and demand in recent years. The growth in demand for liner shipping has rebounded significantly from the gloom of 2009, when concern about the global economic crisis pulled apart

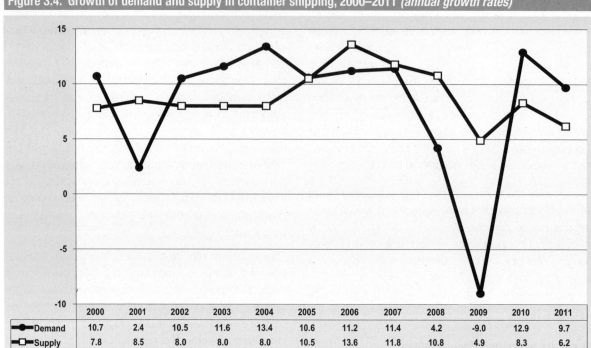

Figure 3.4. Growth of demand and supply in container shipping, 2000–2011 (annual growth rates)

	2000	2001	2002	2003	2004	2005	2006	2007	2008	2009	2010	2011
Demand	10.7	2.4	10.5	11.6	13.4	10.6	11.2	11.4	4.2	-9.0	12.9	9.7
Supply	7.8	8.5	8.0	8.0	8.0	10.5	13.6	11.8	10.8	4.9	8.3	6.2

Source: Compiled by the UNCTAD secretariat on the basis of data from *Clarkson Container Intelligence Monthly,* various issues.

Note: Data refer to total container-carrying fleet, including multi-purpose vessels and other vessels with some container-carrying capacity. The data for 2011 are forecasted figures.

supply and demand to their widest point. For the first time since 2005, growth in demand for liner services has outstripped the growth in supply. Estimates for 2010 show that the difference between the growth in supply and demand reached its widest point at 4.6 percentage points. The forecast for 2011 is that the gap between these two will narrow to 3.5 percentage points, with supply and demand growth being in line with and more stable freight rates.

The idleness of the container fleet, which was around 11.7 per cent, representing some 600 vessels at the start of 2010, declined to 1.9 per cent at the beginning of 2011. Container trade grew by an estimated 12.1 per cent in 2010 after its first-ever contraction in 2009. North–South trade lanes grew about 12.2 per cent because of a growing intra-Asian trade. Freight rates for containers reached an all-time high in early 2010. Freight rates from Shanghai to Europe were $2,164 per TEU in March 2010 and ended the year at $1,401 per TEU.[36]

Container freight rates

Container freight rates in 2010 witnessed a major transformation brought about by an upward trend in exports and measures introduced by operators to

constrain vessel supply. Table 3.6 shows the average yearly rates provided since 2001 by the Hamburg Shipbrokers' Association, also known by its German acronym, VHSS. The table also includes the monthly charter rates for container ships in 2010.[37] It is clear that the average yearly freight rates in the liner market segments performed significantly better in 2010 than 2009, but were still very much below pre-crisis levels. Freight rates climbed steadily in 2010. The smallest container ships, 200–299 TEUs, ended the year up 29 per cent, whereas the largest ships in the table, 1,600–1,999 TEUs, ended the year up 130 per cent. These rises also continued well into 2011.

Figure 3.5 shows the New ConTex Index, which is made up of combined rate freight rates for various container trades.[38] The index shows the dramatic two-thirds decline in container charter rates from mid-2008 to April 2009 and its subsequent rebound to near three quarters of the 2008 level.

Ownership of liner vessels is dominated by German shipowners, who control about two thirds of the container charter market and one third of the total available capacity.[39] Table 3.7 shows the development of liner freight rates on cargoes loaded or discharged by German-owned container vessels for the period

Table 3.6. Container ship time charter rates *(dollars per 14-ton slot/day)*

Ship type (TEUs)	Yearly averages										
	2001	2002	2003	2004	2005	2006	2007	2008	2009	2010	2011
Gearless											
200–299	15.7	16.9	19.6	25.0	31.7	26.7	27.2	26.0	12.5	12.4	14.6
300–500	14.7	15.1	17.5	21.7	28.3	21.7	22.3	20.0	8.8	9.9	12.9
Geared/gearless											
2 000–2 299	8.0	4.9	9.8	13.8	16.4	10.5	11.7	10.0	2.7	4.8	7.4
2 300–3 400[a]		6.0	9.3	13.2	13.0	10.2	10.7	10.7	4.9	4.7	8.5
Geared/gearless											
200–299	17.8	17.0	18.9	27.0	35.4	28.0	29.8	32.1	16.7	18.3	22.5
300–500	14.9	13.4	15.6	22.2	28.8	22.0	21.3	21.4	9.8	11.7	16.5
600–799[b]		9.3	12.3	19.6	23.7	16.6	16.1	15.6	6.6	8.4	12.1
700–999[c]		9.1	12.1	18.4	22.0	16.7	16.9	15.4	6.0	8.5	13.0
800–999[d]									4.9	6.3	11.9
1 000–1 260	8.8	6.9	11.6	19.1	22.6	14.3	13.7	12.2	4.0	5.9	9.1
1 261–1 350[e]									3.7	4.9	8.5
1 600–1 999	8.0	5.7	10.0	16.1	15.8	11.8	12.8	10.8	3.5	5.0	7.5

Ship type (TEUs)	Monthly averages for 2010											
	Jan	Feb	Mar	Apr	May	Jun	Jul	Aug	Sep	Oct	Nov	Dec
Gearless												
200–299	10.4	11.7	13.0	10.4	12.7	11.9	10.8	14.9	10.9	14.7	14.3	13.5
300–500	9.1	8.1	8.3	8.5	9.3	9.6	10.0	10.9	11.3	11.1	11.8	11.4
Geared/gearless												
2 000–2 299	2.6	2.4	2.5	2.8	3.2	5.2	6.2	6.9	8.1	6.6	5.9	5.4
2 300–3 400[a]	2.1	2.6	3.0	5.2	5.5	7.2	7.7					
Geared/gearless												
200–299	16.6	15.2	15.6	15.6	17.4	20.2	17.5	20.3	18.2	21.9	19.6	21.7
300–500	8.8	9.4	9.7	11.6	9.7	9.8	12.6	14.2	13.0	14.9	14.7	12.2
600–799[b]	6.1	5.9	7.4	6.2	7.2	8.5	8.5	10.0	9.9	9.8	11.4	10.3
700–799[c]	6.6	6.2	6.3	6.6	6.9	8.2	9.5	9.3	10.1	10.4	10.8	11.2
800–999[d]	6.4	6.1	5.2	5.3	6.1	7.0	8.3					
1 000–1 260	4.0	3.8	4.0	4.3	4.8	6.2	6.5	7.3	7.6	7.6	7.4	7.3
1 261–1 350[e]				3.8	4.2	5.3	6.3					
1 600–1 999	3.0	3.3	3.0	4.5	3.4	5.0	5.9	6.8	7.0	6.4	5.5	6.8

Table 3.6. Container ship time charter rates *(dollars per 14-ton slot/day)* (concluded)

Ship type (TEUs)	Monthly averages for 2011					
	Jan	Feb	Mar	Apr	May	Jun
Gearless						
200–299	13.3	14.4	14.9	15.6	15.7	13.8
300–500	11.3	12.3	13.4	14.4	14.3	14.1
Geared/gearless						
2 000–2 299	6.6	7.3	7.4	8.2	7.6	7.9
2 300–3 400[a]	7.6	8.5	9.1	8.6	8.7	8.1
Geared/gearless						
200–299	22.1	22.9	22.5		27.2	24.7
300–500	17.2	16.1	17.2	15.5	15.3	18.2
600–799[b]	10.4	12.9	12.6	12.4	13.4	12.7
700–999[c]	11.9	12.7	13.4	13.8	13.5	13.3
800–999[d]	10.3	12.7	12.2	12.3	12.4	12.1
1 000–1 260	7.5	8.7	9.9	10.1	10.4	10.3
1 261–1 350[e]	7.6	8.0	8.9	9.4	9.5	9.6
1 600–1 999	6.7	7.5	7.9	7.8	8.0	8.0

Source: Compiled by the UNCTAD secretariat, from the Hamburg Index produced by the Hamburg Shipbrokers' Association, available at http://www.vhss.de; and from *Shipping Statistics and Market Review*, vol. 52, no. 1/2 2010: 54–55, produced by the Institute of Shipping Economics and Logistics.

a   This category was created in 2002. The data for the first half of the year correspond to cellular ships in the 2,300–3,900 TEU range, sailing at 22 knots minimum.

b   Sailings at 17–17.9 knots.

c   Sailings at 18 knots minimum.

d   This category was created in 2009 by splitting the 700–999 category.

e   This category was created in 2009 by splitting the 1,000–1,350 category.

Figure 3.5. New ConTex 2007–2011 *(indices base: 1,000 – October 2007)*

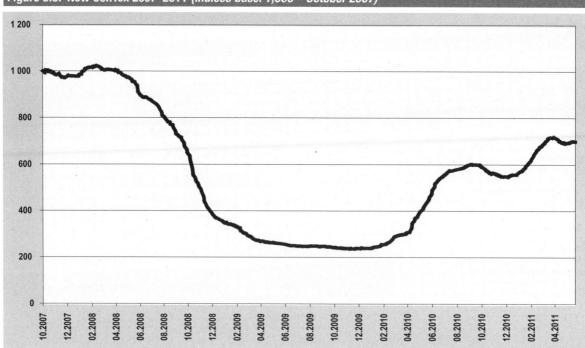

Source: Compiled by the UNCTAD secretariat, using the ConTex Index produced by the Hamburg Shipbrokers' Association. See http://www.vhss.de.

Table 3.7. Liner freight indices, 2007–2011 *(monthly figures: 1995 = 100)*

Month	Overall index					Homebound index					Outbound index				
	2007	2008	2009	2010	2011	2007	2008	2009	2010	2011	2007	2008	2009	2010	2011
January	89	98	62	98	114	98	116	68	138	152	81	83	58	65	82
February	88	95	59	104	108	98	114	64	149	141	80	80	55	67	81
March	86	92	57	111	106	96	110	60	163	136	78	77	55	68	80
April	87	88	56	115	102	100	106	61	161	130	77	74	52	77	80
May	88	89	53	119	103	101	107	58	166	130	76	75	49	82	81
June	92	89	53	125	103	105	106	59	170	129	81	75	48	88	82
July	94	89	60	127		114	104	71	174		80	76	51	88	
August	95	93	65	120		118	107	80	162		81	81	53	86	
September	98	97	69	117		121	113	87	158		84	85	54	83	
October	97	90	75	109		119	105	98	146		84	77	57	79	
November	97	86	75	109		115	101	97	146		86	74	56	79	
December	100	73	84	111		118	83	111	146		88	65	63	83	
Annual average	93	90	64	114		109	106	76	157		81	77	54	79	

Source: Compiled by the UNCTAD secretariat, on the basis of information in various issues of *Shipping Statistics and Market Review*, published by the Institute of Shipping Economics and Logistics.

2007–2011. The average overall index for 2010 increased by 50 points from the 2009 level, to reach 114 points, a rise of 78 per cent. The year 2010 took off with a significant increase, especially on the homebound index (imports into Europe). The annual average figure on the homebound index was up by over 100 per cent in 2010, whereas the outbound index increased by 45 per cent.

At present (2011), freight rates between Asia and Europe are declining. Their average all-inclusive freight rate for dry cargo from Asia to northern Europe fell by 10 per cent in April. Freight rates from Asia to the Western Mediterranean/Northern Africa declined by 7.4 per cent and Eastern Mediterranean/Black Sea regions dropped 9 per cent.[40] The average bunker adjustment factor had risen by approximately $135 per TEU in April 2011, compared with the average for the fourth quarter of 2010. By June 2011, the figure was $250 per TEU. On the Shanghai–Mediterranean route, the bunker adjustment factor was an additional $700 in April 2011 based on a freight rate of around $960 per TEU. At around the same time, all-inclusive freight rates from Shanghai to the United States West Coast were around $1,650–$1,850 per 40-foot equivalent unit (FEU), while prices to the East Coast were $2,980–$3,200 per FEU.[41] [42]

Container prices

Figure 3.6 shows how the purchase prices of containers have evolved over the past few years. During 2010 and into 2011 they continued to climb. At the end of 2009, a standard TEU cost $1,900. By the first quarter of 2011 it had risen to $2,800, an increase of almost 50 per cent. Helping to boost the demand for containers is the increase in container fleet size. While the ratio of container per vessel has declined in recent years, the overall number of containers in circulation has grown (see chapter 2 for more details on the container fleet).

4. Freight cost as a percentage of value of imports

Figure 3.7 illustrates how costs as a percentage of the value of imports have averaged over the last three decades by region. Over the last two decades, maritime freight rates have fallen in all regions. The most significant observation is that transport costs as a percentage of imports for developing countries in the Americas have remained the same, whereas all other areas witnessed a reduction in costs. Transport costs in Africa remain

Figure 3.6. Container prices (2005–2011) *(quarterly averages, in dollars)*

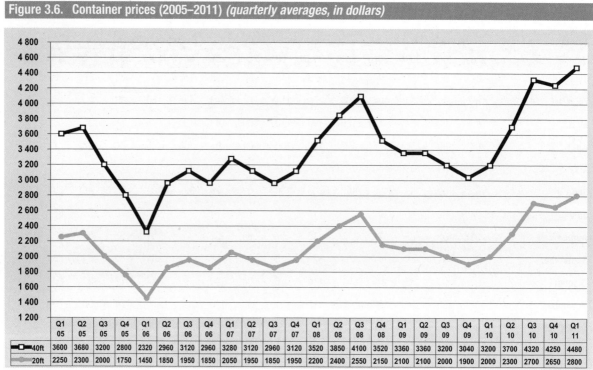

	Q1 05	Q2 05	Q3 05	Q4 05	Q1 06	Q2 06	Q3 06	Q4 06	Q1 07	Q2 07	Q3 07	Q4 07	Q1 08	Q2 08	Q3 08	Q4 08	Q1 09	Q2 09	Q3 09	Q4 09	Q1 10	Q2 10	Q3 10	Q4 10	Q1 11
40ft	3600	3680	3200	2800	2320	2960	3120	2960	3280	3120	2960	3120	3520	3850	4100	3520	3360	3360	3200	3040	3200	3700	4320	4250	4480
20ft	2250	2300	2000	1750	1450	1850	1950	1850	2050	1950	1850	1950	2200	2400	2550	2150	2100	2100	2000	1900	2000	2300	2700	2650	2800

Source: Compiled by the UNCTAD secretariat based on data from *Containerisation International Magazine*, various issues.

Figure 3.7. Freight cost as a percentage of value of imports: long-term trend (1980–89, 1990–99 and 2000–09) *(average percentages for decades)*

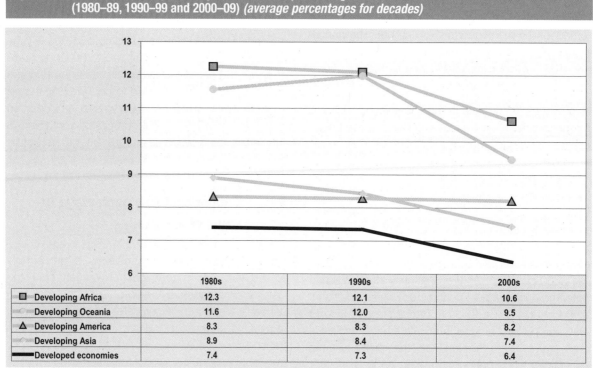

	1980s	1990s	2000s
Developing Africa	12.3	12.1	10.6
Developing Oceania	11.6	12.0	9.5
Developing America	8.3	8.3	8.2
Developing Asia	8.9	8.4	7.4
Developed economies	7.4	7.3	6.4

Source: UNCTAD secretariat.

the highest in the world. Freight costs for African countries constitute a higher proportion of total import value than those of other regions. The data suggest that it costs more to ship to Africa than to developed countries, on average 10.6 per cent of the price of final goods for Africa, as opposed to 6.4 per cent on average for developed countries.[43]

The drop in shipping costs has been influenced by the global transformation of maritime transport spurred by globalization over the past two decades. Several factors have contributed to this decline, including: the growing market of container traffic, which has been the fastest-growing segment of maritime transport. As a result, and in order to benefit from economies of scale, container ships have been growing in size surpassing 10,000 TEUs per vessel, compared with the late 1990s, when the largest vessels had a capacity of 4,400 TEUs – Panamax.[44] Moreover, developments in cargo handling, new technologies and reduced crew sizes have had an impact on the operational costs and per-unit cost of ocean cargo transport. Port reforms and increased investment in information and communication technology, innovation and new technologies have also led to greater efficiency and productivity at the port level, reducing the time of cargo handling, and in turn affecting terminal charges and reducing overall cargo prices.

Outlook for vessel prices and freight rates

Tables 3.8 and 3.9, and figure 3.8 describe world fleet performance. Table 3.8 reveals that the world ratio of world fleet to volume carried was at 1:6, meaning that over the course of the year, each vessel carried on average six times its maximum capacity – six full journeys a year – to produce the total volume of cargo carried by sea. This figure is below 6.6, which was achieved in 2009, and down from the 2006 ratio of 1:8. The increase in the world total of cargo moved by maritime transport shows the expansion of the world fleet with significantly more ships and ship capacity chasing only slightly more cargo.

Table 3.9 and figure 3.8, derived from the same data, provide a breakdown of table 3.8 by general vessel type. For instance, it reveals that the productivity

Table 3.8. Cargo carried per deadweight ton of the total world fleet, selected years

Year	World fleet (millions of dwt, beginning of year)	Total cargo (millions of tons)	Tons carried per dwt
1970	326	2 566	7.9
1980	683	3 704	5.4
1990	658	4 008	6.1
2000	799	5 984	7.5
2006	960	7 700	8.0
2007	1 042	8 034	7.7
2008	1 118	8 229	7.4
2009	1 192	7 858	6.6
2010	1 395	8 408	6.0

Source: Calculated by the UNCTAD secretariat, on the basis of UNCTAD data on seaborne trade (in tons) and IHS Fairplay data on the world fleet (in dwt).

of the tanker and dry bulk sectors has decreased considerably over time. Tankers that used to carry 9.74 tons per dwt in 1970 carried only 6.12 tons in 2010. For the dry bulk sector, the corresponding figures are 6.21 tons per dwt in 1970 to 5.11 tons per dwt in 2010. However, fleet productivity relating to dry cargo almost doubled from the 6.38 tons per dwt that were carried in 1970, to the 11.69 tons per dwt that were carried in 2010. One explanation for the high productivity rate of container ships is that container shipping can often benefit from return cargoes, whereas oil and bulk vessels tend to move cargo from extraction to consumptions points and return in ballast. With an increased number of production centres, the distances between source and consumption have grown, resulting in a lower measured tanker fleet productivity. In 2010, tanker fleet productivity declined, whereas the productivity of dry bulk and containers fleets increased. The year 2010 was the most productive for the container fleet since 2006, suggesting that the container fleet might need to expand.

Table 3.9. Estimated productivity of tankers, bulk carriers and the residual fleet,ª selected years

Year	Oil cargo (millions of tons)	Tanker fleet (millions of dwt, beginning of year)	Tons carried per dwt of tankers	Main dry bulks (millions of tons)	Dry bulk fleet (millions of dwt, beginning of year)	Tons carried per dwt of bulk carriers	All other dry cargoes (millions of tons)	Residual fleetª (millions of dwt, beginning of year)	Tons carried per dwt of the residual fleetª
1970	1 442	148	9.74	448	72	6.21	676	106	6.38
1980	1 871	339	5.51	796	186	4.29	1 037	158	6.57
1990	1 755	246	7.14	968	235	4.13	1 285	178	7.23
2000	2 163	282	7.66	1 288	276	4.67	2 532	240	10.53
2006	2 698	354	7.62	1 836	346	5.31	3 166	260	12.19
2007	2 747	383	7.17	1 957	368	5.32	3 330	292	11.41
2008	2 742	408	6.72	2 059	391	5.26	3 428	319	10.75
2009	2 642	418	6.32	2 094	418	5.01	3 122	355	8.80
2010	2 752	450	6.12	2 333	457	5.11	3 323	284	11.69

Source: Calculated by the UNCTAD secretariat, based on UNCTAD data on seaborne trade (in tons), and IHS Fairplay data on the world fleet (in dwt).

a   The residual fleet refers to general cargo, container ships and other vessels included in annex III (b).

Figure 3.8. Tons carried per deadweight ton (dwt) of the world fleet, selected years

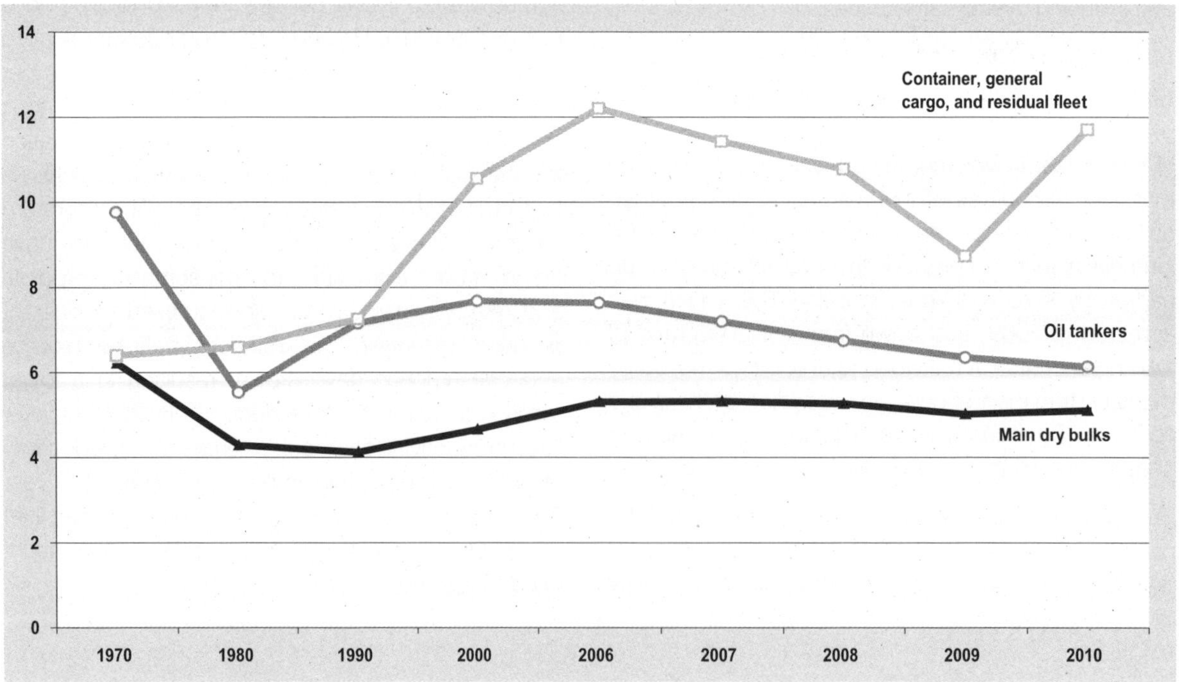

Source: UNCTAD secretariat.

ENDNOTES

[1] See for example, Radelet S and Sachs J (1998), *Shipping Costs, Manufactured Exports, and Economic Growth*, presented at the Annual Meeting of the American Economics Association, Chicago, 3–5 January; Hummels D, (1999), *Towards a Geography of Trade Costs*, University of Chicago; Limao N and Venables AJ (2001), Infrastructure, geographical disadvantage and transport costs, *World Bank Economic Review*, No. 15; UNCTAD Transport Newsletter (2006), Trade, liner shipping supply, and maritime freight rates, No. 33, September; Hummels D, (2007), Transportation costs and international trade in the second era of globalization, *Journal of Economic Perspectives*, 21(3):131–154; UNCTAD Transport Newsletter (2008), The modal split of international goods transport, No. 38, March; Kumar S and Hoffmann J (2010), Globalization: The maritime nexus, in: the *Handbook of Maritime Economics and Business, second edition*.

[2] Other factors, such as competition between shipyards and the residual value of a vessel, will also affect its price.

[3] Around 40 per cent of the operating costs of a 10-year-old bulk carrier in 2005 were capital costs, according to Stopford M (2009). Maritime Economics. Third edition. Routledge. London.

[4] In February 2009, the United Arab Shipping Company introduced a $22 piracy surcharge for containers moving through the port of Aden, Yemen. See http://www.seatradeasia-online.com/News/3728.html.

[5] In April 2011 Hapag-Lloyd was charging a container seal fee of ₩5,000 ($4.6) on all exported containers from the Republic of Korea, whereas in China the fee was RMB 44 ($6.8) on exports from Ningbo.

[6] In January 2011, Maersk Line was charging $16 per container for electronic cargo release.

[7] As freight rates are rarely all-inclusive, it is often difficult for shippers to estimate the final transport cost. Therefore, there is growing pressure to change the billing process. In 2008, the European Union repealed the block exemption previously granted to liner conferences to collectively set freight rates, which meant that liner companies would have to set prices independently. A study of THCs in some 44 ports across Europe showed that the level of those charges increased after the ending of liner conferences, and that there was a high degree of averaging of charges applied. This has led to complaints from shippers that terminal handling charges (a) are not a reflection of the actual costs incurred by terminal operators and (b) are used as a mechanism to compensate for lower freight rates. See Competition reports (2009). *Terminal Handling Charges During and After the Liner Conference Era*. October. European Commission. Brussels.

[8] In July 2010, COSCO announced an "emergency equipment surcharge" of $400 per FEU on its transpacific route because of container shortages brought about by a surge in shipping demand amid the global economic revival. Bloomberg (2010). China shipping container adds surcharges on cargo-box shortage, 25 June.

[9] While Maersk Line lists 107 surcharges on the following link, http://www.maerskline.com/link/?page=brochure&path=/our_services/Related%20services/VAS/ALL (date accessed: 17 June 2011) consultancy firm Seaintel quotes an unnamed carrier with 541 surcharges http://www.seaintel.com/.

[10] Lloyd's List (2011). Box carriers display independence on currency surcharges, 1 June.

[11] See http://www.strategicnine.com/LNG-gas-market.htm.

[12] *Tanker Operator Magazine* (2011). High cost of bunkers impacts on earnings. March, p. 4.

[13] The expansion of the Suez Canal in recent years has meant that some smaller VLCCs can now transit the canal.

[14] *Sea Rates* (2010). DVB bank: Suezmax tanker market outlook newsletter. 25 August. Available online from http://www.searates.com/news/11236/ (accessed 22 June 2011).

[15] Tanker Operator. November/December 2010.

[16] See http://c0182999.cdn1.cloudfiles.rackspacecloud.com/TOJanFeb2011web.pdf.

[17] Lloyd's List (2009). About the fleet, 1 April.

[18] Unlike in Europe, where an extensive network of pipelines feeds gas directly into many homes, thereby creating many sources of demand.

[19] Lloyd's List (2011). LNG spot market boost as few ships to come off charter, 11 May.

[20] Lloyd's List (2011). How high can LNG rates go? 21 May.

[21] Platts (2011). Global spot, short-term LNG trades in 2010 up 40% on year to 727 cargoes, 10 May.

[22] Orissa State, which alone accounts for a quarter of India's annual exports of around 100 million tons of iron ore, has banned exports since July 2010.

[23] Clarkson (2011). *Dry Bulk Trade Outlook*. 17(6):5. June.

[24] Handysize and Handymax vessels are smaller bulk carriers, ranging from 10,000 dwt to 35,000 dwt and 35,000 dwt to 55,000 dwt, respectively. They are preferred because of their flexibility, as they can carry reasonable cargo sizes to almost any port.

[25] The BDI is made up of various vessel types involved in the carry of different cargo types on various routes.

26   Capesize vessels are the largest dry bulk carriers and so named because they had to sail pass the Cape of Good Hope because they were too large to transit the Suez or Panama Canals.

27   Bloomberg (2011). Freight rates poised to tumble as 35-mile line of ships passes coal demand, 10 January.

28   The world's biggest container ship, the *Emma Maersk* (2006), and her seven sister-ships, were constructed here.

29   Business Monitor Online (2010). Mitsubishi yard closure reflects long-term shipbuilding decline, 26 July.

30   See http://www.reclaiming-spaces.org/transformation/archives/302.

31   TR Defence (2011). Turkish shipyards struggle due to financial crisis. 6 February. See http://www.trdefence. com/2011/02/06/turkish-shipyards-struggle-due-to-financial-crisis/.

32   Clarkson (2011). *Shipping Review and Outlook*. Spring, p59.

33   *Ibid.*, p66.

34   The Shippers' Voice (2011). Container freight derivatives, April.

35   Lloyd's List (2010). Container lines on track for $17bn profits in 2010, 14 December.

36   CIMB (2010). Container shipping. 7 June. Available from http://www.remisiers.org/cms_images/research/Jun06-Jun10/REG-CS-070611CIMBOW.pdf.

37   Since 1998, the Hamburg Shipbrokers' Association has published the Hamburg Index, which provides a market analysis of container ship time charter rates of a minimum duration of three months.

38   The New ConTex is a daily index that appears every Tuesday and Thursday and is compiled by a panel of international brokers on charter rate fixtures for six container vessel sizes.

39   Some of the largest German shipowners who charter their tonnage are C-P Offen, Peter Dohle, NSB N'Elbe, Norddeutsche, Rickmers and E.R.Schiff. Between them they represent more than 2 million dwt. (*Source: Clarkson's Container Intelligence Monthly*, May 2011).

40   (2011) Asia-Europe rates shock. *Containerisation International, 3 June.*

41   IFW (2011). Asia to Europe rates still on the slide. 13 April. Available from http://www.ifw-net.com/freightpubs/ifw/article.htm?artid=20017864731&src=rss.

42   JCtrans. (2011). Shanghai container index up on all routes. 16 May. Available from http://info.jctrans.com/jcnet/news/osn/20115161004026.shtml.

43   The data shown are the average for the decade, indicating only the relative price of freight as a percentage to imports, not the actual transport costs per se. Variations by country and over time will undoubtedly exist. The data must be read along with trade volume data to see how they have changed over time.

44   World Bank (2007). Port and maritime transport challenges in West and Central Africa. Sub-Saharan Africa Transport Policy Program (SSATP). Working Paper No. 84, May.

PORT AND MULTIMODAL TRANSPORT DEVELOPMENTS

CHAPTER 4

World container port throughput increased by an estimated 13.3 per cent to 531.4 million TEUs in 2010 after stumbling briefly in 2009. Chinese mainland ports continued to increase their share of total world container port throughput to 24.2 per cent. The UNCTAD Liner Shipping Connectivity Index (LSCI) reveals that China continues its lead as the single most connected country, followed by Hong Kong SAR, Singapore and Germany. In 2011, 91 countries increased their LSCI ranking over 2010, 6 saw no change, and 65 recorded a decrease. In 2010, the rail freight sector grew by 7.2 per cent to reach 9,843 billion freight ton kilometres (FTKs). The road freight sector grew by 7.8 per cent in 2010 over the previous year with volumes reaching 9,721 billion FTKs.

This chapter covers some of the major port development projects under way in developing countries, container throughput, liner shipping connectivity, improvements in port performance, and inland transportation and infrastructure development in the areas of road, rail, and inland waterways, with a special focus on public-private partnerships (PPPs) in financing inland transport infrastructure development and rail transport.

A.   PORT DEVELOPMENTS

1.   Container port throughput

For modern production processes, components of goods are often produced as semi-manufactured goods, re-exported in containers and assembled into final products. These final products may also be exported in a container. Containerized goods are suitable for transhipment, which means more container handling for ports. The growth in semi-manufactured goods and the use of transhipment has thus helped container throughput to thrive in recent decades. In 1990, world container port throughput volumes were around 85 million TEUs, and they have since grown sixfold to 531.4 million TEUs over 20 years. As can been seen from chapter two, the world fleet of container ships also grew by a similar magnitude. In 2010, container port throughput resumed its long climb after a brief stumble in 2009 as a result of the global economic crisis.

Table 4.1 shows the latest figures available on world container port traffic for 76 developing countries and economies in transition with an annual national throughput of over 100,000 TEUs. (An extended list of port throughput for countries can be found in annex V). In 2009, the container throughput rate of change for developing economies was an estimated minus 7 per cent, with a throughput of 325.2 million TEUs. Their share of world throughput remained virtually unchanged at approximately 69 per cent. Out of the 76 developing economies listed in table 4.1, only 23 experienced a positive growth in port throughput in 2009. The 10 countries registering the highest growth were Ecuador (49.2 per cent), Djibouti (45.7 per cent), Namibia (44.7 per cent), Morocco (32.9 per cent), Jordan (15.8 per cent), Lebanon (15.4 per cent), the Syrian Arab Republic (12.2 per cent), Dominican Republic (11 per cent), the Islamic Republic of Iran (10.3 per cent) and Sudan (10.3 per cent). The country with the largest share of container throughput is China, with nine ports in the top 20. Chinese ports, excluding Hong Kong SAR, experienced a negative growth of 6.58 per cent in 2009 to reach 107.5 million TEUs. Preliminary figures for 2010 showed a rebound for Chinese port throughput of around 19.6 per cent, to 128.5 million TEUs. Despite the fall in overall volumes, Chinese ports, with the exception of Hong Kong SAR, accounted for around 24.2 per cent of world container throughput, up from 22.9 per cent in 2009. The share

of Chinese ports of world container throughput has risen steadily in recent years from around 1.5 per cent in 1990 to 9.0 per cent in 2000 and 22.5 per cent in 2008. In 2010, the port of Shanghai for the first time took the title of the world's busiest container port from Singapore, with a throughput of 29.2 million TEUs. This represented a growth rate of over 16 per cent, compared with 2009 and was higher than Singapore's performance of 9.72 per cent. The port of Shanghai previously overtook Singapore to become the world's largest port in 2005 in terms of volume handled by all modes of transport. Singapore has faced growing competition in recent years from its neighbours in the form of existing and new potential port projects, for example, Batam Island (Indonesia), Port Tanjung Pelepas (Malaysia), Thailand (Pak Bara) and Cai Mep (Viet Nam).

Table 4.2 shows the world's 20 leading container ports for 2008–2010. This list includes 14 ports from developing economies, all of which are in Asia; the remaining 6 ports are from developed countries, 3 of which are located in Europe and 3 in North America. In 2010, one Asian port (Laem Chabang, Thailand) fell out of the top 20 and another port from North America (New York/New Jersey) joined the group. This is unusual, given the decline of North American ports in terms of their share of world container throughput. One explanation may be that trade across the Atlantic was less affected by the global economic crisis than trade across the Pacific. Table 4.2 also shows that Ningbo (up two places) and Qingdao (up one place) made gains in their ranking by increasing container throughput 25 and 17 per cent, respectively. Guangzhou (down one place) and Dubai (down two places) slipped in the ranking despite growing 17 and 14 per cent, respectively.

The top 20 container ports combined accounted for approximately 47.9 per cent of world container throughput in 2010, which is up from 47. 1 per cent in 2009 but down from the figure of 48.1 per cent reached in 2008 before the global financial crisis. Combined, these ports showed a 10.7 per cent decrease in throughput in 2009 and a 15.2 per cent increase in 2010. While this is good news for world trade, a closer examination of the numbers reveal that most of the gains reported in 2010 occurred during the first three quarters of the year, weakening significantly in the fourth quarter. In 2009, the top 20 container ports recorded negative growth, except the ports of Guangzhou (China), Tanjung Pelepas (Malaysia) and Tianjin (China).

Table 4.1. Container port traffic for 76 developing countries and economies in transition: 2008, 2009 and 2010 (in TEUs)					
Country	2008	2009	Preliminary estimates for 2010	Percentage change 2009–2008	Percentage change 2010–2009
China	115 060 978	107 492 861	128 544 458	-6.58	19.58
Singapore[a]	30 891 200	26 592 800	29 178 200	-13.91	9.72
China, Hong Kong SAR	24 494 229	21 040 096	23 532 000	-14.10	11.84
Republic of Korea	17 417 723	15 699 161	18 487 580	-9.87	17.76
Malaysia	16 024 829	15 671 296	17 975 796	-2.21	14.71
United Arab Emirates	14 756 127	14 425 039	15 195 223	-2.24	5.34
China, Taiwan Province of	12 971 224	11 352 097	12 302 111	-12.48	8.37
India	7 672 457	8 011 810	8 942 725	4.42	11.62
Indonesia	7 404 831	7 243 557	8 960 360	-2.18	23.70
Brazil	7 238 976	6 574 617	7 979 626	-9.18	21.37
Egypt	6 099 218	6 250 443	6 665 401	2.48	6.64
Thailand	6 726 237	5 897 935	6 648 532	-12.31	12.73
Viet Nam	4 393 699	4 840 598	5 474 452	10.17	13.09
Panama	5 129 499	4 597 112	5 906 744	-10.38	28.49
Turkey	5 218 316	4 521 713	5 508 974	-13.35	21.83
Saudi Arabia	4 652 022	4 430 676	5 313 141	-4.76	19.92
Philippines	4 471 428	4 306 723	5 048 669	-3.68	17.23
Oman	3 427 990	3 768 045	3 774 562	9.92	0.17
South Africa	3 875 952	3 726 313	4 039 241	-3.86	8.40
Sri Lanka	3 687 465	3 464 297	4 000 000	-6.05	15.46
Mexico	3 312 713	2 874 287	3 708 806	-13.23	29.03
Chile	3 164 137	2 795 989	3 162 759	-11.64	13.12
Russian Federation	3 307 075	2 337 634	3 091 322	-29.31	32.24
Iran (Islamic Republic of)	2 000 230	2 206 476	2 592 522	10.31	17.50
Pakistan	1 938 001	2 058 056	2 151 098	6.19	4.52
Colombia	1 969 316	2 056 747	2 443 786	4.44	18.82
Jamaica	1 915 943	1 689 670	1 891 770	-11.81	11.96
Argentina	1 997 146	1 626 351	1 972 269	-18.57	21.27
Bahamas	1 702 000	1 297 000	1 125 000	-23.80	-13.26
Dominican Republic	1 138 471	1 263 456	1 382 601	10.98	9.43
Venezuela (Bolivarian Republic of)	1 325 194	1 238 717	1 228 354	-6.53	-0.84
Peru	1 235 326	1 232 849	1 533 809	-0.20	24.41
Morocco	919 360	1 222 000	2 058 430	32.92	68.45
Bangladesh	1 091 200	1 182 121	1 350 453	8.33	14.24
Ecuador	670 831	1 000 895	1 221 849	49.20	22.08
Lebanon	861 931	994 601	949 155	15.39	-4.57
Guatemala	937 642	906 326	1 012 360	-3.34	11.70
Costa Rica	1 004 971	875 687	1 013 483	-12.86	15.74
Kuwait	961 684	854 044	888 206	-11.19	4.00
Syrian Arab Republic	610 607	685 299	710 642	12.23	3.70
Côte d'Ivoire	713 625	677 029	704 110	-5.13	4.00
Jordan	582 515	674 525	610 000	15.80	-9.57
Kenya	615 733	618 816	643 569	0.50	4.00

**Table 4.1. Container port traffic for 76 developing countries and economies in transition:
2008, 2009 and 2010 *(in TEUs) (concluded)***

Country	2008	2009	Preliminary estimates for 2010	Percentage change 2009–2008	Percentage change 2010–2009
Uruguay	675 273	588 410	671 952	-12.86	14.20
Honduras	669 802	571 720	619 867	-14.64	8.42
Trinidad and Tobago	554 093	567 183	573 217	2.36	1.06
Djibouti	356 462	519 500	600 000	45.74	15.50
Ukraine	1 123 268	516 698	537 366	-54.00	4.00
Ghana	555 009	493 958	513 716	-11.00	4.00
Sudan	391 139	431 232	448 481	10.25	4.00
Tunisia	424 780	418 880	435 636	-1.39	4.00
Qatar	400 000	410 000	346 000	2.50	-15.61
Mauritius	454 433	406 862	412 313	-10.47	1.34
Yemen	492 313	382 445	390 000	-22.32	1.98
United Republic of Tanzania	363 310	370 401	426 847	1.95	15.24
Senegal	347 483	331 076	344 319	-4.72	4.00
Congo	321 000	285 690	297 118	-11.00	4.00
Cuba	319 000	283 910	295 266	-11.00	4.00
Benin	300 000	267 000	237 630	-11.00	-11.00
Namibia	183 605	265 663	256 319	44.69	-3.52
Papua New Guinea	250 252	257 740	268 050	2.99	4.00
Algeria	225 140	247 986	257 906	10.15	4.00
Cameroon	270 000	240 300	249 912	-11.00	4.00
Bahrain	269 331	239 705	249 293	-11.00	4.00
Mozambique	241 237	214 701	223 289	-11.00	4.00
Cambodia	258 775	207 577	224 206	-19.78	8.01
Georgia	253 811	181 613	196 030	-28.45	7.94
Myanmar	180 000	160 200	166 608	-11.00	4.00
Guam	167 784	157 096	183 214	-6.37	16.63
Libyan Arab Jamahiriya	174 827	155 596	161 820	-11.00	4.00
Madagascar	143 371	132 278	141 093	-7.74	6.66
Gabon	158 884	130 758	135 988	-17.70	4.00
Croatia	168 761	130 740	135 970	-22.53	4.00
El Salvador	156 323	126 369	145 774	-19.16	15.36
Aruba	140 000	125 000	130 000	-10.71	4.00
New Caledonia	119 661	119 147	123 913	-0.43	4.00
Sub total	345 812 178	321 448 907	370 510 520	-7.05	15.26
Other reported [b]	4 064 500	3 758 889	3 888 060	-7.52	3.44
Total reported	349 876 678	325 207 796	374 398 580	-7.05	15.13
Total	513 734 943	469 003 339	531 400 672	-8.71	13.30

Source: UNCTAD secretariat, derived from information contained in Containerisation International Online (May 2011), from various Dynamar B.V. publications and from information obtained by the UNCTAD secretariat directly from terminal and port authorities.

Note: Some figures for 2010 are estimates. Port throughput figures tend not to be disclosed by ports until a considerable time after the end of the calendar year. Country totals may conceal the fact that minor ports may not be included; therefore, in some cases, the actual figures may be higher than those given. The figures for 2009 are generally regarded as more reliable and are thus more often quoted in the accompanying text.

[a] In this table, Singapore includes the port of Jurong.

[b] Where fewer than 100,000 TEUs per year were reported or where a substantial lack of data was noted.

Table 4.2. Top 20 container terminals and their throughput for 2008, 2009 and 2010 (in TEUs, and percentage change)					
Port name	2008	2009	Preliminary figures for 2010	Percentage change 2009–2008	Percentage change 2010–2009
Shanghai	27 980 000	25 002 000	29 069 000	-11	16
Singapore[a]	29 918 200	25 866 400	28 430 800	-14	10
Hong Kong	24 494 229	21 040 096	23 532 000	-14	12
Shenzhen	21 413 888	18 250 100	22 509 700	-15	23
Busan	13 452 786	11 954 861	14 157 291	-11	18
Ningbo	11 226 000	10 502 800	13 144 000	-6	25
Guangzhou	11 001 300	11 190 000	12 550 000	2	12
Qingdao	10 320 000	10 260 000	12 012 000	-1	17
Dubai	11 827 299	11 124 082	11 600 000	-6	4
Rotterdam	10 800 000	9 743 290	11 145 804	-10	14
Tianjin	8 500 000	8 700 000	10 080 000	2	16
Kaohsiung	9 676 554	8 581 273	9 181 211	-11	7
Port Klang	7 973 579	7 309 779	8 870 000	-8	21
Antwerp	8 662 891	7 309 639	8 468 475	-16	16
Hamburg	9 737 000	7 007 704	7 900 000	-28	13
Los Angeles	7 849 985	6 748 994	7 831 902	-14	16
Tanjung Pelepas	5 600 000	6 000 000	6 530 000	7	9
Long Beach	6 487 816	5 067 597	6 263 399	-22	24
Xiamen	5 034 600	4 680 355	5 820 000	-7	24
New York/New Jersey	5 265 053	4 561 831	5 292 020	-13	16
Total top 20	247 221 180	220 900 801	254 387 602	-11	15

Source: UNCTAD secretariat and Containerisation International Online (May 2011).
[a]   In this table, Singapore does not include the port of Jurong.

2.   International container terminal operators

Container terminal operation is dominated by a few global players that operate a portfolio of terminals in different ports around the world. In general, these terminal operators experienced increased revenue in 2010 on the back of higher container throughput that slumped in 2009.

The major international container terminal operators are led by Hutchison Port Holding of Hong Kong, China, with a combined throughput of 75 million TEUs in 2010, up 14.9 per cent from the previous year. Following closely behind is APM Terminals, with an estimated 70 million TEUs, up 2 per cent over the previous year. PSA International of Singapore increased its throughput of containers by 14.4 per

cent to 65.1 million TEUs in 2010. China Merchants Holdings International increased its throughput in 2010 by 19.2 per cent to 52.3 million TEUs with the launch of new operations in Viet Nam and Sri Lanka. DP World of Dubai increased its container throughput by 14 per cent to 49.6 million TEUs in 2010. COSCO Pacific container throughput grew by 19 per cent in 2010 to 48.5 million TEUs. Further details on the international container terminal operators can be found in chapter 6.

3.   Liner shipping connectivity

Liner shipping services form a global maritime transport network that caters for most of the international trade in manufactured goods. Thanks to regular container shipping services and transhipment operations in so-called hub ports, basically all coastal countries are connected to each other. The connectivity level of countries to this global network varies, and since 2004, the annual LSCI established by UNCTAD has captured trends and differences in countries' liner shipping connectivity. The LSCI covers 162 coastal countries and is made up of five components: (a) the number of ships, (b) their container carrying capacity, (c) the number of companies, (d) the number of services provided and (e) the size of the largest vessels that provide services from and to each country's seaports.[1]

In July 2011, China continued to lead the LSCI ranking, followed by China (Hong Kong), Singapore and Germany. The best connected LDCs is Djibouti benefiting from recent port reforms and a geographical position next to major trade routes. Between 2010 and 2011, 91 countries increased their LSCI, 6 countries saw no change and 65 recorded a decrease.

With regard to LSCI components, in 2011 the industry continued to consolidate and the average number of companies per country decreased, while the average vessel size grew. While the use of larger vessels makes it possible to achieve economies of scale and thus reduce trade costs, the extent to which cost savings are passed on to importers and exporters depends on the level of competition among carriers. Many developing countries are confronted with the double challenge of having to accommodate larger ships while having access to fewer regular shipping services to and from a country's ports.

Several recent empirical studies have found strong correlations between liner shipping connectivity and trade costs, in particular transport costs.[2] Different connectivity components, such as the number of direct liner services between a pair of countries, the vessel sizes or the level of competition on a given trade route, are all found to be closely related to lower transport costs. A recent research project by the Economic and Social Commission for Asia and the Pacific (ESCAP) included the LSCI in an empirical study on trade costs, and concluded that "about 25% of the changes in non-tariff policy-related trade costs can be explained by the liner shipping connectivity index".[3] For the estimated trade costs between a number of Asian exporters and importers, the ESCAP study found that the exporting country's LSCI had a higher correlation with the trade costs than the importing country's LSCI.

In order to complement the country-level LSCI data and to facilitate further analysis of trade costs and flows, UNCTAD has created a more comprehensive database on pair-of-country connectivity data. The database includes the air and maritime distances between countries' main air- and seaports, combined with data on the liner shipping services between the latter. Using this database to compare the structure of the global liner shipping network of 2006 and 2010, some interesting trends can be observed. In 2006, 18.4 per cent of pairs of countries were connected with each other through direct liner shipping services, while the remaining 81.6 per cent required at least one transhipment. In 2010, the percentage of direct connections increased slightly to 18.9 per cent. Of the routes that had direct services in 2006, 83 per cent were able to retain those direct services in 2010, i.e. 17 per cent of the pairs of countries had lost the direct service connection four years later. By the same token, 19 per cent of the pairs of countries with direct services between them in 2010 did not have a direct connection in 2006.

The average number of service providers per direct route declined from 5.63 in 2006 to 4.96 in 2010, a decrease of 12 per cent. During the same period, the average size of the largest ships deployed per country pair grew by 38 per cent, from 2,774 TEUs to 3,839 TEUs.

The country-pair data thus confirm trends that were already measured with the LSCI at the country level; as the size of deployed vessels increases, the level of competition decreases. The data further suggest that the overall structure of the global liner shipping network is relatively stable, albeit showing some adjustments over time. Shipping companies may add direct services, for example, in response to growing bilateral trade, or they may drop a direct service if, for example, feedering into a transhipment port helps to fill larger ships on the main route.

Shipping connectivity is an important determinant of trade costs, and understanding them will allow policymakers to improve their country's trade competitiveness. Carriers' choices of ports of call are determined by three main considerations: (a) the port's geographical position within the global shipping networks, (b) the port's captive cargo base (hinterland), (c) port pricing and the quality of services and of infrastructure.

4. Recent port developments

In all parts of the world, new port projects or the expansion of existing facilities, are under way. In 2009, there was a brief pause in port developments as uncertainty surrounded trade volumes and the availability of finance. The recovery in trade volumes witnessed during the first half of 2010 gave renewed confidence for the continuation of many of these projects. The following sections give a snapshot of port projects from around the world; based on diverse sources, they illustrate some of the trends in global port development.

Latin America and the Caribbean

Latin America is continuing apace with some of the world's most sizeable port development projects on the back of increased commodity exports. The region is catching up with other regions through larger port investment, which stands at almost $12 billion. The port projects listed in this section do not provide an exhaustive analysis of all port projects in the region.

In *Brazil*, a rise in foreign demand for sugar, soybean and iron ore pushed exports up by 32 per cent to $201.9 billion. Imports also increased by 42 per cent to $181.6 billion as the largest consumer-fuelled demand in two decades took hold.[4] In the south of the country, the ports of Antonina and Paranagua reported exports of soybean, corn and sugar expanding significantly.[5] Despite Brazil's continued port investments of around $1 billion since 1995,[6] the increase in trade led to port congestion, which forced many shipowners to cancel ship calls.[7] To tackle the congestion, the Brazilian Government has announced several major port development projects that are expected to be completed over the next few years.[8] In the port of Santos, international investment of $679 million, for instance, was secured to improve its container and liquid cargo-handling facilities. Facilities capable of handling 1.2 million tons of liquid cargo per annum, primarily for exports of ethanol, are being developed. Container-handling facilities will nearly double with the addition of 2.2 million TEUs in capacity to the existing 2.7 million TEUs of throughput in 2010. Elsewhere in Brazil, the largest Brazilian port and logistics company, Wilson Sons, announced plans to invest $1.8 billion in its facilities, including $247 million to expand Tecon Salvador Container Terminal at Salvador Port and Tecon Rio Grande at Rio Grande Port.[9] Brazil's mining giant, Vale, announced plans to spend $2.9 billion expanding port facilities at Ponta da Madeira to reach 150 million tons.[10] Ponta da Madeira handled the world's largest ore carrier, the 402,347 dwt Vale Brasil, with iron ore destined for Dalian, China, in 2011.

In *Chile*, the concession of the new Terminal 2 project at Valparaiso port has stalled, as none of the three pre-qualified companies, out of the original 18 companies that expressed interest, made a bid.[11] The current development work is estimated to cost $350 million and to be completed by 2014. As well as being a maritime gateway to the world, Valparaiso port is part of a vital land transport link to Argentina through the Libertadores mountain pass. In addition, the area around Valparaiso generates approximately 60 per cent of Chile's GDP.

In *Colombia*, major plans were announced to develop the country's transport infrastructure. The estimated cost is $56 billion up to 2021 and includes updating the country's ports.[12]

In *Uruguay*, plans to develop a $3.5 billion deepwater port in Rocha province near La Paloma have been submitted to the government by a consortium of private companies.[13]

In *Panama*, plans to build two new ports at Balboa and Rodman with international assistance in both construction and operation were announced by the government.[14] The development of a container terminal at Rodman port was previously estimated to cost $100 million and to have a capacity of 450,000 TEUs.[15] Rodman port, built as a United States navy base, is expected to be expanded using waste material excavated from the ongoing Panama Canal expansion. The canal expansion, which is set to be completed in 2014 and cost around $5.25 billion, will allow for much larger – although not the largest – vessels to transit (see chapter 2 for more details).

In the *Dominican Republic*, the port of Caucedo completed its second phase of development in 2011 with an additional 300 metres of quayage. The port, which was originally estimated to cost $300 million, now has a handling capacity of 1.25 million TEUs.[16] The port is located next to the International Airport with free zones and logistics centres nearby and 25 km from the capital, Santo Domingo.[17]

In *Jamaica*, the port of Kingston announced plans to extend the port to cater for the expected increased demand once the Panama Canal enlargement is completed. The $200 million project will see dredging works take the port's entrance channel down to 16 metres deep and the quay area extended by 1.5 km.[18]

In Costa Rica, APMT won a 33-year concession to develop and operate a container terminal at Moin port in Limon province on the Atlantic coast. The project is expected to cost $1 billion and the first phase to be completed by 2016. The port entrance and turning basin will be first dredged to 16 metres and then to 18 metres in a second phase. One thousand direct jobs are expected to be generated during the construction phase and 450, during the first phase of operation, indirect jobs into the local community.[19]

In *El Salvador*, the port of La Unión opened for business in 2010. Its construction, which began in 2005, cost over $180 million and will have an annual container throughput capacity of 500,000 TEUs in phase one, rising to 1.7 million TEUs by completion of a second and third phase.[20] [21] A concession scheme for private companies to operate the port is being finalized.

In *Peru*, APMT won in 2011 a concession to operate the Terminal Muelle Norte in the port of Callao.[22] APMT is expected to invest $749 million in the port, turning it into a multi-purpose port for general cargo, containers, Ro-Ro, break bulk and cruise ships. In 2010, DP World won a concession to operate Muelle Sur pier at Callao and with APMT's arrival more intra-port competition is expected to be beneficial for port users. Among the mains areas for increased competition are the export of metals (Peru is the world's number-one silver producer and the second largest copper producer), natural gas, fishmeal and coffee.

Europe

In Europe there are far fewer new port development projects because the market is more mature and the procedural requirements to build new ports often involve a lengthy public consultation process. Western European ports are predominately privately operated with States controlling only around 7 per cent of container port throughput.[23] In Eastern Europe the figure is around 16 per cent, suggesting that further reform or development of new ports may be more likely to occur here.

In *Greece,* the government revealed plans to privatize the ports of Thessaloniki and Piraeus as part of a wider programme to cut government expenditure and increase revenue.[24] In 2008, COSCO Pacific won a 35-year concession at the port of Piraeus to operate two container terminals.

In *Croatia*, a 30-year concession was awarded to ICTSI to operate and develop the Adriatic Gate Container Terminal at the port of Rijeka. The development plan includes extending the quay by 330 metres and dredging the port to 14.5 metres. Once completed, the port will have a container-handling capacity of 600,000 TEUs.[25]

In *Poland*, the DCT Gdansk container terminal, operated by ICTSI, began receiving its first regular deep-sea vessels in January 2010. In May 2011, it welcomed the 13,092 TEU *Maersk Elba*, the largest container vessel to enter the Baltic Sea.[26] The development of Gdansk as a transhipment hub will have an impact on trade flows within the region and economies of scale should bring savings to importers and exIn *Georgia*, APMT acquired the management of the Black Sea port of Poti. In 2008, Ras Al Khaimah Investment Authority (RAKIA), a sovereign wealth fund of the United Arab Emirates, acquired a 49-year concession to operate the port but failed to attract sufficient investors to the nearby free trade zone. APMT is expected to invest $65 million in the port and the free trade zone.[27]

Africa

In Africa there is still a large State involvement in ports. For instance, around 50 per cent – the highest of all regions – of the continent's container throughput passes through ports in which the State owns part of the operation. Many ports in the bulk sector, which handle the export of raw commodities, are joint ventures between governments and foreign companies wishing to purchase a single commodity. Port development projects in Africa are pushing ahead, as illustrated by a number of projects that have been announced or are under way in several countries. For instance, in *Guinea*, one of the world's largest exporters of bauxite and alumina and where some of the world's highest-grade iron ore deposits can be found, a change in political leaders also heralded change at Conakry's container port. In April 2011, a previous 25-year concession awarded to Getma International in 2008 was cancelled and given to Bolloré Africa Logistics, which had lost out in the initial bidding process. Bolloré Africa Logistics is set to invest €500 ($640) million in the port, which will double the existing quay length, triple the yard area and create a rail connection.[28] In a separate deal, Bolloré Group also announced plans to build a $150 million dry port to help relieve congestion through the country. In 2011, an agreement was also signed between the Guinean Government and the mining giant Rio Tinto to develop a new port in the country by 2015.[29] The port will handle exports from the Simandou iron ore project, which is expected to produce 95 million tons of iron ore. The route from the mine to the coast will involve a 650-km dedicated railway, including 21 km of tunnels to reach a wharf located 11 km offshore from Matakang Island.

In *Togo*, Bolloré Africa Logistics announced plans to build a third quay at Lomé port at a cost of $640 million aimed at doubling container traffic to around 800,000 TEUs within five years. The quay will be 450 metres long, 15 metres deep and will be able to handle vessels up to 7,000 TEUs.[30]

In *Cameroon*, work by the French construction firm Razel got under way to prepare for the construction of a deepwater port at Kribi, some 300 km south of Yaoundé. Once completed, the $1 billion project will provide valuable access to international markets for neighbouring Chad and the Central African Republic.[31]

In *Kenya*, bids for construction of a second 1.2 million TEU container terminal at Mombasa is under review.[32] In 2010, the port handled 695,000 TEUs, up 12 per cent over the previous year. The port was originally designed to handle 250,000 TEUs, hence the severe congestion. Local unions are, however, concerned that there will be significant reductions to the 7,000 personnel currently employed by the Kenya Port Authorities, should the port become privatized.[33]

In *Mozambique*, several port development plans are in progress. In Maputo, the coal terminal is being upgraded to handle 25 million tons by 2014 and developments at the container terminal are nearly completed.[34] The dredging of the port from 9.4 metres to 11 metres was completed in early 2011. The port of Nacala, in the north of the country, is set to benefit from increased coal exports from the Moatize mine. Exports from the mine were planned to be transported by the Sena railway line to the port of Beira but construction delays have meant a diversion of coal to Nacala. The Moatize mine is expected to produce 8 millions tons of hard coking coal and 4 million tons of thermal coal annually by 2013.[35] The port of Beira is presently undergoing an 18-month dredging programme at a cost of $52 million to receive ships of 60,000 dwt.

In the *United Republic of Tanzania*, the construction of two new container terminals at the port of Dar es Salaam is to be completed by the end of 2012, doubling the port's capacity by a further 500,000 TEUs. Dar es Salaam is the country's principal port, boasting a capacity that can handle 4.1 million tons of dry cargo and 6 million tons of bulk liquid cargo. The port also serves the landlocked countries of Malawi, Zambia, Burundi, Rwanda and Uganda, as well as the eastern part of the Democratic Republic of the Congo. Presently the port is operating at maximum container capacity with port congestion reportedly increasing from 11 days in 2010 to around 19 days in 2011.

In *South Africa*, plans are being proposed to develop the county's busiest port, Durban, by increasing its container-handling capacity from 2.5 million to 6 million TEUs. The work is not expected to start until 2015 and will take four years to complete, thereafter involving a PPP.[36] To tackle congestion at Durban port, a new port at Ngqura opened for business at the end of 2009, and is now South Africa's third-deepest port, achieving 28 container moves per hour. In Cape Town, dredging works at two of four terminals was complete. By the end of the planned development phase, container capacity will double to 1.4 million TEU.[37]

Asia

Many Asian ports were early adopters of containerization and private participation in port operations. These factors collectively enabled the region to master container handling and become home to some of the world largest global terminal operators.[38] Asia is the home to the world's largest port (Shanghai), most busiest port (Singapore) and to some of the most efficient ports (e.g. Port Klang in Malaysia and Dubai in the United Arab Emirates).[39] In addition, there are many new greenfield ports being built, and existing facilities, expanded.

In *Israel,* plans were announced to privatize the port of Eilat on the Red Sea to boost container throughput. Presently container throughput at Eilat port remains negligible compared with the country's two other ports, Ashod and Haifa, which together handled 2.2 million TEUs in 2010. Eilat port has a depth of around 11.5 metres, which is sufficient for container vessels of around 3,000 TEUs. If the port is developed to include container handling, it would lower the cost of imports and exports to and from Asia by avoiding the need to use the Suez Canal.

In *Iraq*, there are plans to issue a tender for the construction of a new port south of Basra that will receive containers bound for Europe and transport them overland by rail, thereby avoiding the use of the Suez Canal. The project is expected to cost $6.4 billion; the initial phase should be completed by the end of 2013, and the second phase, four years later. Upon completion, the port will have 7 km of quays. However, just across the border in Kuwait, plans to develop the Mubarak port on Boubyan Island are causing concern about the viability of Iraq's existing and planned ports. The port, to be completed in 2016 at a cost of $1.1 billion, is expected to handle 1.8 million TEUs.[40]

In *Oman*, construction work at the port of Salalah has begun. The $645 million project will see the port increase its capacity to 40 million tons of dry bulk commodities and 5 million tons of liquid cargo.[41] At the port of Sohar, the Brazilian mining company, Vale, is nearing completion of a new 600-metre jetty to receive its iron ore exports from Brazil. Vale is building an iron ore pelletizing plant at the port of Sohar and supplying it with its own iron ore to extract and re-export the iron pellets.

In *Qatar*, work has begun on the first phase of the $4.5 billion New Doha port, which is expected to be completed by 2014.[42] The first phase will handle containers, general cargo, bulk grain, vehicle carriers, livestock and offshore supply support operations, and a facility for the Qatar coast guard and navy. The new container terminal will have a throughput capacity of two million TEUs, and is one of three planned terminals, which will see throughput rise to a maximum of 12 million TEUs. A dry dock and ship repair yard capable of servicing LNG vessels has been completed.

In *Pakistan*, the port of Qasim received its first container vessels as the newly completed first phase, 400,000 TEU Terminal 2, became operational. Phases two and three will see capacity rise to 1.2 million TEUs. The port is operated by DP World and can accommodate vessels up to a capacity of 6,700 TEUs.[43]

In *India*, the newly deepened Dhamra port in the Bay of Bengal became operational to ships with a draft of up to 18 metres. The port will handle India's export of bulk cargoes, such as, coal, iron ore, chromites, bauxite and steel.[44] The operation of container facilities at the port is expected to be taken over by APMT. Elsewhere in India, a number of other port projects, including those at Chennai, Enmore and Vallarpadam, are contributing to the country's growing port capacity.[45] Indian ports reached an annual capacity capable of handling 1 billion tons in January 2011.[46] At the Jawaharial Nehru Port Trust in Mumbai, a new terminal is expected to be built which will add a further 4.8 million TEUs to the port's present 4 million TEU capacity.

In *Indonesia*, plans were announced to develop Belawan port from its present 850,000 TEU capacity to 1.2 million TEUs. The port handles around 60 per cent of the country's palm oil exports, but is suffering from congestion and long loading and unloading times. The plans include extending the quay length by 350 metres and purchasing new cranes to improve productivity. In addition, access to the port is expected to be improved by increased dredging. Further development at Indonesian ports is also expected as legislation on opening up port competition was enacted in 2011.[47]

In *Viet Nam,* the Tan Cang Cai Mep International Terminal with a capacity of 1.15 million TEUs, opened in March 2011.[48] The new terminal, located 50 km from Ho Chi Minh City, has a draft of 15.8 metres allowing it to accommodate some of the world's largest container vessels. Its first customer was the 11,500 TEU CMA CGM *Columba,* which was sailing on her maiden voyage. Elsewhere in Viet Nam, the development of Van Phong port project in the central province of Khanh Hoa has stalled, while costs have reportedly almost doubled to $295 million.[49] A new container port was opened in Hai Cang Ward, Quy Nhon City, Binh Dinh Province, in February 2011 and received its first customer, the *Vsico Pioneer*, with a capacity of 7,055 dwt. The port will help attract goods from the central provinces of Viet Nam and landlocked neighbouring Laos.

In *China*, the world's largest port developer, the focus has shifted from sea ports to inland port development. Plans to spend $2.7 billion on developing Yangtze ports over the period 2011–2015 have been revealed.[50] The works will allow a 50,000-dwt vessel to reach Nanjing and be complete by 2015. The river is currently suffering from severe drought, leaving hundreds of vessels stranded.[51]

B.   INLAND TRANSPORT DEVELOPMENTS

This section highlights some recent key developments in global freight volume movement by main inland transport systems, namely rail, road and waterways.[52] The subsequent section will consider recent developments affecting developing countries' inland transport infrastructure with a special focus on PPPs in financing inland transport infrastructure development.

In 2010, global inland freight transport volumes continued the recovery that had started in late 2009 but remained below pre-crisis volumes. By December 2010, road and rail levels were estimated to have remained 5–15 per cent below pre-crisis volumes.[53]

1.   Rail

In 2010, the global rail freight sector grew by 7.2 per cent to reach 9,843 billion FTKs, or $161,797 million in value terms, a 7.7 per cent increase over the previous year.[54]

By the end of 2010, the *United States*, which accounted for 43.2 per cent of the global rail freight sector value, recorded a strong recovery, albeit with rail freight volumes that were somewhat below pre-crisis levels at the end of the last quarter of 2010.[55] Overall traffic for coal and grain commodity carloads, as well as intermodal traffic, was good in 2010, reflecting the increase in global demand for the goods. Total carloads for the year were 14.8 million, up 7.3 per cent compared with 2009 total carloads, and intermodal volume was 11.3 million trailers and containers, up 14.2 per cent compared with 2009.[56] The recovery continued in 2011, with reported cumulative rail volumes up 3.3 per cent for the first five months of 2011 and 4.5 million trailers and containers, 8.8 per cent higher than the same period in 2010.[57]

In 2010, rail freight volumes in the *European Union (EU)* were estimated to be 16 per cent below the 2008 peak level. Eurostat reported a small recovery in EU-27 freight rail volumes. Data available for the first two quarters in 2010 show increases of 8 per cent and 14 per cent, respectively, compared with the same quarters in 2009. EU-27 rail freight transport suffered significantly in 2009 from the crisis with a 17 per cent reduction in the freight traffic volume, falling to 366 billion ton-kilometres; national and international traffic declined 15 per cent and 20 per cent, respectively. The drop of freight rail transport for the period 2008–2009 has been visible in all EU Member States, except Estonia and Norway, which reported a slight improvement in freight transport, 0.1 per cent and 1.2 per cent, respectively.

The rail freight volumes in China experienced continued growth in 2010, up by 9.6 per cent over the previous year, bringing the total volume to 2,733 billion FTKs.[58] Likewise, rail freight volumes recorded an upward trend in the Russian Federation, countries of Central and Eastern Europe and Central Asia. Data from the Community of European Railway and Infrastructure Companies show that rail freight volume in ton-kilometres increased in Central and Eastern Europe by 7.6 per cent compared with 2009.[59] Freight volumes on rail lines in the Russian Federation rose 7.8 per cent to 2.0 trillion ton-kilometres. Russian rail transport accounts for a substantial share of external trade freight between the Russian Federation and China. During the first 10 months of 2010, the volume of rail freight between the countries increased by 33 per cent to reach 53 million tons. The vast majority (94 per cent) of cargo comprises Russian oil, timber, chemicals and mineral fertilizer exports, but there are also increased volumes of imports of Chinese machinery and technical goods. With direct rail freight with China estimated to grow by 50–100 per cent over next decade, and as part of efforts to develop cooperation in rail container freight, Russian Railways have been developing the main freight routes between the Russian Federation and China through large investments in rail infrastructure in the regions of Siberia and the Russian Federation's Far East.[60] At the end of 2010, an agreement was reached with Chinese and German partners to create a joint venture for container transport.[61]

An emerging trend is the renewed interest in rail freight transport mainly due to the rising price and demand for raw materials (primarily in emerging markets) and the widespread view that rail transport is one of the most optimal modes of transport for large, heavy, bulk freight transfer/haulage over long distances. For instance, coal accounted for 47 per cent of the United States railroad traffic volume in 2009 and generated 25 per cent of railroad gross revenues in that country in 2009.[62] Equally, the Australian Rail Growth in the freight transport industry, led by the resources boom, was 6.9 per cent in the last five years, and was worth $10.5 billion in 2010–11. In Brazil, the world's sixth-largest freight rail market, the freight rail company MRS Logistica[63] experienced an increase in traffic volume of 12 per cent in 2010, surpassing 140 million tons, owing to strong demand worldwide for the country's commodities, including iron ore, steel, cement and other critical commodities. Box 4.1 provides examples of how the boom in minerals is driving Africa's railways development, with more investment targeting dedicated minerals railways.

2.   Road

In 2010, the global road freight sector grew by 7.8 per cent over 2009, with volumes reaching 9,721 billion FTKs. In terms of value, global road freight – the largest segment of inland transport since they are usually reserved for high-value, time-sensitive products – expanded by 8.5 per cent in 2010, compared

Box 4.1. The recent minerals boom and its impact on railway development in Africa

Since late 2009, the mining sector has gathered momentum and the boom in demand has led major railway development in many commodity-producing countries, particularly in Africa.

- China Railway Construction Corporation (CRCC), the second-largest State-owned construction enterprise; Vale SA, a Brazilian mining company, ranked number two after BHP Billiton, Australia; and other companies are investing at least $35 billion in rail projects over the next five years to transport copper and coal out of Africa to power plants in China and India.

- Sinohydro Corporation. China's State-owned hydropower engineering and construction company, is restoring the 1,344-km Benguela railway linking the cobalt reserves in the southern Democratic Republic of the Congo and copper mines in Zambia to Angola's Lobito port, 243 miles south of Luanda, the capital.

- Sundance Resources, an Australian exploration company, has signed an MoU with CRCC Africa Construction (CAC) to develop a railway and the required rolling stock to support Sundance's Mbalam project in Cameroon and the Congo, West Africa. The MoU engages the parties to work together to establish the scope, cost and programme for delivery of railway track and rolling stock sufficient to support a planned output of 35 million tons per annum of iron ore from Sundance's proposed Cameroon and Congo mines, and sets out the terms for CAC's delivery of the mine rail project.

- The Brazilian mining company Vale, signed an MoU for the construction of a new railway across southern Malawi to take Vale's coal from its mining concession in Mozambique's Moatize coal basin (west) to the northern port of Nacala. The railway is necessary because the existing Sena line, from Moatize to the central port of Beira, will be unable to handle the vast amounts of coal exports planned by Vale and the other mining companies exploiting the Moatize coal basin. The total distance from Moatize to Nacala is about 900 km; not all the line will be entirely new, since after passing through Malawi it will join the existing northern railway to Nacala.

- Freeport-McMoRan Copper & Gold Inc., a leading international mining company with headquarters in Phoenix, Arizona, may build rail lines to transport ore from its $2 billion Tenke project in the Democratic Republic of the Congo, possibly connecting with the Benguela line.

- The Trans-Kalahari Rail Line, linking coal deposits in landlocked Botswana to Namibia's Walvis Bay for an estimated cost of $9 billion, has drawn great interest from contract bidders such as Anglo American, Canada's CIC Energy Corporation and South Africa's Exxaro Resources, Ltd.

with the previous year, with levels reaching $1,720 billion.[64] Global road freight volumes are forecast to reach 12,350.5 billion FTKs in 2015, an increase of 27 per cent over 2010. In terms of value, the projected figure amounts to $2,198 billion, an increase in value of 27.8 per cent over 2010. The Americas – United States, Mexico and Canada – account for the largest share of the global road freight sector value, about 56 per cent. The United States road freight sector is estimated to have reached a total volume of 2,918.4 billion FTKs and total revenues of $787 billion in 2010.[65]

Measured in seasonally adjusted ton-kilometres, road freight in the EU-27 area stagnated in 2010, with volumes remaining 14 per cent below pre-crisis levels.[66] The EU's road freight volumes in 2010 were

estimated at 1,658 billion FTKs. Western Europe accounted for the largest share, with a total of 1,229 billion FTKs, while Eastern Europe reached a total of 429 billion FTKs in 2010.[67] In 2009, a little over two thirds of goods carried by road were related to the transportation of goods on national road networks. However, this proportion varied considerably between the EU Member States, with the highest proportion of national road freight transport on Cyprus (98.1 per cent) and the United Kingdom (93.6 per cent in 2007), while the relative importance of national road freight transport was much lower in Slovakia (19.9 per cent), Slovenia (15.4 per cent), Lithuania (14.8 per cent) and Luxembourg (6.3 per cent). For most freight hauliers registered in the EU, international road freight transport mostly relates to intra-EU trade.[68]

3.   Inland waterways

Inland water transport, including rivers and canals, represents an important inland transport alternative and an environmentally friendly means of transporting goods, both in terms of energy consumption and exhaust gas emissions. It is estimated that its energy consumption per km/ton of transported goods is approximately 17 per cent of that of road transport and 50 per cent of rail transport.[69]

Globally, great importance is being given to the inland waterways sector. In the United States, out of 41,000 km of navigable waterways, 24,000 km have a depth of more than 2.75 metres and the modal share of inland waterways transport represents 15 per cent. Although this mode of transport offers the lowest price per ton-mile, this may not be sufficient to guarantee the future of the United States waterway network. Lack of investment and maintenance for aging infrastructure and dredging shortfalls have in recent years been identified as the principal threats to waterway viability and efficiency.[70]

Inland waterway transport also plays an important role in the transport of goods in the EU. More than 37,000 km of waterways connect hundreds of cities and industrial regions. Some 20 out of the 27 EU Member States have inland waterways, 12 of which have an interconnected waterway networks.[71] In 2010, the share of inland waterways in the total transport system was the highest in the Netherlands (42 per cent), followed by France (15 per cent), Hungary (15 per cent), Germany (14 per cent) and Belgium (13 per cent). These shares are likely to grow in the future, particularly in view of Europe-wide policies aimed at promoting its further use. In this respect, the European Commission, through its action programme on the Promotion of Inland Waterway Transport "NAIADES", aims to develop and strengthen the competitive position of inland waterway transport and to facilitate its integration into the intermodal logistic chain so as to create a sustainable, competitive and environmentally friendly European-wide transport network.

Asia is generously endowed with navigable inland waterways representing 290,000 km in length. More than 1 billion tons of cargo are carried annually on these waterways. China contributes approximately 70 per cent or some 690 million tons of freight of volume per year. With an inland waterway system comprising more than 5,600 navigable rivers and a total navigable length of 119,000 km, and 200 inland ports, China

has the most highly developed inland waterways transport subsector in Asia. This mode of transport has been growing in recent years, given China's Inland Transport Development Strategy. For instance, in Hunan province, the inland water container transport volume increased from 1,929 TEUs in 1993 to 101,632 TEUs in 2006 at an average annual growth rate of 36 per cent. In central China, where the Yangtze River is used to transport commodities such as coal and steel to and from river cities, freight volumes have been increasing at 40 per cent per annum.[72]

The aim of China's Inland Transport Development Strategy is to develop a modern, efficient, green inland waterway system, and build more river ports and infrastructure to develop the country's vast interior regions and increase water transport capacity, enabling the freight traffic of the national waterways to expand to more than 3 billion tons by 2020.[73]

Elsewhere in Asia, for example, in Bangladesh, a number of initiatives were launched to enhance the inland waterway mode of transport, which is estimated to carry approximately 35 per cent of the country's annual freight volume. A major project being implemented by the Bangladesh Inland Water Transport Authority (BIWTA) is the first-ever inland container terminal project at Pangaon in Dhaka, a joint venture between BIWTA and Chittagong Port. The project aims to transport at least 50 per cent of containers through waterways. This is expected to reduce time, cut costs by about 30 per cent a day and lessen pressure on the roads. The terminal is likely to handle about 0.115 million TEUs at the initial stage and reach a 0.16 million TEU capacity. Other inland terminals are planned and are expected to handle over 0.5 million TEUs a year.[74] The government will also develop the Ashuganj River port as a container terminal for the smooth transhipment of Indian goods to Tripura through Akhaura.

Africa's inland waterways have long been recommended as part of the solution to the continent's transport development and networks integration, mainly for the 29 African countries with navigable waterways. Yet relatively little effort has been put into developing this energy-efficient mode of transport and promoting its integration with road and rail transport links. According to the August-September 2007 issue of African Business, East African waterways offer cheap and easy access to and from ocean ports, although its transport potential has been neglected in the past. Now, however, governments, mainly in southern and central Africa, are showing interest in the significance of inland waterways, including Lake Malawi and the Zambezi and Shire river system. The Governments of Zambia, Malawi and Mozambique have signed an MoU to promote shipping on the Zambezi–Shire water system. The Shire–Zambezi waterway project, which has been adopted by both the Southern African Development Community (SADC) and the Common Market for Eastern and Southern Africa, aims to develop the waterway as part of regional transport corridors, opening up new outlets to the sea for SADC countries, and promoting regional integration. Another initiative being developed is the establishment of the Commission Internationale du Bassin Congo-Ouabangui-Sangha under the auspices of the Economic and Monetary Community of Central Africa to improve the physical and regulation arrangements for inland navigation between Cameroon, the Congo, the Democratic Republic of the Congo and the Central African Republic.[75]

C. SURFACE TRANSPORT INFRASTRUCTURE DEVELOPMENT IN DEVELOPING COUNTRIES

The following section looks more closely at recent developments affecting inland transport infrastructure, mainly in developing countries. The increasing importance of private-sector entities, including through PPPs in financing transport infrastructure development is also highlighted, with an emphasis on rail transport.

In today's globalized world economy, dominated by interdependent international supply networks, efficient transport systems have come to depend more and more on inland transport networks. They play a crucial role in ensuring the smooth and prompt delivery of goods from production centres or producers' warehouses to the port of loading and the onward forwarding of cargo to final customers. Inefficient inland transport infrastructure and services can seriously undermine a country's connectivity and access to global markets and negatively impact its trade performance and competitiveness. The case of landlocked developing countries (LLDCs), which represent about one third of the LDCs, illustrates this point. For African LLDCs, for example, where inland transport-related bottlenecks are significant, freight expenses are very high, averaging 14 per cent of the value of the traded goods,[76] compared with an average share in developed countries of 6 per cent. The added transport costs, therefore, erode trade competitiveness and can offset advantages like lower

wage rates that are inherent to LLDCs and the benefits that could be derived from access to globalized markets and international trade.

Addressing the transport infrastructure gap to develop efficient and cost-effective transport infrastructure and services, both interregional and international, requires mass investment. Given the limited availability of public-sector funds, developing countries have been increasingly turning to the private sector, seeking the infusion of private-sector finance, innovation and efficiencies in infrastructure provision through PPPs. In the last two decades, these have been used as a mechanism to leverage greater private investment participation and most importantly to access specialized skills, innovations and new technologies associated with infrastructure development, operation and maintenance.

While there is no single universal definition of PPPs, a widely accepted definition refers to PPP in infrastructure as a mechanism for the "creation and/or management of public infrastructure and/or services through private investment and management for a pre-defined period and with specific service level standards".[77] As such, PPPs can vary in shape and size, ranging from small service contracts to full-blown concessions, greenfield projects and divestitures.

The sections that follow give a brief analysis of the pattern of private-sector involvement in transport infrastructure development, mainly inland transport, in developing regions over the past two decades.

1. Types of transport-related public-private partnerships (PPPs) in developing countries[78]

The types of transport-related PPPs that have been developed over the last two decades in developing regions have been mostly concessions and greenfield projects – which may also entail concessions (figure 4.1). The concession model is associated with a long-term contractual arrangement that can be broadly said to signify the private entity taking over an existing State-owned project/providing an infrastructure asset for a given period during which it assumes operation and maintenance of the assets as well as financing and managing all required investment. The government may retain the ultimate legal ownership of the facility and/or right to supply the services. A concession is similar in scope and approach to what is applied in a typical operation and maintenance agreement between parties under a build-operate-transfer-, or BOT-type arrangement. As to greenfield projects, they require a private entity or a public-private joint-venture to build and operate a new project for the period specified in the contract. Greenfield projects may include – but are not limited to – BOT, build-own-operate-transfer (BOOT), build-lease-own (BLO) or design-build-operate (DBO). However, a divestiture agreement entails the government transferring or selling an asset, either in part or in full, to the private sector – synonymous to privatization – though the private stake may or may not imply private management of the enterprise. Countries that have applied divestiture are China, the Russian Federation and some Latin America countries such as the Plurinational State of Bolivia and Chile.

2. Development of PPP transport projects in developing countries

Private investment participation through PPPs in the transport sector of developing countries started in the 1980s, with 13 developing countries awarding 25 projects, mainly toll road projects (Mexico, Malaysia, and Thailand). It grew rapidly in the 1990s with private

participation exceeding $10 billion in 1990, driven mainly by toll road concession projects awarded in Latin America (Argentina and Mexico). In the 1990s, three quarters of toll road concessions involved the expansion or rehabilitation of existing roads rather than the construction of new networks. Very few divestitures have occurred, mostly in China, where minority stakes were sold in several State-owned toll road companies in order to finance future road construction.

Despite the record growth in activity, private participation still remains limited in many developing countries. Private participation in developing countries' PPP transport projects has been fluctuating over the two decades, from 1990 to 2010, with a peak in 2006 reaching about $32 billion. In 2009, private investments directed towards transport remained severely affected by the crisis and fell to $21.7 billion, a 20 per cent drop compared with 2008 (the number of projects dropped by 19 per cent in 2009). Of the 50 new transport projects – medium-sized and large projects – 32 were concessions and represented 65 per cent of investment in new transport projects, while 16 were greenfield projects (mainly BOT contracts) and the remaining two projects were lease contracts. Most of the projects were concentrated in road

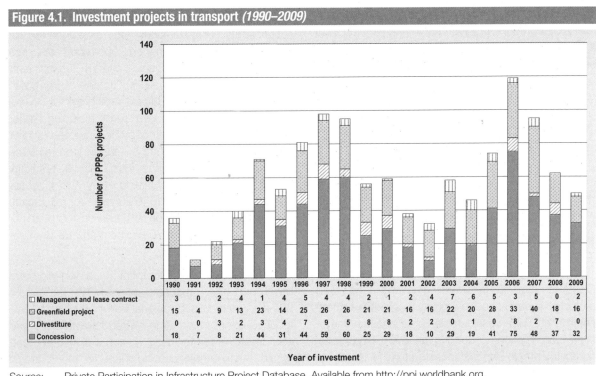

Figure 4.1. Investment projects in transport *(1990–2009)*

	1990	1991	1992	1993	1994	1995	1996	1997	1998	1999	2000	2001	2002	2003	2004	2005	2006	2007	2008	2009
Management and lease contract	3	0	2	4	1	4	5	4	4	2	1	2	4	7	6	5	3	5	0	2
Greenfield project	15	4	9	13	23	14	25	26	26	21	21	16	16	22	20	28	33	40	18	16
Divestiture	0	0	3	2	3	4	7	9	5	8	8	2	2	0	1	0	8	2	7	0
Concession	18	7	8	21	44	31	44	59	60	25	29	18	10	29	19	41	75	48	37	32

Year of investment

Source: Private Participation in Infrastructure Project Database. Available from http://ppi.worldbank.org.

projects and in a few large developing economies, such as Brazil, India and Mexico.

In the first quarter of 2010, the trend of investment commitments to new transport projects had not changed compared with the first quarter of 2009. An estimated 440 projects in 61 developing countries were reported to be at the final tender stage, or had been awarded contracts, or were seeking financing, or were yet to start looking for finance.

Despite the difficult environment and financial market conditions associated with the 2009 crisis, many developing country governments maintained their commitment to their PPP programmes. Projects with strong economic and financial fundamentals and solid support from sponsors were still able to get finance, albeit with more stringent conditions such as lower debt/equity ratios, shorter tenors and more conservative structures. Other implementation issues such as delays in land acquisition or government approvals had become more of an issue.

The role of development banks, as well as bilateral and multilateral agencies, was central in raising substantial finance. For instance, about $1.3 billion was provided in 2010 by the Asian Development Bank for transport infrastructure in central and west Asia, mostly under multitranche financing.[79] This included a $340 million regional road project in Afghanistan, $456 million for the Central Asia Regional Economic Cooperation (CAREC) corridors programme in Kazakhstan and $115 million in Uzbekistan. The financing will also benefit the 75-km railway line from Hairatan dry port located on Afghanistan's border with Uzbekistan to Mazar-e-Sharif, the second largest commercial city in northern Afghanistan.[80] According to the Infrastructure Consortium for Africa (ICA),[81] total commitments to the continent's freight and passenger transport sector increased by 20 per cent between 2008 and 2009, that is, from $5.9 billion to $7.1 billion in 2009.[82] In this regard, a major contribution of some $2 billion[83] was made by the African Development Bank.

South–South cooperation has also been a prominent mechanism for financing the transport infrastructure in developing countries. In Africa, for example, China is involved in financing railway and road projects, spearheaded by highly competitive State enterprises with considerable experience in large-scale construction. According to ICA, China's total commitments to Africa's infrastructure in 2009 are estimated at $5 billion, mainly across Nigeria, Angola, Ethiopia and Sudan. Another example is India's

commitments to infrastructure projects in the region, which averaged $500 million per year from 2003 to 2007. In recent years, India has committed funding to an estimated 20 African infrastructure projects worth a total of $2.6 billion. Like China's financing activities, India's are closely linked to interests in natural resource development.

3. Rail transport

This section explores private-sector participation in transport infrastructure development by focusing on the special case of freight rail transport in Africa.

Railways remain a strategic mode of transport for inland haulage, especially over long distances and for high-volume low-value cargo such as bulk. Rail is also suited to carry container traffic between ports and inland production centres. Over the last two decades, rail transport has grown in tandem with global economic growth and is projected to expand further. By 2015, the global rail freight sector is forecast to carry 12,213 billion FTKs, an increase of 24.1 per cent over 2010. The value of these volumes is expected to reach $199,974 million, 23.6 per cent more than in 2010.[84]

The relevance of freight rail and the merit of focusing on this mode are further heightened by growing environmental concerns and the prominence of sustainability considerations on the agendas of regulators, traders, transport operators, shippers and consumers. Rail transport offers a fuel-efficient, cost-effective and less polluting means of transport. According to the World Bank, "...rail provides several comparative advantages over road, including higher transport capacity per unit of money invested (50 per cent less cost per kilometre of rehabilitated rail track compared with a two-lane road), higher durability (roads need complete rebuilding every 7 to 10 years as compared with every 15 to 20 years for rail tracks), lower energy consumption and carbon footprint per ton transported – up to 75 per cent and 85 per cent less, respectively".[85]

Given the low carbon footprint on a ton-kilometre basis and the prospects of growing rail freight demand, national and regional transport policies have focused on investments in related infrastructure and services to order to foster a modal shift from road to rail. An example can be found in the strategic objectives and policy set forth in the White Paper on Transport adopted by the European Commission in March 2011. The document sets a clear objective to strengthen the role of rail in freight and passenger traffic. This would entail the shifting of 50 per cent of freight transport on medium distances from road to rail and maritime and river transport. This also aims to contribute to the overall objective of reducing by 60 per cent transport-generated emissions by 2050. The White Paper proposes optimizing the performance of multimodal logistics chains by using several more energy-efficient modes of transport on a larger scale. This means that 30 per cent of road freight moving over 300 km would shift to other modes such as rail or waterborne transport by 2030, and more than 50 per cent by 2050, facilitated by efficient and green freight corridors. Meeting this goal implies the development of adequate infrastructure.[86]

PPP railway projects in developing countries

With the growing demand for efficient, low-cost, and low-carbon freight transportation, along with the spread of PPPs, private-sector involvement in the rail business has been revived and looks set to continue growing over the years in many developing regions. Some 39 developing countries have embarked on PPPs for the development of railways (freight and passenger traffic), for the period 1990–2009. As noted earlier, concessions, followed by greenfield

projects, are the most common type of private participation in railways, accounting for 50 per cent of investment.

In the 1990s, many significant PPP railway projects were taking place in Latin America – in particular Argentina, Brazil, Chile and Mexico – through concessions. The peak of private activity in terms of financial volume was in 1996, reaching almost $6 billion (see figure 4.2 below). Concessions were used to improve the management of loss-making railways and to rehabilitate deteriorating infrastructure. The length of railway concessions varied with investment needs. Where the operator invested only in rolling stock, concession contracts ranged from 10 to 15 years. But where the operator had to invest in substantial restorations of the track, contracts were up to 90 years.[87]

Greenfield railway projects were mainly developed in Asia, which was more focused on expanding capacity in response to rapid urbanization and growing demand for infrastructure services rather than improving the efficiency of existing public operators. Greenfield projects were concentrated in metropolitan light or heavy rail systems rather than in long-distance freight lines.[88]

Figure 4.2. Number of railway projects by region *(1990–2009)*

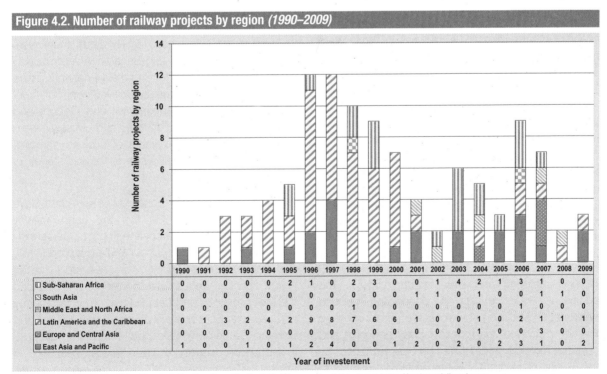

	1990	1991	1992	1993	1994	1995	1996	1997	1998	1999	2000	2001	2002	2003	2004	2005	2006	2007	2008	2009
Sub-Saharan Africa	0	0	0	0	0	2	1	0	2	3	0	0	1	4	2	1	3	1	0	0
South Asia	0	0	0	0	0	0	0	0	0	0	0	1	1	0	1	0	0	1	1	0
Middle East and North Africa	0	0	0	0	0	0	0	0	1	0	0	0	0	0	0	0	1	0	0	0
Latin America and the Caribbean	0	1	3	2	4	2	9	8	7	6	6	1	0	0	1	0	2	1	1	1
Europe and Central Asia	0	0	0	0	0	0	0	0	0	0	0	0	0	0	1	0	0	3	0	0
East Asia and Pacific	1	0	0	1	0	1	2	4	0	0	1	2	0	2	0	2	3	1	0	2

Year of investement

Source: *Private Participation in Infrastructure Project Database. Available from http://ppi.worldbank.org .*

4.   Railways transport development in Africa

Africa has recently been experiencing strong growth, and the rail sector cannot be overemphasized as an enabler of sustainable trade-led growth on the continent.[89] Rail transport is of particular relevance for Africa in view of the following factors: (a) the structure of the continent's trade (i.e. mainly high-volume, low-value goods), (b) its economic and geographical situation (i.e. many LLDCs and high potential for increasing intraregional trade), (c) the prevailing prohibitive cost of inland transport, which drives up overall trade costs (to cite one example, shipping a container from Dubai to Mombasa costs $1,400–$1,700 for a 40-ft container, while inland transport from Mombasa to Kampala costs $3,800), and (d) containerization and the associated developments in multimodal requirements (i.e. if multimodal transport is to be effectively promoted in Africa and if diversification of its trade to include more containerized cargo is to be enabled). Yet, like in many developing regions, historic underinvestment and maintenance in government-owned rail links have resulted in unreliable, inefficient services in many African countries.

Most of the African railways were built at the end of the nineteenth and at the beginning of the twentieth century, linking ports to the production sites of primary commodities – mainly mining – in the hinterland for export. Until the mid-1990s, railways in Africa were mainly run as State monopolies, characterized by cumbersome and bureaucratic administrations. The lack of investment, poor management and maintenance of the railways structure, together with the generally obsolete and inefficient rolling stock and rundown equipment, did not allow the railways to compete adequately with other modes of transport, mainly roads, which had attracted most of the focus of development efforts and private-sector participation in the past two decades. It has been estimated that long-term maintenance neglect has caused a massive investment backlog of approximately $3 billion for Africa's railways.[90]

Beyond restoring and modernizing railways, the additional challenge lies in connecting existing networks and building new lines in order to enhance the connectivity of the African railway networks and develop regional trade. This was underpinned by the Twelfth Session of the African Union Summit in February 2009, which endorsed the Programme for Infrastructure Development in Africa (PIDA).[91] The Programme defined a multisectoral set of infrastructure development plans and identified priority projects, including the interconnecting Africa railways networks as listed in box 4.2.

The private sector remains an essential player in mobilizing the significant investments required to develop, operate and maintain well-performing and reliable railway systems.

The participation of the private sector in railway operations in Africa has taken different forms of PPPs:

- Hybrid rail concession contracts/"affermage" scheme – a type of lease widely used in France, for example, Sitarail in Côte d'Ivoire and Burkina Faso – the first concession that took place in Africa in 1996;

- Full-blown concession contracts, for example, Tanzania Rail Corporation, Railway Systems of Zambia and Camrail in Cameroon;

- Management contracts such as the one with Société Nationale des Chemins de Fer du Congo (Democratic Republic of the Congo).

Today more than 70 per cent of rail activities are in the hands of private operators. An overview of cases in which the private sector was involved in PPP railways in Africa is set out in box 4.2. By 2010, there were 14 concessions in the sub-Saharan African railway systems (arrangements for 3 of the 14 networks were cancelled and subsequently revived with different operators, including Senegal/Mali and Gabon, and Kenya/Uganda). Côte d'Ivoire and Malawi were affected by conflict and years of cyclone damage, respectively. Another four were at varying stages of progress. [92]

Generally, PPP railway concessions in Africa have shown mixed results. On the one hand, railway concessions did provide positive impacts, particularly with respect to increased labour and asset productivity and traffic volumes. Further, they resulted in better freight services and safety conditions, and reduced the financial strain and debt burden on governments. For example, Sitarail (Côte d'Ivoire/Burkina Faso) and Camrail (Cameroon) have both witnessed increases in labour productivity of over 50 per cent and in freight traffic of around 40 per cent following their concessioning.[93]

Box 4.2. PIDA approved inter-connecting Africa railways networks projects development and implementation

This box describes the development and implementation of approved transport infrastructure projects to promote interconnecting African railway networks between 2010 and 2015.

East Africa. One project, which includes the United Republic of Tanzania, Rwanda and Burundi, involves the extension of the railway line (691 km) from Isaka (United Republic of Tanzania) to Kigali (Rwanda) and Bujumbura (Burundi) and is estimated to cost $4 billion (including a $1.5 million feasibility study that is under way) with support from the African Development Bank. This project is part of the Dar es Salaam–Kigali–Bujumbura Central Transport Corridor. The new line would provide an alternative route to the seaport of Dar es Salaam for landlocked countries Rwanda and Burundi, promoting inter-State trade and integration.

West Africa. The AfricaRail project in West Africa links Benin, Togo, Burkina Faso, Niger and Chad. This project, supported by the Economic Community of West African States, as formulated under a PPP (2,000 km.). The estimated cost was $1–$1.5 billion (for phase 1, Cotonou–Parakou–Dosso–Niamey) and $4 million for detailed studies. AfricaRail is a project that aims to rehabilitate and construct 2,000 km of new railway to link the railway systems of Côte d'Ivoire, Burkina Faso, Niger, Benin and Togo (all 1,000-mm narrow gauge), including a train service linking the ports of Lomé and Cotonou. Specifically, the project involves the following sections: Benin to Niger, Burkina to Niger, Dori-Tambao (90 km), Togo to Benin and Burkina to Togo. A future stage of the project would link Mali, Nigeria (1,067-mm gauge changing to 1,435-mm gauge) and Ghana.

Central Africa. Brazzaville–Kinshasa Rail/Road Bridge and Railway Extension Kinshasa–Ilebo Central. This rail and road bridge will link the two capital cities, Brazzaville (the Congo) and Kinshasa (the Democratic Republic of the Congo), across the Congo River. The bridge will complete a missing road link of the Trans-African Highway 3 from Tripoli–Windhoek–Cape Town, and with the railway extension will fill a major gap of 700 km in the Point Noire–South-Eastern Africa railway network. The bridge and extension will promote regional integration and economic development in both countries and also serve as an inter-State and subregional Trans-African link. A feasibility study is under way, with $7.7 million funded by the African Development Bank.

Horn of Africa. Regional transport network improvements, including $500,000 for identification studies and the construction of a ring road and connections to seaports, are being planned to link the countries of the Horn of Africa, including the connections Sudan–Kenya, Kenya–Ethiopia, Sudan–Uganda, and Berbera Corridor Somalia–Ethiopia. Two rail connections (Uganda–Sudan and Djibouti–Ethiopia) and a trade and transport facilitation programme have been proposed to encourage integration.

On the other hand, many concessions have not yielded the desired objectives. The basic model followed by the concession countries was one developed by the World Bank. The challenges faced were mainly in the way the concessions were negotiated and the agreement achieved, which did not necessarily lead to the expected outcome. The main problems were linked to the following issues: [94]

- The overestimation of available rail freight markets. Traffic gains were much lower than expected because of strong road competition. Host governments failed to implement an appropriate competition strategy between rail and road;

- The underestimation of investment needs and the miscalculation of freight-sector requirements. The concession bidding underestimated the dilapidated state of rail infrastructure and equipment, which required massive maintenance and rehabilitation investments, and many concessions did not deliver the investment required or the expected improvement and technologies;

- The undercapitalization of concessions. Concession companies had to provide limited capital bases and many were faced with a cash shortage since the projected cash flows did not materialize. This led concession companies to borrow from donors and increased their long-term debt.

Moreover, governments have on occasion set high fixed and floating licence fees, taxes, duties and social contributions, which in turn have undermined the ability of private partners to invest in infrastructure and develop the rolling stock fleet.

Despite these challenges, PPP rail concessions in Africa remain an economically plausible and viable

Box 4.3. Private-sector participation in African railways

Country	PPP type	Company	PPP subtype	Segment	Financial closure year
Algeria	Management and lease contract		Management contract	Fixed assets and passenger	2007
Burkina Faso/Côte d'Ivoire	Concession	Sitarail	Rehabilitate, lease or rent, and transfer	Fixed assets and freight	1995/1996
Cameroon	Concession	Camrail	Rehabilitate, operate and transfer	Fixed assets, freight and passenger	1999
Democratic Republic of the Congo	Management and lease contract	Sizarail (from 1995–1997) and SNCC (Société Nationale des Chemins de Fer du Congo) as of 2011	Management contract	Freight	1995
Gabon	Concession		Rehabilitate, operate and transfer	Fixed assets	2005
Gabon	Concession	Transgabonais - change in concession	Rehabilitate, operate and transfer	Freight and passenger	1999
Kenya/Uganda	Concession	RVRC (Rift Valley Rail Corporation) – change in concession	Rehabilitate, operate and transfer	Fixed assets, freight and passenger	2006
Madagascar	Concession	Madarail	Rehabilitate, operate and transfer	Fixed assets, freight and passenger	2003
Malawi	Concession	CEAR (Central East African railways Corporation) – severely affected for some years by cyclone damage	Management contract	Fixed assets, freight and passenger	1999/2000
Mali/Senegal	Concession	Transrail - change in concession	Rehabilitate, operate and transfer	Fixed assets, freight and passenger	2003
Mozambique	Concession	CCFB (Companhia dos Caminhos de Ferro da Beira)	Rehabilitate, lease or rent and transfer	Fixed assets, freight and passenger	2004/2005
Mozambique	Concession	CDN (Corredor de Desenvolvimento do Norte)	Rehabilitate, lease or rent and transfer	Freight and passenger	2004/2005
Mozambique	Concession	Maputo Corridor	Rehabilitate, operate and transfer	Freight	2002
Togo	Management and lease contract	Canac/WACEM (1995–2002)	Management contract	Fixed assets, freight and passenger	1996
United Republic of Tanzania	Concession	TRL /Tanzania Railways (cancelled in 11/2010)	Rehabilitate, operate and transfer	Fixed assets, freight and passenger	2007
United Republic of Tanzania	Greenfield project		Build, operate and transfer	Fixed assets	1998
Zambia	Concession	RSZ (Railway Systems of Zambia)	Rehabilitate, operate and transfer	Fixed assets, freight and passenger	2003
Zimbabwe	Greenfield project	BBR (Beitbridge Bulawayo Railway)	Build, operate and transfer	Fixed assets and freight	1998
Planned railways Concessions					
Congo		CFCO (Congo - Ocean Railway)			2012
Nigeria		NRC (Nigerian Railway Corporation)			2012

Source: Private Participation in Infrastructure (PPI) Project Database (available from http://ppi.worldbank.org), Richard Bullock 2010, and Pozzo di Borgo 2010.

solution to promote private participation in the rail sector; lessons can be drawn from the long history of rail concessioning in Africa and thus help optimize PPPs. It has been noted, for instance, that African rail markets such as those in sub-Saharan Africa, are sometimes too small in terms of traffic volumes to ensure a profitable concession and sustainable rail business to cover the financing of both rail track infrastructure and rolling stock. In this respect, the government should play a crucial role in shouldering some of the costs such as investment in infrastructure and rail rehabilitation to ensure positive public and private economic returns on investments, while ensuring a framework for fair rail/road competition and putting in place an enabling environment for sustained partnerships For example, governments should be ready whenever necessary to surrender higher concession fees for more investment.

Today, second-generation contract concessions are making their appearance in Africa with a more prominent role for the government. This is illustrated by new concession agreements concluded by Camrail (Cameroon) and Madarail (Madagascar), where the scope of the partnership and share of the investments are redefined in a more balanced manner. In this type of concessions, private operators have taken the responsibility for financing rolling stock maintenance and renewal, and governments have agreed to finance infrastructure track renewal, partially securitized by an infrastructure renewal fee paid by the concessionaire. In such a case, private operators bear the cost of track maintenance.

ENDNOTES

[1]   See annex VI. The underlying data are provided by Containerisation International Online, www.ci-online.co.uk . The UNCTAD LSCI is also included in the World Bank database of World Development Indicators 2010, http://data.worldbank.org/indicator/IS.SHP.GCNW.XQ . It can be found on the UNCTAD website under http://unctadstat.unctad.org/TableViewer/tableView.aspx?ReportId=92 . The Index is generated as follows: For each of the five components, a country's value is divided by the maximum value of that component in 2004, and the average of the five components is calculated for each country. This average is then divided by the maximum average for 2004 and multiplied by 100. In this way, the index generates the value for the country with the highest average index of the five components in 2004.

[2]   For recent empirical studies with comprehensive literature overviews, see Wilmsmeier G (2011), *Explaining Maritime Transport Costs*, Ashgate Publishing, Farnham, Surrey; Kumar S and Hoffmann J (2010), Globalization – the maritime nexus, in: Grammenos C, ed., *The Handbook of Maritime Economics and Business*, Second Edition, Informa Law, London; and Korinek J (2009), *Determinants of Maritime Transport Costs*, TAD/TC/WP(2009)4, OECD, Paris.

[3]   Duval Y and Utoktham C (2011). Trade Facilitation in Asia and the Pacific: Which Policies and Measures Affect Trade Costs the Most? Asia-Pacific Research and Training Network on Trade Working Paper Series, No. 94, January 2011, Bangkok. Available from www.unescap.org/tid/artnet/pub/wp9411.pdf.

[4]   Bloomberg (2011). Exports Brazil: Brazil port stocks quadruple on record shipping: Freight markets, 13 April.

[5]   Corn exports tripled and leather increased by 45 per cent; see Fairplay (2011), Brazil ports unveil rises, 13 January.

[6]   Dredging Today (2010). Latin America's countries invest in port development, 27 August.

[7]   Brazil's 17 leading ports generated 850 cancellations in 2010 and an increase of 86 per cent from the previous year's figure of 457; see Dredging Today (2011), Brazil's ports face lack of investment in infrastructure, 3 May.

[8]   See the UNCTAD *Review of Maritime Transport 2010* for more details on Brazil's port development programme.

[9]   Business News Americas (2011). Brazil: Wilson, Sons launches USD 1.8 billion ports investment plan, 17 May.

[10]   Fairplay (2011). Vale to spend $2.9bn expanding port, 25 May.

[11]   Port Strategy (2011). Valparaiso tender dead in the water. May.

[12]   Business News Americas (2011). Colombia's Transport Ministry plans $56 billion investment up to 2021, 6 May.

13   BusinessNews Americas (2011). Uruguay's government aims to declare $3.5 bn deepwater port of public interest, 12 January.

14   Moveforward (2011). Two mega ports to be built to cope with Panama Canal expansion, 31 March.

15   Business News Americas (2007). Mici, PSA ink agreement for Rodman port development, 17 October.

16   Dominican Today (2007). Caucedo Port lowers Dominican freight costs, executive says, 3 August.

17   TradeArabia (2011). DP World launches second phase of Caucedo port, 20 March.

18   Port Technology (2011). Port of Kingston prepares for Panama Canal expansion, 21 March.

19   Cargo Systems (2011). APM terminals wins Costa Rica concession, 1 March.

20   Cocatram (2010). *Central American Ports Handbook 2010–2011*. Land & Marine Publications Ltd.:41 Essex, United Kingdom.

21   South East Shipping News (2010). Operarán Puerto La Unión mientras reparan Acajutla, 30 June.

22   Cargonews Asia (2011). APM gets nod to bid for India terminal project, 13 May.

23   Drewry (2010). *Annual Review of Global Container Terminal Operators*. August. Drewry Shipping Consultants Limited. London. Available from http://www.drewry.co.uk/publications/view_publication.php?id=356.

24   Economics NewsPaper (2011). Privatization: Greece plans sale of shares in Ports, 23 May.

25   Dredging Today (2011). Croatia: ICTSI inks port of Rijeka deal, 8 March.

26   Marine-Cafe.com (2011). Baltic record for Rickmers boxship, 18 May.

27   Reuters (2011). APM terminals buys Georgia port from RAKIA-official. 4 April.

28   Bolloré Africa Logistics (2011). Bolloré Africa Logistics wins container terminal management contract at Conakry, 29 March.

29   Port Technology International (2011). New Guinean port construction as part of Rio Tinto mining agreement, 26 April.

30   Reuters (2011). Bollore confirms $640 mln Lomé port expansion plan, 7 March.

31   Transport Weekly (2011). Cameroon plan for ultramodern deep seaport moves ahead, 12 January.

32   Cargo Systems (2011). Second Mombasa box terminal imminent, 10 May.

33   Dredging Today (2011). Kenya: Mombasa port expansion unlikely before 2013, 10 May.

34   Ftwonline.co.za (2011). Maputo port expansion plans on track, 7 March.

35   Reuters (2011). Mozambique's CDN to invest $200 mln in port upgrade, 2 March.

36   Cargo Systems (2011). New 6 million TEU terminal for Durban, 17 March.

37   Transnet Limited (2011). Milestone for Cape Town container terminal expansion, 6 May.

38   For example, DP World (United Arab Emirates), COSCO Pacific (China), Evergreen (Taiwan Province of China), HPH (Hong Kong, China), ICTSI (Philippines) and PSA (Singapore).

39   Malaysia's Port Klang is often cited in the news for breaking productivity records in container handling.

40   Dredging Today (2011). New Kuwait port to cut Iraq's main port traffic by 60 per cent, 16 May.

41   Oman Daily Observer (2011). Port expansion projects to boost Oman's industrial and shipping capability, 10 March.

42   Dredging News Online (2010). Ports expansion key to Qatar $100 billion economic investment, 4 March.

43   Containershipping.com (2011). DP World opens terminal 2 in Port Qasim, 12 January.

44   Press Trust of India (2011). Dhamra Port to go operational in April, says its CEO, 13 March.

45   Ship-technology.com (2011). Vallarpadam Container Terminal to open. 9 February. Available from http://www.ship-technology.com/news/news109567.html.

46   IFW (2011). Indian ports reach a milestone. 8 February. Available from http://www.cargosystems.net/freightpubs/ifw/analysis/indian-ports-reach-a-milestone/20017847105.htm;jsessionid=F6B8ADB37D807DE0DBA398FFFFABDB CD.cb1a6af26f4f089d0d4cce62279dcbca5a310b19.

47   In Indonesia, a new law came into force in 2011 limiting port operators Pelindo I, II, III and IV acting as port regulators. See Port & Shipping News (2011), *Indonesia: New regulation throws open ports to private competition*, 4 May.

48   Dredging Today (2011). Viet Nam: CMA CGM arrives at newly opened Cai Mep International Terminal, 30 March.

49   Cargonews Asia (2011). Viet Nam asks line to speed up port project, 8 May.

50   Dredging Today (2011). China to invest USD 2.7 billion in Yangtze River dredging, 3 May.

51   Associated Press (2011). Drought in China snags Yangtze River shipping, 8 May.

52   Whenever possible, data on road and inland waterways have been provided.

53   Recovery continues in global freight transport – uncertainties remain. *International Transport Forum*, March 2011. Available from http://www.oecd.org/document/48/0,3746,en_2649_35131810_47354672_1_1_1_1,00.html.

54   Rail Freight: Global Industry Guide. *Datamonitor*. January 2011. Available from http://www.datamonitor.com/store/Product/rail_freight_global_industry_guide_2010?productid=4AAF392A-F290-443B-9C1E-FDE5878CA897.

55   See International Transport Forum, *Statistics Brief,* May 2011, available from http://www.internationaltransportforum.org/statistics/StatBrief/2011-05.pdf; Rail freight: global industry guide, *Datamonitor*, January 2011.

56   See *Great Expectations 2011*, a publication by the Association of American Railroads, available from http://www.aar.org/AAR/GreatExpectations.aspx.

57   According to data compiled by the Association of American Railroads in May 2011, http://www.aar.org/AAR/NewsAndEvents/Freight-Rail-Traffic/2011/05/26-railtraffic.aspx.

58   Data extracted from the statistics centre of China Ministry of Railways, http://www.china-mor.gov.cn/.

59   The Community of European Railway and Infrastructure Companies, March 2011, http://www.cer.be/index.php?option=com_content&view=article&id=2124:rail-freight-grows-by-more-than-5-in-2010-in-further-sign-of-recovery-in-rail-markets&catid=918.

60   In 2009 alone, more than 12 billion rubles ($425 million) were spent on developing rail infrastructure in the Far East regions, compared with some 13 billion rubles ($461 million) in 2010. The project is being carried out on the basis of a PPP, and is directly linked to the creation of an ore mining and smelting cluster in the Amur area. Under the project, the parties plan to deliver around 20 million tons of iron ore and other commodities to China annually by 2020. A potential area for expanding cooperation is container freight from north-western Chinese provinces with no direct access to the coast via Russian Far East ports, for subsequent delivery to south China, Japan, the Republic of Korea and other countries. Sources: Russian Railways, http://eng.rzd.ru/isvp/public/rzdeng?STRUCTURE_ID=4092&layer_id=4839&refererPageId=704&refererLayerId=4537&id=105604 and http://www.ftnnews.com/other-news/10929-rail-freight-traffic-with-china-could-double-in-coming-decade.html.

61   Ibid.

62   Association of American Railroads estimate.

63   MRS Logística S.A. is a freight rail company located in Brazil that operates 1,643 km of track. It is the concessionary company that operates the South-eastern Federal Railroad Network. The operation started in 1996, combining the lines Rio de Janeiro–São Paulo, Rio de Janeiro–Belo Horizonte, São Paulo–Santos and Ferrovia do Aço. These lines are in the richest and most populous area of Brazil (54 per cent of Brazil's GDP), and MRS Logistica has a connection to three of Brazil's leading seaports, Rio de Janeiro, Itaguaí and Santos. The company also has a connection to the privately owned iron ore terminal of MBR in Ilha de Guaíba on Angra dos Reis Bay.

64   See http://www.researchandmarkets.com/reportinfo.asp?report_id=1215443&tracker=related.

65   Road Freight in North America. *Datamonitor*, March 2011.

66   International Transport Forum. *Statistics Brief*, May 2011. Available from http://www.internationaltransportforum.org/statistics/StatBrief/2011-05.pdf.

67   Data extracted from the International Transport Forum, *Statistics Brief*, May 2011, and from Road freight in Europe, Road freight in Western Europe, and Road freight in Eastern Europe, *Datamonitor*, March 2011.

68   See http://epp.eurostat.ec.europa.eu/statistics_explained/index.php/Freight_transport_statistics.

69   See http://ec.europa.eu/transport/inland/index_en.htm.

70   See http://www.envisionfreight.com/modes/default.aspx?id=waterway#fn1.

71   See http://ec.europa.eu/transport/inland/index_en.htm and http://www.naiades.info/.

72   UNESCAP, available from http://www.unescap.org/ttdw/Publications/TPTS_pubs/pub_2307/pub_2307_ch11.pdf, and *Hindustan Chamber Review*: 44(9), February 2011.

73   See http://news.xinhuanet.com/english2010/china/2011-01/30/c_13713969.htm.

74   Rupayun, a private company, has received approval to set up another river terminal in Narayanganj and the government will set up more terminals – one in Khanpur under a PPP – and AK Khan Group and Kumudini Trust have already submitted proposals to set up two other terminals in the Narayanganj area. Sources: http://proquest.umi.com/pqdweb?did=2252346091&sid=1&Fmt=3&clientId=23038&RQT=309&VName=PQD and http://www.thefinancialexpress-bd.com/more.php?date=2011-03-06&news_id=128152n.

75   *African Development Report 2010: Ports, Logistics and Trade in Africa*. African Development Bank and Oxford University Press: 2011. Oxford.

76   Reaching over 45 per cent in many countries, such as Malawi (56 per cent), Chad (52 per cent) and Rwanda (4 per cent).

77   From the presentation, "Public Private Partnerships in Infrastructure in India", delivered by Dr. Arvind Mayaram, Additional Secretary, Ministry of Rural Development, Government of India, at the UNCTAD Multi-year expert meeting on investment, February 2011.

78   This and the following section draw from the Private Participation in Infrastructure Projects Database (joint product of the World Bank's Infrastructure Economics and Finance Department and the Public-Private Infrastructure Advisory Facility – PPIAF, a multi-donor technical assistance facility). The database divides transport infrastructure projects into

four sectors: (a) airports (runways and terminals), (b) railways (including fixed assets, freight, intercity passenger and local passenger), (c) roads (toll roads, bridges, highways and tunnels) and (d) ports (port infrastructure, superstructures, terminals and channels). See www.ppiaf.org.

[79]   Asian Development Bank. *Annual Report 2010*, volume 1.

[80]   The CAREC corridors link Central Asia's key economic hubs and connect the region to other Eurasian markets. The line is under construction by Uzbek Railway through a design-and-build contract. It will save transport costs and freight time for commodities (such as fuel) and general cargo.

[81]   Bilateral members of ICA include the G-8 countries – Canada, France, Germany, Italy, Japan, the Russian Federation, the United States and the United Kingdom, and multilateral institutions such as the African Development Bank Group, the European Commission, the European Investment Bank, the Development Bank of Southern Africa and the World Bank Group. The ICA secretariat is located at the African Development Bank.

[82]   ICA *Annual Report 2009.*

[83]   See http://www.icafrica.org/en/infrastructure-issues/transport/.

[84]   Rail Freight: Global Industry Guide, *Datamonitor*. January 2011. Available from http://marketpublishers.com/report/ services/transport_logistics/rail_freight_global_industry_guide.html.

[85]   Pierre Pozzo di Borgo, 2011. Available from http://www.afd.fr/jahia/webdav/site/proparco/shared/PORTAILS/ Secteur_prive_developpement/PDF/SPD%209/Proparco%20SPD_9_UK_A-balance-between-public-and-private- sector-roles-the-key-to-a-succesful-rail-concession.pdf.

[86]   European Commission White Paper 2011. Available from http://ec.europa.eu/transport/strategies/2011_white_paper_ en.htm.

[87]   *Private Participation in Infrastructure: Trends in Developing Countries in 1990–2001.* Available from http://ppi. worldbank.org/book/Chapter11.pdf.

[88]   Ibid.

[89]   This section draws mainly from: Africa's Infrastructure: A Time for Transformation, http://www.infrastructureafrica.org/ system/files/WB147_AIATT_CH11.pdf, Assessing Regional Integration in Africa IV: Enhancing Intra-African Trade by the Economic Commission for Africa – http://www.uneca.org/aria4/chap9.pdf, and Africa Review Report on Transport, United Nations Economic and Social Council, Economic Commission for Africa, Sixth Session of the Committee on Food Security and Sustainable Development (CFSSD-6) FCA/FSSD/CFSSD/6/12, Ethiopia, August 2009.

[90]   See http://www.icafrica.org/en/infrastructure-issues/transport/railways/.

[91]   The Programme is designed to be a successor to the Medium- to Long-Term Strategic Framework of the New Partnership for Africa's Development (NEPAD), to develop a vision and strategic framework for the development of regional and continental infrastructures (energy, transport, information and communication technologies, and transboundary water resources). The PIDA initiative is being led by the African Union Commission, the NEPAD Secretariat and the African Development Bank, which serves as the executing agency.

[92]   Richard Bullock. African railway concessions, a step forward but not the whole answer. *Proparco's Magazine*. Issue No. 9. March 2011.

[93]   Ibid.

[94]   "Africa railway concessions: Lessons learned and potential solutions for a revival of the sector", presentation by Pierre Pozzo di Borgo, the World Bank, March 2011.

5

LEGAL ISSUES AND REGULATORY DEVELOPMENTS

This chapter provides information on some important legal issues and recent regulatory developments in the fields of transport and trade facilitation, together with information on the status of ratification of some of the main maritime conventions. Important developments include the entry into force, on 14 September 2011, of the International Convention on Arrest of Ships, which had been adopted at a joint United Nations/ International Maritime Organization (IMO) Diplomatic Conference, held in 1999, under the auspices of UNCTAD. Moreover, during 2010 and the first half of 2011, important discussions continued at IMO regarding the scope and content of a possible international regime to control greenhouse gas (GHG) emissions from international shipping. Finally, there were a number of recent regulatory developments in relation to maritime security and safety, as well as in respect of trade facilitation agreements at both the multilateral and regional levels.

A.   IMPORTANT DEVELOPMENTS IN TRANSPORT LAW

This section highlights two significant legal developments that may be of interest to the parties engaged in international trade and to the shipping industry. First, an overview is provided about some of the key features of the International Convention on Arrest of Ships 1999, which recently entered into force and now represents the most modern international regulatory regime relating to ship arrest. Secondly, attention is drawn to the entry into force of the 2008 "e-CMR Protocol" to the Convention on the Contract for the International Carriage of Goods by Road, 1956 (as amended), which establishes the legal framework for the use of electronic means of recording and handling of consignment note data for such contracts.

1.   Entry into force of the International Convention on Arrest of Ships 1999

Arrest of ships – a key mechanism to secure and enforce maritime claims – is an issue of considerable importance to the international shipping and trading community. While the interests of owners of ships and cargo lie in ensuring that legitimate trading is not interrupted by the unjustified arrest of a ship, the interests of claimants lie in being able to obtain security for their claims. The International Convention on Arrest of Ships 1999, like its predecessor, the Brussels Convention on the Arrest of Sea-Going Ships 1952, aims at striking a balance between these interests, bearing in mind the different approaches adopted by various domestic legal systems.[1]

On 14 March 2011, Albania was the 10th State to accede to the 1999 Arrest Convention, following earlier accession by Algeria, Benin, Bulgaria, Ecuador, Estonia, Latvia, Liberia, Spain and the Syrian Arab Republic. The latest accession triggered the entry into force of the Convention on 14 September 2011.[2]

The 1999 Arrest Convention refines and updates the principles of the 1952 Arrest Convention, regulating the circumstances under which ships may be arrested or released from arrest. It covers issues such as claims for which a ship may be arrested, ships that can be subject to arrest, release from arrest, right of re-arrest and multiple arrest, liability for wrongful arrest and jurisdiction on the merits of a claim. The new international rules on arrest apply to all ships within

the jurisdiction of a State Party, whether or not they are sea-going and whether or not they are flying the flag of a State Party; however, State Parties may enter a reservation in this respect when acceding to the Convention.

The 1999 Arrest Convention was adopted by consensus on 12 March 1999, at the Joint United Nations/IMO Diplomatic Conference, held in Geneva from 1 to 12 March 1999, under the auspices of UNCTAD.[3] The preparatory work on a new international instrument on arrest of ships began following the adoption in 1993 of the International Convention on Maritime Liens and Mortgages (MLM Convention) by the United Nations/IMO Conference of Plenipotentiaries on Maritime Liens and Mortgages. Arrest of ships being a means of enforcing maritime liens and mortgages, it was considered necessary to revise the 1952 Convention on Arrest of Ships so as to closely align the two conventions and to ensure that all claims giving rise to a maritime lien under the 1993 MLM Convention would give rise to a right of arrest under the Arrest Convention. Furthermore, some of the provisions of the 1952 Convention had become out of date, requiring amendment, while others were considered ambiguous, giving rise to conflicting interpretations. An overview of the key features of the 1999 Arrest Convention will be provided below.[4]

As the 1999 Arrest Convention has now entered into force, Contracting States need to ensure effective national implementation of the new international legal regime. Contracting States to both the 1999 and 1952 Arrest Conventions[5] would also need to denounce the 1952 Convention, so as to avoid undesirable overlap between the two international legal instruments.[6] In view of the fact that the international regulatory landscape for ship arrest is to change soon, other States may too wish to consider the merits of accession more closely. In particular, Contracting States to the 1993 MLM Convention that are not parties to the 1999 Arrest Convention may wish to give the matter of accession particular consideration, with a view to strengthening the relevant legal regime for the enforcement of maritime liens and mortgages. The 1993 MLM Convention entered into force in 2004 and, as at 31 July 2011, had 16 Contracting States.[7]

It should be noted that, in some respects, the 1999 Arrest Convention may offer particular advantages from the perspective of developing countries. For instance, express reference in the list of maritime claims under the 1999 Arrest Convention to disputes arising in relation to ownership or possession of a ship, or contracts of sale of a ship, as well as to claims regarding mortgages, hypothèques or charges of the same nature,[8] may indirectly promote ship financing and purchase of second-hand ships – an important issue for developing countries. Moreover, in connection with a wide maritime lien of the highest priority under the 1993 MLM Convention in relation to crew claims,[9] the possibility of arrest of ships for such claims under the 1999 Arrest Convention[10] will be of particular interest to developing countries, from which the vast majority[11] of the maritime workforce originates.

Key features of the 1999 Arrest Convention

The 1999 Arrest Convention now represents the most modern international regime that regulates the circumstances under which ships may be arrested or released from arrest. Among the key features of the new Convention are a wider definition of arrest, a wider scope of application and an extended list of maritime claims, as compared with the existing international legal framework under the 1952 Arrest Convention. In addition, a range of other matters relating to arrest of ships has been clarified in the new Convention.

Wider definition of arrest: The definition of arrest in the 1999 Arrest Convention has been amended and is now wider, referring not only to the detention of a ship but also to the restriction on a ship's removal (article 1(2)). This means that other forms of pre-trial security, such as freezing orders, have been brought within the definition of arrest. This amendment aims to preclude the possibility of a claimant obtaining additional pre-trial security once a ship has been arrested.

Wider scope of application: The 1999 Arrest Convention applies to any ship within the jurisdiction of a Contracting State, whether or not that ship is flying the flag of a Contracting State. Also, in contrast to the 1952 Arrest Convention, the 1999 Convention is not limited to sea-going ships.[12] States may, however, reserve the right to exclude the application of the Convention to non-sea-going ships and/or ships not flying the flag of a Contracting State.[13] Declarations may also be made in respect of treaties on navigation on inland waterways to the effect that they would prevail over the 1999 Arrest Convention (see articles 8 and 10).

Extended list of maritime claims: The 1999 Arrest Convention provides a closed list of maritime claims which give rise to the right of arrest, adopting a similar approach to that of the 1952 Convention (article 1(1)). The list has been updated and expanded, however, and now extends to 22 types of claim,[14] with completely new provisions in respect of (a) insurance premiums, including mutual insurance calls; (b) commissions, brokerage or agency fees; and (c) disputes arising out of a contract for the sale of the ship. "Bottomry" has been deleted, however, from the list of maritime claims.[15] Given that the list is more extensive than that in the 1952 Convention, it is likely that, in practice, the number of claims giving rise to a right to arrest will significantly increase.

It is important to note that, during the Diplomatic Conference, there had been a strong divergence of opinion between certain delegations that preferred a closed list of claims, and other delegations that favoured an open-ended list of claims to ensure that no genuine maritime claims were excluded. After an extensive discussion, the Drafting Committee had succeeded in reaching a compromise solution where a closed list of claims giving rise to the right of arrest was adopted, while flexibility was allowed in respect of certain categories of claim. For example, in relation to environmental damage, various claims are identified along with the possibility of adding "damage, costs, or loss of a similar nature" to those already included in the provision (article 1(1)(d)). Such an approach reflects the fact that this specific area of law is still developing. Claims may also be made in respect of "a mortgage or a 'hypothèque' or a charge of the same nature on the ship" (article 1(1)(u)). In contrast to the 1952 Convention, there is, however, no longer a requirement for such charges to be registered or registrable, as this condition was also removed as part of the compromise solution. As a consequence, arrest may be made for various forms of debt obligations.

Powers of arrest: The 1999 Convention clarifies that a ship may only be arrested or released from arrest under the authority of a court of the State Party in which the arrest is effected. Furthermore, it should be noted that arrest of a vessel is only possible for claims of a maritime nature, and vessels cannot be arrested for any other type of claim. The procedure relating to arrest and release from arrest is governed by the law of the forum of arrest, although the Convention makes clear that arrest may be used to obtain security for a claim which may be adjudicated or arbitrated in another jurisdiction. However, the exercise of the right of arrest, release from arrest and the right of re-arrest are governed by the Convention (see article 2).

Exercise of the right of arrest: Arrest of a ship is permissible following assertion of a maritime claim; there is no requirement to prove liability beforehand. However, a link between the person against whom the maritime claim is made and the ship to be arrested is generally required for the purposes of arrest. Accordingly, an arrest is only possible where the relevant person is the shipowner or demise charterer of the vessel at the time the claim arose and also at the time of arrest. Arrest of a ship for debts owed by a time charterer, for instance, is therefore excluded; an option which may have otherwise been available under the national law of some States (see article 3(1) (a) and (b)).

There are, however, a limited number of exceptions to this general rule, where arrest of a ship is permitted in other circumstances. These include cases where (a) the claim is based upon a mortgage or a *hypothèque* or a charge of the same nature on the ship;[16] (b) it relates to the ownership or possession of the ship; or (c) the claim is against the owner, demise charterer, manager or operator of the ship and is secured by a maritime lien available under the law of the State where the arrest is applied for. Accordingly, all maritime liens granted or arising under the law of the *forum arresti* are covered (see article 3(1)(c)-(e)).

Sister-ship arrest: The possibility of arresting other ships that are owned by the person or company against whom a maritime claim is brought (sister-ship arrest) is retained in the 1999 Arrest Convention, although the provision has been drafted more clearly (article 3(2)). There is, however, no definition of an "owner" or of what constitutes "ownership" in the 1999 Arrest Convention, an issue which was debated at length during the Diplomatic Conference.[17]

By way of background, certain delegations were concerned that the proliferation of single-ship companies since 1952 had typically precluded the possibility of sister-ship arrest, which meant that the only option available to claimants was to arrest the particular ship in respect of which a maritime claim arose. Several jurisdictions have attempted to combat this problem by allowing, under national law, for the corporate form to be disregarded where, for example, two companies are under the full control of the same person or persons, or in the case of fraud.[18] This has come to be known as "lifting" or "piercing" the corporate veil. Even though most delegations considered that a problem did exist, they were of the opinion that it was a problem of a more general nature,

with implications for other areas of law. As such, certain delegations did not believe that the problem could be solved in the context of the Convention. By contrast, other delegations considered that the issue was of particular importance for the shipping industry, and should not be left to national law. A number of proposals to counter this problem were put forward at the Conference, but were rejected on various grounds. As a result, no uniformity has been achieved on the questions of whether and in which circumstances the corporate veil can be pierced and, consequently, whether ships owned by companies having a different corporate identity from that of the company against whom a maritime claim has been brought may be arrested.[19] It should, however, be noted that the Convention does not prohibit piercing the corporate veil, and States will therefore need to refer to their national law in order to determine such questions.

Release from arrest: The provisions regarding release from arrest are based on those in the 1952 Arrest Convention. Release of a ship from arrest is mandatory when sufficient security has been provided in a satisfactory form. Where the parties cannot agree on the sufficiency and the form of the security, it will be left to the Court to determine its nature and the amount necessary, to a sum not exceeding the value of the arrested ship (see article 4).

Re-arrest and multiple arrest clarified: The circumstances that allow a ship to be re-arrested have been expressly clarified by the 1999 Arrest Convention. For example, a ship may be re-arrested where the initial security provided is inadequate, as long as the aggregate amount of security does not exceed the value of the ship. Also, a ship may be re-arrested if the insurer or person providing financial security is unlikely to fulfill his obligations, or, if the ship arrested or the security previously provided was released with the consent of the claimant or because the claimant could not prevent the release (see article 5(1)).

Furthermore, other ships which would be subject to arrest, i.e. sister-ships, may also be arrested to provide additional security to "top-up" the security already provided. Several arrests may be made to reach the amount of the maritime claim, so long as the additional security does not exceed the value of ship arrested (see article 5(2)).

Remedies of the shipowner: The 1999 Convention leaves at the discretion of the Court the question of whether the claimant must provide security for any loss or damage that may be incurred by the shipowner (or demise charterer), as a consequence of the arrest having been wrongful or unjustified, or where excessive security has been demanded and provided. In such circumstances, the liability of the claimant, if any, will be determined by the courts of the State in which the arrest was effected, in accordance with the national law of that State (see article 6).

Jurisdiction and judgments: As a general rule, jurisdiction to determine the merits of the case is now granted only to the courts of the State in which the arrest was effected or security to obtain release of the ship was provided, unless there is a valid jurisdiction or arbitration clause. Such courts, however, may decline jurisdiction if permitted to do so by national law and a court of another State accepts jurisdiction. Regarding recognition of judgments, the courts of the State in which an arrest has been effected are required to recognize a final judgment of the courts of another State by releasing the security to the successful claimant. That is, so long as the defendant has been given reasonable notice of such proceedings and a reasonable opportunity to present his case, and such recognition is not against public policy (see article 7).

2. Entry into force of the e-CMR Protocol

The main international Convention governing liability arising from carriage of goods by road is the Convention on the Contract for the International Carriage of Goods by Road (CMR), 1956 (as amended in 1978[20]), which, as at 31 July 2011, was in force in 55 States.[21] The CMR standardizes conditions governing contracts for the international carriage of goods by road to or from a Contracting State, in particular by providing for mandatory minimum standards of carrier liability.[22] Other issues, too, are regulated in the Convention, such as the obligation of a carrier to issue a consignment note in respect of the goods which complies with certain requirements and fulfils an important evidentiary function.

In order to better adapt the CMR Convention to the demands of modern transportation and to ensure the equivalent treatment of electronic alternatives to traditional paper-based transport documents, an amending Protocol was adopted on 20 February 2008, the so-called "e-CMR Protocol". Following ratification of the e-CMR Protocol by Lithuania on 7 March 2011, the Protocol has now entered into force,

with effect from 5 June 2011, for those Contracting States to the CMR which have ratified or acceded to the new Protocol.[23]

The e-CMR Protocol establishes the legal framework for the use of electronic means of recording and handling of consignment note data, allowing for the faster and more efficient transfer of information. As a consequence, the consignment note, along with any demand, declaration, instruction, request, reservation or other communication relating to the performance of a contract of carriage to which the CMR Convention applies, may be carried out by way of electronic communication. Electronic consignment notes that comply with the e-CMR Protocol are to be considered as equivalent to consignment notes referred to in the CMR Convention, having the same evidentiary value and producing the same effects.

By introducing electronic consignment note procedures, transport operators are likely to save time and money, and to benefit from streamlined procedures and secure data exchange. Widespread adoption of the e-CMR Protocol could, in the longer term, significantly facilitate transactions by reducing the scope of error in dealing with the identification and authentication of signatures.

B. REGULATORY DEVELOPMENTS RELATING TO THE REDUCTION OF GREENHOUSE GAS EMISSIONS FROM INTERNATIONAL SHIPPING

GHG emissions from international shipping – which carries over 80 per cent of world trade by volume and almost 60 per cent by value – are not regulated under the Kyoto Protocol.[24] Rather, IMO, at the request of parties to the United Nations Framework Convention on Climate Change (UNFCCC), 1992, is currently leading international efforts in developing a regulatory regime for the reduction of CO_2 emissions from international shipping, including the various technical aspects. While maritime transport compares favourably to other modes of transport, both in terms of fuel efficiency and GHG emissions (per unit/ton-kilometre), its global carbon footprint is likely to continue to grow in view of the heavy reliance of international shipping on oil for propulsion and the expected growth in world demand for shipping services, driven by expanding global population and trade. Recent IMO data shows that international shipping emitted 870 million tons of CO_2 in 2007, or about 2.7 per cent of the global CO_2 emissions from fuel combustion.[25] In the absence of effective reduction measures, emissions from international shipping are expected to treble by 2050.[26]

Against this background, ongoing efforts, in particular those under the auspices of IMO, aimed at reaching agreement on a package of measures to reduce GHG emissions from international shipping are of particular interest. Before providing a more detailed overview of the most recent developments under the auspices of IMO, it should be recalled, by way of background, that IMO's Marine Environment Protection Committee has been considering a range of measures aimed at reducing emissions of GHG from international shipping, including **technical, operational and market-based measures.**[27]

The most important **technical** measure for the reduction of CO_2 emissions is the Energy Efficiency Design Index (EEDI), which establishes a minimum energy efficiency requirement for new ships depending on ship type and size. On the **operational** side, a mandatory management tool for energy efficient ship operation, the Ship Energy Efficiency Management Plan (SEEMP) has been developed to assist the international shipping industry in achieving cost-effective efficiency improvements in their operations, as well as the Energy Efficiency Operational Indicator (EEOI) as a monitoring tool and benchmark.[28]

Discussions continue on a number of proposals for **market-based measures** to regulate emissions from international shipping, which had been submitted to the Marine Environment Protection Committee for consideration.[29] The different proposals under consideration were briefly described in chapter 6 of the *Review of Maritime Transport 2010,*[30] and an overview of deliberations over the past year is provided below. As the relevant deliberations are ongoing, they are subject to further development. However, it should be noted that there appears to be increasing controversy, with diverging views among IMO member States on whether there is a need for market-based measures at all and which, if any, of the proposals under consideration may be most suitable.

An important issue arising from the ongoing deliberations is an apparent divide in respect of the question of how any measures developed under the auspices of IMO, in particular any potential market-based measure that may be adopted, may reconcile the seemingly conflicting principles of UNFCCC and IMO.

While the UNFCCC regime is based on the principle of "Common but Differentiated Responsibilities and Respective Capabilities" (CBDR) of States, policies and measures adopted under the auspices of IMO are guided by its major principle of non-discrimination and equal treatment of ships (flag neutrality). All of the market-based proposals currently under consideration by IMO assume application to all ships. However, also under consideration is a proposal for a "Rebate Mechanism" tabled by the International Union for Conservation of Nature which aims to reconcile the different principals by compensating developing countries for the financial impact (incidence) of any market-based measure that may be adopted.

The sixty-first session of the Marine Environment Protection Committee was held from 27 September to 1 October 2010 in London. While the report of the meeting[31] should be considered for further detail, a summary of the deliberations relevant to the reduction of GHG emissions form shipping is provided below.

1.   Technical and operational measures on energy efficiency measures for ships

Speed reductions

The Committee noted that speed reduction was the most immediate single factor to increase energy efficiency and reduce emissions, and that slow steaming was widely deployed by some sections of the shipping industry to reduce fuel costs. Following consideration of whether speed reduction should be pursued as a regulatory option in its own right,[32] the Committee agreed that speed considerations would be addressed indirectly though the EEDI and SEEMP, and any possible market-based measure, and thus further investigation of speed reductions as a separate regulatory path was not needed.

The use of correction factors in the EEDI

The Committee agreed to a proposal[33] in relation to the use of correction factors[34] in the EEDI, and decided that the matter should be further considered by the Working Group on Energy Efficiency Measures for Ships. The proposal suggested that correction factors should be used carefully to minimize the risk of creating loopholes in the EEDI requirements and proposed six criteria that must be met before any new correction factor is added to the EEDI equation.

Safety issues related to the EEDI

A proposal[35] was put forward by the International Association of Classification Societies (IACS), which aimed at ensuring that safety was not sacrificed, as a consequence of a ship being constructed to comply with the EEDI. In order to avoid any adverse affects on safety, such as under-powered ships, it was suggested that the necessary safeguard should be added to the draft EEDI guidelines. While the substance of the proposal attracted support from many delegations, others expressed the view that the guidelines needed to be developed before the Committee would be in a position to make a final decision. The IACS undertook to develop a first draft of the guidelines to be submitted at the next session of the Committee for further consideration.

EEDI and ships trading to LDCs and SIDS

Consideration was given by the Committee to a proposal[36] for alternative calculation or exemption of the EEDI, and the minimum efficiency thereby required, for ships whose trade was critical, either economically or materially, to support least developed countries (LDCs) and small island developing States (SIDS). Such countries may have less developed port facilities or limited infrastructure and thus require the support of vessels outfitted with self-loading and unloading appliances. The proposal therefore aimed to provide an exemption for vessels of such design, which might face a disadvantage if the current EEDI formulation is used as projected. The Committee agreed that the Working Group on Energy Efficiency Measures for Ships, if time allowed, should consider how the special needs and circumstances of remotely located States and SIDS might be accommodated. It was also agreed that thorough investigation of the implications of any exemptions from the EEDI framework was required before any action was taken, and delegations were invited to submit further proposals and input to future sessions.

CO_2 abatement technologies

The Committee discussed a proposal on CO_2 abatement technologies,[37] where it was suggested that a new provision to allow for alternative CO_2 reduction compliance methods, i.e. CO_2 abatement technologies, should be added to the draft EEDI regulations. It was also proposed that guidelines be developed for type approval of CO_2 abatement technologies and reduction factors for the EEDI and EEOI formulas. The Committee agreed to instruct the Working Group on Energy Efficiency Measures for Ships to include provisions on CO_2 abatement technologies in the EEDI framework. It also noted that development of relevant guidelines was not at present an urgent matter and invited delegations to submit further input to future sessions.

Capacity-building

Regarding the assessment of the need for capacity-building related to mandatory EEDI and SEEMP, the Committee noted, inter alia, that to accurately assess the capacity-building implications, all aspects of the mandatory EEDI and SEEMP regimes would need to be finalized, including supporting guidelines, as they could influence the additional burden for maritime administrations; accordingly, the assessment needed to be kept alive. If the EEDI and SEEMP were to be made mandatory as proposed, the Integrated Technical Cooperation Programme of IMO for the 2012-2013 biennium should allocate the applicable funding for the training and capacity-building activities, and those activities should be implemented before entry into force of the amendments.[38]

In this context, it should also be noted that on 21 April 2011, a Cooperation Agreement was signed between IMO and the Republic of Korea International Cooperation Agency, for implementation of a pioneering technical cooperation project on Building Capacities in East Asian countries to address GHG emissions from ships.[39] The Republic of Korea International Cooperation Agency will make available approximately $700,000 to fund 10 activities to be implemented by IMO over a two-year period. The selected activities will focus on enhancing the capacities of developing countries in East Asia to develop and implement, at the national level, appropriate action on CO_2 emissions from shipping, in addition to promoting sustainable development.

Working Group on Energy Efficiency Measures for Ships

The Committee noted with approval the report[40] of the first intersessional meeting of the Working Group on Energy Efficiency Measures for Ships, which was held from 28 June to 2 July 2010, and decided to re-establish the Working Group, to finalize the draft regulatory text on EEDI and SEEMP with a view to approval by the Committee at the end of its current session. The Working Group was also asked to finalize the EEDI associated guidelines and to address other issues related to technical and operational measures.

A report of the Working Group[41] was duly submitted to the Committee before the end of the session. In concluding its consideration of the report, The Committee agreed, among other things, to establish an Intersessional Correspondence Group on Energy Efficiency Measures for Ships which would submit its report to the sixty-second session of the Committee in July 2011. The Intersessional Correspondence Group was tasked, inter alia, to (a) finalize the draft guidelines on the method of calculation of the attained energy design index for ships; (b) further develop the guidelines for the SEEMP; and (c) develop a work plan with timetable for development of EEDI frameworks for ships not covered by the draft regulations.[42]

No consensus was achieved, however, in respect of the fundamental question of the appropriate legal format in which draft regulations on energy efficiency for ships should be introduced, in particular whether this should be done by way of amendments to Annex VI[43] of the International Convention for the Prevention of Pollution from Ships (MARPOL), 1973/1978.[44] This question gave rise to considerable debate among delegates along with an intervention by the Secretary-General.[45] "A number of delegations supported the inclusion of the energy efficiency measures in MARPOL Annex VI as the appropriate legal instrument and in line with the decision made at the last session. However, a number of other delegations opposed this as they maintained the view that MARPOL Annex VI was not the appropriate legal instrument to regulate energy efficiency measures and that a new instrument would be needed".[46] In conclusion, the Committee noted that no consensus view on the issue could be reached.

In this respect, it is worth noting that, following the Committee's sixty-first session, two *IMO Circular Letters* were distributed, one of which made proposals for amendments to Annex VI of MARPOL 73/78[47] and another, prepared by a number of developing countries, expressed serious legal concerns about the proposed amendments.[48] A further document considering a number of potential legal issues arising out of the proposal to amend Annex VI of MARPOL 73/78 was subsequently submitted for consideration at the sixty-second meeting of the Committee.[49] Thus, at the time of writing, there is clearly no consensus among the IMO membership on the issue of adopting energy efficiency measures for ships by way of amendments to Annex VI of MARPOL 73/78.[50]

It should be noted that, following completion of the Review of Maritime Transport 2011, important developments in respect of technical and operational measures took place at the sixty-second session of the Marine Environment Protection Committee in July 2011. As a result of a roll-call vote, the Committee adopted, by majority, amendments to MARPOL Annex VI, incorporating, within that Annex, a new chapter 4 regulating energy efficiency for ships. The amendments, as adopted by the Committee, are set out in resolution MEPC.203(62).[51]

2.   UNFCCC matters

In respect of UNFCC matters,[52] the Marine Environment Protection Committee at its sixty-first session noted that there seemed to be general agreement among UNFCCC parties that IMO was the appropriate international organization to develop and enact regulations aimed at controlling GHG emissions from international shipping.[53] However, there were still three questions that needed to be resolved:

(a) Should a reduction target be set for emissions from international shipping, and if so, what should the target be, how should it be articulated, and should it be set by UNFCCC or IMO?

(b) Should a new legally binding agreement or a Conference of Parties decision state how revenues from a market-based instrument under IMO should be distributed and used (for climate change purposes in developing countries in general, for specific purposes only (e.g. adaptation) or in certain groups of developing countries (LDCs and SIDS))? and

(c) How should the balance between the basic principles under the two Conventions be expressed in the new legally binding agreement text or the Conference of Parties' decision (UNFCCC and its fundamental principle of "Common but Differentiated Responsibilities and Respective Capabilities" and, on the other hand, the IMO constitutive Convention with its non-discriminatory approach)?[54]

3.   Market-based measures

(a) Deliberations at the sixty-first session of the IMO Marine Environment Protection Committee

At its sixty-first session, the Marine Environment Protection Committee, assisted by the report of the Expert Group on Feasibility Study and Impact Assessment of Possible Market-based Measures,[55] which had been completed in August 2010,[56] also held an extensive debate on how to progress the development of a market-based measure (MBM) for international shipping. The MBM proposals under review ranged from proposals envisaging a contribution or levy on all CO_2 emissions from all ships or only for those generated by ships not meeting the EEDI requirement, to emissions trading schemes and to schemes based on a ship's actual efficiency both by design (EEDI) and operation (EEOI).[57]

The Committee exchanged views on which measure to build upon or the elements that should be included in such a measure. There was however no majority view on a particular MBM. It should be noted that a number of documents had been submitted for consideration, but, due to time constraints, they were not considered at the meeting.[58] These included submissions by some large developing countries' delegations, expressing concerns about the uncertainties associated with MBMs as well as the potential inherent in some of the proposals of placing developing countries at a competitive disadvantage, and their failure to reflect the principle of "Common but Differentiated Responsibilities and Respective Capabilities".[59]

Following the discussions, the Committee agreed to hold an *Intersessional* Working Group Meeting, tasking it with providing an opinion on the compelling need and purpose of MBMs as a possible mechanism to reduce GHG emissions from international shipping. The Intersessional Working Group Meeting was also tasked to further evaluate the proposed MBMs considered by the Expert Group on Feasibility Study and Impact Assessment of Possible Market-based Measures, against the same criteria as used by the Expert Group, including (a) their impact on, among other things, international trade, the maritime sector of developing countries, as well as the corresponding environmental benefits; and (b) the principles and provisions of relevant conventions such as the UNFCCC and its Kyoto Protocol, as well as their compatibility with the World Trade Organization (WTO)

Rules and customary international law, as depicted in the United Nations Convention on the Law of the Sea (UNCLOS), 1982.[60] In addition to relevant terms of reference, the Committee also agreed on a list of nine criteria for use by the Intersessional Working Group.[61]

(b) The third Intersessional Meeting of the Working Group on Greenhouse Gas Emissions from Ships

The third Intersessional Meeting of the Working Group on Greenhouse Gas Emissions from Ships was held from 28 March to 1 April 2011 and was attended by more than 200 representatives from member Governments and observer organizations. The report of the meeting[62] was published in April 2011, and submitted to the sixty-second session of the Marine Environment Protection Committee in July 2011, to enable the Committee to make further progress in accordance with its work plan. Given the importance of the substantive issues debated at the meeting, a brief summary of the deliberations is provided below.

Need and purpose of a MBM

In the context of an examination of the compelling need and purpose of a MBM as a possible mechanism to reduce GHG emissions from international shipping, a number of documents submitted by IMO members and observer organization were considered,[63] followed by an extensive debate on the matter.[64]

Several delegations took a critical approach to the need for MBMs, stating a view[65] that MBMs could not achieve direct reduction of emissions, as they depended on a market mechanism to deliver reduction, and that technical and operational measures were the only means by which a vessel could achieve an immediate effect upon CO_2 emissions. Many also shared serious concerns[66] regarding the introduction of MBMs for international shipping on the no more favourable treatment basis of IMO, due to the disparity in economic and social development status between developed and developing countries. GHG reduction targets for international shipping under IMO should be in consonance with those being set by the UNFCCC;[67] otherwise, an MBM could negatively impact world trade and development, as it could disadvantage consumers and industries in developing countries and could further lead to an increase in the price of food, hampering food security in developing countries.

By contrast, a number of other delegations supported the view, expressed also in a joint submission,[68] that a global MBM for international shipping was needed to ensure that the international shipping community did its part to reduce the total amount of anthropogenic CO_2 emissions; although technical and operational measures could deliver CO_2 reductions for individual vessels, these measures were not sufficient and additional measures were needed to ensure that the shipping sector could deliver the requisite combined CO_2 reductions. Several delegations also expressed the view that there was a compelling need for an MBM for international shipping under IMO, which would provide the most cost effective emission reduction strategy for the sector, as well as an incentive to adopt new technology and make further efficiency gains. Some delegations also stated that there was a need to adopt an MBM sooner rather than later, otherwise the cost to society and developing countries in particular would be greater.

Thus, the debate revealed two groups of opinion: one which considered that a compelling need for an MBM under IMO had been clearly demonstrated with the purpose of reducing GHG emissions from international shipping; and another group which, by contrast, did not consider that a compelling need and purpose had been established.[69] The Intersessional Meeting agreed to put forward both opinions to the Committee; an extensive summary of supporting arguments, put forward by each group, is set out in the report of the meeting.[70]

Review of the proposed MBMs

Based on a number of presentations[71] and additional documents commenting on the different proposals,[72] the Working Group on Greenhouse Gas Emissions from Ships proceeded to debate in some detail different aspects of the MBM Proposals. Some of the relevant submissions considered that, ultimately, a levy (GHG Fund) was considered preferable to an emissions trading scheme (ETS), in particular as it would provide price certainty and investors would respond to a price rather than an emissions cap[73] – a view which has since been formally endorsed by the global shipping industry association, the International Chamber of Shipping.[74] Others identified an ETS as a robust emission reduction mechanism.[75] In conclusion, it was noted that some delegations indicated a preference for certainty in emissions reductions, whereas other delegations opted for a certainty in price, with some delegations

considering the two as equally important and other delegations believing that certain MBM proposals had the potential to achieve both outcomes. In relation to the possible uses for revenues generated by MBMs, options identified include incentives for the shipping industry to achieve improved energy efficiency, offsetting, providing a rebate for developing countries, finance adaptation and mitigation activities in developing countries, finance improvement of maritime transport infrastructure in developing countries, research and development, and support for IMO's Integrated Technical Cooperation Programme. As part of the debate, the potential of MBMs to provide incentives for new technology and operational changes was also considered, as was the question of out-of-sector emissions reductions (offsetting).[76] By way of background, it should be noted that the different proposals for market-based measures under consideration have different ways of reducing GHG emissions; some focus on "in-sector" reductions and others also utilize reductions in other sectors. The extent of such reductions either within the sector (in-sector) or from outside the sector (out-of-sector) is detailed within the individual evaluation of each proposal in the report of the Expert Group on Feasibility Study and Impact Assessment of possible Market-based Measures,[77] which should be consulted for further information.

Grouping and evaluation of proposed MBMs

Following extensive debate on the desire and preferable approach to grouping the different proposals for MBMs, the Working Group on Greenhouse Gas Emissions from Ships agreed that the proposals should be grouped according to whether the mechanism delivers reductions in GHG emissions specifically within the sector, or also utilizes reductions in other sectors. Accordingly, the proposals were grouped in the following manner: (a) "focus on in-sector" and (b) "in-sector and out-of-sector"; strengths and weaknesses as understood by the proponents of the MBMs were identified and listed in a matrix, set out in the report of the meeting.[78] Other delegations which were not proponents of the MBMs were also invited to provide input and identified the following weaknesses of the proposals: (a) not compatible with UNFCCC principles and provisions; (b) not compatible with WTO Rules; (c) would adversely affect the export competitiveness of developing countries; (d) impose a financial burden on developing countries that are least responsible for global warming and consequent climate change;

(e) lack sufficient details for necessary evaluation; and (f) do not take into account the needs and priorities of developing countries.[79]

Relation to relevant conventions and rules

Following consideration of a number of documents[80] and extensive debate, the Working Group on Greenhouse Gas Emissions from Ships concurred with the findings of the Expert Group on Feasibility Study and Impact Assessment of Possible Market-based Measures that no incompatibilities existed between IMO establishing an MBM for international shipping, and customary international law as depicted by UNCLOS. As regards concerns about possible inconsistencies with WTO Rules,[81] shared by a number of delegations, further submissions were invited for consideration at a future session. With respect to the relation of any potential MBM with UNFCCC, opinions were also divided, with some delegations reiterating their key concerns regarding a conflict between the UNFCCC principle of "Common but Differentiated Responsibilities and Respective Capabilities" and IMO's approach of no more favourable treatment. No consensus view was reached on how to reconcile the two. In conclusion,[82] it was agreed that further discussion was required on the relation to relevant conventions and rules and that focus on the goal, the reduction of GHG emissions from ships, should not be lost.

Impact evaluation

Due to lack of time, the Working Group on Greenhouse Gas Emissions from Ships did not further evaluate the impacts of the proposed MBMs on international trade and the maritime sectors of developing countries, LDCs and SIDS, and the corresponding environmental benefits.[83] It did, however, agree that a further impact study[84] was urgently needed, and that further studies would be more meaningful and comprehensive when proposals were more detailed and matured. Proponents were urged to fully develop their proposals in the shortest possible time. Certain delegations did not consider that it was appropriate to await the completion of further studies before making a decision on an MBM, noting that the resolution of the issue was a critical and urgent test of competency for IMO. A number of delegations expressed interest in the Rebate Mechanism proposal that had been initiated by International Union for Conservation of Nature and elaborated upon by World Wide Fund for Nature and supported its further development and consideration either as an integral or add-on element to a future MBM.

C. OTHER LEGAL AND REGULATORY DEVELOPMENTS AFFECTING TRANSPORTATION

This section touches upon some key issues in the field of maritime security and safety, which may be of particular interest to parties engaged in international trade and the shipping industry. These include notable developments relating to piracy and maritime and supply-chain security, as well as a new inspection regime adopted under the most recent amendment to the Paris Memorandum of Understanding on Port State Control and amendments to the International Convention on Standards of Training, Certification and Watchkeeping for Seafarers, 1978.

1. Piracy

With pirate attacks at an all-time high, piracy at sea remains a fundamental international maritime security concern. In the first five months of 2011 alone, there were a total of 211 attacks worldwide, with 24 successful hijackings.[85] The majority of these events have been reported off the coast of Somalia, with 139 incidents in that area, 21 hijackings, 362 persons being taken hostage and 7 killed. According to the International Maritime Bureau's Piracy Reporting Centre, 26 vessels and 522 hostages are currently being held by Somali pirates. In 2010, the number of actual or attempted acts of piracy and armed robbery against ships, which were reported to IMO, was 489, an increase of 83 (20.4 per cent) over the figure for 2009.[86] These reports mark 2010 as the fourth successive year that the number of reported incidents increased. The total number of actual or attempted incidents of piracy and armed robbery against ships, reported from 1984 to 2010, has risen to 5,716. The geographical reach of piracy has also expanded, as a consequence of the use of larger, so-called, "mother ships". Even though the majority of incidents in 2010 occurred off East Africa, attacks in the Indian Ocean and the Arabian Sea also increased. Moreover, the number of attacks in the South China Sea increased significantly, along with a smaller rise in incidents in South America and the Caribbean.[87]

Given the worsening situation, there has been a movement by the industry in favour of the use of private armed guards on board ships, as a means of protection against pirate attacks. In response to this movement, the IMO Maritime Safety Committee (MSC), at its eighty-ninth session, in May 2011,[88] adopted various forms of guidance on the use of privately contracted armed security personnel,[89] building upon its previous work aimed at preventing and suppressing piracy and armed robbery against ships.[90] It is recommended, inter alia, that Flag States should have in place a policy on whether or not the use of private armed security personnel is authorized under national law and, if so, under which conditions. Consequently, such laws and regulations of the vessel's Flag State should be considered by shipowners before opting to use armed personnel, and the laws of Port and Coastal States should also be taken into account when entering their territorial waters.[91] It is also noted that the use of armed guards should not be considered as an alternative to best management practices (BMP) and other protective measures.[92]

The MSC also adopted Guidelines to Assist in the Investigation of the Crimes of Piracy and Armed Robbery Against Ships,[93] to be read in conjunction with the Code of Practice for the Investigation of the Crimes of Piracy and Armed Robbery against Ships.[94] The Guidelines are intended to assist an investigator in collecting and recording evidence, with a view to assisting the capture, prosecution and sentencing of pirates and armed robbers. An Intersessional meeting of the "Working Group on Maritime Security including Piracy and Armed Robbery against Ships" was planned for September 2011, to develop further recommendations and review, as necessary, the Interim Guidance that has already been adopted.[95]

Piracy has also been a key issue on the agenda of IMO's Legal Committee.[96] Following its ninety-eighth session in April 2011,[97] the Legal Committee requested the secretariat to issue IMO Circular Letter No. 3180, which includes a number of documents that the Committee agreed might be useful to States that are either developing national legislation or reviewing existing legislation on piracy.[98] The documents identify the key elements that may be included in national law to facilitate full implementation of international conventions applicable to piracy, in order to assist States in the uniform and consistent application of the provisions of these conventions. It should, however, be noted that the documents do not constitute definitive interpretations of the instruments referred to, nor do they limit, in any way, the possible interpretations by State Parties of the provisions of those instruments. Information had also been provided at the Committee meeting on the seventh session of Working Group 2 of

the Contact Group on Piracy off the Coast of Somalia, held in March 2011.[99] The Working Group had, in particular, focused on the report prepared by Mr. Jack Lang, special advisor of the United Nations Secretary-General on piracy, which dealt with the prosecution and imprisonment of persons responsible for acts of piracy and armed robbery at sea off the coast of Somalia.[100]

In addition, the United Nations Division for Ocean Affairs and the Law of the Sea (UNDOALOS), together with IMO and the United Nations Office on Drugs and Crime, has continued to collect information on national legislation relating to piracy, to serve as a resource for States. Such legislation has been included in the UNDOALOS database of national legislation.[101]

Efforts have also been made to combat piracy at the regional level. As reported in the Review of Maritime Transport 2009, the Code of conduct concerning the repression of piracy and armed robbery against ships in the Western Indian Ocean and the Gulf of Aden (Djibouti Code of Conduct) was adopted at a high-level meeting of States from the Western Indian Ocean, Gulf of Aden and Red Sea areas, which was convened by IMO in Djibouti in January 2009.[102] Signatories to the Code of Conduct declare their intention to cooperate to the fullest possible extent, and in a manner consistent with international law, in the repression of piracy and armed robbery against ships. Following signature by the United Arab Emirates on 18 April 2011, the Code of Conduct had 18 signatories.[103] Furthermore, on 30 May 2011, a Memorandum of Understanding (MoU) was signed to allow IMO to fund the building of a regional training centre in Djibouti, to promote the implementation of the Code of Conduct.

For the shipping industry, an additional problem related to piracy is the potential repercussions that the capture and detention of vessels by pirates may have for various maritime contracts. Given that many standard form contracts are governed by English law and practice, certain recent decisions of the Courts of England and Wales are, in this context, particularly worth noting.

In relation to marine insurance, an important question that was recently examined is whether any depreciation in the value of a cargo, as a result of delay caused by detention by pirates, was covered by the insurance contract. The case referred, in particular, to the Institute Cargo Clauses and the Marine Insurance Act 1906. The Court of Appeal of England and Wales confirmed that capture by pirates does not render a ship or cargo an actual total loss (ATL) for the purpose of a marine insurance policy.[104] The Court considered that such capture does not constitute an ATL, as there was no "irretrievable deprivation" of property, since the vessel and cargo were likely to be recovered following a payment of a comparatively small ransom.[105] Although not an issue on appeal, it was further stated by the Court that the facts of the case would not even support a claim for a constructive total loss (CTL), as it was doubtful that the test of "unlikelihood of recovery" would to be satisfied. In the light of the decision, cargo owners who are concerned that they may suffer an economic loss as a result of prolonged detention of their cargo in connection with a piracy incident may therefore wish to obtain market alternatives in addition to standard insurance cover. A brief review of options that are currently available on the market suggests, however, that such specific cover is not at present widely available.[106]

Another private law issue arising in the context of piracy incidents is the question of whether a vessel remains on-hire during the vessel's detention by pirates, i.e. whether hire remains payable by the charterer. In a decision of the High Court of England and Wales,[107] it was held that the terms of a widely-used time charter-party, namely the 1946 version of the New York Produce Exchange (NYPE) Form, did not constitute an off-hire event and the charterers were obliged to pay outstanding hire to the shipowners. The High Court held that if parties wished to treat capture by pirates as an off-hire event under a time charter-party, they should agree to express provision in a "seizures" or "detention" clause that would clarify their intention to do so. In this regard, it is worth noting that BIMCO, an independent international shipping association, has developed various piracy clauses for incorporation into time and voyage charter-parties, in a bid to allocate responsibility between the parties in the unfortunate event of a pirate attack. BIMCO have also published Industry Guidelines on Private Maritime Security Contractors, Best Management Practices to deter piracy off the Coast of Somalia and in the Arabian Sea and other related documents that may serve as a useful resource for shipowners.[108]

2. Maritime and supply-chain security

There have been a number of developments in relation to existing maritime and supply-chain security standards that had been adopted under the auspices of various international organizations, such as the World Customs Organization (WCO), IMO and the International Organization for Standardization (ISO), as well as at the European Union (EU) level.

(a) WCO–SAFE Framework of Standards

As will be recalled from previous editions of the *Review of Maritime Transport,* WCO adopted, in 2005, the Framework of Standards to Secure and Facilitate Global Trade (the SAFE Framework),[109] with the objective of developing a global supply-chain framework. The SAFE Framework provides a set of standards and principles that must be adopted as a minimum threshold by national customs administrations. It has fast gained widespread international acceptance, and as of 1 March 2011, 164 WCO members had expressed their intention to implement the SAFE Framework.[110]

The SAFE Framework was developed on the basis of four core principles – advance electronic information, risk management, outbound inspection and business partnerships – and rests on two related twin pillars: (a) customs-to-customs network arrangements, and (b) customs-to-business partnerships. A key aspect of the SAFE Framework is the accreditation of Authorized Economic Operators (AEOs), who are essentially parties that have been approved by national customs administrations as complying with WCO or equivalent supply-chain security standards. Given that AEOs adhere to security and compliance criteria, customs administrations are able to focus on potentially risky trade flows and, as such, AEOs are typically rewarded by way of trade facilitation benefits. Over the course of recent years, a number of Mutual Recognition Agreements have been adopted between customs administrations, usually on a bilateral basis. In January 2011, a Mutual Recognition Agreement was concluded between Andorra and the EU and in May 2011, Japan and the Republic of Korea also concluded a Mutual Recognition Agreement. A number of other Mutual Recognition Agreements are currently being negotiated between, respectively, China-EU, China-Japan, China-the Republic of Korea, China-Singapore, EU-San Marino, EU-United States, Japan-Singapore, the Republic of Korea-New Zealand, New Zealand-Singapore, Norway-Switzerland, and Singapore-United States.[111]

Recently, WCO has placed on its website the "SAFE package" i.e. a compilation of a number of instruments and guidelines, published in 2010, to further support implementation of the SAFE Framework.[112] As part of the SAFE package, for example, guidance has been provided on how to implement an AEO programme, and a compendium of such programmes and Mutual Recognition Agreements has been created. Furthermore, in accordance with WCO AEO guidelines, national AEO programmes need to include a means of appeal against decisions by customs administrations regarding AEO authorization, including denial, suspension, revocation or withdrawal. In this context, Model AEO Appeal Procedures have been developed for consideration by members. WCO is currently in the process of updating the SAFE package, and a 2011 version will be adopted shortly, along with a 2011 edition of the AEO Compendium.

In April 2010, the Private Sector Consultative Group that had been established under the auspices of WCO issued a statement in respect of benefits being offered to accredited AEOs.[113] The Group emphasized that it was imperative to establish a core set of internationally accepted trade facilitation benefits that could be offered to AEOs, and provided a list of example benefits as guidance to customs administrations implementing AEO programmes. The Group also believed that such benefits should be transparent and meaningful, should justify the additional costs sustained by economic operators in meeting prescribed AEO requirements, and should bring those operators real improvements and facilitation gains, above and beyond the normal procedures enjoyed by non-AEOs.

(b)   European Union (EU)

At the regional level, the EU has continued to strengthen its measures to enhance maritime and supply-chain security. Given the particular importance for many developing countries of trade with the EU, certain developments in this context are worth noting here. Previous editions of the *Review of Maritime Transport* have provided information on the Security amendment to the Customs Code (Regulation 648/2005 and its implementing provisions), which aims to ensure an equivalent level of protection through customs controls for all goods brought into or out of the EU's customs territory. The amendment has introduced four major changes to the Customs Code, in respect of which there have been some developments over the past year.

First, a significant consequence of the amendment is the obligation on traders to provide customs authorities with advance safety and security data on goods prior to import to or export from the EU customs territory. As reported in the *Review of Maritime Transport 2010*, the advance cargo data reporting requirements continued to be an option for traders for a transitional period from 1 July 2009 to 31 December 2010. It should be noted that, since 1 January 2011, this advance declaration has been an obligation for traders and is no longer optional. As a consequence, relevant security data must be sent before the arrival of the goods in the EU customs territory. If goods are not declared in advance, i.e. if safety and security data is not sent in advance, then the goods will need to be declared immediately on arrival at the border. This may delay the customs clearance of consignments pending the results of risk analysis for safety and security purposes.

In a second major change, the amendment introduced provisions regarding so-called Authorized Economic Operators (AEO), a status which reliable traders may be granted and which entails benefits in terms of trade facilitation measures. Further information on the AEO concept is provided in the *Review of Maritime Transport 2009;* however a number of relevant recent developments are worth noting. For instance, it has strongly been recommended that economic operators perform a self-assessment to be submitted together with the application for AEO status. A revised self-assessment questionnaire[114] has been agreed between EU member States and the European Commission in order to guarantee a uniform approach throughout all member States in respect of AEOs. A transitional period was agreed in order to allow member States to adapt their internal procedure to the new self-assessment questionnaire. This transitional period ended on 31 December 2010, and the new self-assessment questionnaire should now be used. Furthermore, Regulation 197/2010[115] has established new time limits for issuing the AEO certificate.

As regards customs procedures, the amendment introduced uniform risk-selection criteria for controls, supported by computerized systems for goods brought into, or out of, the EU customs territory. Guidelines on entry and summary declarations in the context of Regulation (EC) No 648/2005[116] and Guidelines on export and exit in the context of Regulation (EC) No 648/2005[117] have recently been developed.

As all economic operators established in the EU need to have an Economic Operators Registration and Identification (EORI) number, the final major change to the Customs Code introduced a Community data base allowing the consultation of all national registration numbers.[118] Guidelines[119] have recently been established in respect of EORI implementation.

(c) International Maritime Organization (IMO)

One of the main tasks of the IMO Maritime Safety Committee is the consideration of measures to enhance maritime security. In this respect, certain developments at the most recent sessions of the Committee over the past year,[120] which relate to the International Convention for the Safety of Life at Sea (SOLAS), 1974, as amended, are worth noting. As will be recalled, Chapter XI-2 of SOLAS in particular provides special measures to enhance maritime security and includes the International Ship and Port Facilities Security (ISPS) Code. The ISPS Code represents the main international maritime security regime, which has been mandatory for all SOLAS member States since 1 July 2004. For ease of reference, the main obligations under the ISPS Code are briefly summarized in Box 5.1 below. Further information on the ISPS Code is also available in the *Review of Maritime Transport 2005,* as well as two UNCTAD Reports, which were published in 2004 and 2007 respectively.[121]

In accordance with SOLAS, Contracting States are obliged to communicate relevant security-related information to IMO. In this context, to improve the maritime security module of the Global Integrated Shipping Information System (GISIS), the Committee, at its eighty-eighth session, supported a proposal[122] by the secretariat to add the following two fields in the section relating to port facilities: (a) the date of the most recent review or approval of the Port Facility Security Plan (PFSP) pursuant to SOLAS regulation XI-2/10.2; and (b) the date of the most recent Statement of Compliance of the Port Facility (SoCPF) issued, if applicable. Moreover, SOLAS Contracting States were urged by the Committee at its eighty-ninth session to meet their obligations under the provisions of SOLAS regulation XI-2/13 by reviewing the information which had been provided to the maritime security module of GISIS to ensure that it was complete and accurate, and to continue to update such information as and when changes occurred.[123]

The Report[124] of the Correspondence Group on the Maritime Security Manual (the MSM Correspondence Group) was also submitted at the eighty-ninth session of the Committee. Among other tasks, the Group

had been required to (a) review the draft Maritime Security Manual – Guidance for port facilities, ports and ships[125] to ensure that all relevant material was reflected; to add explanatory text where required; (b) make recommendations on the development of any supplementary materials; and (c) make recommendations with respect to expansion or revocation of existing IMO material.[126] The purpose of the manual is to consolidate existing IMO maritime security-related material into an easily-read companion guide to SOLAS chapter XI-2 and the ISPS Code, intended both (a) to assist SOLAS Contracting Governments in the implementation, verification of compliance with, and enforcement of the provisions of SOLAS chapter XI-2 and the ISPS Code; and (b) to serve as an aid and reference for those engaged in delivering capacity-building activities in the field of maritime security.

In addition, at its eighty-ninth session, the Committee considered the necessity of periodical surveys of the Ship Security Alert System (SSAS).[127] It was agreed that the reliability of Alert System equipment was an important issue and two main questions needed to be resolved: namely, whether to make the surveys of such systems mandatory, and if so, by whom this should be done. Views were expressed by delegations on (a) the need for confidentiality; (b) the difficulty of introducing clear regulations; (c) whether a periodic testing regime mandated by the ISPS Code was an adequate substitute for an inspection; and (d) national regulation by the Flag State as opposed to global regulation. Consequently, the "Working Group on Maritime Security" was instructed by the Committee to further consider the issue and to provide recommendations on the need to conduct such periodical surveys, and, if appropriate, advise on how the issue should be taken forward.

Previously, at its eighty-fifth session in 2008, the Committee had approved the Non-mandatory Guidelines on security aspects of the operation of vessels which do not fall within the scope of SOLAS Chapter XI-2 and the ISPS Code.[128] In this regard, it was noted at the eighty-ninth session of the Committee that, on 24 January 2011, the United States had released its DHS Small Vessel Security Implementation Plan (SVS–IP), which was intended to reduce the risk of a small vessel being used by a terrorist for an attack on the maritime transportation system. The SVS–IP had been developed from the goals and objectives of the Small Vessel Security Strategy (SVSS) that had previously been released by the United States in 2008.

Box 5.1. The International Ship and Port Facilities Security Code

The ISPS Code imposes a wide range of responsibilities on governments, port facilities and ship-owning and operating companies. Since 1 July 2004, the ISPS Code applies mandatorily to all cargo ships of 500 gross tons or above, passenger vessels, mobile offshore drilling units and port facilities serving such ships engaged in international voyages. Part (A) of the Code establishes a list of mandatory requirements, and Part (B) provides recommendations on how to fulfil each of the requirements set out in Part (A).

Responsibilities of Contracting Governments

The principal responsibility of Contracting States under Part (A) of the ISPS Code is to determine and set security levels. Responsibilities also include, inter alia:

- The approval of Ship Security Plans;
- The issuance of International Ship Security Certificates (ISSCs) after verification;
- The carrying out and approval of Port Facility Security Assessments
- The approval of Port Facility Security Plans
- The determination of port facilities which need to designate a Port Facility Security Officer, and
- The exercise of control and compliance measures.

Governments may delegate certain responsibilities to Recognized Security Organizations (RSOs) outside Government.

Responsibilities of vessel-owning and/or operating companies

A number of responsibilities apply to vessel-owning and/or operating companies, whose principal obligation it is to ensure that each vessel they operate obtains an ISSC from the administration of a flag state or an appropriate RSO, such as a classification society. In order to obtain an ISSC, the following measures must be taken:

- Designation of a Company Security Officer (CSO);
- Carrying out Ship Security Assessments (SSA) and development of Ship Security Plans (SSP);
- Designation of a Ship Security Officer (SSO); and
- Training drills and exercises.

A number of special mandatory requirements in SOLAS chapters V, X-1 and X-2 are applicable to ships and create additional responsibilities for vessel-owning companies and for governments. These include in particular the following:

- Automatic Identification System (AIS);
- Ship Identification Number (SIN);
- Ship Security Alert System (SSAS); and
- Continuous Synopsis Record (CSR).

Responsibilities of port facilities

Depending on size, there may be, within the legal and administrative limits of any individual port, several or even a considerable number of port facilities for the purposes of the ISPS Code.

- Port Facility Security Plans (PFSP): based on the Port Facility Security Assessment carried out and – upon completion – approved by the relevant national government, a Port Facility Security Plan needs to be developed;
- Port Facility Security Officer (PFSO): For each port facility, a Security Officer must be designated;
- Training drills and exercises.

The Committee, at MSC 88, also considered further proposals in relation to SOLAS chapter XI-2 and the ISPS Code.[129] For instance, the Committee did not agree with the proposal of incorporating the provisions of the 2008 Code of Safety for Special Purpose Ships in SOLAS Chapter XI-2 and the ISPS Code, as it did not find that a compelling need to amend the instruments had been established.[130] In respect of the development of guidance on port facility security inspections in order to ensure the quality of implementation of SOLAS Chapter XI-2 and the ISPS Code, it was concluded that, in the absence of any feedback on the use of the existing self-assessment guidance,[131] there was no merit in establishing a correspondence group on the matter. The Committee did, however, urge SOLAS Contracting Governments and international organizations to bring to the attention of the Committee the results of the experience gained from the use of the existing guidance, for consideration of action to be taken.

(d) International Organization for Standardization (ISO)

The development of the ISO 28000 series of standards, to specify the requirements for security management systems to ensure security in the supply-chain, has been reported in previous editions of the *Review of Maritime Transport*. Over the last year, revised standards have been published,[132] and work has continued to progress in respect of new security-related standards.[133]

Furthermore, following consultations with all of ISO's developing country members worldwide, the ISO Action Plan for developing countries 2011-2015 has been adopted,[134] with a view towards achievement of ISO's key objective that the capacity and participation of developing countries in international standardization is significantly enhanced. Under the Action Plan, ISO's stated goal is "to contribute to improving developing countries' economic growth and access to world markets, enhancement of the lives of citizens, fostering innovation and technical progress and achieving sustainable development when considered from each of the economic, environmental and societal perspectives." Accordingly, the stated purpose of the Action Plan is to "strengthen the national standardization infrastructure in developing countries in order to increase their involvement in the development, adoption and implementation of International Standards." The Action Plan sets out a range of activities which aim at:

(a) Increasing participation of developing countries in ISO technical work;

(b) Enhancing capacity-building efforts in standardization and related matters for ISO members and their stakeholders;

(c) Raising awareness of the role and benefits of standardization and the need for involvement in standardization activities;

(d) Strengthening ISO members in developing countries at the institutional level;

(e) Encouraging better regional cooperation; and

(f) Introducing the subject of standardization in educational curricula.

As reported in the *Review of Maritime Transport 2010*, during 2005-2009, ISO carried out more than 250 activities covering the five key objectives of its Action Plan for developing countries 2005-2010, and more than 12,000 participants from developing countries benefited.[135] The implementation of such activities will continue to be funded by donors and by ISO member contributors.

3. "New Inspection Regime" adopted under the Paris Memorandum of Understanding on Port State Control

Port State Control is an extremely important tool for the monitoring and enforcement of compliance with international conventions and codes on minimum standards for safety, pollution prevention and seafarers living and working conditions. Compliance with such standards is one of the main responsibilities of the shipowner or operator, and the Flag State of the vessel must ensure that the shipowner conforms to the applicable instrument. However, Port States may also inspect visiting foreign vessels that enter their territorial waters to ascertain whether the shipowner and Flag State have performed their respective obligations. Where necessary, the Port State can require defects to be corrected, and detain the ship for this purpose.

Following a major oil spill that resulted from the grounding of the Amoco Cadiz in 1978, political and public outcry in Europe for more stringent regulations with regard to ship safety led to the adoption of a new[136] Memorandum of Understanding on Port State Control among 14 European Countries, which entered into force on 1 July 1982. Since then, the Paris

Memorandum of Understanding (MoU) has been amended several times and the organization has expanded to 27 member States, including Canada and numerous European Coastal States.[137] The aim of the Paris MoU is to eliminate the operation of substandard ships through a harmonized system of Port State Control in the territorial waters of each member State.[138]

In an effort to reward quality shipping and to focus Port State Control inspections, a New Inspection Regime has been adopted by the 32nd Amendment to the Paris MoU, which entered into force on 1 January 2011. The New Inspection Regime is aligned with the legislative requirements of EU Directive 2009/16/EC on Port State Control, and the national legislation of the Paris MoU member States. Foreign vessels entering the Paris MoU region will accordingly be inspected to ensure compliance with the standards laid down in the various instruments listed in the Memorandum.[139] It goes without saying that shipowners and operators visiting ports or anchorages in the Paris MoU region need to familiarize themselves with the New Inspection Regime, but more importantly, that each vessel complies with all of the legal instruments applicable to it. Ships may otherwise face multiple detentions and may ultimately be banned from entering the Paris MoU region, if infringements are not rectified.[140]

Further information on the New Inspection Regime is provided in Box 5.2. Briefly, under the New Inspection Regime, every ship calling at a port or anchorage in a member State of the Paris MoU must be inspected. The type and frequency of each inspection will be determined by the classification awarded to each ship, in accordance with its "Ship Risk Profile". The classification of each ship will decide whether a ship must undergo an "initial", "more detailed" or "expanded" inspection, as well as how often such inspections must take place, unless an "overriding"[141] or "unexpected"[142] factor warrants an intermediate inspection. As mentioned above, ships that do not comply with the various standards laid down in the Paris MoU may be detained or refused access to the Paris MoU region. Furthermore, the requirement for arrival notifications has been extended, and member States are now required to report the actual time of arrival and departure of any ship calling at its ports or anchorages in the Paris MoU region.

4. 2010 Manila amendments to the International Convention on Standards of Training, Certification and Watchkeeping for Seafarers, 1978

The safety of persons at sea and the protection of the marine environment are, to a considerable extent, dependent on the professionalism and competence of seafaring personnel. Against this background, the International Convention on Standards of Training, Certification and Watchkeeping for Seafarers (STCW Convention), adopted in 1978, establishes basic requirements on training, certification and watchkeeping for seafarers at the international level.[143] The STCW Convention entered into force on 28 April 1984 and, as at 31 July 2011, has 154 Contracting Parties, representing 99.15 per cent of world tonnage.[144]

The STCW Convention was subjected to an extensive revision and updating process in 1995 to clarify the standards of competence required and to provide effective mechanisms for enforcement of its provisions. One major outcome of the 1995 revision was the development of the STCW Code, which contains various technical regulations that were previously listed in the Convention's technical annex. The STCW Code provides mandatory minimum standards of competence for seafarers along with recommended guidance for implementation of the Convention.

A number of significant amendments to the STCW Convention and Code were adopted at a Conference of Parties held in Manila, Philippines on 21–25 June 2010, under the auspices of IMO.[145] These amendments will enter into force on 1 January 2012 under the tacit acceptance procedure, and will provide enhanced standards of training for seafarers. The STCW Convention and Code have also been amended on several other occasions,[146] however, the 2010 amendments constitute the second major revision of the Convention. Some of the important changes include:

(a) Improved measures to prevent fraudulent practices associated with certificates of competency and strengthen the evaluation process (monitoring of Parties' compliance with the Convention);

(b) Revised requirements on hours of work and rest and new requirements for the prevention of drug and alcohol abuse, as well as updated standards relating to medical fitness of seafarers;

Box 5.2. The New Inspection Regime under the Paris Memorandum of Understanding on Port State Control (Paris MoU)

The 32nd Amendment to the Paris MoU, which introduced the New Inspection Regime, entered into force on 1 January 2011. An overview of the key features of the New Inspection Regime is provided below.

New target of full coverage: Under the New Inspection Regime, each member State commits to inspect every ship calling at its ports and anchorages in the Paris MoU region, in comparison with its previous target of inspecting 25 per cent of individual ships calling at each member State.

New "Ship Risk Profile": All ships will be classified as "low-risk ships" (LRSs), "standard-risk ships" (SRSs) or "high-risk ships" (HRSs) on the basis of generic and historic parameters taken from inspections carried out in the Paris MoU area in the last three years. Each criterion has a weighting which reflects the relative influence of each parameter on the overall risk of the ship. Parameters include:

- Type and age of ship;
- Performance of the flag of the ship as reflected by the Black, Grey and White list for Flag State Performance adopted by the Paris MoU Committee;
- Development of a corrective action plan drawn up in accordance with the Framework and Procedures for the Voluntary IMO Member State Audit Scheme;
- Performance of recognized organizations, and performance of the company responsible for ISM management;
- Number of deficiencies and number of detentions.

The classification awarded to a ship will ultimately determine the type and frequency of inspection imposed upon a ship.

New inspection and selection scheme: The New Inspection Regime includes two categories of inspection: a "periodic inspection" which is determined by a set time window, and an "additional inspection", which is triggered by overriding and unexpected factors depending on the severity of the occurrence. Ships become due for periodic inspection in the following time windows:

- HRS – between 5-6 months after the last inspection in the Paris MoU region;
- SRS – between 10-12 months after the last inspection in the Paris MoU region;
- LRS – between 24-36 months after the last inspection in the Paris MoU region.

Once a time window has passed or an overriding factor is apparent, a ship will become a "Priority I" and must be inspected. Alternatively, a ship will become a "Priority II" when the time window opens or an unexpected factor warrants inspection, and they may be inspected. Other ships will not have a priority status and member States are not obliged to perform an inspection, although they are at liberty to choose otherwise. The time span for the next periodic inspection re-starts after any inspection, as periodic and additional inspections have equal status.

Extended inspection to all ship types: Three types of inspection are provided by the New Inspection Regime – "initial", "more detailed" and "expanded" – which will be imposed according to the Ship Risk Profile. "Initial" inspections will consist of a visit on board the ship in order to verify the numerous certificates that are listed in the Paris MoU, and to check the overall condition and hygiene of the ship. A "more detailed" inspection will be triggered where there are clear grounds for believing that the condition of the ship or of its equipment or crew does not substantially meet the relevant requirements of an applicable instrument. It will include an in-depth examination of areas where such clear grounds are established, areas relevant to any overriding or unexpected factors, and other areas at random from explicit risk areas detailed in the Paris MoU. An "expanded inspection" will require a check of the overall condition, including the human element where relevant, of a specific list of risk areas contained in the memorandum.

For periodic inspections, LRS and SRS will have to undergo an "initial" inspection unless clear grounds are established for a "more detailed" inspection. HRS, as well as chemical tankers, gas carriers, oil tankers, bulk carriers and passenger ships more than 12 years old, will be subject to an "expanded" inspection. Additional inspections are required to be "more detailed" inspections, except where the ship is a HRS or is one of the ship risk types mentioned above. In such cases, it is at the discretion of the Member State whether or not to perform an "expanded" inspection.

Widened refusal of access (banning): Multiple detentions will lead to ships being refused access to a port or anchorage within the region of the Paris MoU. In brief, ships that fly a blacklisted flag will be banned after more than 2 detentions in the last 36 months, and ships that fly a grey-listed flag will be banned after more than 2 detentions in the last 24 months. The time period that applies before bans may be lifted is as follows: 3 months after the first ban; 12 months after the second ban; 24 months after the third ban; followed by a permanent ban. Any subsequent detentions after the second banning will lead to refusal of access, regardless of the ship's flag.

Widened requirement for arrival notifications: All HRS, as well as chemical tankers, gas carriers, oil tankers, bulk carriers and passenger ships more than 12 years old that are eligible for an "expanded" inspection are required to notify a port or anchorage in a member State 72 hours in advance, or earlier if required by national law, of its arrival (ETA72). In addition, all ships are required to provide a pre-arrival notification 24 hours in advance (ETA24). Furthermore, member States are now required to report the actual time of arrival (ATA) and the actual time of departure (ATD) of any ship calling at its ports or anchorages in the Paris MoU region.

(c) New certification requirements for able seafarers;

(d) New requirements relating to training in modern technology such as electronic chart display and information systems (ECDIS);

(e) New requirements for marine environment awareness training and training in leadership and teamwork;

(f) New training and certification requirements for electro-technical officers;

(g) Updating of competence requirements for personnel serving on board all types of tankers, including new requirements for personnel serving on liquefied gas tankers;

(h) New requirements for security training, as well as provisions to ensure that seafarers are properly trained to cope if their ship comes under attack by pirates;

(i) Introduction of modern training methodology including distance learning and web-based learning;

(j) New training guidance for personnel serving on board ships operating in polar waters; and

(k) New training guidance for personnel operating Dynamic Positioning Systems.

It is worth noting that, once the amendments enter into force in 2012, several aspects of the Maritime Labour Convention, adopted by the International Labour Organization (ILO) in February 2006, will also become mandatory for Contracting States to the STCW Convention. As reported in previous issues of the *Review of Maritime Transport*,[147] the Maritime Labour Convention consolidates and updates over 68 international labour standards related to the Maritime sector that have been adopted by ILO over the last 80 years, including no fewer than 36 maritime Conventions and 1 Protocol.[148] It is hoped that the Maritime Labour Convention will represent the "fourth pillar" of the international maritime regulatory regime, alongside three other key IMO Conventions, namely, the International Convention for the Safety of Life at Sea (SOLAS), 1974; the International Convention on Standards of Training, Certification and Watchkeeping for Seafarers (STCW), 1978; and the International Convention for the Prevention of Pollution from Ships (MARPOL), 1973, as amended by the Protocol of 1978 (73/78).

The Maritime Labour Convention 2006 has so far been ratified by 12 States representing approximately 48 per cent of world tonnage, although a further 18 ratifications are needed to satisfy its conditions for entry into force.[149] At the ninety-eighth session of the IMO Legal Committee in April 2011, several States indicated that they were working to ratify the Convention before the end of 2011, to enable it to enter into force at the same time as the 2010 Manila amendments to the STCW Convention and Code.[150] The Maritime Labour Convention requires widespread ratification in order for the enforcement and compliance system established under the Convention to be effective.

D.   TRADE FACILITATION IN INTERNATIONAL AGREEMENTS

1.   Towards the multilateral rules on trade facilitation at the WTO: different start, same finishing lines?

Through trade facilitation trading nations can achieve greater efficiency of processes and operations involved in international trade. With the aim to clarify and improve existing Articles V, VIII and X of the General Agreement on Tariffs and Trade 1994 (GATT)[151] and develop multilateral trade facilitation rules, WTO members have been engaged in negotiations on trade facilitation under the Doha Development Agenda trade talks. Since their launch in 2004, the negotiations have made progress toward the draft text of a future WTO trade facilitation agreement. The draft text of the agreement currently comprises two parts.[152]

The first part is devoted to commitments on substantive trade facilitation measures related to transparency in administration of trade rules, fees and formalities at the border and transit matters. The second part of the draft text addresses the provisions that deal with the principle of special and differential treatment providing developing countries, particularly least-developed countries, with flexibilities in implementing certain commitments.

In practice, implementing some trade facilitation measures can be complex and costly. For example, establishing a single window requires substantial financial resources and having certain preconditions met such as legislative and regulatory reforms, strong political support, close collaboration among involved agencies, the prior analysis and simplification of trade control processes, the adoption of international standards on trade data elements and a sound information and communication infrastructure. Some developing country members have been reluctant to make such measures a WTO binding rule. The special and differential treatment provisions would provide flexibility for these countries to introduce such measures and thus could offer an incentive to implementing the commitments contained in the first part of the draft WTO trade facilitation agreement.

In the draft text of the WTO trade facilitation agreement, the special and differential treatment principle extends beyond the granting of traditional transition periods for the implementation of commitments.[153] The extent and time of entering into commitments of developing countries, particularly least developed countries, would depend on their acquired capacity to implement them. The agreement also contains provisions covering technical assistance, capacity-building, and financial support to these country members of WTO. Such assistance, it is hoped, will help overcome technical and financial obstacles to implement trade facilitation reforms, and will also support policy makers in their efforts to obtain the necessary political will for reform.

The capacity acquisition can be ensured with domestic resources and through the provision of technical assistance by the international community. The assistance provided by bilateral donors and international organizations can be expected to be channeled mostly to those trade facilitation commitments that are legally binding in the agreement ("shall" language). Where the trade facilitation agreement contains a "soft" provision in the form of best-endeavor language ("should", "may", "shall endeavor" or "shall to the extent possible"), developing countries will not be obliged to implement such a measure. In such case, the probability of receiving technical assistance and capacity-building support may be reduced.

Locking in trade facilitation reforms through mandatory commitments would allow WTO members to shelter from possible attempts from future governments to amend them. Binding WTO members to such reforms offers benefits to each country and significant advantages to the trading community with greater legal certainty for conducting international trade transactions.

2.   Regionalism and trade facilitation

In parallel with trade facilitation negotiations at WTO, trade facilitation has also been agreed at a regional level. Many trade facilitation measures are easier to agree upon, and even to implement among the neighbouring or like-minded countries pursuing common economic, political or other interests. It would not, therefore, come as a surprise that trade facilitation measures have been increasingly included in regional trade agreements (RTAs).[154]

By their nature, RTAs grant a more favourable treatment to the parties of such agreements than to other WTO members. Therefore, RTAs represent a departure from one of the core principles of the multilateral trading system: the most favoured nation (MFN) principle. The MFN principle establishes that a WTO member shall apply the same conditions on its trade of like products or services with other WTO members (i.e. prohibits discrimination among WTO members).[155] There are two sets of WTO provisions that allow for an exception from the MFN principle for the purposes of creating RTAs with regards to trade in goods:

(a) Article XXIV of the GATT 1994 providing for preferential treatment through creating a customs union or a free trade area, which were an inherent part of the original GATT 1947, that built the basis of the multilateral trading system;

(b) The decision on differential and more favorable treatment, reciprocity, and fuller participation of developing countries, known as "Enabling Clause", which allows developed countries to grant a more favorable tariff treatment to products from developing country Members. Furthermore, it permits RTAs on trade in goods among developing countries.[156]

By mid-2011, WTO had received 474 RTAs' notifications on goods and services, of which 351 RTAs were notified under Article XXIV of the GATT, and 31 under the Enabling Clause. Of all the notified RTAs, 283 agreements were in force.[157] Traditional RTAs concluded in early stages in the GATT era (before 1995) mainly aimed at creating free trade areas or customs unions through dismantling customs duties and non-tariff barriers to trade. The scope of RTAs has gradually expanded to further areas, such as services, intellectual property rights, investment, competition, government procurement and trade facilitation. Inclusion of separate chapters on trade facilitation and customs matters in RTAs reflects the growing importance attached to these issues in national and regional development strategies. Trade facilitation aims to make movement of goods across the border easier and faster, therefore, its commitments are included in either in trade in goods chapters, or stand-alone chapters of RTAs.

Evolution of scope and depth of trade facilitation measures in RTAs

Between 2000 and 2010, the number of RTAs with trade facilitation provisions grew six-fold (see figure 5.1). About one third of all RTAs in force today contain some kind of trade facilitation measures. The scope of such measures has evolved significantly over the years. Initially, RTAs mainly included provisions narrowly focused on customs procedures. Nowadays, these provisions expand to other areas such as transparency measures, simplification and harmonization of trade documents by other border agencies than customs, and coordination among border agencies, as well as with the business community.

Provisions dealing with customs matters have also evolved by presenting a deeper content. Nowadays, these provisions cover a wide range of measures including risk management, right of appeal, advance rulings, periodic review, release of goods, temporary admission, and express shipment, among others.

Drivers for the scope expansion and depth of trade facilitation measures in RTAs

Several drivers can exist behind the expansion of the scope and the depth of trade facilitation measures in RTAs. These include: (a) specificities and common interests of trading partners; (b) harmonization with international standards; and (c) WTO negotiations on trade facilitation.

(a) Specificities and common interests of trading partners

An important factor that affects the nature of trade facilitation provisions contained in RTAs lies in the specificities and common interests of trading partners. These can include, for instance, economic development, the level of information technology maturity or geographical location. If an RTA involves a landlocked country, it usually includes transit-related provisions sometimes linked to provisions on development of transport infrastructure and logistics. Freedom of transit is of vital importance for landlocked developing countries trade with overseas markets

using land transport and seaports systems in coastal transit neighboring states. Some interesting examples of RTAs with detailed provisions on transit, transport policies and/or transport infrastructure development include the Common Market for Eastern and Southern African States (COMESA) and the Southern African Customs Union (SACU) treaties.

RTAs concluded between parties that are leading countries in development and use of information technology (IT) contain also provisions encouraging the use of IT solutions, such as paperless trading and electronic commerce transactions. Provisions on paperless trading as solution to facilitate trade through electronic filling and transfer of trade-related information and electronic versions of documents (e.g. such as bills of lading, invoices, letters of credit, and insurance certificates) can be found in RTAs in some bilateral RTAs by Japan (e.g. with the Philippines, Singapore and Thailand).

(b) Harmonization with international standards

Many RTAs refer to the international trade facilitation standards with the most cited ones including those developed by the World Customs Organization (WCO).[158] A significant number of RTAs refer to the WCO International Convention on the Simplification and Harmonization of Customs Procedures (the revised Kyoto Convention),[159] which provides a comprehensive set of rules and standards for efficient customs procedures and controls to comply with. It deals with key principles of simplified and harmonized customs procedures, such as predictability, transparency, due process, maximum use of information technology, and modern customs techniques, including risk management, pre-arrival information, and post-clearance audit, which are echoed in specific chapters on customs procedures and administration in a large number of RTAs. Thus, it may have influenced the way the provisions on customs procedures in those RTAs were crafted.

Adherence to such international standards would more likely ensure that the countries align their procedures and documents to the same internationally agreed benchmarks. The use of international instruments could provide for application of the same customs procedures and practices for all traders, not only for those under preferences. It could also contribute to convergence between potentially overlapping RTAs.

Figure 5.1. Increasing number of RTAs with trade facilitation measures *(cumulative)*

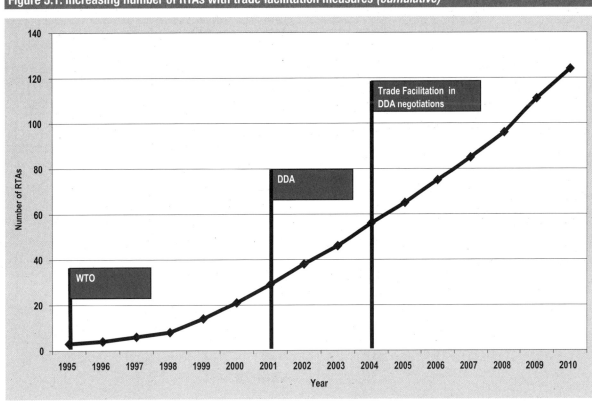

Source: UNCTAD secretariat.

(c) WTO negotiations on trade facilitation

The majority of the RTAs concluded after the launch of the WTO negotiations on trade facilitation in July 2004 contain measures which are very similar or identical in their content to those considered at WTO – the so-called WTO-like trade facilitation measures. In this case, a parallel can be drawn between regional commitments and multilateral trade facilitation negotiations at WTO. It appears that, to some extent, trade facilitation commitments that are contained in existing RTAs have provided a basis to those currently negotiated at WTO, while on other occasions the draft WTO text may have served as basis for newly negotiated RTAs.[160] For example, a well-established pattern by the United States of including provisions on express shipment in RTAs is mirrored at WTO in the negotiating draft text agreement. Similar observations can be made in the case of the EU's interest in dealing with authorized traders. Provisions addressing this issue can be found in most of the Closer Economic Partnership Agreements by the EU and likewise advocated by the EU at WTO. Furthermore, a closer look at the Framework Agreement on Trade Facilitation

under the Asia-Pacific Trade Agreement (formerly known as the Bangkok Agreement) reveals that its trade facilitation measures are to a large extent similar to those negotiated at WTO. Figure 5.2 provides a breakdown of WTO-like trade facilitation measures contained in RTAs.

3. The interplay between trade facilitation commitments at the regional and multilateral level

Trade facilitation at the regional level can be beneficial also to trading partners outside the region that are not part of the RTAs. It has been argued that trade facilitation measures undertaken regionally rarely have a preferential effect against non-RTA parties, when implemented on the ground. Some trade facilitation measures under RTAs indeed appear to be applied to all the trading partners, not only to those under RTAs.[161] Such measures, for instance, include some transparency provisions, such as public availability of trade-related laws, regulations and rulings, and the use of international instruments to simplify procedures

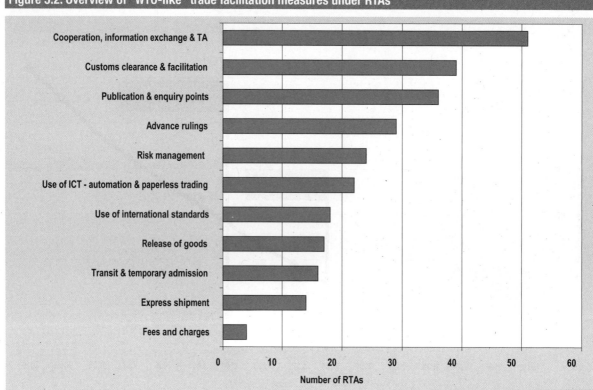

Figure 5.2. Overview of "WTO-like" trade facilitation measures under RTAs

Source: UNCTAD secretariat.

and documents. It is not only more efficient, but also more practical to introduce one Internet portal where all the necessary trade-related information is available in one place for all the trading partners, rather than publicizing information on a preferential basis. Another example might include creation of a paperless trading environment or a national single window under an RTA, both of which in practice are usually applied equally to trade flows from all trading partners and not only those under an RTA.

Are regional trade facilitation commitmets always discriminatory?

On the other hand, due to the inherent nature of RTAs, many other trade facilitation provisions have shown to be applied on a preferential basis, i.e. solely among the parties to the RTA in question. This may potentially lead to discrimination against other trading partners. Such discrimination can be found in two forms:

(a) The first type of potential discrimination lies in the nature of an agreed trade facilitation commitment that is exclusively agreed between members of an RTA. For example, this can include the provision of advance

rulings, harmonized customs procedures, fees and charges, or the application of regional standards. Trade facilitation measures discriminate against non-trading partners that are WTO members by lowering trade and non-trade barriers within their RTA partners;

(b) The second type of discrimination could potentially be in the differentiated level of preferential trade facilitation measures, which vary across a maze of different RTAs. This means that individual countries or regional groupings are parties to two or even more RTAs that apply similar trade facilitation measures with a different scope, depth and language. Put differently, trade facilitation measures covered by different RTAs, which include the same countries, if not harmonized, might potentially discriminate among the different trading partners under different RTAs, and at the same time against the non-members of RTAs.

An interesting example of the second type of discrimination is the procedure and administration of advance rulings. Some remarkable differences and divergences were found in the scope, depth and language across various RTAs, involving the same country and different trading partners. For example, the period of issuing the advance ruling in three different RTAs involving the same country, Australia, is 30 days in the Thailand-Australia RTA, 120 days in the United States–Australia RTA, and the Association of Southeast Asian Nations (ASEAN)–Australia–New Zealand RTA requires that an advance ruling be "issued to the applicant expeditiously, within the period specified in each Party's domestic laws, regulations or administrative determinations". The latter has a basis in a domestic regulation and diminishes any flavour of the potential discrimination, as it is equally applied to all trading partners.

As stated above, RTAs allow for preferential treatment among trading partners under RTAs against WTO members that are non-RTA countries. Then, instead of looking into whether trade facilitation measures under RTAs can discriminate under GATT Article XXIV against trading partners that are WTO members but not RTA members, a more relevant question is whether such application of differentiated trade facilitation measures would be permitted under the future WTO trade facilitation agreement. If, under the WTO trade facilitation agreement, developing countries commit to put in place a trade facilitation measure, which they already apply under an RTA but refuse to apply multilaterally, for example, due to the lack of capacity, this would be considered as a WTO plus in RTAs in relation to trade facilitation commitments. In such a case, as it happens with WTO plus obligations, those trade facilitation obligations would be considered as WTO discriminatory.

The commitment to facilitate trade

The primary objective of trade facilitation is to reduce the complexity and cost of formalities involved in international trade. The multiple RTAs concluded by a country or a regional grouping with other countries may lead to a new type of a "spaghetti bowl" of overlapping customs procedures and trade facilitation measures. Such phenomena could potentially arise, if a maze of different preferential customs procedures and other trade facilitation measures is applied by one country or a regional grouping to different trading partners under different RTAs.

Independent of whether trade facilitation measures adopted under regional initiatives are applied differently to different trading partners, these should in practice be applied in such a manner that would minimize the potential discrimination and not contradict the primary objective of trade facilitation.

One possible solution to avoid such potential problems in the future is to apply as much preferential trade facilitation measures to all trading partners as possible. This "multilateralization" of regional trade facilitation measures can be done either through policymaking or national laws and regulations which would not differentiate among preferential and non-preferential trading partners. Another option is to use international conventions and standards, which provide the same internationally agreed basis to harmonize similar trade facilitation measures across different countries.

Since the majority of trade facilitation commitments under RTAs go deeper and broader than the current WTO provisions under GATT Articles V, VIII and X, they are probably WTO consistent. RTAs can serve as an experiment on how to reflect certain measures at the multilateral level. In particular, the WTO-like trade facilitation measures which are in the spirit of the measures negotiated at WTO could provide a useful basis for the implementation of the future multilateral agreement on trade facilitation. Adopting a coherent approach to the negotiation and implementation of the new or existing regional and multilateral trade facilitation commitments by countries is critical in this respect.

E.   STATUS OF CONVENTIONS

There are a number of international conventions affecting the commercial and technical activities of maritime transport, prepared or adopted under the auspices of UNCTAD. Box 5.3 provides information on the status of ratification of each of these conventions, as at 31 July 2011.[162]

Box 5.3. Contracting States parties to selected conventions on maritime transport, as at 31 July 2011

Title of Convention	Date of entry into force or conditions for entry into force	Contracting States
United Nations Convention on a Code of Conduct for Liner Conferences, 1974	Entered into force 6 October 1983	Algeria, Bangladesh, Barbados, Belgium, Benin, Burkina Faso, Burundi, Cameroon, Cape Verde, Central African Republic, Chile, China, Congo, Costa Rica, Côte d'Ivoire, Cuba, Czech Republic, Democratic Republic of the Congo, Egypt, Ethiopia, Finland, France, Gabon, Gambia, Ghana, Guatemala, Guinea, Guyana, Honduras, India, Indonesia, Iraq, Italy, Jamaica, Jordan, Kenya, Kuwait, Lebanon, Liberia, Madagascar, Malaysia, Mali, Mauritania, Mauritius, Mexico, Montenegro, Morocco, Mozambique, Netherlands*, Niger, Nigeria, Norway, Pakistan, Peru, Philippines, Portugal, Qatar, Republic of Korea, Romania, Russian Federation, Saudi Arabia, Senegal, Serbia, Sierra Leone, Slovakia, Somalia, Spain, Sri Lanka, Sudan, Sweden, Togo, Trinidad and Tobago, Tunisia, Turkey, United Republic of Tanzania, Uruguay, Venezuela (Bolivarian Republic of), Zambia. **(78)**
United Nations Convention on the Carriage of Goods by Sea, 1978 (Hamburg Rules)	Entered into force 1 November 1992	Albania, Austria, Barbados, Botswana, Burkina Faso, Burundi, Cameroon, Chile, Czech Republic, Dominican Republic, Egypt, Gambia, Georgia, Guinea, Hungary, Jordan, Kazakhstan, Kenya, Lebanon, Lesotho, Liberia, Malawi, Morocco, Nigeria, Paraguay, Romania, Saint Vincent and the Grenadines, Senegal, Sierra Leone, Syrian Arab Republic, Tunisia, Uganda, United Republic of Tanzania, Zambia. **(34)**
International Convention on Maritime Liens and Mortgages, 1993	Entered into force 5 September 2004	Albania, Benin, Ecuador, Estonia, Lithuania, Monaco, Nigeria, Peru, Russian Federation, Spain, Saint Kitts and Nevis, Saint Vincent and the Grenadines, Syrian Arab Republic, Tunisia, Ukraine, Vanuatu. **(16)**
United Nations Convention on International Multimodal Transport of Goods, 1980	Not yet in force – requires 30 contracting parties	Burundi, Chile, Georgia, Lebanon, Liberia, Malawi, Mexico, Morocco, Rwanda, Senegal, Zambia. **(11)**
United Nations Convention on Conditions for Registration of Ships, 1986	Not yet in force – requires 40 contracting parties with at least 25 per cent of the world's tonnage as per annex III to the Convention	Albania, Bulgaria, Côte d'Ivoire, Egypt, Georgia, Ghana, Haiti, Hungary, Iraq, Liberia, Libyan Arab Jamahiriya, Mexico, Oman, Syrian Arab Republic. **(14)**
International Convention on Arrest of Ships, 1999	Entered into force 14 September 2011	Albania, Algeria, Benin, Bulgaria, Ecuador, Estonia, Latvia, Liberia, Spain, Syrian Arab Republic. **(10)**
United Nations Convention on Contracts for the International Carriage of Goods Wholly or Partly by Sea, 2008	Not yet in force – requires 20 contracting parties	Spain **(1)**

Source: For official status information, see http://www.un.org/law.

*Following the modification in the structure of the Kingdom of the Netherlands, from 10 October 2010, the Kingdom will consist of four autonomous countries: the Netherlands (European part and Caribbean part, the latter comprising Bonaire, Sint Eustatius and Saba), Aruba, Curaçao and Sint Maarten.

ENDNOTES

1. See further, Berlingieri F (2006). *Berlingieri on Arrest of Ships*. London: Informa, 4th ed.; Berlingieri F (2005). "The 1952 Arrest Convention revisited." L.M.C.L.Q., 3 August, 327-337; Gaskell N and Shaw R (1999), "The Arrest Convention." L.M.C.L.Q., 4 November, 470-490.

2. The official text and status of the 1999 Arrest Convention can be found on the UNCTAD website at www.unctad.org/ttl/legal.

3. For further information on the Diplomatic Conference see http://www.unctad.org/Templates/meeting.asp?intItemID=1942&lang=1&m=5674.

4. See also the Report of the Chairman of the Main Committee, which highlights issues that had been the subject of considerable debate within the Committee, *Report of the United Nations/International Maritime Organization Diplomatic Conference on the Arrest of Ships* (A/CONF.188/5) at pp. 19-23, available on the UNCTAD website at www.unctad.org/ttl/legal.

5. As at 31 July 2011, the following States are Contracting Parties to both Arrest Conventions: Algeria, Benin, Latvia, Spain and the Syrian Arab Republic, although Spain has denounced the Convention with effect from 28/03/2012. For further status information on the 1952 Arrest Convention see http://diplomatie.belgium.be/fr/.

6. Denunciation of the 1952 Arrest Convention will take effect 12 months after its deposit with the Belgian Government. Contracting States to both Conventions will, therefore, for a transitional period at least, continue to be bound by the 1952 Convention after the 1999 Arrest Convention enters into force.

7. For the official text and current status of the 1993 MLM Convention, see www.unctad.org/ttl/legal.

8. See Articles 1(1)(s), 1(1)(u) and 1(1)(v), 1999 Arrest Convention.

9. In particular, "claims for wages and other sums due to the master, officers and other members of the vessel's complement in respect of their employment on the vessel, including costs of repatriation and social insurance contributions payable on their behalf", see Article 4, 1993 MLM Convention.

10. See Article 1(1)(o), 1999 Arrest Convention.

11. For further information, see the *BIMCO/ISF Manpower 2010 Update*, available for a fee from www.bimco.org.

12. Berlingieri debates the question of whether the 1952 Arrest Convention was limited to sea-going ships, as the only reference to such ships is in the title of the Convention, see Berlingieri F "The 1952 Arrest Convention revisited", at pp. 327-328.

13. Spain has reserved the right to exclude the application of the 1999 Arrest Convention in respect of ships not flying the flag of a Contracting State.

14. For the purposes of the 1999 Arrest Convention, "Maritime Claim" means a claim arising out of one or more of the following: (a) loss or damage caused by the operation of the ship; (b) loss of life or personal injury; (c) salvage operations; (d) environmental damage; (e) wreck removal; (f) any agreement relating to the use of hire of the ship; (g) carriage of goods or passengers; (h) carriage of goods, including luggage; (i) general average; (j) towage; (k) pilotage; (l) goods, materials, provisions, bunkers, equipment supplied or services rendered to the ship; (m) construction, reconstruction, repair, converting or equipping of the ship; (n) waterway dues and charges; (o) crews' wages; (p) disbursements; (q) insurance premiums; (r) any commissions, brokerages or agency fees payable in respect of the ship; (s) any dispute as to ownership or possession of the ship; (t) any dispute as to the employment or earnings of the ship; (u) a mortgage, hypothèque or a charge of the same nature on the ship; and (v) any dispute arising out of a contract for the sale of the ship (see Article 1).

15. "Bottomry" refers to a maritime contract (now almost obsolete) by which the owner of a ship borrows money for equipping or repairing the vessel and, for a definite term, pledges the ship as security – it being stipulated that if the ship be lost in the specified voyage or period, by any of the perils enumerated, the lender shall lose his money.

16. A significant deletion in this provision is the words "registered" or "registrable" in relation to mortgages or hypothèques. Their previous inclusion in the 1952 Arrest Convention was deemed to prevent the holder of an equitable mortgage from enforcing his security by arrest; an important type of security in container leasing and certain yacht financing agreements. It has been noted that a potential consequence of this change might be to allow a ship to be arrested for an unregistered mortgage or charge, even where that ship has been sold to a bona fide purchaser, as there is no link required between the person liable for the debt secured by a mortgage or charge and the owner at the time of arrest; see Gaskell N and Shaw R, at pp. 477-478.

17. See further the Report of the Chairman of the Main Committee contained in the *Report of the United Nations/International Maritime Organization Diplomatic Conference on the Arrest of Ships* (A/CONF.188/5) at pp. 19-23, available on the UNCTAD website at www.unctad.org/ttl/legal.

18. For further information and a brief overview of the position of selected jurisdictions on the matter, see Berlingieri on Arrest of Ships, Chapter 10.

19   *Berlingieri on Arrest of Ships*, at para. 99.130.

20   On 5 July 1978, a Protocol to the Convention was adopted which establishes the Special Drawing Right (SDR) as the currency for the settlement of compensation rather than the gold franc used in the original CMR Convention. The Protocol entered into force on 28 December 1980 and as at 31 July 2011, had 41 Contracting Parties.

21   For the official text and ratification status of the CMR Convention and its Protocols, see http://live.unece.org/trans/conventn/legalinst.html#25.

22   For further information, see Clarke M (2008). *International Carriage of Goods by Road: CMR*. London: Informa, 5th ed.; and Clarke M and Yates D (2008). Contracts of Carriage by Land and Air, London: Informa, 2nd ed..

23   Subsequently, as at 31 July 2011, the Czech Republic and Spain have also acceded to the e-CMR Protocol. Other Contracting States include Bulgaria, Latvia, the Netherlands and Switzerland.

24   The Kyoto Protocol was adopted in Kyoto, Japan, on 11 December 1997. It came into force on 16 February 2005, and, as at 31 July 2011, had 192 Parties. It is an international agreement linked to the United Nations Framework Convention on Climate Change (UNFCCC), 1992, which provides the overall framework for international efforts to tackle climate change. While UNFCCC encourages developed countries to stabilize greenhouse gas (GHG) emissions, the Kyoto Protocol sets specific commitments, binding 37 developed countries to cut GHG emissions by about 5 per cent from 1990 levels over the five-year period from 2008 to 2012. The Protocol places a heavier burden on developed countries, as the largest contributors to GHG emissions over the years, under the principle of *Common but Differentiated Responsibilities and Respective Capabilities (CBDR)*. For more information, see the UNFCCC website at http://www.unfccc.int.

25   Overall GHG emissions from international shipping are estimated at 2.7 per cent of global GHG emissions from fuel combustion in 2007, or more than double the GHG emissions from international air transport.

26   See the Second IMO GHG Study 2009, available at http://www5.imo.org/SharePoint/blastDataHelper.asp/data_id%3D27795/GHGStudyFINAL.pdf.

27   For an overview of the MEPC's work in recent years, see Chapter 6 of the 2008, 2009 and 2010 editions of the *Review of Maritime Transport.*

28   For further information on the package of technical and operational reduction measures for ships that was agreed at MEPC 59, see http://www.imo.org/OurWork/Environment/PollutionPrevention/AirPollution/Documents/Technical%20 and%20operational%20reduction%20measures.pdf.

29   For an overview of a range of potential approaches to mitigation in maritime transport, see also the Summary of Proceedings from the *UNCTAD Multi-year Expert Meeting on Transport and Trade Facilitation: Maritime Transport and the Climate Change Challenge*, 16–18 February 2009, Geneva. UNCTAD/DTL/TLB/2009/1, at pp. 11-15, available on the UNCTAD website at www.unctad.org/ttl/legal.

30   See the *Review of Maritime Transport 2010*, at pp. 118-123.

31   MEPC 61/24, *Report of the Marine Environment Protection Committee on its sixty-first session (secretariat).*

32   See the submission by the Clean Shipping Coalition (CSC): MEPC 61/5/10, *Speed Reduction – the key to the fast and efficient reduction of greenhouse gas emissions from ships.*

33   MEPC 61/5/17, *Decision criteria for establishing EEDI correction factors (United States).*

34   Correction factors, in this context, are mathematical components that may be used while calculating the EEDI of a ship. These factors will allow the calculation of the minimum energy efficiency requirement for ships to vary, where necessary, to take into account special characteristics of particular ships, e.g. ice-classed ships, or particular weather conditions, e.g. wave and wind factors.

35   MEPC 61/5/32. *Consideration of the Energy Efficiency Design Index for New Ships – Minimum installed power to maintain safe navigation in adverse conditions (IACS).*

36   MEPC 61/5/12. *Consideration of a principle for alternate calculation or exemption of EEDI in ships with special circumstances (Vanuatu).*

37   MEPC 61/5/20. *Consideration of CO2 abatement technologies (Singapore).*

38   MEPC 61/5. *Preliminary assessment of capacity-building implications (Vice-Chairman).*

39   See further. http://www.imo.org/MediaCentre/PressBriefings/Pages/Republic-of-Korea-to-assist-IMO-in-building-capacity-in-developing-countries-to-address-Greenhouse-Gas-Emissions-from-Ships.aspx.

40   MEPC 61/5/3, *Report of the outcome of the Intersessional Meeting of the Working Group on Energy Efficiency Measures for Ships.*

41   MEPC 61/WP.10.

42   See MEPC 61/24, at p. 41.

43   Annex VI of MARPOL 73/78 deals with the prevention of air pollution from ships. Annex VI entered into force on 19 May 2005 and, as at 31 July 2011, has 65 Contracting States, representing 89.82 per cent of world tonnage.

44   MARPOL 73/78 is the main international convention dealing with prevention of pollution of the marine environment

by ships from operational or accidental causes. It includes six technical annexes that aim to prevent specific types of pollution including pollution caused by oil (Annex I), chemicals (Annex II), harmful substances in packaged form (Annex III), sewage (Annex IV), garbage (Annex V) and air pollution (Annex VI). The Convention, along with Annexes I and II, entered into force on 2 October 1983. As at 31 July 2011, it has 150 Contracting States, representing 99.14 per cent of world tonnage. The remaining Annexes have been ratified separately by States, with all Annexes having gained widespread acceptance. For the status of each Annex, see www.imo.org.

45 See further MEPC 61/24, at pp. 37-42.

46 See MEPC 61/24, at paras. 5.53-5.55.

47 IMO Circular Letter No.3128, dated 24 November 2010.

48 IMO Circular Letter No.3170, dated 1 March 2011.

49 MEPC 62/6/9, *Consideration and adoption of amendments to mandatory instruments (India)*.

50 In this context, it is interesting to note that the International Chamber of Commerce (ICC) issued recommendations for CO2 reduction for ships giving support to adoption of a package of measures by way of amendments to MARPOL Annex VI.

51 For further information, see MEPC 62/64, Report of the *Marine Environment Protection Committee on its sixty-second session (secretariat);* and MEPC 62/24/Add.1. The outcome of the roll-call vote can be found at MEPC 62/24, at p. 57.

52 For further information, see MEPC 61/24, at pp. 42-44; MEPC 61/5/1, *Outcome of the United Nations Climate Change Talks held in Bonn, Germany in May/June 2010 (secretariat)*; MEPC 61/5/18 and MEPC 61/5/18/Rev.1, *High-Level Advisory Group of the United Nations Secretary-General on Climate Change Financing (secretariat)*.

53 In this context, the MEPC considered the outcome of the August 2010 session of the UNFCCC Ad Hoc Working Groups: *Ad Hoc Working Group on Further Commitments for Annex I Parties under the Kyoto Protocol* (AWG-KP) 13 and *Ad Hoc Working Group on Long-term Cooperative Action under the Convention* (AWG-LCA) 11. See further MEPC 61/5/1/Add.1.

54 MEPC 61/24, at p. 43.

55 A technical report by the UNCTAD secretariat, *Oil Prices and Maritime Freight Rates: An Empirical Investigation,* UNCTAD/DTL/TLB/2009/2, focusing on the effect of oil prices as a determinant of maritime freight rates, served to assist in the work of the *IMO Expert Group on Feasibility Study and Impact Assessment of Possible Market-based Measures.* The technical report is available on the UNCTAD website at www.unctad.org/ttl/legal.

56 MEPC 61/INF.2, *Full report of the work undertaken by the Expert Group on Feasibility Study and Impact Assessment of possible Market-based Measures (secretariat).* For the Executive Summary, see MEPC 61/5/39 (Secretary-General). See also the *Review of Maritime Transport 2010*, at pp. 122-123, where the conclusions of the report are reproduced in full.

57 For a concise summary of the proposals, see Chapter 6 of the *Review of Maritime Transport 2010.*

58 Comments on the use of credits of the Clean Development Mechanism in market-based measures for international shipping (Republic of Korea); MEPC 61/5/19, *Market-Based Measures – inequitable burden on developing countries (India)*; MEPC 61/5/24, *Uncertainties and Problems in Market-based Measures (China and India).*

59 See also MEPC 61/24/Annex 8, *Statements by the Delegations of India and China on the Report of the Expert Group on Market-based Measures to Reduce Green-house Gas Emissions from the Maritime Sector.*

60 See MEPC 61/24/Annex 7, *Terms of Reference for the Third Intersessional Meeting of the Working Group on GHG Emissions from Ships (GHG-WG 3).*

61 See MEPC 61/24/Annex 7, Appendix, *Criteria agreed by MEPC 60 for use by the MBM-EG.*

62 MEPC 62/5/1.

63 GHG-WG 3/2, *Alternatives to Market-based Measures (Bahamas)*; GHG-WG 3/2/1, *International Greenhouse Gas Fund (Cyprus, Denmark, the Marshall Islands and Nigeria)*; MEPC 61/5/19, *Market-Based Measures – inequitable burden on developing countries (India).*

64 The views expressed by individual delegations are reflected in MEPC 62/5/1, *Report of the third Intersessional Meeting of the working group on greenhouse gas emissions from ships (secretariat),* at pp. 6-7. See also the separate statements of the delegations of Brazil, Australia, Greece and India, which are reproduced in Annex 1 of MEPC 62/5/1.

65 GHG-WG 3/2, *Alternatives to Market-based Measures (Bahamas).*

66 MEPC 61/5/19, *Market-Based Measures – inequitable burden on developing countries (India).*

67 See also the general statement by the delegation of Brazil which expresses the view that no measures should be imposed mandatorily on non-Annex 1 (of the Kyoto Protocol) countries, MEPC 62/5/1, Annex 1.

68 See GHG-WG 3/2/1, *International Greenhouse Gas Fund (Cyprus, Denmark, the Marshall Islands and Nigeria).*

69 See MEPC 62/5/1, at para. 2.22.

70 For a summary of 12 supporting arguments put forward by each group, see further MEPC 62/5/1, at pp. 8-10.

138

REVIEW OF MARITIME TRANSPORT 2011

71 Summaries of the proposals along with the presentations can be found in Annex 2 of MEPC 62/5/1.

72 GHG-WG 3/3/7 (Germany); GHG-WG 3/3/8 (United Kingdom); GHG-WG 3/INF.2 (the Netherlands); GHG-WG 3/INF.3 (European Commission); GHG-WG 3/3/1 (Republic of Korea); MEPC 61/5/19 (India); MEPC 61/5/21 (China and India); MEPC 61/5/28 (Republic of Korea).

73 GHG-WG 3/3 (Greece).

74 In a press release on 20 May 2011 by the newly merged International Chamber of Shipping (ICS) and the International Shipping Federation (IFS), the ICS gave express preference to a levy/compensation fund-based MBM rather than an emissions trading scheme. See http://www.marisec.org/pressreleases.htm#20may11.

75 GHG-WG 3/3/35 (Norway).

76 For further information on the various debates, see MEPC 62/5/1, at pp. 13-17.

77 MEPC 61/INF.2, *Full report of the work undertaken by the Expert Group on Feasibility Study and Impact Assessment of possible Market-based Measures (secretariat).*

78 See further, MEPC 62/5/1, at pp. 16-17, and Annex 3.

79 The above mentioned weaknesses are noted in Annex 5 of MEPC 62/5/1.

80 For references to the documents consulted see MEPC 62/5/1, at pp. 18-21.

81 See only the statement of India, which is reproduced in Annex 1 of MEPC 62/5/1.

82 See MEPC 62/5/1 at para. 3.63.

83 Vivid Economics, an external consultant, had already provided detailed analysis on the economic impact on trade, for illustrative products and markets, due to the introduction of a MBM for reduction of GHG emissions from international shipping for the meeting of the Expert Group. The full report can be found at http://www.imo.org/OurWork/Environment/PollutionPrevention/AirPollution/Documents/VividEconomicsIMOFinalReport.pdf. A presentation on the outcome on its assessment was provided at the Intersessional Meeting of the Working Group, see GHG-WH 3/WP.4.

84 It is envisaged that a further impact study will build upon the earlier study of the *Expert Group on Feasibility Study and Impact Assessment of Possible Market-based Measures* (MEPC 61/INF.2).

85 Figures have been taken from the International Maritime Bureau's (IMB) Piracy Reporting Centre (PRC), http://www.icc-ccs.org/piracy-reporting-centre/piracynewsafigures. Figures are correct as of 23 May 2011. Quarterly and Annual Reports from the PRC are available free of charge, upon request at http://www.icc-ccs.org/. For further statistics on international piracy and armed robbery at sea, see the website of the United States Department of Transportation, Research and Innovative Technology Administration, Bureau of Transport Statistics, in particular, http://www.bts.gov/publications/special_reports_and_issue_briefs/special_report/2010_04_22/html/entire.html.

86 For the IMO 2010 Annual Report on acts of piracy and armed robbery against ships, see MSC.4/Circ.169, 1 April 2011. Information on all acts reported to have occurred or to have been attempted in 2010 can be found in the Annexes to the Circular along with a regional analysis of acts and a graphical presentation by area of reports received during 2010 alone, and of reports received between 1984 and 2010. Quarterly and Annual reports on piracy and armed robbery are available from the IMO at http://www.imo.org/OurWork/Security/PiracyArmedRobbery/Pages/PirateReports.aspx.

87 For further information on piracy prone areas, see http://www.icc-ccs.org/piracy-reporting-centre/prone-areas-and-warnings.

88 MSC 89/25, *Report of the Maritime Safety Committee on its eighty-ninth session (secretariat).*

89 *Interim Guidance to shipowners, ship operators and shipmasters on the use of privately contracted armed security personnel on board ships in the High Risk Area (MSC.1/Circ.1405); and Interim Recommendations for Flag States regarding the use of privately contracted armed security personnel on board ships in the High Risk Area (MSC.1/Circ.1406).* The "High Risk Area" is an area defined by the Best Management Practices (BMP) unless otherwise defined by the Flag State. The latest edition of the BMP states that "the High Risk Area for piracy attacks defines itself by where the piracy attacks have taken place. For the purposes of the BMP, this is an area bounded by Suez to the North, 10°S and 78°E," see BMP3, at Section 2.

90 IMO has previously adopted *Recommendations to governments for preventing and suppressing piracy and armed robbery against ships (MSC.1/Circ.1333); Guidance to shipowners and ship operators, shipmasters and crew on preventing and suppressing piracy and armed robbery against ships (MSC.1/Circ.1334); and Piracy and armed robbery against ships in waters off the coast of Somalia: Best Management Practices to Deter Piracy off the Coast of Somalia and in the Arabian Sea Area developed by the industry (MSC.1/Circ.1337).*

91 It should be noted in this respect that ships calling at South African Ports which do not have a license for any arms that are on board the vessel will risk arrest and detention by the South African Police Service. The 21-day rule for obtaining a permit is being strictly enforced by South African authorities, without exception. For further information see http://www.skuld.com/News/News/South-Africa-Guns-and-ammunition-on-ships-calling-at-South-African-ports/?MyMode=print.

92 The latest edition of BMP can be accessed at http://www.icc-ccs.org/images/stories/pdfs/bmp3.pdf.

93 See MSC.1/ Circ.1404.

94   See Assembly resolution A.1025(26).

95   See above, FN 89.

96   For a discussion of the numerous issues that arise when considering a legal definition of sea piracy see Dubner B H (2011). On the Definition of the Crime of Sea Piracy Revisited: Customary vs. Treaty Law and the Jurisdictional Implications Thereof. *Journal of Maritime Law and Commerce*. Vol. 42, No. 1, January, and the references therein.

97   See further the Report of the Legal Committee on the Work of its 98th Session, document LEG 98/14, at pp. 18-22. See also the Report of the Legal Committee on its 97th Session, document LEG 97/15, at pp. 19-23.

98   The documents attached at annex to Circular Letter No.3180 include *Piracy: elements of national legislation pursuant to the United Nations Convention on the Law of the Sea, 1982* (documents LEG 98/8/1 and LEG 98/8/3, submitted by the United Nations Division for Ocean Affairs and the Law of the Sea); *Establishment of a legislative framework to allow for effective and efficient piracy prosecutions* (document LEG 98/8/2, submitted by the UN Office on Drugs and Crime); *Uniform and consistent application of the provisions of international conventions relating to piracy* (document LEG 98/8, submitted by the IMO secretariat); and *Establishment of a legislative framework to allow for effective and efficient piracy prosecutions* (document LEG 98/8/4, submitted by Ukraine).

99   See further, LEG 98/14, at pp. 18-19.

100   See Annex to the Letter dated 24 January 2011 from the Secretary-General to the President of the Security Council (S/2011/30), 25 January 2011.

101   Access to national legislation on piracy, as provided by Member States to the United Nations, is available at http://www.un.org/Depts/los/piracy/piracy_national_legislation.htm.

102   For further information on the Djibouti Code of Conduct, along with the full text and current signatories to the code, see http://www.imo.org/OurWork/Security/PIU/Pages/DCoC.aspx.

103   As at 31 July 2011, signatories to the Djibouti Code of Conduct include Comoros, Djibouti, Egypt, Eritrea, Ethiopia, Jordan, Kenya, Madagascar, Maldives, Mauritius, Oman, Saudi Arabia, Seychelles, Somalia, Sudan, the United Arab Emirates, the United Republic of Tanzania and Yemen. There are now three countries that remain eligible to sign the Code, namely, France, Mozambique and South Africa.

104   See *Masefield AG v Amlin Corporate Member Ltd.* [2011] EWCA Civ 24 (26 Jan 2011), on appeal from the decision of the High Court [2010] EWHC 280 (Comm) (18 Feb 2010).

105   The Court of Appeal also confirmed that, under national law, the payment of a ransom is not illegal.

106   It may be of interest to note that MARSH, a global insurance broker and risk adviser, has published a document titled *Piracy – the insurance implications*, intended to be used as a practical guide to shipping companies based on the situation in June 2011. The guide can be accessed at http://documents.marsh.com/documents/piracywhitepaper07-11-11.pdf.

107   *Cosco Bulk Carrier Co. Ltd. V Team-Up Owning Co. Ltd. (The Saldanha)* [2010] EWHC 1340 (Comm) (11 June 2010).

108   For further information on BIMCO's piracy-related work, see https://www.bimco.org.

109   For further information on the SAFE Framework, see http://www.wcoomd.org/files/1.%20Public%20files/PDFandDocuments/Procedures%20and%20Facilitation/safe_package/safe_package_I.pdf.

110   For the list of WCO members who have expressed their intention to implement the SAFE Framework, see http://www.wcoomd.org/files/1.%20Public%20files/PDFandDocuments/Enforcement/FOS_bil_05.pdf.

111   According to information provided by the WCO secretariat.

112   The current SAFE Package can be accessed at http://www.wcoomd.org/home_pfoverviewboxes_safepackage.htm.

113   For the PSCG Statement on AEO Benefits see http://www.wcoomd.org/files/1.%20Public%20files/PDFandDocuments/Procedures%20and%20Facilitation/safe_package/safe_package_VI.pdf.

114   For the self-assessment questionnaire, see http://ec.europa.eu/taxation_customs/resources/documents/customs/policy_issues/customs_security/aeo_self_assessment_en.pdf. Explanatory notes are also available at http://ec.europa.eu/taxation_customs/resources/documents/customs/policy_issues/customs_security/aeo_self_assessment_explanatory_en.pdf.

115   Commission Regulation (EU) No 197/2010 of 9 March 2010 amending Regulation (EEC) No 2454/93 laying down provisions for the implementation of Council Regulation (EEC) No 2913/92 establishing the Community Customs Code.

116   For the import/entry Guidelines, see http://ec.europa.eu/ecip/documents/procedures/import_entry_guidelines_en.pdf.

117   For the export/exit Guidelines, see http://ec.europa.eu/ecip/documents/procedures/export_exit_guidelines_en.pdf.

118   For access to the various databases in relation to the Taxation and Customs Union, see http://ec.europa.eu/ecip/information_resources/databases/index_en.htm.

119   See http://ec.europa.eu/ecip/documents/who_is/taxud1633_2008_rev2_en.pdf. For further information in respect of national implementation see http://ec.europa.eu/ecip/documents/who_is/eori_national_implementation_en.pdf.

120 The 88th session of the MSC was held in November/December 2010, and the 89th session was held in May 2011.

121 For further information on maritime security, see the following reports of the UNCTAD secretariat, *Container Security: Major Initiatives and related International Developments* (UNCTAD/SDTE/TLB/2004/1), and *Maritime Security: ISPS Code Implementation, Costs and related Financing* (UNCTAD/SDTE/TLB/2007/1), available on the UNCTAD website at www.unctad.org/ttl/legal. See also Asariotis, R., 'Implementation of the ISPS Code: an overview of recent developments', J.I.M.L. 2005, 11(4), 266-287.

122 MSC 88/4, *Developments since MSC 87 (secretariat).*

123 See further MSC 89/4, *Need for updating the information provided in the GISIS Maritime Security Module (secretariat)*, and MSC 88/26, at pp. 17-18.

124 MSC 89/4/1, *Report of the Correspondence Group on the Maritime Security Manual (Canada).*

125 MSC 89/INF.13, *Maritime Security Manual – Guidance for port facilities, ports and ships (Canada).*

126 The MSM Correspondence Group had been established at MSC 88. For its Terms of Reference see MSC 88/26, at paragraph 4.40.

127 Document MSC 89/4/2, *Consideration of periodical survey to Ship Security Alert System (SSAS)*, submitted by the Republic of Korea was also considered by the Committee.

128 MSC.1/Circ.1283, 22 December 2008.

129 See MSC 88/4/2, *Enhancements to the ISPS Code (Canada).*

130 See further the *Interim scheme for the compliance of special purpose ships with the special measures to enhance maritime security* (MSC.1/Circ.1189).

131 See *Guidance on voluntary self-assessment by SOLAS Contracting Governments and by Port Facilities* (MSC.1/Circ.1192); *Guidance on voluntary self-assessment by administrations and for ship security* (MSC.1/Circ.1193); and *Effective implementation of SOLAS Chapter XI-2 and the ISPS Code* (MSC.1/Circ.1194).

132 See, for example, ISO/PAS 28002:2010: Security management systems for the supply chain – Development of resilience in the supply chain – Requirements with guidance for use; and ISO 28005-2:2011: Security management systems for the supply chain – Electronic port clearance (EPC) – Part 2: Core data elements. For further information, see www.iso.org.

133 In particular, work continues on ISO 28004 and ISO 28005.

134 The ISO Action Plan for developing countries 2011-2015 can be accessed at http://www.iso.org/iso/iso_strategy_and_policies. See also the ISO Strategic Plan 2011-2015.

135 See the *Review of Maritime Transport 2010*, at pp. 128-130. The ISO Action Plan for developing countries 2005-2010 can be accessed at http://www.iso.org/iso/actionplan_2005.pdf.

136 Prior to the oil spill, the "Hague Memorandum" had been agreed in 1978 between a number of maritime administrations in Western Europe, which dealt mainly with enforcement of shipboard living and working conditions as required by ILO Convention no. 147.

137 As at 31 July 2011, the 27 member States of the Paris MoU are Belgium, Bulgaria, Canada, Croatia, Cyprus, Denmark, Estonia, Finland, France, Germany, Greece, Iceland, Ireland, Italy, Latvia, Lithuania, Malta, Netherlands, Norway, Poland, Portugal, Romania, the Russian Federation, Slovenia, Spain, Sweden and the United Kingdom. Further information on the Paris MoU, as well as the full text including the 32nd amendment can be found at http://www.parismou.org/.

138 For further information, see the Paris MoU Annual Reports, https://www.parismou.org/Publications/Annual_reports/.

139 The 15 international conventions listed in the Memorandum include the International Convention on Load Lines, 1966 and its 1988 Protocol; the International Convention for the Safety of Life at Sea, 1974 (SOLAS) and its Protocols of 1978 and 1988; the International Convention for the Prevention of Pollution from Ships, 1973, as modified by the Protocol of 1978, and as further amended by the Protocol of 1997 (MARPOL); the International Convention on Standards of Training, Certification and Watchkeeping for Seafarers, 1978; the Convention on the International Regulations for Preventing Collisions at Sea, 1972; the International Convention on Tonnage Measurement of Ships, 1969; the Merchant Shipping (Minimum Standards) Convention, 1976 and its 1996 Protocol; the International Convention on Civil Liability for Oil Pollution Damage, 1969; Protocol of 1992 to amend the International Convention on Civil Liability for Oil Pollution Damage, 1969; the International Convention on the Control of Harmful Anti-Fouling Systems on Ships, 2001; and the International Convention on Civil Liability for Bunker Oil Pollution Damage, 2001.

140 For a list of ships currently banned from the Paris MoU region see https://www.parismou.org/Inspection_efforts/Bannings/Banning_list/.

141 "Overriding factors" are considered sufficiently serious to trigger an additional inspection at Priority I and include, inter alia, ships involved in a collision, grounding or stranding; ships accused of violating the provisions on discharge of harmful substances or effluents; and ships which have been withdrawn or suspended from their Class for safety reasons.

142 "Unexpected factors" are those that may indicate a serious threat to the safety of the ship, crew or the environment, such as ships that do not comply with reporting obligations; ships reported with outstanding deficiencies or previously

detained ships; ships operated in a manner to pose danger; or ships reported with problems concerning their cargo, in particular noxious or dangerous cargo. The need to undertake an additional inspection is, however, left to the discretion of the Member State.

143 Prior to the adoption of the STCW Convention, such standards were determined by national law irrespective of practices in other countries, which resulted in widespread differences in standards and procedures.

144 For the ratification status of the STCW Convention, see www.imo.org.

145 For further information, see a press release by IMO on the Conference http://www.imo.org/MediaCentre/PressBriefings/Pages/STCW-revised-adopted.aspx. The International Shipping Federation has produced new *Guidelines to the IMO STCW Convention* that take account of the recent amendments. See further http://www.marisec.org/pressreleases.htm#22march.

146 See further http://www.imo.org/OurWork/HumanElement/TrainingCertification/Pages/STCW-Convention.aspx.

147 See in particular, the *Review of Maritime Transport 2006,* at pp. 90-91, along with the applicable references to the *Maritime Labour Convention* in Chapter 6 of the subsequent editions of the *Review of Maritime Transport.*

148 For a list of the Conventions revised by the MLC 2006, see http://www.ilo.org/global/standards/maritime-labour-convention/WCMS_150389/lang--en/index.htm.

149 For status information of the *Maritime Labour Convention 2006*, see http://www.ilo.org/ilolex/cgi-lex/ratifce.pl?C186.

150 See document LEG 98/14, *Report of the Legal Committee of the work at its ninety-eighth session (secretariat)*, at paragraph 5.1.

151 The mandate of the trade facilitation negotiations at the WTO is "to clarify and improve relevant aspects of Articles V, VIII and X of the GATT 1994 with a view to further expediting the movement, release and clearance of goods, including goods in transit". GATT Articles V (freedom of transit), VIII (fees and formalities connected with importation and exportation) and X (publication and administration of trade regulations), are therefore the main focus of the ongoing negotiations and the substantive measures in the draft text of trade facilitation agreement are crafted along these three existing articles.

152 Draft consolidated negotiating Text, Negotiating Group on Trade Facilitation (TN/TF/W/165/Rev.8), of 21 April 2011.

153 UNCTAD (2011). *Reflections on a Future Trade Facilitation Agreement: Implementation of Future WTO Obligations, A comparison of Existing WTO Provisions,* http://www.unctad.org/tlb20102.pdf.

154 For purposes of this publication we will make reference to the term of Regional Trade Agreements as the document that creates free trade zones and/or customs union between countries and/or territories.

155 With respect to trade in goods, this principle is contained in Article I of GATT.

156 *Decision on differential and more favorable treatment reciprocity and fuller participation of developing countries,* 28 November 1979 (L/4903).

157 See http://www.wto.org/english/tratop_e/region_e/region_e.htm.

158 Such as SAFE Framework of Standards to Secure and Facilitate Global Trade, ATA and Temporary Admission Conventions, and the WCO Data Model.

159 The International Convention on the Simplification and Harmonization of Customs procedures (Kyoto Convention) entered into force in 1974 and was revised and updated to ensure that it meets the current demands of governments and international trade. The WCO Council adopted the revised Kyoto Convention in June 1999 as the blueprint for modern and efficient customs procedures in the 21st century. More information can be found at http://www.wcoomd.org/home_pfoverviewboxes_tools_and_instruments_pfrevisedkyotoconv.htm.

160 UNCTAD (2011). *Trade Facilitation Measures in Regional Trade Arrangements.* Working Paper presented at the Ad Hoc Expert Meeting on Trade Facilitation in Regional Trade Arrangements, 30-31 March 2011, Geneva.

161 Ibid.

162 Up-to-date and authoritative information on the status of international conventions is available from the relevant depository. For United Nations conventions, see the United Nations website at http://www.un.org/law. This site also provides links to a number of websites of other organizations, such as IMO (www.imo.org), ILO (www.ilo.org) and the United Nations Commission on International Trade Law (www.uncitral.org), containing information on conventions adopted under the auspices of each of them. Since the last reporting period, Albania and Ecuador acceded to the International Convention on Arrest of Ships, 1999. In addition, Spain was the first country to ratify the United Nations Convention on Contracts for the International Carriage of Goods Wholly or Partly by Sea (the "Rotterdam Rules").

DEVELOPING COUNTRIES' PARTICIPATION IN MARITIME BUSINESSES

CHAPTER 6

Developing countries are expanding their participation in a range of different maritime businesses. They already hold strong positions in ship scrapping, registration, and the supply of seafarers, and they have growing market shares in more capital-intensive or technologically advanced maritime sectors such as ship construction and owning. China and the Republic of Korea alone built 72.4 per cent of the world's ship capacity (in dwt) in 2010, and nine out of the twenty largest shipowning nations are developing countries.

Ship financing, insurance services and vessel classification are among the few maritime sectors that have, until today, been dominated by the more advanced economies. Here too, however, developing countries have recently been demonstrating their potential to become major market players. India, for instance, has joined the International Association of Classification Societies, and through this gains easier access to the global ship classification market. China now hosts two of the world's largest banks dealing with ship financing.

This chapter analyses these and other maritime businesses. It discusses the current and potential participation of developing countries based on a wide range of sector data, and provides examples illustrating the growth paths of selected developing countries in different maritime businesses. Furthermore, the chapter explores the linkages between maritime sectors, as some develop more autonomously than others. It also assesses how policy measures and a country's stage of development may influence its involvement in a maritime sector.

A.   MARITIME BUSINESSES IN DEVELOPING COUNTRIES

1.   Introduction

Forty years ago, when UNCTAD first produced the *Review of Maritime Transport,* the maritime industry as a whole was mostly located in developed countries, whereas today, developing countries have gained large market shares in many maritime businesses.[1] One example of this trend is shipbuilding – an industry that used to be dominated by members of the Organization for Economic Cooperation and Development (OECD). Today, the world's largest shipbuilding countries are China and the Republic of Korea, and the vessels built in these two countries are purchased by shipping companies worldwide. In 2001, the value of vessels exported from developed countries was higher than that exported from developing countries; however, in 2009, the total value of vessels exported from developing countries stood at $91 billion, compared to vessel exports worth $53 billon from developed countries (figure 6.1).

Traditionally, developed countries covered the entire maritime value chain or a large part of it, whereas today most maritime champions in both developing and developed countries specialize in a limited number of sectors (see also annex VII for a table with each country's market share in key maritime businesses). For example, Panama and Liberia are the largest open ship registries. Containers are mostly built in China. Dubai Ports is among the largest container terminal operators, with concessions on all continents. Bangladesh specializes in ship recycling. Many ships operate with crews from India, Indonesia and the Philippines.

The remainder of this chapter analyses the structure, intensity, and future prospects of selected maritime sectors in developing countries.

Section A introduces the maritime sectors that fall within the scope of this chapter, and refers to the different maritime businesses along a ship's lifecycle.

In Section B, a number of key maritime sectors are described individually, and country case studies illustrate examples of the growth paths of maritime businesses in developing countries.

Section C presents a cross-sector comparison which looks at the market concentration levels and market shares of developing countries. It also discusses linkages between different maritime sectors.

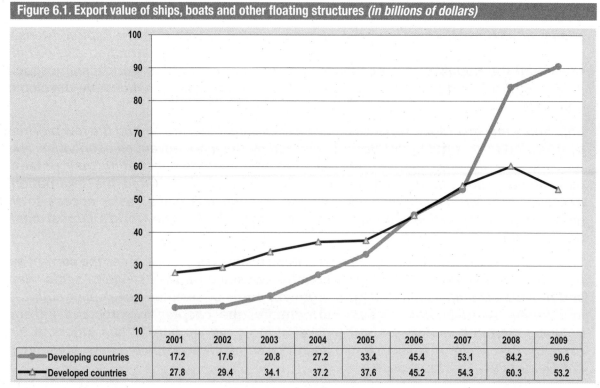

Figure 6.1. Export value of ships, boats and other floating structures *(in billions of dollars)*

	2001	2002	2003	2004	2005	2006	2007	2008	2009
Developing countries	17.2	17.6	20.8	27.2	33.4	45.4	53.1	84.2	90.6
Developed countries	27.8	29.4	34.1	37.2	37.6	45.2	54.3	60.3	53.2

Source: International Trade Centre. Trade Map. http://www.trademap.org/tradestat/Country_ SelProduct_TS.aspx (accessed in September 2011).

2.   Maritime shipping

Maritime shipping comprises a large variety of different businesses, a selection of which will be analysed in this chapter. Following Porter's value chain concept, the sectors are structured in chronological order.[2] Porter chooses a single business unit as the appropriate level to construct his value chain. Products pass through this sequence of functions and gain value at each activity.

For the purposes of this chapter, a selection of key maritime businesses is presented along a ship's lifecycle, starting from the building of the ship and continuing until its scrapping (figure 6.2).[3] The sectors are divided into (a) the core ship lifecycle industries and (b) the supporting industries, with an emphasis on container shipping. Conceptually, the object of the analysis is a cluster of maritime businesses, rather than a single business unit. The core businesses in the ship lifecycle industries include:

(a) *Ship building*: A manufacturing industry that conceptualizes and assembles different vessel types.

(b) *Ship owning*: The company purchases the ship through its own or external financial resources, and becomes the legal proprietor of the ship.

(c) *Ship operation*: A ship operator is usually responsible for management of the crew, route planning, servicing and maintenance. It also takes the entrepreneurial risks related to

capacity utilization and operational efficiency. Particularly in the case of containerized liner shipping, operation and ownership of ships often lie in different companies.

(d) *Ship scrapping*: Includes the breaking up of a ship at the end of its lifecycle and is often referred to as "ship recycling". The ship scrapping company mostly benefits from the reuse of the scrapped steel and some other components, although hazardous elements have to be recycled or disposed of.

During this lifecycle, the ship will require numerous support services, six of which are discussed in further detail in this chapter:

(a) *Ship financing*: The process whereby a lender, such as a bank, provides the financial resources to a shipowning company to purchase and maintain a vessel.

(b) *Ship classification*: Classification societies verify and certify compliance with technical rules and safety and other national and international standards for ship construction and operation. They work on behalf of the shipbuilder, the flag state, or other interested parties.

(c) *Ship registration*: This includes the process of national registration of a ship by a country under whose flag the vessel sails.

(d) *Ship insurance (P&I)*: This section focuses on protection and indemnity (P&I) clubs. A P&I club is a non-profit association that typically consists of

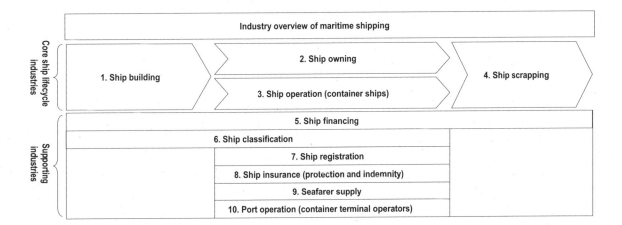

Figure 6.2. Maritime sectors along a ship's lifecycle

Source: UNCTAD secretariat.

shipowners, ship operators and ship charterers. It provides its members with mutual ship insurance services that also cover third-party liabilities, such as cargo or environmental damage.

(e) *Seafarers*: A ship's crew consists of officers (e.g. masters and engineers) and ratings (such as able seamen, oilers and cooks).

(f) *Terminal operators*: Terminal operators carry out the logistical processing of containers between ships and other modes of transports. Particularly in the case of container shipping, loading and unloading operations are mostly undertaken by private stevedoring companies which are often also responsible for the terminal operations, superstructure and IT systems.

Section B below examines these ten maritime sectors in more detail, and evaluates the participation of developing countries. In addition, it briefly introduces some other maritime and related businesses, such as container construction, leasing, ship repair, bunkering, brokering, and ship management.

B.   ANALYSIS OF SELECTED MARITIME BUSINESSES

This section analyses the current participation of developing countries within ten selected maritime businesses. A case study from a developing country, for each sector, aims to illustrate possible growth paths and corresponding influencing factors.

1. Ship building

Most large cargo-carrying vessels are now built in developing countries in Asia, while shipyards in Australia, Europe, and North and South America specialize in smaller vessels (e.g. tugboats and offshore supply ships) or other specialized non-cargo-carrying vessels (e.g. ferries and cruise ships).

Ship building has become a highly concentrated business (table 6.1). China and the Republic of Korea together built more than 72 per cent of dwt in 2010, with China specializing in dry bulk carriers and the Republic of Korea specializing more in container ships. Japan was the third-largest player, with 22 per cent. These three major producers combined reached a market share of 94 per cent of world tonnage. The Philippines, in fourth position with a market share of 1.2 per cent, focuses on bulk carriers. Production by South-East Asian shipbuilders concentrates on small types of

ships or on specific elements of ships. Singapore, for instance, is a world leader in oil rig building.

China has emerged as the world's largest shipbuilder, and expanded its dry bulk shipbuilding capacity by a factor of six between 2008 and 2010.[4] The country is also the world's largest importer of ship engines, with a value of $2.4 billion in 2009.[5] In addition to dry bulk carriers, China builds a large number of smaller ships, including tugboats and product tankers.

Country case study: The Republic of Korea expanding its product portfolio in shipbuilding

The diversification of the Republic of Korea's shipbuilding business and its competitiveness are a result of support policies for manufacturing industries at the "infant industry" stage. Such policies during the third and fourth five-year plans (1971–1981) allowed for accelerated development of the sector. To this day, the strategic importance of the sector is reflected in the structure of the country's Government, which includes a maritime affairs ministry with various supporting bodies.[6]

Table 6.2. shows the distribution of imports and exports to/from the Republic of Korea in different shipbuilding sectors. Dry cargo ships (including container ships) and passenger ships account for the largest share. The second most important sector includes the construction of light vessels, dredgers, floating docks and drill platforms. The fastest-growing export sector comprises warships and lifeboats, however these vessels remain at a comparatively low level, with a total value of $0.5 billion in 2010.

Shipbuilding companies from the Republic of Korea are often also active in other manufacturing industries – this is the case of Daewoo, Hyundai and Samsung. The Republic of Korea is the world's sixth-largest producer of steel, which is a crucial input for ship construction.[7] The country's Hanjin and Hyundai Merchant Marine (HMM) carriers, which are among the world's top 20 liner shipping companies, have most of their ships built in shipyards in the Republic of Korea, which specialize in container ships, offshore vessels, oil tankers, and LNG tankers.

The country's shipbuilding sector is currently confronted by rising labour costs, which it is partly able to offset by achieving constant increases in productivity. The Republic of Korea's average labour costs for the manufacture of transportation equipment tripled between 1998 ($7.90 per hour) and 2007 ($23.30 per hour), whereas unit labour costs had an average annual growth rate of only 1.67 per cent from 2000 until 2009.[8]

Table 6.1. Top 20 economies for shipbuilding, 2010 deliveries[a] (percentage of built tonnage)

Rank		Tankers	Bulk carriers	Other dry cargo/ passenger	Offshore	Others	Total 1000 dwt	Accumulated market share percentage	Number of ships
1	China	23.8	65.7	9.7	0.4	0.3	61 499	41.1	1 413
2	Republic of Korea	40.6	34.7	23.0	1.6	0.0	46 924	72.4	526
3	Japan	29.7	59.2	11.0	0.0	0.0	32 598	94.2	580
4	Philippines	12.5	64.2	23.4	0.0	0.0	1 859	95.4	34
5	Romania	12.7	60.0	16.8	9.6	0.8	897	96.0	43
6	Viet Nam	1.9	75.4	20.8	0.9	1.1	840	96.6	132
7	Denmark	0.0	97.0	3.0	0.0	0.0	751	97.1	8
8	Taiwan Province of China	0.0	0.0	99.3	0.0	0.7	661	97.5	21
9	Croatia	67.5	19.6	11.8	0.0	1.0	531	97.9	16
10	Germany	7.1	6.3	82.3	2.3	2.0	524	98.2	36
11	Turkey	58.6	18.7	16.8	4.6	1.2	497	98.6	94
12	United States	71.3	0.0	1.0	25.7	2.0	332	98.8	76
13	Russian Federation	87.6	0.0	7.5	3.3	1.5	252	98.9	30
14	Spain	15.5	0.0	19.0	21.5	44.0	225	99.1	56
15	Indonesia	12.8	27.7	13.8	40.3	5.4	180	99.2	135
16	Netherlands	2.5	0.0	49.9	16.6	31.1	174	99.3	29
17	India	29.7	41.8	21.4	1.2	5.9	136	99.4	37
18	Poland	0.0	0.0	27.8	47.1	25.1	116	99.5	52
19	Italy	3.8	0.0	68.5	22.9	4.7	116	99.6	34
20	Bulgaria	4.8	70.0	25.1	0.0	0.0	103	99.7	6
-	World	30.1	53.1	15.3	1.2	0.3	149 746	100.0	3 748

Source: Compiled by the UNCTAD secretariat on the basis of data supplied by IHS Fairplay.

[a] Seagoing propelled merchant ships of 100 gross tons and above.

TABLE 6.2. Structure of ship imports and exports in the Republic of Korea, 2001 and 2010

Ship type	2001 Imports $1 000	2010 Imports $1 000	2001–2010 Increase/ decrease percentage	2001 Exports $1 000	2010 Exports $1 000	2001–2010 Increase/ decrease percentage	2001 Trade balance $1 000	2010 Trade balance $1 000
Cruise ships, cargo ships, barges	294 913	2 486 422	843%	8 168 147	37 073 448	454%	7 873 234	34 587 024
Light vessels, dredgers, floating docks, floating / submersible drill platforms	32 294	732 527	2268%	1 331 953	9 996 550	751%	1 299 659	9 264 023
Tugs and pusher craft	18 671	40 395	216%	159 235	54 463	-66%	-4 721	39 822
Warships, lifeboats and other rowing boats	8 634	37 381	433%	2 423	53 885	2224%	140 564	14 068
Vessels and other floating structures for breaking-up	3 463	24 973	721%	481	5 902	1227%	661	101
Floating structures (rafts, tanks, coffer dam, landing stages)	9 043	22 940	254%	10 993	4 517	-59%	-8 562	-17 038
Yachts and other vessels for pleasure or sports	7 144	14 063	197%	25 227	808	-97%	7 530	-20 456
Fishing vessels and factory ships	45	39	-13%	706	140	-80%	16 593	-36 573
Total	374 207	3 358 740	798%	9 699 165	47 189 713	387%	9 324 958	43 830 971

Source: Compiled by the UNCTAD secretariat on the basis of data from the International Trade Centre.

2.   Ship owning

The three largest shipowners are developed countries, namely Greece, Japan and Germany. Together, they account for 41 per cent of the world's deadweight tonnage. China ranks fourth, with an owned capacity of 108 million dwt. While the four largest shipowning countries together control about half of the world fleet, ownership of the other half is spread among a large number of countries, including many developing countries (see also chapter 2, and in particular, table 2.5).

The order book in table 6.3 shows that China can be expected to climb the ownership ranking in the future; the country's order book ranks second in the world. As a group, developing countries have a larger order book than developed countries, suggesting a growing market for developing countries in the future.

Country case study: Largest order book in Brazilian history

The case of Brazil shows how shipowning can be linked to a country's international trade in goods.

Building on the boom in its commodity exports, Brazil is expected, in the coming years, to achieve the highest fleet growth out of the top 35 shipowning countries. Underlying this projection is the country's order book, which is the world's largest order book in relation to its current fleet (table 6.3). It is also the largest order book in Brazilian history.

As at January 2011, Brazilian shipowners had a fleet which comprised 152 vessels and had a capacity of 10.9 million dwt. At a global level, Brazil's market share is below 1 per cent, ranking twenty-third in the world. In terms of deadweight tonnage, 38 per cent of the Brazilian fleet is made up of bulk carriers and 41 per cent is made up of tankers (table 6.4). These ship types mainly serve the demand created by the country's exports such as oil and iron ore and by the offshore industry. The largest oil-producing company in Brazil is the state-owned Petrobras, which operates 172 vessels, 52 of which are owned by the company.[9]

Table 6.4 analyses Brazil's fleet in terms of ship registration. More than 70 per cent of the country's

TABLE 6.3. Top 20 ship orderbooks by country of ownership, 1 January 2011

Rank		Number of ships	Value (billions of dollars)	Gross tonnage (millions of GT)	GT, world percentage	GT, accumulated world percentage	GT, ownership rank	GT orderbook as a % share of the owned fleet
1	Greece	715	42.3	39.2	13.6	13.6	1	28.2
2	China	801	36.0	36.7	12.7	26.4	4	45.0
3	Japan	535	31.2	26.7	9.3	35.6	2	19.5
4	Germany	714	33.8	24.9	8.6	44.3	3	29.4
5	Republic of Korea	310	17.3	17.2	6.0	50.3	7	42.8
6	Taiwan Province of China	179	13.6	11.7	4.1	54.3	10	50.7
7	Norway	322	20.7	8.7	3.0	57.3	5	17.5
8	Turkey	251	10.2	8.1	2.8	60.2	16	52.8
9	Italy	168	9.4	6.9	2.4	62.6	8	21.3
10	Brazil	106	12.1	6.9	2.4	65.0	27	108.1
11	Denmark	201	10.0	6.7	2.3	67.3	9	22.0
12	China, Hong Kong SAR	150	6.6	6.6	2.3	69.6	11	20.0
13	Singapore	281	7.5	6.5	2.3	71.8	12	28.8
14	United States	181	20.2	6.3	2.2	74.0	6	14.4
15	Israel	81	6.9	6.2	2.2	76.2	13	39.2
16	India	138	5.4	5.1	1.8	77.9	17	41.0
17	France	132	4.8	2.6	0.9	78.8	23	28.6
18	United Arab Emirates	102	4.0	2.5	0.9	79.7	25	31.0
19	Canada	58	3.2	2.3	0.8	80.5	14	14.6
20	Netherlands	204	3.9	1.9	0.7	81.2	20	19.9
-	World	7456	376.8	287.9	100.0	100.0	-	-

Source: Clarkson Research Services. *World Fleet Monitor.* As at 1 January 2011. Seagoing cargo-carrying vessels only.

TABLE 6.4. Brazilian-owned fleet, 1 January 2011							
	Total	Percentage of total					
		Brazil	Panama	Liberia	Bahamas	Marshall Islands	Others
Total number of ships	152	70.4	5.3	16.5	1.3	0.0	6.6
Total dwt	10 866 503	19.9	11.7	56.9	3.3	3.1	8.1
Bulk carriers, dwt	4 690 527	8.8	2.9	81.2	0.0	0.0	7.1
Cargo/passenger ships, dwt	270 289	100.0	0.0	0.0	0.0	0.0	0.0
Offshore, dwt	1 428 141	7.4	59.8	0.0	18.1	4.3	14.8
Tankers, dwt	4 466 352	30.6	6.3	53.2	2.4	6.3	7.6
Miscellaneous, dwt	11 194	59.7	0.0	0.0	0.0	0.0	40.3

Source: Compiled by the UNCTAD secretariat on the basis of data provided by IHS Fairplay.

vessels sail under the Brazilian flag. However, based on tonnage, Liberia is the most used flag for the Brazilian-owned fleet, with a share of 57 per cent. Next are the Brazilian flag (20 per cent) and the Panamanian flag (12 per cent). Large vessels such as bulk carriers and tankers are involved in international transport and are mostly listed at Liberia's registry, while offshore platforms and general cargo and passenger vessels often need to be registered in Brazil. Cabotage, for instance, can only be carried out by Brazilian-flagged vessels.

3.   Ship operation

In container shipping especially, the companies that provide liner shipping services tend to own only a part of their fleet. The liner shipping companies charter in additional ships, which are then operated and deployed under their own name.

A total of 405 containership operators are reported to provide international liner shipping services. The three countries with the highest containership operating capacity (in terms of total TEU vessel capacity) are Denmark, Switzerland and France, which jointly have a market share of almost 30 per cent.[10] It is also noteworthy that the largest shipowning country, Greece, is not host to any major containership operators.[11]

Among the top 20 operating countries are 10 developing economies, which have a combined share of 37 per cent. After the selling in the 1990s of major United States liner shipping companies, it is Chilean companies which today operate the largest containership fleet in the Western Hemisphere (tables 2.6 and 6.5).

Country case study: Chilean containership operators

Chile is home to three international containership operators, which in January 2011 had a combined capacity of 449,913 TEU. Compañía Sudamericana de Vapores (CSAV) dominates the sector in Chile, with an 85 per cent share among the Chilean carriers and a ranking of tenth in the world (table 2.6). The other Chilean carriers are Compañía Chilena de Navegación Interoceánica, and Nisa Navegación (table 6.6).

As illustrated in figure 6.3, CSAV's growth has outpaced the world market for containerized cargo in recent decades. From 1981 to 2009, global transport of containerized cargo increased approximately 3.3 times faster than the world's GDP, while the cargo carried by CSAV grew almost 11 times faster during the same period. In 2009, during the economic crisis, the company lost market share. This was the year with the highest net loss in the company's history (-$633 million). CSAV was able to generate a positive net income in 2010 ($171 million), but in early 2011 it was again reporting losses. The Lucksic family is now a major shareholder and they are trying to accomplish a sustainable turnaround.

Founded in 1872, CSAV is one of the oldest shipping companies in the world. Initially, the company's business consisted of national coastal shipping services; these were then extended along the whole west coast of South America as far as the Panama Canal. Today, CSAV, through its subsidiary Sudamericana Agencias Aéreas y Marítimas (SAAM), also has interests in terminal operations, stevedoring, tugboats, agency and other logistics-related services in 11 countries in North, Central and South America. On the shipping side, the CSAV group includes liner companies in Brazil and Uruguay, as well as interests in dry bulk and reefer shipping.

Table 6.5. The 20 largest containership-operating economies, January 2011

Country	Total fleet			
	Vessel capacity TEU	Vessel capacity, percentage of world capacity	Accumulated market share, percentage of world capacity	Number of ships, 2010
Denmark	1 891 051	11.6%	11.6%	485
Switzerland	1 771 621	10.9%	22.5%	439
France	1 190 894	7.3%	29.9%	383
China	1 141 708	7.0%	36.9%	398
Singapore	1 117 000	6.9%	43.8%	492
Taiwan Province of China	1 113 598	6.9%	50.6%	337
Japan	1 085 802	6.7%	57.3%	296
Germany	1 025 650	6.3%	63.6%	412
Republic of Korea	906 259	5.6%	69.2%	336
China, Hong Kong SAR	661 531	4.1%	73.2%	190
Chile	449 913	2.8%	76.0%	149
United States	318 297	2.0%	78.0%	337
Israel	281 532	1.7%	79.7%	73
Kuwait	178 599	1.1%	80.8%	47
Belgium	137 090	0.8%	81.6%	163
Netherlands	132 483	0.8%	82.5%	191
Iran, Islamic Republic of	90 288	0.6%	83.0%	42
Malaysia	85 967	0.5%	83.5%	74
Italy	80 080	0.5%	84.0%	95
United Arab Emirates	69 896	0.4%	84.5%	47
World	16 253 988	100%	100.0%	9 688

Source: Compiled by the UNCTAD secretariat on the basis of data from Containerisation International Online (accessed in March 2011).

Table 6.6. Chilean ship operators

Company	Total fleet					Order book in 2010	
	2010 Ranking position	2009 Ranking position	2010 TEU	Share of TEU, as a % of Chilean TEU	2010 Number of ships	TEU	Ships
Compañia Sud Americana de Vapores SA	10	10	382 786	85.1	119	6 316	1
Compañía Chilena de Navegación Interoceánica S.A.	28	29	65 530	14.6	27	0	0
Nisa Navegacíon S.A.	230	311	1 597	0.4	3	0	0
Total Chile			449 913		149	6 316	1

Source: Compiled by the UNCTAD secretariat on the basis of data from Containerisation International Online (accessed in March 2011).

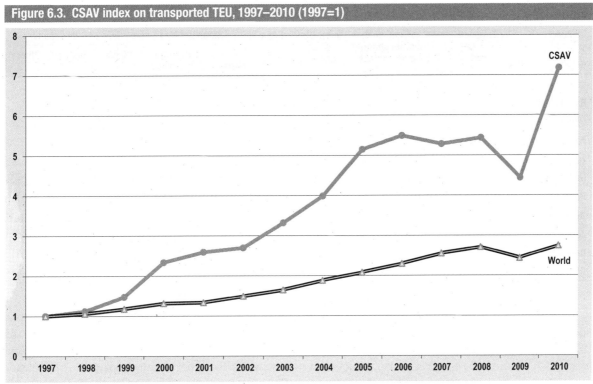

Figure 6.3. CSAV index on transported TEU, 1997–2010 (1997=1)

Source: Compiled by the UNCTAD secretariat on the basis of data from various CSAV web pages, (accessed in March 2011).

With regard to its liner shipping operations, CSAV controls 80 per cent of its sales through its own 105 agencies worldwide. A specific characteristic of the company is the comparatively low share of owned ships in terms of TEU capacity; more than 90 per cent of its capacity is chartered-in tonnage. By comparison, the other top 10 liner shipping companies own almost half of their operated fleet.[12]

The expansion of CSAV has also been driven by geographical factors. With 6,435 km of coastline, extending 4,270 km from North to South, Chile had to develop long-distance national maritime transportation networks in order to reach remote regions at affordable freight rates. Chile has a high demand for maritime transport, sending 95 per cent of its exports (mostly agricultural products and copper) by sea. Owing to its geographical location, Chilean ship operators have been able to optimize the capacity utilization of vessels by loading and discharging cargo at stopovers along the coast of South America located on regional and international trade routes. Moreover, the country's containerized international trade is relatively balanced, with slightly more exports than imports, whereas other countries on the west coast of South America have a trade deficit in containerized transport.[13] Chile adopted policies that aimed to liberalize international transport

services earlier than most other Latin American countries did, and this has given impetus for national ship operators to modernize and internationalize their businesses.

4. Ship scrapping

The competitiveness of a country's scrapping industry is mostly influenced by labour costs and the regulatory environment. All major ship scrapping countries are developing countries. Ship scrapping has reached a similar level of market concentration as ship building. The four largest ship scrapping countries covered 98.1 per cent of the activity in terms of recycled dwt in 2010 (table 6.7). India ranked first with 9.3 million dwt, followed by Bangladesh with 6.8 million dwt, and then China with 5.8 million dwt and Pakistan with 5.1 million dwt. Each of these countries is home to more then 100 companies that are involved in the ship scrapping business, through which competition is sustained within the sector.[14]

The types of ship scrapped vary from one country to another: India focuses on tankers (representing a 46 per cent share of its dwt) and on dry cargo and passenger ships (33 per cent share of its dwt); China

Table 6.7. Top 10 ship-scrapping nations, 2010

Country	Scrapped amount, dwt	Accumulated market share, as a percentage	Number of ships scrapped	Rank	Scrapped ships, percentage of total volume				
					Bulk carriers	Dry cargo / passenger	Offshore	Tankers	Others
India	9 287 775	32.4	451	1	9.7	32.8	5.3	46.2	5.9
Bangladesh	6 839 207	56.3	110	2	15.1	5.5	5.7	71.1	2.5
China	5 769 227	76.5	189	3	46.6	36.3	2.5	12.2	2.4
Pakistan	5 100 606	94.3	111	4	8.1	2.9	6.2	80.6	2.2
Turkey	1 082 446	98.1	226	5	24.3	48.7	0.2	14.1	12.8
United States	217 980	98.8	15	6	0.0	19.9	0.0	80.1	0.0
Romania	16 064	98.9	4	7	0.0	100.0	0.0	0.0	0.0
Denmark	15 802	98.9	25	8	0.0	53.4	22.7	0.0	23.9
Japan	13 684	99.0	1	9	0.0	100.0	0.0	0.0	0.0
Belgium	8 807	99.0	12	10	0.0	100.0	0.0	0.0	0.0
World	28 637 092	100.0	1 324		18.6	22.7	4.7	50.0	4.1

Source: Compiled by the UNCTAD secretariat on the basis of data from IHS Fairplay

specializes in bulk carriers (47 per cent share of its dwt); Pakistan scraps tankers (81 per cent share of its dwt). These differences are also reflected in the average vessel sizes scrapped in the different countries – the size of the average vessel scrapped in Bangladesh is approximately 62,000 dwt, while the average size in China is 31,000 dwt.

Strong steel prices and the recovery of maritime business increased costs for ship procurement but at the same time tripled the margins in the ship scrapping business from 8 per cent in 2009 to 30 per cent in 2010.[15] Indian shipbuyers left Asian scrapyards behind, with rates that were lower by about $50 per ldt. Thus, tonnage opening up in Asia was bought by Indian shipbreakers and delivered to their yards.[16]

Country case study: Bangladesh reopening ship scrapping yards

Bangladesh's ship scrapping industry provides direct and indirect employment, and is also important to cover the country's demand for steel. It contributes approximately 50 per cent to the country's steel-using industries and 20–25 per cent to national steel consumption. In total, approximately 1.5 million tons are supplied by the national ship scrapping industry.[17]

Bangladesh's ship scrapping industry came to a halt in 2010 due to an explosion in 2009 that led to the death of four workers. The High Court forced more than 100 shipyards to stop their activities for most of 2010. Only about 20 scrapping yards that acquired certificates guaranteeing better environmental standards were

allowed to continue their operations. The result was temporary job loss for an estimated 100,000 workers who were directly or indirectly employed in the industry. Since a large proportion of the labour force working in ship scrapping is unskilled or even illiterate, these job losses especially affected the poorest households in the country.[18]

The court ruled that the scrapyards could reopen on 7 March 2011. The reopening of the yards can be expected to have a positive influence on the competitiveness of other heavy industries in the country, since the price of imported steel is higher than the price of steel purchased from national scrapyards. The precise way in which the reopening process and regulatory changes will proceed is still being defined.[19]

5. Ship financing

The economic crisis had a severe effect on ship financing. Many banks had to write off a large amount of bad assets from their balance sheets, and were very reluctant to enter into any new ship financing deals. In addition, the demand for maritime freight transport collapsed, as did freight rates and vessel values, which put pressure on shipowners' and ship operators' profit margins (see chapters 2 and 3). This led to a downturn in business in the fourth quarter of 2008, with new ship finance deals amounting to only $14.1 billion, compared with $33.2 billion one quarter earlier in the same year. The market began to recover in the third quarter of 2010 with a deal value of $25.7 billion (see figure 6.4).

Restricted access to bank loans made shipbuyers seek alternative sources of funding. By way of example, bond finance volume in Asia reached $7.49 billion in 2009 – an increase of 370 per cent over 2008. Asia accounted for 68 per cent of global shipping bond issuances, with a record value of $11 billion in 2009. This trend continued in the beginning of 2010, with shipping companies from the Republic of Korea alone raising $1.4 billion through bond financing.[20]

A ranking of the largest 25 banks in ship financing indicates the limited participation by developing countries in the lending business. China is the only developing country represented, with two banks and a lending value of $17 billion (table 6.8).[21] The major players in the market are European banks. Germany is the largest ship financing country, hosting 8 banks with a ship finance portfolio worth $144 billion. The United States is the only non-European developed country which has a bank in the top 25 with a lending value of $8 billion. Ship financing in developing countries is often state-led and focuses on supporting the national maritime industry, as is the case in Brazil, China and the Republic of Korea.

Country case study: China expanding into international ship financing

The Chinese finance market is to a large extent state-controlled, with 57 per cent of all of its corporate lending provided by publicly owned commercial banks

and publicly owned policy banks.[22] Chinese ship financing helps with the provision of a sufficient and cheap money supply to national maritime industries such as ship construction and ship owning and operation. For instance, all of the major lenders to the largest Chinese state-controlled ship operator COSCO are publicly owned banks (table 6.9). But state lending also aims at providing loans to foreign customers of China's shipbuilding industry. For example, the Government has pledged $5 billion for a special fund to assist Greek shipowners in accessing finance for vessels built in Chinese yards.[23]

Although, on average, the volume of lending for shipping decreased by 10 per cent from 2008 to 2009 (figure based on the top 25 banks only), the Chinese bank ICBC was among the few banks to record positive growth during that period (table 6.8).

6.   Ship classification

Originating in eighteenth-century England when the Register Society was created, marine classification is an activity that aims at promoting safety and environmental protection through compliance with technical standards for the design, construction and maintenance of ships. Private companies, such as shipbuilders, shipowners or insurance companies, as

Figure 6.4. Global marine finance loan volume (in billions of dollars)

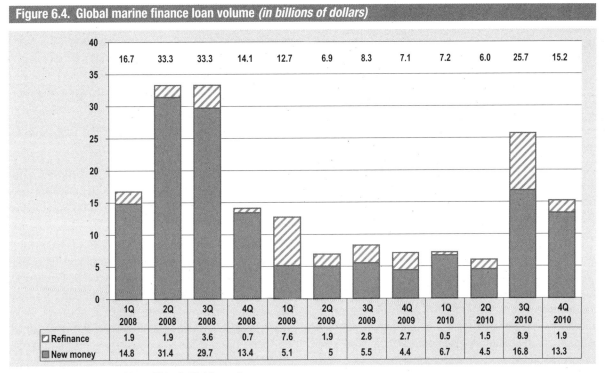

	1Q 2008	2Q 2008	3Q 2008	4Q 2008	1Q 2009	2Q 2009	3Q 2009	4Q 2009	1Q 2010	2Q 2010	3Q 2010	4Q 2010
	16.7	33.3	33.3	14.1	12.7	6.9	8.3	7.1	7.2	6.0	25.7	15.2
Refinance	1.9	1.9	3.6	0.7	7.6	1.9	2.8	2.7	0.5	1.5	8.9	1.9
New money	14.8	31.4	29.7	13.4	5.1	5	5.5	4.4	6.7	4.5	16.8	13.3

Source: Data received from Dialogic Holdings plc.

Table 6.8. World's largest ship-financing banks, total lending portfolio, 2009

Bank	Country	2009 (billions of dollars)	2008–2009 increase / decrease percentage
HSH Nordbank	Germany	49.3	-8.7
Deutsche Schiffsbank	Germany	33.3	-11.5
DnB NOR	Norway	28.0	-8.0
Royal Bank of Scotland	United Kingdom	23.0	-7.0
KfW IPEX-Bank	Germany	20.3	-0.4
Nordea	Sweden	18.4	-1.1
BNP Paribas	France	18.0	6.0
Lloyds Banking Group	United Kingdom	16.9	4.7
CA-CIB	France	13.9	-4.8
DVB	Germany	13.1	-1.5
Bank of China	China	12.2	0.0
UniCredit (ex-HVB)	Italy	11.4	0.2
Danish Ship Finance	Denmark	11.3	0.0
Bremer Landesbank	Germany	9.8	-0.2
Deutsche Bank	Germany	9.5	-1.8
Citi	United States	8.0	-1.5
Danske/Focus Bank	Norway	8.0	-0.2
SEB	Germany	6.1	-0.4
Natixis	France	4.8	-0.2
ICBC	China	4.7	2.5
Fortis	Belgium	4.2	-0.9
Helaba	Germany	3.0	-0.5
Alpha Bank	Greece	2.8	0.1
Marfin Bank	Cyprus	1.9	0.0
Bank of Ireland	Ireland	1.4	-0.4
Total (25 banks)	-	333.3	-10.0

Source: Data from Marine Money. Available at http://www. marinemoney.com (accessed in April 2011).

well as government authorities, rely on "classification societies" for these purposes. In particular, the flag state authority will require that a marine classification society has a ship "classed" before it can be admitted for registration in the country's national fleet.

The market for ship classification is effectively dominated by a group of service providers that are members of the International Association of. Classification Societies (IACS). IACS currently has 12 members and accounts for the classification of more than 90 per cent of world tonnage. The entire classification market is estimated to be worth $5 billion each year.[24] Three classification societies from developing countries are members of IACS

(China, India and the Republic of Korea) and together account for less than 15 per cent of IACS tonnage (table 6.10). The largest ship classification society is Nippon Kaiji Kyokai (Japan) with a classed tonnage in 2010 of 177 million GT. The largest provider from a developing country is Korean Register of Shipping, which has a classed tonnage of 42 million GT. Klasifikasi Indonesia ranks first among the non-members of IACS, and accounts for approximately 0.6 per cent of the global market.

Being a member of IACS brings several benefits, notably that flag states prefer to work with IACS members. IACS has also consultative status with the International Maritime Organization (IMO) and contributes to the interpretation and formulation of maritime regulations adopted by IMO member states. IACS participates in the development of classification standards for the maritime industry.

In previous years, criticism was levelled at IASC for its restrictive policies regarding entry to the organization and for a lack of transparency in the setting of classification standards. This came to an end with a European Commission antitrust investigation that wound up in 2009. The investigation led to several commitments from IACS members. Transparency on membership criteria had to be increased. In addition, IACS committed itself to integrate non-IACS members into the technical working groups and to publish all technical background documents on classification standards. Furthermore, the organization created an independent body that can settle disputes with regard to the granting or withdrawal of IACS membership.[25] The Indian Register of Shipping (IRS) was the first applicant to receive IACS membership after conclusion of the European Commission's antitrust investigation.

Country case study: India joining the International Association of Classification Societies

The Indian Register of Shipping is a relatively small classification society, which in 2009 classified 961 ships totalling 7.6 million dwt. Its world market share is approximately 0.8 per cent.

IRS applied for membership of IACS in 1991, and was initially given associate member status. This was converted into full membership in 2010. Previously, most Indian shipowners went through a dual classification process, with approval from an IACS member and from IRS.[26] With full IACS membership, IRS can now provide all necessary services and can grow its classification business in foreign markets more easily.

Table 6.9. Lenders to COSCO *(in billions of yuan)*

Bank	Committed credit	Shareholder	Amount drawn	Balance
China Merchant Bank	6.6	public	2.8	3.8
Agricultural Bank of China	8.7	public	3.5	5.2
Bank of China	11.0	public	6.1	4.9
Bank of Communications	6.5	public	0.8	5.7
China Everbright Bank	0.5	public	0.0	0.5
China CITIC Bank	3.3	public	0.6	2.7
Bank of Construction	3.0	public	0.6	2.4
Shenzhen Development Bank	1.2	public	1.2	0.0
Industrial and Commercial Bank of China	1.4	public	0.7	0.7
Other lenders	8.8	-	4.6	4.2
Total	51.0		21.1	29.9

Source: Data from Marine Money. Available at http://www.marinemoney.com (accessed in April 2011).

Table 6.10. Top 20 classification societies, 2010

Society	IACS member	Average ship age in years	Number of ships	Millions of GT	GT share, percentage	Accumulated GT share, percentage	2006 millions of GT	Increase in GT 2006–2010 percentage
Nippon Kiji Kyokai	Yes	10.8	7 000	177.3	18.4	18.4	144.5	22.7
Lloyd's register	Yes	15.3	6 433	155.4	16.1	34.5	132.4	17.4
American Bureau	Yes	15	7 351	152.5	15.8	50.4	110.1	38.5
Det Norske Veritas	Yes	12.9	4 831	141.3	14.7	65.0	113.5	24.5
Germanischer Lloyd	Yes	12.7	5 763	93.9	9.7	74.8	62.8	49.5
Bureau Veritas	Yes	13.1	6 385	73.0	7.6	82.4	53.1	37.5
Korean Register	Yes	14.5	2 023	42.1	4.4	86.7	29.7	41.8
China Class	Yes	13.1	2 220	42.0	4.4	91.1	26.9	56.1
Registro Italiano	Yes	19.4	2 020	28.0	2.9	94.0	20.2	38.6
Russian Register	Yes	25.3	3 214	13.5	1.4	95.4	14.3	-5.6
Indian Register	Yes	16.1	961	7.6	0.8	96.2	7.9	-3.8
Klasifikasi Indonesia	No	20.4	2 984	5.2	0.5	96.7	4.3	20.9
Vietnam Register	No	14.4	893	3.9	0.4	97.1	2.8	39.3
Polski Rejestr	No	30.3	366	2.7	0.3	97.4	3.3	-18.2
Hellenic Register	No	30	418	2.3	0.2	97.7	2.7	-14.8
Türk Loydu	No	27.1	613	1.5	0.2	97.8	1.5	0.0
Croatia	Yes	32.4	208	0.9	0.1	97.9	1.1	-18.2
Bulgarian Register	No	32.8	148	0.7	0.1	98.0	1.1	-36.4
China, Corporation	No	25	37	0.3	0.0	98.0	0.7	-57.1
Russian River	No	33.9	111	0.3	0.0	98.0	0.3	0.0
Total	-	15.3	53 979	944.4	98.0	98.0	733.2	28.8
World Fleet	-	21.1	83 670	963.3	100.0	100.0	726.2	32.6

Source: Clarkson Research Services. World Fleet Monitor. As at 1 January 2011.

The case of India's classification society suggests that having access to a national market of considerable size facilitates the process of admission to IACS. This allowed IRS to build up expertise and sufficient organizational size and experience in order to meet the exacting IACS membership criteria.[27]

7. Ship registration

The four largest vessel registries are in developing economies: Panama, Liberia, the Marshall Islands, and Hong Kong (China). Together, these four territories provide their flag to 47.5 per cent of the world fleet (in dwt, see table 2.7 in chapter 2). These are "open registries", which also provide registration services to non-national shipowners and ship operators. Over time, there has been a significant rise in the share of foreign-flagged tonnage, which indicates the competitiveness and increasing relevance of this type of registry in the business (see also figure 2.4). Thus, the major ship registries in developing economies have grown at the pace of the global fleet or faster than it. Liberia, the Marshall Islands and Hong Kong (China) have seen annual growth of approximately 10 per cent between 2006 and 2011.

A recent cost comparison of major open registries, undertaken by Combined Maritime Limited, concluded that no flag offers the lowest fees for all vessel types, sizes and ages.[28] Accordingly, different registries specialize in different market segments (see also figure 2.5).

Many of the countries that have established open registries are also important providers of other services (including offshore banking), or have attracted company headquarters by offering low corporate tax rates. These include several small island developing States, which may find in ship registration a source of income that their geographical location and small population could not otherwise provide.

Running an open registry implies relatively high fixed costs to maintain a network of offices. In addition, strategic partnerships with classification societies have to be built up. This has prevented major newcomers in this business in recent years. Registration fees need to be kept competitive in a market where shipowners can change their vessel's flag relatively easily. It is also important to run a registry on high safety standards in order to avoid port state control inspections or higher insurance premiums for shipowners.

Entering the business of vessel registration in practice requires close cooperation with partner firms in developed countries. The registry of Panama, for example, has received technical assistance from the Government of Japan; and the registries of Liberia and the Marshall Islands are both effectively managed by companies based in the United States. Also, the certification of ships is usually outsourced to foreign classification societies.

Country case study: Panama, the world's first open registry

Panama is the largest provider of ship registration services, with a market share of 21.9 per cent of the world's dwt. Panama's ship registration services experienced an annual growth rate of 7.4 per cent between 2006 and 2011. The structure of the ship types registered in Panama, which is dominated by dry bulk carriers and oil tankers, has not undergone significant changes in the past fifteen years (figure 6.5).

Panama was the first modern open registry. It was set up in 1917, and mostly targeted owners from the United States. At that time, the geographical location near the United States–administered Panama Canal, with a large amount of ship traffic and therefore contact with potential customers, may have been a comparative advantage. Benefiting from a first mover advantage, the country established consular networks and built up cooperation with classification societies, shipowners and nautical schools. This allowed Panama to provide round-the-clock services at competitive prices.

Panama has recently moved up to the white list of the Paris Memorandum of Understanding on Port State Control (Paris MOU) regime.[29] Inclusion on the white, grey or black list of the Paris MOU reflects the results of random ship inspections. Inclusion on the white list implies that Panama-flagged ships are less likely to be found with deficiencies. For shipowners who have registered their ships in Panama, it means that their vessels are less likely to be physically inspected when calling at European ports.

8. Ship insurance (protection and indemnity)

The global maritime liability insurance market is highly concentrated in developed countries, and mostly in the hands of the 13 members of the International Group of P&I Clubs (IGP&I) which accounts for approximately 90 per cent of the world's seagoing tonnage.[30] Private companies that offer fixed-premium insurance

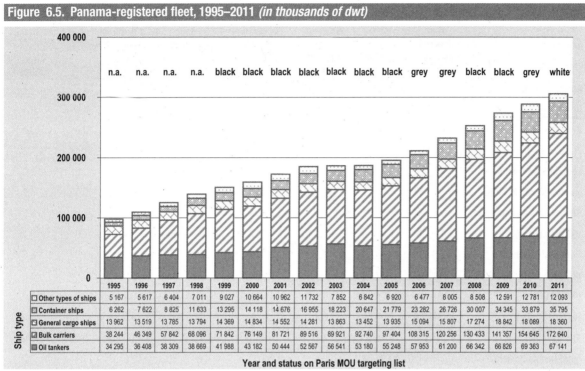

Figure 6.5. Panama-registered fleet, 1995–2011 *(in thousands of dwt)*

Ship type	1995	1996	1997	1998	1999	2000	2001	2002	2003	2004	2005	2006	2007	2008	2009	2010	2011
Other types of ships	5 167	5 617	6 404	7 011	9 027	10 664	10 962	11 732	7 852	6 842	6 920	6 477	8 005	8 508	12 591	12 781	12 093
Container ships	6 262	7 622	8 825	11 633	13 295	14 118	14 676	16 955	18 223	20 647	21 779	23 282	26 726	30 007	34 345	33 879	35 795
General cargo ships	13 962	13 519	13 785	13 794	14 369	14 834	14 552	14 281	13 863	13 452	13 935	15 094	15 807	17 274	18 842	18 089	18 360
Bulk carriers	38 244	46 349	57 842	68 096	71 842	76 149	81 721	89 516	89 921	92 740	97 404	108 315	120 256	130 433	141 357	154 645	172 640
Oil tankers	34 295	36 408	38 309	38 669	41 988	43 182	50 444	52 567	56 541	53 180	55 248	57 953	61 200	66 342	66 826	69 363	67 141

Year and status on Paris MOU targeting list

Source: Compiled by the UNCTAD secretariat on the basis of data supplied by IHS Fairplay.

policies struggle to compete with the P&I clubs. Only a few relatively small players manage to grasp some market share, such as British Marine, whose size is comparable to the tonnage of the American Club of Shipowners (based on entered GT) – the smallest P&I club in the International Group.

Each P&I club is an independent, not-for-profit, mutual insurance association that provides risk coverage for its shipowner and charterer members against third-party liabilities including personal injury to crew, passengers and others on board, cargo loss and damage, oil pollution, wreck removal and dock damage.

P&I clubs often accept members from beyond their head-office country. For instance, almost half of the tonnage in the UK P&I Club is from Asian members, and two thirds of the members of the Japan P&I Club are, in terms of dwt, are from the Americas (table 6.11).

As not-for-profit organizations, the P&I clubs invest savings on behalf of their members. Clubs also provide a wide range of services to their members on claims, legal issues and loss prevention, and often play a leading role in the management of casualties. Mutual insurance associations depend on a large membership to spread the risk.

The main entry barrier to new shipping insurance companies lies in the large reserves that need to be

built up to avoid having to look for reinsurance on the open market at relatively high costs. In addition, building up reserves requires financial commitment from the new members. Comparing the $14 million reserves of the Korea P&I Club with the $1.9 billion of Gard illustrates the finance gap between large and small P&I clubs. The P&I clubs that are members of the IGP&I can also share claims exceeding $8 million, arrange reinsurance programmes, and negotiate contract terms at a competitive price level.[31] The established P&I clubs can rely on a worldwide network of offices that are familiar with the local regulatory framework and are in a position to deliver legal advice. With their historical data and accumulated experience, established P&I clubs have the required capacities to assess the fleets of new and existing members and to maintain a balanced risk structure among members.

The location of the headquarters of today's major clubs is mostly driven by historical reasons and from cluster benefits that stem from being close to banks, insurance companies, law firms and other marine service providers. Only a few developing – or even developed – countries are in a position to offer a comparable competitive setting. However, the following country case studies, which look at China and the Republic of Korea, show that new

Table 6.11. Membership of the International Group of P&I Clubs

P&I club	2008 Entered tonnage, 1 000 GT	2010 Entered tonnage, 1 000 GT	Share of entered tonnage, percentage	2009/10 Calls and premiums, $ million	GT by nationality of management as percentages				
					Europe	Asia	Africa (Middle East)	Americas	Others/ not defined
American Club	13 300	15 283	1.4	115.7	58.2	22.8	1.6	13.6	3.8
Britannia	129 000	138 000	12.6	289.6	41.7	48.9	2.6	6.4	0.4
Gard (Norway)	170 100	184 900	16.9	447.6	68.0	22.0	0.0	10.0	0.0
Japan P&I Club	96 080	102 030	9.3	231.0	0.0	24.4	3.1	67.8	4.7
London Steam-Ship	40 156	40 615	3.7	121.0	64.0	29.0	2.0	3.0	2.0
North of England Club	90 000	114 400	10.4	285.1	44.0	26.0	14.0	10.0	6.0
Shipowners (Luxembourg)	15 614	16 933	1.5	174.2	31.0	36.0	9.0	24.0	0.0
Skuld (Norway)	91 142	n.a.	0.0	255.4	63.0	28.0	2.0	7.0	0.0
Standard (Bermuda)	73 020	110 000	10.0	250.3	50.0	20.0	0.0	22.0	8.0
Steamship (Bermuda)	71 800	82 800	7.6	305.4	30.1	40.1	9.0	20.8	0.0
UK P&I Club	161 000	176 500	16.1	447.2	46.0	36.0	0.0	12.0	6.0
West of England	69 700	68 800	6.3	239.6	45.6	33.0	8.3	13.1	0.0
The Swedish Club	37 930	45 300	4.1	78.7	45.0	54.0	1.0	0.0	0.0
Total (available data)	1 058 842	1 095 561	100.0	3 240.8	44.4	32.0	3.6	17.1	3.0

Source: Willis Group. *Protection and Indemnity: Market Review 2010/2011.* Available at http://www.willis.com/Documents/Pu-blications/Industries/Marine/AnimatedPDF/dec2010/index.html (accessed in September 2011).

market players from developing countries are emerging which have the potential to grab market share from the established P&I clubs of the International Group.

Country case study: China and the Republic of Korea strengthening their P&I business

As developing countries expand their own banking, insurance and services sectors, it is to be expected that, at some point in time, shipowners will consider it beneficial to be members of local clubs closer to home or in which most fellow members have similar interests and backgrounds. In recent years, several developing countries in Asia – notably China and the Republic of Korea – have built up their own P&I clubs. The China P&I Club and the Korea P&I Club are both willing to join the IGP&I. Reportedly, formal approval of the China P&I Club joining IGP&I is expected in February 2012, and observers anticipate that the Korea P&I Club will be approved in the near future too.[32]

The China P&I Club, which was set up in 1984, hosts members from China, Hong Kong SAR, Singapore, and elsewhere in Asia. The club holds a free reserve of around $355 million, and it insures some 24 million GT. Compared to the UK P&I Club's 176.5 million GT,

this is still a relatively small account. The Korea P&I Club comprises more than 900 ships with around 9 million GT, and at the end of 2010 had free reserves estimated at $14 million.[33]

9. Seafarer supply

The 20 biggest suppliers of seafarers, as per the definition of the Baltic and International Maritime Council (BIMCO), are displayed in table 6.12. This table covers two different employment groups: officers and ratings.

Seven out of the ten biggest suppliers of ratings are developing countries. China ranks first with 90,295 ratings and a share of 12.1 per cent, followed by Indonesia with 61,821 ratings.

Increasingly, developing countries are also supplying officers. While the largest academies for marine officers have traditionally been in developed countries, the six largest suppliers today are in developing/transition economies. The Philippines leads the ranking with 57,688 officers (2010 figures); China comes second with 51,511 officers. Next is India, with 46,497 officers employed. Taken together, these three countries account for one quarter of the world's supply.

Table 6.12. The 20 biggest suppliers of officers and ratings in 2010

Country	Number of officers supplied	Market share officers, percentage of world	Accumulated market share, percentage of world	Country	Number of ratings supplied	Market share ratings, percentage of world	Accumulated market share, percentage of world
Philippines	57 688	9.2	9.2	China	90 296	12.1	12.1
China	51 511	8.3	17.5	Indonesia	61 821	8.3	20.4
India	46 497	7.5	24.9	Turkey	51 009	6.8	27.2
Turkey	36 734	5.9	30.8	Russian Federation	40 000	5.4	32.5
Ukraine	27 172	4.4	35.2	Malaysia	28 687	3.8	36.4
Russian Federation	25 000	4.0	39.2	Philippines	23 492	3.1	39.5
United States	21 810	3.5	42.7	Bulgaria	22 379	3.0	42.5
Japan	21 297	3.4	46.1	Myanmar	20 145	2.7	45.2
Romania	18 575	3.0	49.1	Sri Lanka	19 511	2.6	47.8
Poland	17 923	2.9	52.0	United States	16 644	2.2	50.0
Norway	16 082	2.6	54.5	India	16 176	2.2	52.2
Indonesia	15 906	2.5	57.1	Honduras	15 341	2.1	54.3
United Kingdom	15 188	2.4	59.5	Cambodia	12 004	1.6	55.9
Canada	13 994	2.2	61.8	Viet Nam	11 438	1.5	57.4
Croatia	11 704	1.9	63.6	Italy	11 390	1.5	58.9
Myanmar	10 950	1.8	65.4	Ukraine	11 000	1.5	60.4
Bulgaria	10 890	1.7	67.1	Pakistan	9 327	1.2	61.6
Viet Nam	10 738	1.7	68.8	France	9 316	1.2	62.9
Greece	9 993	1.6	70.5	Egypt	9 000	1.2	64.1
Republic of Korea	9 890	1.6	72.0	United Kingdom	8 990	1.2	65.3
World	624 062	100.0	100.0	World	747 306	100.0	100.0

Source: Compiled by the UNCTAD secretariat on the basis of data supplied by BIMCO in *Manpower Update* (2010).

The evolution confirms the changing role of developing nations in this business. Developing countries now supply crews with broader and higher educational profiles. Notably, Cambodia and Myanmar (two LDCs) are among the major suppliers, with Myanmar in the top 20 for supply of officers. This suggests that the education of seafarers is also a development opportunity for LDCs, providing access to foreign currency revenue.[34]

Country case study: Philippines becoming the world's largest supplier of maritime officers

The Philippines is a typical example of an economy that has diversified its maritime industry. According to the Philippine Overseas Employment Administration (table 6.13), approximately 330,000 Philippine seafarers were employed on maritime vessels in 2009 (note that this is not fully comparable with the data provided by BIMCO, which only includes seafarers currently registered and licensed in accordance with the IMO STCW convention).

According to the Philippine Joint Manning Group, almost 30 per cent of the world's employed seafarers come from the Philippines, and this group has set a target of increasing the share to 50 per cent in 2016.[35]; [36] The territory of the Philippines comprises 7,107 islands and 36,289 km of coastline, which historically has led to high national levels of demand for seafarers. In addition, the Philippines has invested in an educational infrastructure of 100 maritime academies which graduate some 40,000 seafarers each year. In addition, there are 421 licensed crewing agents in the country.[37]

This sector is also important to the country's economic welfare. Out of the $16 billion generated by Philippine nationals employed outside the country, $7 billion is contributed by seafarers.[38] Remittances from workers employed overseas prevent up to 3 million Philippine nationals from falling below the poverty line.[39]

Table 6.13 specifies the flags employing Philippine seafarers. Panama is first, employing 67,000

Table 6.13. Top 10 flags employing Philippine seafarers, and top 10 occupations of Philippine seafarers

Country	2007	2008	2009	Occupation	2007	2008	2009
Panama	51 619	53 912	67 362	Able Seaman	31 818	34 563	45 338
Bahamas	29 681	29 177	36 054	Oiler	19 491	20 941	27 483
Liberia	21 966	21 632	29 796	Ordinary Seaman	17 355	18 715	23 737
Marshall Islands	9 772	11 859	18 068	Chief Cook	7 778	9 022	12 651
Singapore	10 308	12 130	15 674	Second mate	7 873	8 694	12 119
Malta	7 513	11 025	14 786	Bosun	7 737	8 603	11 555
Norway	8 188	8 883	11 447	Messman	7 810	8 320	10 536
United Kingdom	8 172	8 232	10 313	Third engineer officer	7 056	7 995	11 307
Cyprus	7 052	7 446	9 425	Third mate	6 559	7 349	9 857
Netherlands	7 017	7 796	9 281	Second engineer officer	6 369	6 878	9 557
Total top 10	161 288	172 092	222 206	Total top 10	119 846	131 080	174 140
Total	226 900	244 144	329 728	Total	226 900	244 144	329 728

Source: Compiled by the UNCTAD secretariat based on data from the Philippine Overseas Employment Administration.
Note: Data not fully comparable with that in table 6.12.

Philippine seafarers, followed by the Bahamas with 36,000 and Liberia with 30,000. But flags from developed countries are in the top 10 list too – such as Malta, the Netherlands and the United Kingdom. The total number of Philippine seafarers employed has experienced continuous growth, with an increase of 45 per cent between 2006 and 2009.

10. Port operation (container terminal operators)

With the increased containerization of manufactured goods trade, and the extended use of transshipment "hubs", containerized port traffic has grown at high annual rates (see also chapter 4). Today, containerized port traffic is mostly handled by global operators, many of which are companies from developing countries. Table 6.14 lists the world's largest container terminal operators. The three largest service terminal operators are Hutchison Port Holdings (HPH), APM Terminals, and the Port of Singapore Authority (PSA). Together they handle about 34 per cent of the world's container traffic.

None of the major container terminal operators entered the business as a complete newcomer. Several of them were initially operating in a home port and subsequently took on concessions in foreign ports; this is the case of HPH and PSA, coming from two of the world's busiest container ports, namely Hong Kong (China) and Singapore. Other operators

were linked to a shipping company that initially focused on dedicated terminal operations for the mother company. Today, the distinction is becoming less relevant. APM Terminals, for example, although belonging to the same group as the Maersk shipping line, provides services to all shipping companies.

Country case study: United Arab Emirates: Recovery of Dubai Ports World from the economic crisis

The case of Dubai and port operator Dubai Ports World (DP World) is an example of a logistics provider expanding its operations abroad. DP World started taking on concessions in foreign ports slightly later than most of its main competitors. Its growth was partly realized through the purchase of P&O from the United Kingdom in 2006, which at that time was the world's fourth-largest ports operator. Today, DP World operates around 50 terminals in more than 30 countries.[40]

DP World has realized relatively stable profits during the past four years, managing to preserve them despite a fall in TEU throughput of 7.9 per cent between 2008 and 2009, which was still better than the total world decline of almost 10 per cent.[41]

One reason for the company's resilience to economic turbulence lies in its geographical presence, which is evenly spread over all continents, with a focus on the Middle East (figure 6.6). DP World has grown faster than the market during the economic recovery that began in 2009, increasing its market share to

Table 6.14. Top 20 port operators, 2009

	Name	Economy	Country Type	Throughput (millions of TEU)	World percentage	Terminal capacity (millions of TEU)	World terminal capacity as a percentage
1	HPH	China, Hong Kong SAR	DC	64.2	12.2	93.9	12.5
2	APMT	Netherlands	IN	56.9	10.9	105.4	14.0
3	PSA	Singapore	DC	55.3	10.5	84.4	11.2
4	DPW	United Arab Emirates	DC	45.2	8.6	63.1	8.4
5	Cosco	China	DC	32.5	6.2	68.1	9.1
6	MSC	Switzerland	IN	16.4	3.1	23.6	3.1
7	Eurogate	Germany	IN	11.7	2.2	21.1	2.8
8	Evergreen	Taiwan Province of China	DC	8.6	1.6	16.6	2.2
9	SSA Marine	United States	IN	7.7	1.5	18.0	2.4
10	CMA-CGM	France	IN	7.0	1.3	14.5	1.9
11	Hanjin	Republic of Korea	DC	6.0	1.1	15.8	2.1
12	NYK Line	Japan	IN	5.2	1.0	19.0	2.5
13	HHLA	Germany	IN	5.0	1.0	9.2	1.2
14	Dragados	Spain	IN	4.9	0.9	9.1	1.2
15	APL	Singapore	DC	4.6	0.9	7.7	1.0
16	K Line	Japan	IN	4.3	0.8	8.7	1.2
17	OOCL	China, Hong Kong SAR	DC	4.2	0.8	5.5	0.7
18	Yang Ming	Taiwan Province of China	DC	4.1	0.8	7.9	1.1
19	ICTSI	Philippines	DC	3.6	0.7	7.4	1.0
20	MOL	Japan	IN	2.7	0.5	5.7	0.8
Total				350.1	66.8	604.7	80.4
World				524.4	100.0	751.9	100.0

Source: Compiled by the UNCTAD secretariat on the basis of data supplied by Drewry Publishing in *Global Container Terminal Operators Annual Review 2010*.

an estimated 10 per cent of world container port throughput, from 8.9 per cent in 2008 (table 6.15).

Even during the economic crisis, and in spite of financial difficulties of the parent company Dubai World, DP World did not significantly change its long-term growth strategy. It maintains a focus on new port projects and capacity expansions in Africa, Asia, Europe and South America – with a total scheduled investment value of $2.5 billion from 2010 to 2012.[42] The geographical portfolio of DP World, and of three other port operators, is shown in figure 6.6. All of them have a strong position in their regional home markets, and internationalize to other locations worldwide, increasing their capacity on several continents. The home ports of Dubai (United Arab Emirates), Hong Kong (China) and Singapore are all regional hub ports, providing transit and transshipment services to neighbouring countries. They cannot rely solely on the captive cargo of imports and exports. This obliges the

port operators to continuously modernize and to offer their services at competitive prices, which is a basis for their subsequent expansion into foreign container terminals.

11.   Other maritime-related sectors

Several other maritime-related businesses have seen growing participation by developing countries, too.

Container construction. Most containers today are built in China. China has the manufacturing capacity; it is also the country where empty containers are most needed, in view of its surplus in containerized trade.

Container leasing. About one third of containers are not owned by the shipping companies but by container lessors. Most container lessors are based in the United States and also engage in leasing of other capital goods and equipment.

Figure 6.6. Regional focus of major port operators

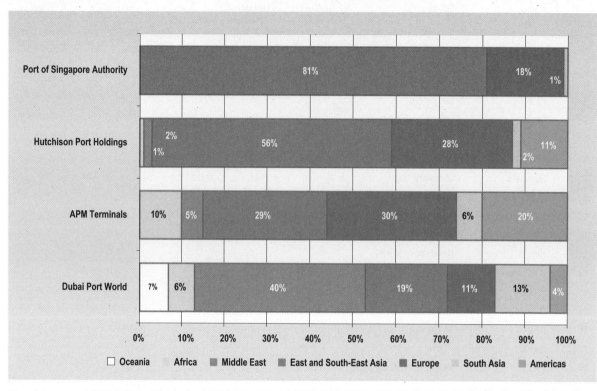

Source: DP World company presentations, available at http://www.dpworld.com and accessed in April 2011.

Table 6.15. Performance figures of Dubai Ports World

Performance Indicators Dubai Ports World	2007	2008	2009	2010
Consolidated throughput TEU million	24.0	27.8	25.6	27.8
Terminal utilization rate, percentage	81.0	80.0	74.0	80.0
Revenue, $ million	2 613	3 283	2 821	3 078
Adjusted EBITDA, $ million	1 063	1 340	1 072	1 240
Adjusted EBITDA margin, percentage	40.7	40.8	38.0	40.3
TEU throughput world market, percentage	8.8	8.9	9.5	10.0

Source: DP World company presentations, available at http://www.dpworld.com and accessed in April 2011. Also, data received directly from DP World.

Ship repair. Ships need to undergo maintenance and repair work. Several developing countries provide such services. For example, Colombia, benefiting from its geographical location near the Panama Canal, has recently made plans to expand its ship-repair capacity.

Bunkering. Ships need to bunker fuel at bunkering stations not too far from their trading routes. Thus, in principle, there is potential for providing bunkering fuel at any port of call. The largest bunkering port in the world is Singapore, followed by Rotterdam.

Brokering. The buying or chartering of ships is usually carried out through ship brokers, who act as intermediaries between the shipowners and the charterers who use the vessels to transport cargo, or between sellers and buyers of the ships themselves. The Institute of Chartered Ship Brokers, the Baltic Exchange, and Clarksons – the world's largest ship broker – are all based in London.

Ship agencies. Most shipping companies, especially in tramp shipping, do not have their own network of representative offices. When their ships call at a foreign port, they depend on ship agents to arrange for services such as bunkering, dealings with the authorities, or assistance to the crew. The largest network of independent ship agents is Multiport, which has its secretariat in London. Many ship agents are relatively small, local companies, however there are some that have global coverage, notably GAC (United Arab Emirates), Inchcape (United Kingdom) and Wilhelmsen Ship (Norway).

C. COMPARATIVE ANALYSIS OF MARITIME BUSINESSES

1. Participation of developing countries in maritime businesses

Over the past decades, developing countries have substantially expanded their fields of expertise into maritime sectors of higher business sophistication and technical complexity. First they became major market players in the provision of seafarers and in vessel registration, and now they are expanding into practically all major maritime sectors.

As illustrated in table 6.16, developing countries today have more than a 50 per cent market share in 6 of the 11 sectors covered in the table. In shipbuilding, ship scrapping, and the provision of seafarers, developing

countries account for more than three quarters of the supply. In 3 of the 11 sectors, developed countries continue to dominate, with around 90 per cent of the market – notably in P&I insurance services, ship financing and ship classification.

2. Possible barriers to participation in a maritime business

The possibility for newcomers to enter the market of a specific maritime business depends on numerous geographical, political, historical and economic factors – as illustrated by the different case studies presented in section B of this chapter. At the same time, there are also some general aspects that allow for a comparison of different maritime businesses and an appraisal of the possibilities for newcomers to enter a particular market. One such aspect is the level of market concentration; it may potentially be more difficult for a country to develop a sector if the business is already dominated by only a small number of countries. Another possible barrier to entry is the country's general level of development; setting up or strengthening a maritime sector may require certain institutional, technical and human capacities that developing countries may not necessarily have.

Market concentration: Given that countries specialize in different maritime businesses, a process of market concentration tends to occur (table 6.16). In shipbuilding, ship scrapping and insurance services, four countries together account for more than 90 per cent of the world market. Sectors that are more evenly spread over a larger number of countries are seafarer supply and containership operation, where the combined market share of the top four countries is less than 40 per cent.

Level of economic development: Table 6.16 also shows, for each maritime sector, the average GDP per capita, as an indicator of the stage of economic development.[43] Ship scrapping takes place in countries with the lowest average GDP per capita ($2,094); going up the scale, the next activities are ship registration and the provision of ratings. At the other end of the spectrum, the average GDP per capita is highest in the countries hosting the P&I clubs ($48,628), followed then by ship financing, containership operation and container terminal operation.

Figure 6.7 is a matrix that combines these two indicators with GDP per capita on the X-axis and

Table 6.16. Comparison of maritime sectors

Maritime sector	Share of the top 4 countries/ economies percentage	Share of the top 10 countries/ economies percentage	Market share of developing countries in the top 10, percentage	Number of developing countries/ economies in top 10	Average GDP per capita, (dollars)	Multiplicator world average per capita GDP
Ship building (dwt)	95.4	98.2	76.4	6	19 368.8	2.3
Ship scrapping (dwt)	94.3	99.0	99.0	5	2 094.0	0.2
Insurance services : P&I (dwt)	91.2	74.62	2.4	2	48 628.0	5.7
Ship financing ($)	70.2	98.1	8.7	1	41 198.0	4.8
Ship classification (dwt)	65.0	95.4	10.6	2	36 629.3	4.3
Ship owning (dwt)	49.7	69.1	26.1	4	31 150.1	3.6
Ship registration (dwt)	45.9	72.0	53.2	6	9 219.6	1.1
Port operation : Container terminals (TEU)	43.9	61.7	67.4	5	35 639.6	4.1
Ship operation: Container ships (TEU)	36.9	73.24	41.5	5	35 847.1	4.2
Ratings (Headcount)	35.1	50.0	89.5	8	10 603.6	1.2
Officers (Headcount)	30.8	52.0	75.4	6	15 314.8	1.8

Source: See section 6.B. Estimates are based on the latest year available.

Figure 6.7. Market-entry barriers into maritime businesses, for developing countries

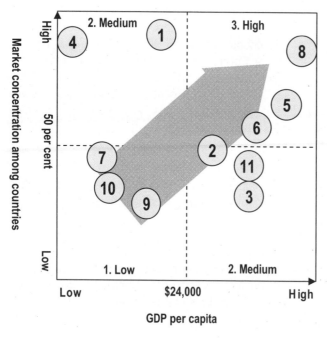

1. Ship building
2. Ship owning
3. Ship operation (container ships)
4. Ship scrapping
5. Ship financing
6. Ship classification
7. Ship registration
8. Ship insurance (protection and indemnity)
9. Officers
10. Ratings
11. Port operation (container terminal operators)

Source: UNCTAD secretariat, based on data from Table 6.16.

market concentration among countries on the Y-axis. The sector-specific data used to create this graph were taken from table 6.16. The matrix groups the observed sectors into four quadrants that evaluate barriers to market entry by developing countries into each maritime business. A high level of concentration combined with a high average GDP per capita (quadrant 3) implies that only a few countries (principally developed countries) participate in the business (e.g. ship financing and ship insurance). It is likely that it will be more difficult for developing countries to enter these sectors than to establish maritime industries with a low market concentration located in economies with a lower level of economic development (quadrant 1).

3. Linkages between maritime businesses

Increasingly, maritime businesses are geographically spread among different countries, with each country specializing in one or a few sectors. As a result of the increasing distance between most industries, it may seem that they are developing ever more independently from each other. While this is true for some sectors, linkages between them remain. Such linkages can be twofold.

Firstly, one sector may provide services to another, and geographical closeness can be an advantage. While this is less relevant today than it was in past decades, there may still be advantages to a shipowner in having, for example, insurance and financing services in the same country. Another example is ship classification, where the societies may find it convenient to be closer to their clients in ship building and operation and in the banks that finance the ships that require classification.

Secondly, different sectors may require the same type of inputs and framework. Low labour costs may be a cost advantage both for ship scrapping and for seafaring. An industrial base is important for manufacturing, be it of ships or port cranes. A developed services sector and a strong legal framework are preconditions for competitive banking and insurance services.

In view of these two possible linkages, it is to be expected that several maritime businesses will be found in the same country. The data on the maritime sectors covered in the analysis suggest that this is indeed the case. Table 6.17 shows the partial correlation coefficients between pairs of sectors. A positive value means that when a country's participation in one sector increases, its participation in the other will also tend to increase. The partial correlation coefficient lies between -1 (complete negative correlation) and +1 (complete positive correlation).[44]

Table 6.17. Correlation analysis between maritime sectors and economic indicators

	Ship building	Ship owning	Ship operation	Ship scrapping	Ship financing	Ship clas-sification	Ship registration	Ship insurances	Seafarer supply (officers)	Seafarer supply (ratings)	Port operation
Ship building	1.00										
Ship owning	0.52	1.00									
Ship operation	0.43	0.47	1.00								
Ship scrapping	0.33	0.20	0.15	1.00							
Ship financing	-0.04	0.25	0.30	-0.07	1.00						
Ship classification	0.37	0.57	0.32	0.05	0.40	1.00					
Ship registration	0.10	0.22	0.13	0.07	-0.07	0.10	1.00				
Ship insurance	0.08	0.20	0.03	-0.00	0.13	0.68	0.10	1.00			
Seafarer supply (officers)	0.36	0.38	0.19	0.53	-0.08	0.33	0.12	0.18	1.00		
Seafarer supply (ratings)	0.37	0.29	0.20	0.49	-0.03	0.19	0.11	0.06	0.73	1.00	
Port operation	0.22	0.30	0.50	0.15	0.37	0.12	0.23	-0.00	0.15	0.15	1.00
Legend:			≤ 0.4			≥ 0.5					

Source: UNCTAD secretariat calculations, based on data from annex VII.

The correlation coefficient between officers and ratings is 0.73, implying that countries that provide officers are also highly likely to provide ratings. Countries such as the Philippines have built up their educational infrastructure for ratings, and now supply officers with a higher qualification profile. There is also a correlation between ship operation and shipowning (0.47). One of the reasons for this is that ship operators often own a share of their fleet and charter the missing capacity in order to react more flexibly to demand volatilities. Some other sectors, on the other hand, are rarely located in the same country; for example, the correlation coefficient between ship scrapping and insurance is zero.

More examples of countries that are active in different groups of sectors that correlate with each other can be found in annex VII, which shows the market shares of individual countries. For instance, Bangladesh and Pakistan are both leading countries in ship scrapping, and also have some participation in the provision of seafarers. Liberia and Saint Vincent and the

Grenadines have open registries, but are not active in any other maritime sector. Apart from being of different sizes in economic terms, Argentina, Brazil and China have similar maritime profiles: all three countries are active in shipbuilding, and have national shipowners and containership operators.

The linkages between different maritime sectors from the previous correlation analysis have been extracted and can be seen in figure 6.8. Correlations of moderate strength or higher (r > 0.4) are illustrated by a solid line. The graph groups the sectors according to the intensity of the barriers to entry into each maritime business, based on the results in figure 6.7. It indicates the probability for a developing country to establish each maritime industry. Establishing a maritime business from group 3, for instance, appears to be difficult for developing countries. Firstly, they face high market barriers when entering the sector. Secondly, few linkages to sectors with lower market-entry barriers exist that may encourage the businesses to be located in the same country.

Figure 6.8. Linkages between maritime sectors

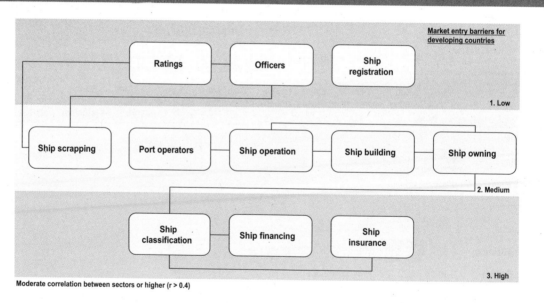

Moderate correlation between sectors or higher (r > 0.4)

Source: UNCTAD secretariat, based on data from tables 6.16 and 6.17.

4.   The globalization of shipping

Within the globalized production of maritime transport services, developing countries are expanding into more and more sectors. They almost entirely dominate labour-intensive low-cost domains such as ship scrapping and the provision of seafarers. They also have an important and growing market share in manufacturing and in more capital-intensive maritime sectors such as ship building, owning and operation. Only the service sectors such as insurance, ship financing and ship classification have so far remained largely in the hands of developed countries, although developing countries are expanding in this area, too.

Shipping companies from both developed and developing countries alike increasingly rely on goods and services from developing countries in order to remain competitive. As far back as the 1970s, shipowners have been making use of open registries, enabling them to hire crews from countries with lower labour costs. In more recent decades, shipping companies have also started purchasing their vessels from shipyards in developing countries, as vessels constructed in European or United States shipyards may be too expensive. Today, the globalization of maritime businesses allows shipping companies to source from the most cost-effective suppliers. This has led to a reduction of international transport costs, which benefits global merchandise trade.

The participation of developing countries in global maritime and related businesses has followed different paths and strategies, depending on the sectors and on comparative advantages and policy choices. Some developing countries have relied on the cost advantage of low wages, others have offered fiscal incentives, and yet others have chosen to support the development of national maritime sectors through industrial policies and targeted aid. For many developing countries, participation in different maritime businesses has been a trigger for economic progress.

Policymakers who aim at further strengthening their country's participation in different maritime businesses need to understand the possible linkages between them. They also need to take into account the already existing level of market concentration, as well as possible linkages between a country's level of development and its capacity to be a competitive player in a particular market. It is hoped that the data and experiences presented and discussed in this chapter may contribute to this endeavour.

ENDNOTES

1   The classification of countries as "developing" in this chapter follows the official terminology of the United Nations (see also annex I).

2   Porter M (1998). *Competitive Advantage: Creating and Sustaining Superior Performance.* New York. Free Press: 30 et seqq.

3   Ibid.

4   *Lloyd's List* (2011). Chinese yards churn out record bulk newbuilders. 12 January. Available at http://www.lloydslist.com/ll/sector/dry-cargo/article353837.ece (accessed in April 2011).

5   Germany Trade and Invest (2010). VR Chinas Schiffsbau mit positivem Jahresergebnis. Available at http://www.gtai.de/fdb-SE,MKT201003168012,Google.html (accessed in April 2011).

6   Ciccantell PS and Shin K-H (2009). The steel and shipbuilding industries of South Korea: Rising East Asia and globalization. Available at http://jwsr.ucr.edu/archive/vol15/Shin_Ciccantell-vol15n2.pdf (accessed in May 2011).

7   World Steel Association (2010). World crude steel output increases by 15 per cent in 2010. Available at http://www.worldsteel.org/?action=newsdetail&id=319 (accessed in April 2011).

8   Bureau of Labour Statistics (2011). Unit labour costs in national currency, compensation, and output. Available at http://www.bls.gov/news.release/prod4.t02.htm (accessed in April 2011) Also: Hourly compensation costs for all employees: Transportation equipment manufacturing. Available at ftp://ftp.bls.gov/pub/special.requests/ForeignLabor/aeind336naics.txt (accessed in April 2011).

9   Petrobras (2011). Petrobras in numbers. Available at http://www.petrobras.com/en/about-us/profile/ (accessed in May 2011).

10   UNCTAD secretariat, on the basis of fleet statistics from Containerisation International Online. Available at http://www.ci-online.co.uk (accessed in May 2011).

[11] Based on data from Containerisation International Online.

[12] The data in this paragraph are based on CSAV company presentations. Available at http://www.csav.cl/ir/presentations-en.htm (accessed in March 2011).

[13] United States Commercial Service (2009). Chile: Maritime ports. Available at http://www.amchamchile.cl/sites/default/files/maritime_ports_io.pdf (accessed in September 2011). Also: ECLAC (2009). Port planning in Latin America and the evolution of container traffic with Asia-Pacific. FAL Bulletin. Edition no. 277, issue 9. Available at http://www.eclac.org/Transporte/noticias/bolfall/4/38994/FAL_277_port_planning.pdf.

[14] Numbers based on presentations and websites of national shipbreaking associations.

[15] Profit margins estimated by Xu Hui, Executive Manager, China Ship Fund. Article available at http://www.chinadaily.com.cn/bizchina/2010-04/08/content_9703387.htm (accessed in April 2011).

[16] UNCTAD (2010). Review of Maritime Transport 2010. United Nations publication. Sales no. E.10.II.D.4. New York and Geneva.

[17] World Bank (2010). The Ship Breaking and Recycling Industry in Bangladesh and Pakistan. Available at http://siteresources.worldbank.org/SOUTHASIAEXT/Resources/223546-1296680097256/Shipbreaking.pdf (accessed in April 2011).

[18] Ibid.

[19] Lloyd's List (2011). The return of Bangladesh. Available at http://www.lloydslist.com/ll/sector/dry-cargo/article357812.ece (accessed in April 2011).

[20] Marine Money (2010). Shipping China. Presentation. Available from http://www.marinemoney.com.

[21] Clarkson Research Services (2010). Will Chinese banks make significant inroads into the international ship financing arena? Article is available from http://www.marinemoney.com.

[22] Standard Chartered (2010). Presentation. Available from http://www.marinemoney.com.

[23] Ince & Co. (2011). Chinese fund for Greek shipowners. Available at http://incelaw.com/news-and-events/News/ch-greek-fund (accessed in May 2011).

[24] BIMCO (2009): Ship classification in the world of free competition. Available at https://www.bimco.org/en/News/2009/10/21_Feature_Week_43.aspx (accessed in April 2011).

[25] Europa Press Releases (2009). Antitrust: Commission paves way for more competition in ship classification market by making IACS's commitments legally binding. Available at http://europa.eu/rapid/pressReleasesAction.do?reference=IP/09/1513&format=HTML&aged=0&language=EN&guiLanguage=en (accessed in April 2011).

[26] Maritime Professional (2010). IRS membership of IACS will put an end to dual class. Available at http://www.maritimeprofessional.com/Blogs/IRS-membership-of-IACS-will-put-an-end-to-dual-cla/June-2010/IRS-membership-of-IACS-will-put-an-end-to-dual-cla.aspx (accessed in April 2011).

[27] Lloyd's List (2010). Class societies wait in line as IACS admits Indian Register. Available at http://www.lloydslist.com/ll/sector/regulation/article171956.ece (accessed in April 2011).

[28] CombinedMar supplied UNCTAD with its results of a recent flag cost comparison.

[29] http://www.parismou.org/.

[30] http://www.igpandi.org/.

[31] Ibid.

[32] Omni (2010). P&I Report 2010. Available at http://omniltd.ca/PDFS/OMNI_PandI_Report_2010.pdf (accessed in April 2011).

[33] Ibid.

[34] UN-OHRLLS (2011). Role of shipping in sustainable development. Available at http://www.un.org/special-rep/ohrlls/UN_system/imo.htm (accessed in September 2011).

[35] Philippine News (2011). Philippines targets to capture 50 per cent of global seafarer demand by 2016. Available at http://www.megascene.net/?p=6229 (accessed in October 2011).

[36] The Joint Manning Group is an organizational body that represents the five leading Philippine manning associations.

[37] Safety4Sea (2011). Philippines in bid to stamp out illegal seafarer recruitment. Available at http://safewaters.wordpress.com/2010/10/20/shipping-philippines-in-bid-to-stamp-out-illegal-seafarer-recruitment/ (accessed in October 2011).

[38] ABS-CBN News (2010). RP likely to ratify ILO convention for seafarers. Available at http://www.abs-cbnnews.com/global-filipino/10/07/10/rp-likely-ratify-ilo-convention-seafarers (accessed in May 2011).

[39] ABS-CBN News (2011). Remittances saved up to 3-M Pinoys from poverty. Available at http://www.abs-cbnnews.com/business/05/03/11/remittances-saved-2-3m-pinoys-poverty (accessed in May 2011).

[40] DP World (2010). Company presentations. Available at http://www.dpworld.com (accessed in April 2011). Also: data received directly from port operator.

[41] Drewry Publishing (2010). Global Container Terminal Operators: Annual Review and Forecast 2010. London.

42   DP World (2010). Company presentations. Available at http://www.dpworld.com (accessed in April 2011). Also: data received directly from port operator.

43   The average GDP per capita for each sector has been calculated by (a) multiplying each country's market share in the business with its average GDP per capita; and (b) adding the results for all countries participating in the business.

44   The correlations are calculated by Excel, using the Pearson correlation. This calculates the correlation coefficient between two measurement variables (here, maritime sector data) when measurements on each variable are observed for each of N subjects (countries). Any missing observation for any subject causes that subject to be ignored in the analysis. The formula applied is shown below:

$$r = \frac{\sum XY - \dfrac{\sum X \sum Y}{N}}{\sqrt{\left(\sum X^2 - \dfrac{(\sum X)^2}{N}\right)\left(\sum Y^2 - \dfrac{(\sum Y)^2}{N}\right)}}$$

The following list includes the data behind each variable of the correlation analysis:

1.   Ship building. Ships built in country, in GT (2009).
2.   Ship owning. Owned ships of companies with nationality of country, in dwt (2010).
3.   Ship operation. Containership operators from country, in TEU (2010).
4.   Ship scrapping. Ships scrapped in country, in GT (2010).
5.   Ship finance. Ship-financing portfolio of banks in country, in dollars; the data only comprise the 25 largest ship-financing banks (2010).
6.   Ship classification. Ships classified by classification society from the country, in GT (2010).
7.   Ship registration. Ships registered by registries from country, in dwt (2010).
8.   Ship insurance. Ships insured by P&I club from country, in GT (2010).
9.   Seafarer supply (officers). Number of officers supplied by country (2010).
10.   Seafarer supply (ratings). Number of ratings supplied by country (2010).
11.   Port operation. Container terminal port operators headquartered in country, port traffic in TEU (2009).

STATISTICAL ANNEX

Annex I. Classification of countries and territories [a b c d]

I.   Developed economies

Code 1

Bermuda
Canada
Greenland

Saint Pierre and Miquelon
United States of America

Code 2

Andorra
Austria
Belgium
Bulgaria
Cyprus
Czech Republic
Denmark
Estonia
Faroe Islands
Finland
France
French Guiana
Germany
Gibraltar
Greece
Guadeloupe
Hungary
Iceland
Ireland
Italy

Latvia
Lithuania
Luxembourg
Malta
Martinique
Monaco
Netherlands
Norway
Poland
Portugal
Réunion
Romania
Slovakia
Slovenia
Spain
Sweden
Switzerland
United Kingdom of Great Britain and
   Northern Ireland

Code 3

Israel

Japan

Code 4

Australia

New Zealand

II.   Transition economies

Code 5.1
in Europe

Albania
Belarus
Bosnia and Herzegovina
Croatia
Montenegro
Republic of Moldova

Russian Federation
Serbia
The former Yugoslav Republic of
   Macedonia
Ukraine

Code 5.2
in Asia

Armenia
Azerbaijan
Georgia
Kazakhstan

Kyrgyzstan
Tajikistan
Turkmenistan
Uzbekistan

Annex I. Classification of countries and territories [a b c d] *(continued)*

III. Developing economies

Code 6.1 Northern Africa	Algeria Egypt Libya	Morocco Tunisia
Code 6.2 Western Africa	Benin Burkina Faso Cape Verde Côte d'Ivoire Gambia Ghana Guinea Guinea-Bissau Liberia	Mali Mauritania Niger Nigeria Saint Helena Senegal Sierra Leone Togo
Code 6.3 Eastern Africa	Burundi Comoros Djibouti Eritrea Ethiopia Kenya Madagascar Malawi Mauritius Mayotte	Mozambique Rwanda Seychelles Somalia Sudan Uganda United Republic of Tanzania Zambia Zimbabwe
Code 6.4 Central Africa	Angola Cameroon Central African Republic Chad Congo	Democratic Republic of the Congo Equatorial Guinea Gabon Sao Tome and Principe
Code 6.5 Southern Africa	Botswana Lesotho Namibia	South Africa Swaziland
Code 7.1 Caribbean	Anguilla Antigua and Barbuda Aruba Bahamas Barbados British Virgin Islands Cayman Islands Cuba Dominica Dominican Republic Grenada	Haiti Jamaica Montserrat Netherlands Antilles Saint Kitts and Nevis Saint Lucia Saint Vincent and the Grenadines Trinidad and Tobago Turks and Caicos Islands United States Virgin Islands

Annex I. Classification of countries and territories [a b c d] (continued)

Code 7.2 Central America	Belize Costa Rica El Salvador Guatemala	Honduras Mexico Nicaragua Panama
Code 7.3 South America – Northern seaboard	Guyana Suriname	Venezuela (Bolivarian Republic of)
Code 7.4 South America – Western seaboard	Chile Colombia	Ecuador Peru
Code 7.5 South America – Eastern seaboard	Argentina Bolivia (Plurinational State of) Brazil	Falkland Islands (Malvinas) Paraguay Uruguay
Code 8.1 Western Asia	Bahrain Iraq Jordan Kuwait Lebanon Oman	Qatar Saudi Arabia Syrian Arab Republic Turkey United Arab Emirates Yemen
Code 8.2 Southern Asia	Afghanistan Bangladesh Bhutan India Iran (Islamic Republic of)	Maldives Nepal Pakistan Sri Lanka
Code 8.3 Eastern Asia	China China, Hong Kong SAR China, Macao SAR China, Taiwan Province of	Democratic People's Republic of Korea Mongolia Republic of Korea
Code 8.4 South-Eastern Asia	Brunei Darussalam Cambodia Indonesia Lao People's Democratic Republic Malaysia Myanmar	Philippines Singapore Timor-Leste Thailand Viet Nam
Code 9 Oceania	American Samoa Christmas Island (Australia) Fiji French Polynesia Guam Kiribati Marshall Islands Micronesia (Federated States of) Nauru	New Caledonia Papua New Guinea Samoa Solomon Islands Tonga Tuvalu Vanuatu Wake Island

Annex I. Classification of countries and territories [a][b][c][d] *(concluded)*

Notes to Annex I

[a] This classification is for statistical purposes only and does not imply any judgement regarding the stage of development or the political situation of any country or territory.

[b] The following are groups of countries or territories used for presenting statistics in this review:

Developed economies:	Codes 1, 2, 3 and 4
Transition economies:	Codes 5.1 and 5.2
Developing economies:	Codes 6, 7, 8 and 9

of which:	in Africa:	Codes 6.1, 6.2, 6.3, 6.4 and 6.5
	in America:	Codes 7.1, 7.2, 7.3, 7.4 and 7.5
	in Asia:	Codes 8.1, 8.2, 8.3 and 8.4
	in Oceania:	Code 9

[c] In certain tables, where appropriate, open-registry countries are recorded in a separate group.

[d] Trade statistics are based on data recorded at the ports of loading and unloading. Trade originating in or destined for neighbouring countries is attributed to the country in which the ports are situated; for this reason, landlocked countries do not figure in these tabulations. On the other hand, statistical tabulations on merchant fleets include data for landlocked countries that possess fleets.

Annex II. World seaborne trade[a] by country group *(in millions of tons)*

Area [a]	Year	Goods loaded			Total goods loaded	Goods unloaded			Total goods unloaded
		Oil		Dry		Oil		Dry	
		Crude	Products [b]	cargo		Crude	Products [b]	cargo	
Developed economies									
North America	2006	22.2	86.4	436.8	545.4	501.0	155.7	492.1	1 148.7
Code 1	2007	24.9	91.3	516.7	632.9	513.5	156.1	453.1	1 122.7
	2008	24.1	119.0	549.4	692.5	481.3	138.9	414.3	1 034.5
	2009	23.9	123.8	498.5	646.1	445.2	132.0	306.4	883.6
	2010	25.5	126.9	523.1	675.5	463.5	135.2	335.0	933.7
Europe	2006	100.9	235.8	768.6	1 105.2	535.6	281.9	1 245.2	2 062.7
Code 2	2007	96.9	253.3	776.6	1 126.8	492.2	262.2	1 154.7	1 909.2
	2008	88.2	261.5	751.1	1 100.8	487.9	273.0	1 213.1	1 974.0
	2009	78.1	236.0	693.8	1 008.0	467.9	281.8	935.0	1 684.6
	2010	83.6	262.8	720.3	1 066.6	478.0	280.5	1 012.2	1 770.7
Japan and Israel	2006	0.0	10.0	153.1	163.1	219.3	84.4	559.6	863.3
Code 3	2007	0.0	14.4	161.2	175.7	213.3	88.5	560.9	862.6
	2008	0.0	21.0	162.0	183.0	254.7	92.8	548.8	896.2
	2009	0.0	19.3	139.8	159.0	190.7	102.3	417.0	710.0
	2010	0.0	24.5	151.2	175.7	192.1	110.6	480.4	783.2
Australia and New Zealand	2006	9.9	4.2	632.7	646.8	26.2	13.5	50.2	90.0
Code 4	2007	13.3	4.0	656.3	673.6	27.0	17.3	51.7	96.0
	2008	16.7	3.8	718.5	739.1	27.3	19.2	56.7	103.2
	2009	12.9	4.8	723.4	741.1	21.5	13.8	60.8	96.1
	2010	16.7	4.3	893.6	914.6	24.8	18.7	60.9	104.5
Subtotal: Developed economies	2006	132.9	336.4	1 991.3	2 460.5	1 282.0	535.5	2 347.2	4 164.7
	2007	135.1	363.0	2 110.8	2 608.9	1 246.0	524.0	2 220.5	3 990.5
	2008	129.0	405.3	2 181.1	2 715.4	1 251.1	523.8	2 233.0	4 007.9
	2009	115.0	383.8	2 055.5	2 554.3	1 125.3	529.9	1 719.2	3 374.4
	2010	125.7	418.5	2 288.2	2 832.5	1 158.5	545.1	1 888.5	3 592.1
Economies in transition	2006	123.1	41.3	245.9	410.3	5.6	3.1	61.9	70.6
	2007	124.4	39.9	243.7	407.9	7.3	3.5	66.0	76.8
Codes 5.1 and 5.2	2008	138.2	36.7	256.6	431.5	6.3	3.8	79.2	89.3
	2009	142.1	44.4	318.8	505.3	3.5	4.6	85.3	93.3
	2010	150.2	45.9	319.7	515.7	3.5	4.6	114.0	122.1
Developing economies									
North Africa	2006	117.4	63.8	77.2	258.5	6.0	13.3	142.0	161.3
Code 6.1	2007	116.1	61.8	80.2	258.1	7.5	14.6	155.4	177.4
	2008	113.2	61.3	77.2	251.8	11.3	16.1	151.1	178.5
	2009	101.1	64.9	71.3	237.3	12.2	14.3	156.2	182.7
	2010	103.6	64.5	76.2	244.3	11.3	14.4	171.1	196.8
Western Africa	2006	110.6	12.6	39.8	162.9	5.4	14.2	62.4	82.0
Code 6.2	2007	110.1	10.3	46.5	166.9	7.6	17.1	67.8	92.6
	2008	111.8	9.1	54.2	175.1	6.8	13.5	61.5	81.8
	2009	104.4	10.5	41.4	156.2	6.8	10.8	66.2	83.8
	2010	96.3	9.1	53.8	159.2	6.5	11.0	73.2	90.7

Annex II. World seaborne trade[a] by country group *(in millions of tons) (continued)*

Area [a]	Year	Goods loaded			Total goods loaded	Goods unloaded			Total goods unloaded
		Oil		Dry cargo		Oil		Dry cargo	
		Crude	Products [b]			Crude	Products [b]		
Eastern Africa	2006	11.8	1.1	29.0	42.0	2.1	7.7	18.2	28.0
Code 6.3	2007	13.6	1.2	23.3	38.1	2.1	8.3	19.8	30.3
	2008	19.7	0.8	27.8	48.2	1.8	7.9	23.8	33.5
	2009	19.0	0.6	18.3	37.8	1.7	9.2	24.4	35.3
	2010	19.0	0.5	29.5	49.1	1.9	8.6	26.3	36.8
Central Africa	2006	114.0	2.6	6.3	122.8	2.1	1.7	7.3	11.2
Code 6.4	2007	122.7	2.6	7.8	133.1	2.8	1.9	7.7	12.3
	2008	134.2	5.8	9.0	149.0	1.7	2.8	8.9	13.5
	2009	129.3	2.0	8.5	139.7	1.9	2.7	10.9	15.5
	2010	124.5	2.0	9.2	135.7	1.6	2.7	11.4	15.8
Southern Africa	2006	0.0	5.9	129.9	135.8	25.6	2.6	39.1	67.4
Code 6.5	2007	0.0	5.9	129.9	135.8	25.6	2.6	39.1	67.4
	2008	0.3	6.2	136.0	142.5	23.4	3.1	42.8	69.3
	2009	0.3	5.1	131.5	136.8	22.0	2.7	44.8	69.4
	2010	0.3	5.4	139.5	145.1	20.8	2.5	35.9	59.2
Subtotal: Developing Africa	2006	353.8	86.0	282.2	721.9	41.3	39.4	269.1	349.8
	2007	362.5	81.8	287.6	732.0	45.7	44.5	289.8	380.0
	2008	379.2	83.3	304.2	766.7	45.0	43.5	288.1	376.6
	2009	354.0	83.0	271.0	708.0	44.6	39.7	302.5	386.8
	2010	343.6	81.5	308.2	733.3	42.0	39.3	318.0	399.3
Caribbean and Central America	2006	108.4	34.6	73.5	216.6	18.5	42.1	101.5	162.2
Codes 7.1 and 7.2	2007	100.4	32.4	75.2	208.1	38.8	44.5	103.1	186.5
	2008	89.1	41.0	84.4	214.5	35.7	47.0	103.5	186.2
	2009	75.1	27.4	71.0	173.4	33.6	46.8	87.2	167.6
	2010	79.1	26.6	86.9	192.6	34.5	49.7	98.2	182.3
South America: Northern	2006	110.8	49.1	499.5	659.4	16.9	10.3	116.2	143.5
and eastern seaboards	2007	120.2	47.8	530.7	698.7	19.9	10.8	125.3	156.1
Codes 7.3 and 7.5	2008	112.6	40.5	560.2	713.2	22.7	13.9	128.3	165.0
	2009	119.0	38.8	524.4	682.2	19.6	14.5	94.8	128.9
	2010	118.3	37.8	592.9	749.0	20.2	14.6	105.0	139.9
South America:	2006	32.1	10.2	112.4	154.8	14.1	7.7	45.9	67.8
Western seaboard	2007	31.6	10.5	118.3	160.4	17.2	8.7	47.5	73.4
Code 7.4	2008	32.9	11.5	136.0	180.4	15.8	9.0	60.9	85.7
	2009	31.7	7.8	134.7	174.2	11.1	12.3	52.0	75.4
	2010	33.6	8.8	145.6	187.9	14.6	12.3	58.4	85.4
Subtotal: Developing America	2006	251.3	93.9	685.5	1 030.7	49.6	60.1	263.7	373.4
	2007	252.3	90.7	724.2	1 067.1	76.0	64.0	275.9	415.9
	2008	234.6	93.0	780.6	1 108.2	74.2	69.9	292.7	436.8
	2009	225.7	74.0	730.1	1 029.8	64.4	73.6	234.0	371.9
	2010	231.0	73.2	825.4	1 129.6	69.3	76.6	261.6	407.5

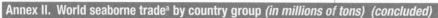

Annex II. World seaborne trade[a] by country group *(in millions of tons)* *(concluded)*

Area [a]	Year	Goods loaded			Total goods loaded	Goods unloaded			Total goods unloaded
		Oil		Dry		Oil		Dry	
		Crude	Products [b]	cargo		Crude	Products [b]	cargo	
Western Asia	2006	729.1	158.1	151.0	1 038.2	27.0	50.3	296.5	373.8
Code 8.1	2007	753.7	155.2	179.5	1 088.5	34.4	51.2	344.4	430.0
	2008	714.0	159.8	181.9	1 055.7	30.6	54.5	349.8	434.9
	2009	717.0	135.8	172.4	1 025.2	22.3	53.1	320.1	395.6
	2010	742.0	154.1	177.6	1 073.7	23.3	53.1	331.4	407.8
Southern and Eastern Asia	2006	132.3	102.5	922.6	1 157.3	411.3	104.0	1 482.0	1 997.4
Codes 8.2 and 8.3	2007	128.1	104.7	959.7	1 192.5	455.0	106.9	1 674.7	2 236.7
	2008	130.7	103.0	943.0	1 176.7	420.5	124.3	1 811.2	2 356.0
	2009	107.6	115.2	823.7	1 046.5	498.8	126.1	2 034.0	2 659.0
	2010	123.2	113.9	919.9	1 156.9	519.7	139.7	2 211.7	2 871.1
South-Eastern Asia	2006	59.8	96.5	721.3	877.6	114.4	94.4	326.8	535.6
Code 8.4	2007	56.4	98.2	779.0	933.6	131.3	102.6	363.0	596.9
	2008	58.1	75.8	837.3	971.2	114.6	108.0	348.5	571.0
	2009	47.7	94.7	840.3	982.7	115.2	90.7	332.0	537.9
	2010	67.8	80.2	812.0	960.1	122.6	107.1	334.8	564.5
Subtotal: Developing Asia	2006	921.2	357.0	1 794.8	3 073.1	552.7	248.8	2 105.3	2 906.8
	2007	938.2	358.1	1 918.3	3 214.6	620.7	260.8	2 382.1	3 263.6
	2008	902.7	338.6	1 962.2	3 203.6	565.6	286.8	2 509.5	3 361.9
	2009	872.3	345.8	1 836.3	3 054.3	636.3	269.9	2 686.2	3 592.4
	2010	932.9	348.2	1 909.5	3 190.7	665.6	300.0	2 877.9	3 843.5
Developing Oceania	2006	1.2	0.1	2.5	3.8	0.0	6.7	6.2	12.9
Code 9	2007	0.9	0.1	2.5	7.1	0.0	7.0	6.5	13.5
	2008	1.5	0.1	2.6	4.2	0.0	7.1	6.7	13.8
	2009	1.5	0.2	4.6	6.3	0.0	3.6	9.5	13.1
	2010	1.5	0.2	4.8	6.5	0.0	3.7	9.7	13.4
Subtotal: Developing	2006	1 527.5	537.1	2 765.0	4 829.5	643.6	355.1	2 644.3	3 642.9
economies and territories	2007	1 553.9	530.7	2 932.6	5 020.8	742.4	376.3	2 954.3	4 073.0
	2008	1 518.0	515.1	3 049.6	5 082.6	684.9	407.2	3 097.0	4 189.1
	2009	1 453.5	502.9	2 842.0	4 798.4	745.3	386.9	3 232.1	4 364.2
	2010	1 509.0	503.1	3 047.9	5 060.1	776.9	419.6	3 467.1	4 663.7
World total	2006	1 783.4	914.8	5 002.1	7 700.3	1 931.2	893.7	5 053.4	7 878.3
	2007	1 813.4	933.5	5 287.1	8 034.1	1 995.7	903.8	5 240.8	8 140.2
	2008	1 785.2	957.0	5 487.2	8 229.5	1 942.3	934.9	5 409.2	8 286.3
	2009	1 710.5	931.1	5 216.4	7 858.0	1 874.1	921.3	5 036.6	7 832.0
	2010	1 784.9	967.5	5 655.8	8 408.3	1 938.9	969.3	5 469.7	8 377.8

Source: Compiled by the UNCTAD secretariat on the basis of data supplied by reporting countries, as published on the relevant government and port industry websites and by specialist sources. The data for 2006 onwards have been revised and updated to reflect improved reporting, including more recent figures and better information regarding the breakdown by cargo type. Figures for 2010 are estimates based on preliminary data or on the last year for which data were available.

[a]   See annex I for the composition of groups.

[b]   Including LNG, LPG, naphtha, gasoline, jet fuel, kerosene, light oil, heavy fuel oil and others.

Annex III. (a) Merchant fleets of the world by flags of registration,[a] groups of countries and types of ship,[b] as at 1 January 2011 *(in thousands of GT)*

	Total fleet	Oil tankers	Bulk carriers	General cargo ships[c]	Container ships	Other types
DEVELOPING ECONOMIES OF AFRICA						
Algeria	790	21	121	66	0	582
Angola	71	6	0	11	0	54
Benin	1	0	0	0	0	1
Cameroon	17	0	0	2	0	15
Cape Verde	34	3	0	9	0	22
Comoros	912	62	277	449	8	116
Congo	4	0	0	0	0	4
Côte d'Ivoire	8	1	0	0	0	7
Democratic Republic of the Congo	12	1	0	0	0	10
Djibouti	3	0	0	0	0	3
Egypt	1 114	223	439	203	55	193
Equatorial Guinea	41	8	0	9	0	23
Eritrea	13	2	0	10	0	1
Ethiopia	112	0	0	112	0	0
Gabon	15	0	0	5	0	9
Gambia	33	4	0	27	0	2
Ghana	107	3	0	17	0	87
Guinea	27	0	0	1	0	26
Guinea-Bissau	6	0	0	1	0	5
Kenya	10	1	0	0	0	9
Libya	865	788	0	27	0	50
Madagascar	15	0	0	6	0	9
Mauritania	47	1	0	1	0	45
Mauritius	73	0	0	14	0	59
Morocco	390	14	0	16	47	314
Mozambique	40	0	0	6	0	34
Namibia	126	0	0	3	0	123
Nigeria	661	437	0	10	0	214
Saint Helena	2	0	0	0	0	2
Sao Tome and Principe	14	1	4	5	0	4
Senegal	49	0	0	2	0	46
Seychelles	201	122	0	43	0	36
Sierra Leone	824	132	144	425	29	95
Somalia	6	0	0	3	0	3
South Africa	169	13	0	0	0	155
Sudan	24	0	0	20	0	3
Togo	247	26	60	121	23	17
Tunisia	189	16	17	50	0	106
United Republic of Tanzania	331	68	28	214	5	16
DEVELOPING ECONOMIES OF AFRICA						
Total	7 603	1 955	1 091	1 888	167	2 503

Annex III. (a) Merchant fleets of the world by flags of registration,[a] groups of countries and types of ship,[b] as at 1 January 2011 *(in thousands of GT) (continued)*

	Total fleet	Oil tankers	Bulk carriers	General cargo ships[c]	Container ships	Other types
DEVELOPING ECONOMIES OF AMERICA						
Anguilla	1	0	0	1	0	0
Argentina	623	284	40	42	13	244
Aruba	0	0	0	0	0	0
Barbados	1 283	431	367	249	157	80
Belize	1 374	36	258	800	0	280
Bolivia (Plurinational State of)	136	7	52	68	0	10
Brazil	2 393	915	459	254	277	487
British Virgin Islands	20	0	0	0	0	19
Cayman Islands	3 024	1 222	632	957	0	213
Chile	871	215	246	71	23	315
Colombia	90	4	0	39	0	47
Costa Rica	5	0	0	0	0	5
Cuba	54	0	1	7	0	45
Curaçao	1 263	99	81	911	6	166
Dominica	908	268	512	81	0	46
Dominican Republic	6	0	0	1	0	5
Ecuador	334	199	0	6	0	130
El Salvador	11	0	0	0	0	11
Falkland Islands (Malvinas)[d]	46	0	0	0	0	46
Grenada	2	0	0	1	0	1
Guatemala	4	0	0	0	0	4
Guyana	42	6	0	23	0	14
Haiti	1	0	0	1	0	0
Honduras	522	81	39	191	2	210
Jamaica	170	0	98	41	28	4
Mexico	1 459	631	126	50	0	652
Nicaragua	5	1	0	1	0	3
Paraguay	46	2	0	30	7	8
Peru	454	206	0	20	0	228
Saint Kitts and Nevis	972	119	285	410	8	150
Suriname	5	2	0	1	0	1
Trinidad and Tobago	52	3	0	1	0	48
Turks and Caicos Islands	2	0	0	0	0	2
Uruguay	98	13	2	6	0	77
Venezuela (Bolivarian Republic of)	1 062	462	121	34	0	445
DEVELOPING ECONOMIES OF AMERICA *Total*	17 339	5 207	3 320	4 295	521	3 996
DEVELOPING ECONOMIES OF ASIA						
Bahrain	532	108	33	1	247	144
Bangladesh	880	65	478	266	35	35
Brunei Darussalam	493	5	0	3	0	484

Annex III. (a) Merchant fleets of the world by flags of registration,[a] groups of countries and types of ship,[b] as at 1 January 2011 (in thousands of GT) (continued)

	Total fleet	Oil tankers	Bulk carriers	General cargo ships[c]	Container ships	Other types
Cambodia	1 776	42	207	1 313	19	195
China	34 705	6 772	15 727	4 430	5 208	2 569
China, Hong Kong SAR	55 543	11 904	28 858	3 129	10 411	1 242
China, Macao SAR	2	0	0	0	0	2
China, Taiwan Province of	2 869	654	1 155	115	689	255
Democratic People's Republic of Korea	814	56	102	583	22	51
India	9 244	4 935	2 576	315	254	1 164
Indonesia	9 279	2 689	1 444	2 442	738	1 965
Iran (Islamic Republic of)	755	80	200	217	30	228
Iraq	19	17	0	0	0	2
Jordan	217	137	0	38	0	42
Kuwait	1 908	1 272	46	96	269	225
Lao People's Democratic Republic	0	0	0	0	0	0
Lebanon	128	0	19	106	0	3
Malaysia	8 073	3 344	222	473	670	3 364
Maldives	111	6	1	92	0	12
Mongolia	655	2	466	144	5	38
Myanmar	195	3	14	147	1	29
Oman	29	1	0	2	0	26
Pakistan	340	175	103	37	0	25
Philippines	5 256	452	2 286	1 525	308	686
Qatar	960	302	70	1	300	287
Republic of Korea	12 513	868	7 955	1 335	741	1 615
Saudi Arabia	1 661	880	0	272	204	304
Singapore	44 870	17 622	9 045	4 203	9 922	4 078
Sri Lanka	197	11	45	101	16	24
Syrian Arab Republic	178	0	51	124	0	3
Thailand	2 941	1 116	594	688	234	309
Timor-Leste	1	0	0	0	0	1
Turkey	5 947	1 028	2 407	1 548	503	461
United Arab Emirates	1 087	377	63	79	345	222
Viet Nam	3 704	933	1 079	1 367	131	194
Yemen	35	17	0	5	0	13
DEVELOPING ECONOMIES OF ASIA						
Total	207 917	55 876	75 246	25 197	31 301	20 296
DEVELOPING ECONOMIES OF OCEANIA						
Fiji	34	0	0	8	0	26
Kiribati	548	89	197	196	0	66
Micronesia (Federated States of)	13	0	0	6	0	6
Papua New Guinea	104	4	17	65	0	17
Samoa	12	0	0	8	0	4
Solomon Islands	11	0	0	2	0	9

	Total fleet	Oil tankers	Bulk carriers	General cargo ships[c]	Container ships	Other types
Tonga	53	1	6	32	0	15
Tuvalu	763	373	138	145	11	97
Vanuatu	2 435	4	1 099	266	25	1 040
DEVELOPING ECONOMIES OF OCEANIA						
Total	3 974	471	1 458	729	36	1 280
DEVELOPING ECONOMIES TOTAL	236 832	63 509	81 115	32 108	32 025	28 075
DEVELOPED ECONOMIES						
Australia	1 698	122	298	154	0	1 124
Austria	10	0	0	10	0	0
Belgium	4 501	1 010	1 585	203	99	1 603
Bulgaria	422	8	271	125	0	18
Canada	3 060	530	1 260	114	16	1 140
Denmark	12 259	3 517	215	414	6 557	1 556
Estonia	375	8	0	11	0	356
Finland	1 450	364	4	474	29	581
France	6 668	2 704	181	154	1 833	1 796
Germany	15 283	366	418	434	13 335	729
Greece	40 795	23 437	12 638	288	2 169	2 264
Guernsey	0	0	0	0	0	0
Iceland	155	0	0	1	0	154
Ireland	218	13	0	129	5	71
Israel	283	3	0	2	268	9
Italy	17 044	5 164	3 468	2 638	949	4 825
Japan	16 858	3 292	5 561	2 711	115	5 179
Jersey	1	0	0	0	0	1
Latvia	264	48	0	23	0	193
Lithuania	418	1	0	213	10	194
Luxembourg	1 030	132	51	253	207	387
Netherlands	6 738	443	40	3 054	1 123	2 078
New Zealand	405	57	38	136	7	167
Norway	16 529	5 012	2 389	4 174	5	4 948
Poland	162	5	0	15	0	142
Portugal	1 225	360	51	310	57	448
Romania	92	5	0	16	0	70
Slovakia	56	0	10	46	0	0
Slovenia	2	0	0	0	0	2
Spain	3 073	592	27	330	52	2 073
Sweden	3 561	221	26	2 045	0	1 269
Switzerland	705	55	448	82	114	6
United Kingdom	18 542	1 683	1 512	3 462	8 981	2 904
United States	11 941	2 314	1 172	1 882	3 354	3 220
DEVELOPED ECONOMIES Total	185 824	51 465	31 665	23 903	39 286	39 506

	Total fleet	Oil tankers	Bulk carriers	General cargo ships[c]	Container ships	Other types
TRANSITION ECONOMIES						
Albania	57	0	3	52	0	2
Azerbaijan	741	248	0	112	0	382
Croatia	1 510	667	663	40	0	139
Georgia	711	21	132	480	8	70
Kazakhstan	117	60	0	5	0	52
Montenegro	5	0	0	2	0	4
Republic of Moldova	363	22	66	266	0	9
Russian Federation	7 711	1 391	440	2 871	143	2 866
Turkmenistan	74	24	0	17	0	33
Ukraine	787	25	73	368	0	321
TRANSITION ECONOMIES Total	12 076	2 457	1 377	4 213	151	3 877
MAJOR 10 OPEN AND INTERNATIONAL REGISTRIES						
Antigua and Barbuda	10 738	15	901	3 797	5 892	133
Bahamas	50 370	18 847	8 007	6 845	1 599	15 072
Bermuda	10 536	1 259	1 800	118	564	6 795
Cyprus	20 732	5 397	8 480	1 355	4 164	1 336
Isle of Man	11 621	6 345	2 923	363	95	1 895
Liberia	106 708	37 381	26 611	4 156	33 415	5 146
Malta	38 738	12 795	16 425	3 054	3 540	2 925
Marshall Islands	62 011	27 190	17 753	1 475	5 643	9 950
Panama	201 264	36 925	94 752	23 554	31 963	14 071
Saint Vincent and the Grenadines	4 707	181	1 590	2 173	178	585
MAJOR 10 OPEN AND INTERNATIONAL REGISTRIES	517 425	146 334	179 241	46 891	87 053	57 907
Unknown flag	5 957	682	982	2 107	201	1 986
World total[e]	958 115	264 446	294 379	109 222	158 717	131 351

Annex III. (a) Merchant fleets of the world by flags of registration,[a] groups of countries and types of ship,[b] as at 1 January 2011 *(in thousands of GT) (concluded)*

Annex III. (b) Merchant fleets of the world by flags of registration,[a] groups of countries and types of ship,[b] as at 1 January 2011 *(in thousands of dwt)*

	Total fleet	Oil tankers	Bulk carriers	General cargo ships [c]	Container ships	Other types
DEVELOPING ECONOMIES OF AFRICA						
Algeria	809	30	204	66	0	509
Angola	58	10	0	14	0	34
Benin	0	0	0	0	0	0
Cameroon	10	0	0	4	0	6
Cape Verde	22	5	0	12	0	6
Comoros	1 217	105	458	553	12	90
Congo	1	0	0	0	0	1
Côte d'Ivoire	4	1	0	0	0	3
Democratic Republic of the Congo	14	2	0	1	0	12
Djibouti	1	0	0	0	0	1
Egypt	1 596	388	776	210	63	159
Equatorial Guinea	35	14	0	11	0	11
Eritrea	14	3	0	10	0	1
Ethiopia	146	0	0	146	0	0
Gabon	9	0	0	5	0	4
Gambia	11	5	0	5	0	2
Ghana	81	5	0	22	0	55
Guinea	13	0	0	0	0	12
Guinea-Bissau	2	0	0	0	0	2
Kenya	8	2	0	0	0	6
Libya	1 522	1 461	0	33	0	28
Madagascar	12	0	0	8	0	4
Mauritania	25	2	0	1	0	21
Mauritius	66	1	0	12	0	54
Morocco	217	20	0	14	55	127
Mozambique	35	0	0	11	0	25
Namibia	71	0	0	2	0	70
Nigeria	952	729	0	17	0	206
Saint Helena	1	0	0	0	0	1
Sao Tome and Principe	18	1	7	7	0	2
Senegal	21	0	0	3	0	17
Seychelles	287	201	0	56	0	30
Sierra Leone	1 089	214	225	536	38	76
Somalia	7	0	0	4	0	2
South Africa	102	18	0	0	0	84
Sudan	26	0	0	25	0	1
Togo	347	40	99	166	32	10
Tunisia	113	24	26	35	0	27
United Republic of Tanzania	472	117	45	295	7	8
DEVELOPING ECONOMIES OF AFRICA						
Total	9 436	3 398	1 841	2 283	206	1 708

Annex III. (b) Merchant fleets of the world by flags of registration,[a] groups of countries and types of ship,[b] as at 1 January 2011 (in thousands of dwt) (continued)

	Total fleet	Oil tankers	Bulk carriers	General cargo ships [c]	Container ships	Other types
DEVELOPING ECONOMIES OF AMERICA						
Anguilla	1	0	0	1	0	0
Argentina	905	538	88	59	18	202
Aruba	0	0	0	0	0	0
Barbados	1 882	674	618	321	211	58
Belize	1 628	61	394	943	0	230
Bolivia (Plurinational State of)	193	12	83	88	0	11
Brazil	3 418	1 471	794	301	358	494
British Virgin Islands	11	1	0	1	0	10
Cayman Islands	3 688	2 026	1 015	397	0	249
Chile	1 127	363	411	85	30	239
Colombia	109	7	0	55	0	48
Costa Rica	1	0	0	0	0	1
Cuba	49	1	1	9	0	38
Curaçao	1 698	172	148	1 137	8	232
Dominica	1 603	477	969	115	0	42
Dominican Republic	2	0	0	1	0	1
Ecuador	416	339	0	5	0	72
El Salvador	2	0	0	0	0	2
Falkland Islands (Malvinas)[d]	34	0	0	0	0	34
Grenada	1	0	0	1	0	0
Guatemala	3	1	0	0	0	2
Guyana	45	9	0	28	0	7
Haiti	1	0	0	1	0	0
Honduras	550	146	67	252	2	83
Jamaica	232	0	156	41	35	1
Mexico	1 862	1 046	228	35	0	553
Nicaragua	3	1	0	1	0	1
Paraguay	53	4	0	39	8	2
Peru	471	327	0	30	0	114
Saint Kitts and Nevis	1 300	187	472	550	10	82
Suriname	6	3	0	2	0	1
Trinidad and Tobago	20	4	0	0	0	16
Turks and Caicos Islands	0	0	0	0	0	0
Uruguay	63	19	3	8	0	32
Venezuela (Bolivarian Republic of)	1 530	789	201	45	0	496
DEVELOPING ECONOMIES OF AMERICA *Total*	22 907	8 676	5 647	4 551	681	3 352
DEVELOPING ECONOMIES OF ASIA						
Bahrain	622	192	44	1	271	113
Bangladesh	1 369	113	813	370	48	24
Brunei Darussalam	433	7	0	3	0	423

Annex III. (b) Merchant fleets of the world by flags of registration,[a] groups of countries and types of ship,[b] as at 1 January 2011 *(in thousands of dwt) (continued)*

	Total fleet	Oil tankers	Bulk carriers	General cargo ships [c]	Container ships	Other types
Cambodia	2 185	64	300	1 694	24	103
China	52 741	11 702	27 225	5 698	6 243	1 873
China, Hong Kong SAR	91 733	21 456	52 925	4 125	12 061	1 166
China, Macao SAR	2	0	0	0	0	2
China, Taiwan Province of	4 310	1 112	2 121	157	775	145
Democratic People's Republic of Korea	1 194	96	171	852	31	44
India	15 278	8 907	4 497	352	328	1 194
Indonesia	12 105	4 440	2 406	3 084	978	1 197
Iran (Islamic Republic of)	993	120	346	277	41	209
Iraq	29	27	0	0	0	2
Jordan	343	290	0	41	0	13
Kuwait	3 006	2 330	78	74	292	233
Lao People's Democratic Republic	2	0	0	2	0	0
Lebanon	130	1	30	96	0	3
Malaysia	10 725	5 889	389	512	820	3 115
Maldives	145	12	2	125	0	7
Mongolia	1 050	3	792	200	7	48
Myanmar	220	5	24	178	0	14
Oman	15	2	0	2	0	11
Pakistan	593	322	189	55	0	26
Philippines	6 946	723	3 640	1 859	371	354
Qatar	1 296	546	116	0	331	303
Republic of Korea	20 155	1 470	14 707	1 736	938	1 304
Saudi Arabia	2 246	1 519	0	272	221	234
Singapore	67 287	31 351	16 603	3 211	11 670	4 452
Sri Lanka	267	20	75	139	17	16
Syrian Arab Republic	253	0	84	169	0	0
Thailand	4 564	2 001	970	988	319	285
Timor-Leste	0	0	0	0	0	0
Turkey	8 745	1 759	4 160	1 913	631	283
United Arab Emirates	1 376	633	87	86	378	193
Viet Nam	5 899	1 540	1 834	2 210	175	140
Yemen	36	28	0	2	0	6
DEVELOPING ECONOMIES OF ASIA Total	318 294	98 679	134 630	30 481	36 969	17 535
DEVELOPING ECONOMIES OF OCEANIA						
Fiji	16	0	0	6	0	10
Kiribati	815	151	348	267	0	49
Micronesia (Federated States of)	10	0	0	6	0	4
Papua New Guinea	122	6	23	80	0	12
Samoa	10	0	0	9	0	1
Solomon Islands	8	0	0	2	0	6
Tonga	58	1	7	40	0	10

Annex III. (b) Merchant fleets of the world by flags of registration,[a] groups of countries and types of ship,[b] as at 1 January 2011 (in thousands of dwt) (continued)						
	Total fleet	Oil tankers	Bulk carriers	General cargo ships [c]	Container ships	Other types
Tuvalu	1 202	683	228	182	15	94
Vanuatu	3 023	6	1 805	274	29	909
DEVELOPING ECONOMIES OF OCEANIA						
Total	5 265	847	2 412	866	44	1 095
DEVELOPING ECONOMIES Total	355 902	111 600	144 529	38 181	37 901	23 691
DEVELOPED ECONOMIES						
Australia	1 947	202	482	145	0	1 118
Austria	12	0	0	12	0	0
Belgium	6 800	1 940	3 057	119	122	1 562
Bulgaria	597	13	439	133	0	11
Canada	3 465	889	1 893	102	17	565
Denmark	14 739	5 724	420	330	7 186	1 080
Estonia	97	13	0	15	0	69
Finland	1 157	610	4	385	37	122
France	8 336	4 987	348	86	1 993	921
Germany	17 566	554	828	458	15 341	385
Greece	71 420	43 883	23 712	315	2 371	1 139
Guernsey	0	0	0	0	0	0
Iceland	66	0	1	1	0	64
Ireland	242	18	0	188	7	27
Israel	343	5	0	3	330	5
Italy	19 440	8 814	6 435	1 646	1 054	1 492
Japan	22 201	6 098	10 220	2 472	126	3 285
Jersey	1	0	0	1	0	0
Latvia	159	81	0	21	0	57
Lithuania	350	2	0	262	14	72
Luxembourg	1 135	201	85	144	237	468
Monaco	0	0	0	0	0	0
Netherlands	7 036	677	49	3 899	1 316	1 096
New Zealand	387	89	56	171	8	63
Norway	20 081	8 672	4 248	3 176	7	3 978
Poland	103	7	0	20	0	75
Portugal	1 212	632	81	270	73	157
Romania	65	8	0	14	0	43
Slovakia	74	0	15	58	0	0
Slovenia	0	0	0	0	0	0
Spain	2 750	1 076	42	214	66	1 353
Sweden	1 762	326	36	1 115	0	285
Switzerland	1 129	87	772	106	157	7
United Kingdom	19 352	2 659	2 799	2 405	10 012	1 476
United States of America	12 662	3 949	2 233	978	3 618	1 884
DEVELOPED ECONOMIES Total	236 682	92 214	58 254	19 261	44 092	22 861

Annex III. (b) Merchant fleets of the world by flags of registration,[a] groups of countries and types of ship,[b] as at 1 January 2011 *(in thousands of dwt) (concluded)*

	Total fleet	Oil tankers	Bulk carriers	General cargo ships [c]	Container ships	Other types
TRANSITION ECONOMIES						
Albania	82	0	4	77	0	1
Azerbaijan	660	353	0	122	0	184
Croatia	2 480	1 244	1 154	49	0	33
Georgia	929	35	207	629	12	45
Kazakhstan	143	103	0	5	0	36
Montenegro	3	0	0	2	0	1
Republic of Moldova	477	38	101	332	0	6
Russian Federation	7 400	2 006	615	3 266	149	1 364
Turkmenistan	75	34	0	15	0	25
Ukraine	789	43	118	440	0	188
TRANSITION ECONOMIES Total	13 038	3 856	2 200	4 937	161	1 884
MAJOR 10 OPEN AND INTERNATIONAL REGISTRIES						
Antigua and Barbuda	13 892	23	1 454	4 824	7 448	144
Bahamas	67 465	34 764	14 113	6 219	1 804	10 566
Bermuda	10 860	2 336	3 471	119	577	4 357
Cyprus	32 321	9 729	15 070	1 679	4 964	880
Isle of Man	19 422	11 403	5 521	417	124	1 958
Liberia	166 246	67 826	48 578	4 305	39 646	5 891
Malta	61 294	22 886	29 533	3 482	4 087	1 307
Marshall Islands	98 757	49 585	32 248	1 497	6 772	8 655
Panama	306 032	67 141	172 641	18 360	35 796	12 094
Saint Vincent and the Grenadines	6 701	340	2 804	2 844	243	469
MAJOR 10 OPEN AND INTERNATIONAL REGISTRIES	782 990	266 034	325 433	43 744	101 460	46 319
Unknown flag	7 130	1 142	1 622	2 847	246	1 273
World Total	1 395 743	474 846	532 039	108 971	183 859	96 028

Annex III. (c) Merchant fleets of the world by flags of registration,[a] groups of countries and types of ship,[b] as at 1 January 2011 *(number of ships)*						
	Total fleet	Oil tankers	Bulk carriers	General cargo ships[c]	Container ships	Other types
DEVELOPING ECONOMIES OF AFRICA						
Algeria	134	12	6	12	0	104
Angola	175	6	0	15	0	154
Benin	7	0	0	0	0	7
Cameroon	66	0	0	6	0	60
Cape Verde	40	3	0	11	0	26
Comoros	308	21	20	145	2	120
Congo	20	0	0	0	0	20
Côte d'Ivoire	32	2	0	0	0	30
Democratic Republic of the Congo	18	1	0	1	0	16
Djibouti	11	0	0	0	0	11
Egypt	351	40	12	35	3	261
Equatorial Guinea	43	4	0	5	0	34
Eritrea	13	1	0	4	0	8
Ethiopia	9		0	8	0	1
Gabon	51	1	0	11	0	39
Gambia	12	1	0	3	0	8
Ghana	233	3	1	16	0	213
Guinea	45	0	0	2	0	43
Guinea-Bissau	24	0	0	7	0	17
Kenya	29	2	0		0	27
Libya	167	19	0	9	0	139
Madagascar	66	1	0	14	0	51
Mauritania	139	1	0	3	0	135
Mauritius	54	1	0	5	0	48
Morocco	508	3	0	7	6	492
Mozambique	121	0	0	8	0	113
Namibia	171	0	0	1	0	170
Nigeria	528	87	0	13	0	428
Saint Helena	2	0	0	0	0	2
Sao Tome and Principe	23	1	1	9	0	12
Senegal	193	1	0	5	0	187
Seychelles	49	6	0	7	0	36
Sierra Leone	363	54	14	192	6	97
Somalia	14	0	0	3	0	11
South Africa	258	7	0	1	0	250
Sudan	17	0	0	3	0	14
Togo	107	12	5	57	2	31
Tunisia	76	1	1	5	0	69
United Republic of Tanzania	48	7	0	11	0	30
DEVELOPING ECONOMIES OF AFRICA						
Total	4 625	309	65		20	3 529

Annex III. (c) Merchant fleets of the world by flags of registration,[a] groups of countries and types of ship,[b] as at 1 January 2011 (number of ships) (continued)

	Total fleet	Oil tankers	Bulk carriers	General cargo ships[c]	Container ships	Other types
DEVELOPING ECONOMIES OF AMERICA						
Anguilla	3	0	0	2	0	1
Argentina	484	34	2	12	1	435
Aruba	1	0	0	0	0	1
Barbados	140	23	20	63	6	28
Belize	426	15	39	197	0	175
Bolivia (Plurinational State of)	47	3	3	32	0	9
Brazil	617	49	22	54	12	480
British Virgin Islands	18	1	0	2	0	15
Cayman Islands	158	64	17	29		48
Chile	560	14	12	45	2	487
Colombia	149	6	0	28	0	115
Costa Rica	16	0	0	0	0	16
Cuba	63	1	3	7	0	52
Curaçao	152	4	2	104	1	41
Dominica	108	10	11	37	0	50
Dominican Republic	21		0	2	0	19
Ecuador	267	38	0	6	0	223
El Salvador	16	0	0	0	0	16
Falkland Islands (Malvinas)[d]	26	0	0	0	0	26
Grenada	8	0	0	3	0	5
Guatemala	12	1	0	0	0	11
Guyana	121	5	0	39	0	77
Haiti	4		0	3	0	1
Honduras	926	83	18	241	1	583
Jamaica	36		5	6	4	21
Mexico	854	36	5	13	0	800
Nicaragua	28	1	0	2	0	25
Paraguay	43	2	0	20	4	17
Peru	796	16	0	2	0	778
Saint Kitts and Nevis	268	51	17	110	3	87
Suriname	15	3	0	3	0	9
Trinidad and Tobago	130	1	0	1	0	128
Turks and Caicos Islands	7		0	1	0	6
Uruguay	116	7	0	4	0	104
Venezuela (Bolivarian Republic of)	333	24	5	22	0	282
DEVELOPING ECONOMIES OF AMERICA						
Total	6 969	492	182	1 090	34	5 171
DEVELOPING ECONOMIES OF ASIA						
Bahrain	215	7	2	3	4	199
Bangladesh	331	75	20	113	5	118
Brunei Darussalam	81	3	0	8	0	70

Annex III. (c) Merchant fleets of the world by flags of registration,[a] groups of countries and types of ship,[b] as at 1 January 2011 (number of ships) (continued)

	Total fleet	Oil tankers	Bulk carriers	General cargo ships[c]	Container ships	Other types
Cambodia	878	20	44	606	5	203
China	4 080	528	624	1 167	214	1 547
China, Hong Kong SAR	1 736	317	686	215	275	243
China, Macao SAR	2	0	0	0	0	2
China, Taiwan Province of	677	29	39	71	29	509
Democratic People's Republic of Korea	258	23	9	174	3	49
India	1 404	125	99	159	15	1 006
Indonesia	5 763	420	146	1 708	118	3 371
Iran (Islamic Republic of)	581	13	14	224	3	327
Iraq	3	2	0	0	0	1
Jordan	19	1	0	5	0	13
Kuwait	201	19	2	15	6	159
Lao People's Democratic Republic	1		0	1	0	
Lebanon	43	1	3	32	0	7
Malaysia	1 391	170	11	195	42	973
Maldives	86	13	1	44	0	28
Mongolia	109	7	22	44	1	35
Myanmar	120	5	1	43	1	70
Oman	44	1	0	8	0	35
Pakistan	52	5	3	3	0	41
Philippines	1 946	182	86	662	15	1 001
Qatar	116	6	3	2	13	92
Republic of Korea	2 913	297	224	420	69	1 903
Saudi Arabia	322	48	0	19	4	251
Singapore	2 667	708	207	178	329	1 245
Sri Lanka	92	9	4	18	1	60
Syrian Arab Republic	46		5	27		14
Thailand	888	250	32	189	32	385
Timor-Leste	1	0	0	0	0	1
Turkey	1 334	186	101	494	41	512
United Arab Emirates	530	43	5	83	7	392
Viet Nam	1 451	104	130	949	21	247
Yemen	50	4	0	4	0	42
DEVELOPING ECONOMIES OF ASIA						
Total	30 431	3 621	2 523	7 883	1 253	15 151
DEVELOPING ECONOMIES OF OCEANIA						
Fiji	56	0	0	15	0	41
Kiribati	117	23	9	59	0	26
Micronesia (Federated States of)	29	0	2	10	0	17
Papua New Guinea	137	4	7	61	0	65
Samoa	11	0	0	4	0	7
Solomon Islands	34	0	0	12	0	22

Annex III. (c) Merchant fleets of the world by flags of registration,[a] groups of countries and types of ship,[b] as at 1 January 2011 (number of ships) (continued)

	Total fleet	Oil tankers	Bulk carriers	General cargo ships[c]	Container ships	Other types
Tonga	42	2	1	16	0	23
Tuvalu	174	29	6	43	3	93
Vanuatu	497	1	37	38	1	420
DEVELOPING ECONOMIES OF OCEANIA						
Total	1 097	59	62	258	4	714
DEVELOPING ECONOMIES Total	43 122	4 481	2 832	9 933	1 311	24 565
DEVELOPED ECONOMIES						
Australia	738	12	13	63	0	650
Austria	2	0	0	2	0	0
Belgium	245	14	22	20	4	185
Bulgaria	92	11	14	20	0	47
Canada	984	30	66	36	2	850
Denmark	987	159	6	119	93	610
Estonia	113	5	0	5	0	103
Finland	275	13	1	82	3	176
France	799	51	6	55	25	662
Germany	931	41	7	92	293	498
Greece	1 433	429	267	105	32	600
Guernsey	3	0	0	0	0	3
Iceland	220	1	1	4	0	214
Ireland	233	2	0	35	1	195
Israel	37	6	0	1	5	25
Italy	1 649	250	89	141	21	1 148
Japan	6 150	638	441	1 560	15	3 496
Jersey	5		0	1	0	4
Latvia	140	7	0	8	0	125
Lithuania	115	1	0	44	1	69
Luxembourg	133	17	2	14	10	90
Monaco	1	0	0	0	0	1
Netherlands	1 302	56	2	548	68	628
New Zealand	270	4	6	51	1	208
Norway	1 995	179	62	379	1	1 374
Poland	314	7	0	12	0	295
Portugal	464	23	7	59	7	368
Romania	76	7	0	6	0	63
Slovakia	19	0	1	17	0	1
Slovenia	7	0	0	0	0	7
Spain	1 469	38	9	51	6	1 365
Sweden	488	43	8	88	0	349
Switzerland	37	5	18	9	4	1
United Kingdom	1 938	170	39	340	216	1 173
United States	6 371	65	60	95	84	6 067
DEVELOPED ECONOMIES Total	30 035	2 284	1 147	4 062	892	21 650

Annex III. (c) Merchant fleets of the world by flags of registration,[a] groups of countries and types of ship[b] as at 1 January 2011 *(number of ships) (concluded)*

	Total fleet	Oil tankers	Bulk carriers	General cargo ships[c]	Container ships	Other types
TRANSITION ECONOMIES						
Albania	65	0	1	56	0	8
Azerbaijan	298	49	0	34	0	215
Croatia	305	18	28	38	0	221
Georgia	280	13	18	172	1	76
Kazakhstan	114	10	0	8	0	96
Montenegro	11	0	0	1	0	10
Republic of Moldova	134	4	8	113	0	9
Russian Federation	3 485	353	62	967	13	2 090
Turkmenistan	61	6	0	8	0	47
Ukraine	528	17	4	150	0	357
TRANSITION ECONOMIES Total	5 281	470	121	1 547	14	3 129
MAJOR 10 OPEN AND INTERNATIONAL REGISTRIES						
Antigua and Barbuda	1 293	7	51	767	406	62
Bahamas	1 384	305	241	366	56	416
Bermuda	158	21	23	10	15	89
Cyprus	1 014	132	275	184	198	225
Isle of Man	385	140	49	64	7	125
Liberia	2 726	734	580	278	899	235
Malta	1 724	439	528	424	107	226
Marshall Islands	1 622	577	457	95	211	282
Panama	7 986	1 099	2 441	1 984	738	1 724
Saint Vincent and the Grenadines	942	19	72	362	19	470
MAJOR 10 OPEN AND INTERNATIONAL REGISTRIES Total	19 234	3 473	4 717	4 534	2 656	3 854
Unknown flag	5 720	384	138	1 323	24	3 851
World total[e]	103 392	11 092	8 955	21 399	4 897	57 049

Notes to Annex III

Source: IHS Fairplay.

[a]   The designations employed and the presentation of material in this table refer to flags of registration and do not imply the expression of any opinion by the Secretariat of the United Nations concerning the legal status of any country or territory, or of its authorities, or concerning the delimitation of its frontiers.

[b]   Seagoing propelled merchant ships of 100 gross tons and above, excluding the Great Lakes fleets of the United States and Canada and the United States Reserve Fleet.

[c]   Including passenger/cargo.

[d]   A dispute exists between the Governments of Argentina and the United Kingdom of Great Britain and Northern Ireland concerning sovereignty over the Falkland Islands (Malvinas).

[e]   Excluding estimates of the United States Reserve Fleet and the United States and Canadian Great Lakes fleets.

Annex IV. True nationality of the 20 largest fleets by flag of registration, as at 1 January 2011[a]

Country or territory of ownership	Antigua and Barbuda			Bahamas			China		
	Number of vessels	1 000 dwt	%	Number of vessels	1 000 dwt	%	Number of vessels	1 000 dwt	%
Belgium	0	0	-	9	122	0.2	1	59	0.1
Bermuda	0	0	-	17	1 907	2.8	0	0	-
Brazil	0	0	-	3	637	0.9	0	0	-
Canada	1	17	0.1	101	10 883	16.1	0	0	-
China	0	0	-	4	242	0.4	2 044	46 207	90.2
China, Hong Kong SAR	0	0	-	3	102	0.2	16	108	0.2
China, Taiwan Province of	0	0	-	0	0	-	1	3	0.0
Cyprus	0	0	-	23	932	1.4	0	0	-
Denmark	17	88	0.6	70	1 245	1.8	0	0	-
France	0	0	-	19	625	0.9	0	0	-
Germany	1 088	12 498	90.1	36	2 777	4.1	0	0	-
Greece	4	57	0.4	229	12 887	19.1	0	0	-
India	0	0	-	1	8	0.0	0	0	-
Indonesia	0	0	-	2	82	0.1	3	3	0.0
Iran (Islamic Republic of)	0	0	-	0	0	-	0	0	-
Isle of Man	0	0	-	0	0	-	0	0	-
Italy	0	0	-	7	443	0.7	0	0	-
Japan	0	0	-	103	6 587	9.8	2	2	0.0
Kuwait	0	0	-	2	85	0.1	0	0	-
Malaysia	0	0	-	15	186	0.3	0	0	-
Netherlands	17	71	0.5	41	2 798	4.2	0	0	-
Norway	9	75	0.5	225	4 671	6.9	0	0	-
Qatar	0	0	-	0	0	-	0	0	-
Republic of Korea	0	0	-	1	6	0.0	0	0	-
Russian Federation	3	8	0.1	1	2	0.0	1	3	0.0
Saudi Arabia	0	0	-	19	4 948	7.3	0	0	-
Singapore	0	0	-	9	55	0.1	0	0	-
Spain	0	0	-	7	671	1.0	0	0	-
Sweden	0	0	-	10	504	0.7	0	0	-
Thailand	0	0	-	4	99	0.1	0	0	-
Turkey	7	38	0.3	3	155	0.2	0	0	-
United Arab Emirates	0	0	-	30	1 372	2.0	0	0	-
United Kingdom	1	3	0.0	32	489	0.7	1	3	0.0
United States	9	53	0.4	114	4 532	6.7	0	0	-
Viet Nam	0	0	-	0	0	-	0	0	-
Total 35	1 156	12 909	93.0	1 140	60 051	89.1	2 069	46 388	90.5
Other owners	61	577	4.2	88	4 208	6.2	0	0	-
Unknown owners	42	391	2.8	75	3 131	4.6	324	4 858	9.5
TOTAL	1 259	13 877	100.0	1 303	67 391	100.0	2 393	51 246	100.0

Annex IV.	True nationality of the 20 largest fleets by flag of registration, as at 1 January 2011[a]								
Cyprus			**DIS**			**Germany**			**Country or territory of ownership**
Number of vessels	1 000 dwt	%	Number of vessels	1 000 dwt	%	Number of vessels	1 000 dwt	%	
2	14	0.0	0	0	-	0	0	-	Belgium
7	322	1.0	0	0	-	1	43	0.2	Bermuda
0	0	-	0	0	-	0	0	-	Brazil
2	64	0.2	0	0	-	0	0	-	Canada
7	199	0.6	0	0	-	0	0	-	China
2	36	0.1	0	0	-	0	0	-	China. Hong Kong SAR
0	0	-	0	0	-	0	0	-	China, Taiwan Province of
129	4 016	12.5	0	0	-	0	0	-	Cyprus
7	72	0.2	362	14 094	98.8	0	0	-	Denmark
19	786	2.4	0	0	-	0	0	-	France
191	4 314	13.4	9	28	0.2	442	17 149	98.0	Germany
200	11 257	35.1	0	0	-	1	40	0.2	Greece
3	111	0.3	0	0	-	0	0	-	India
2	151	0.5	0	0	-	0	0	-	Indonesia
10	3 179	9.9	0	0	-	0	0	-	Iran (Islamic Republic of)
0	0	-	0	0	-	0	0	-	Isle of Man
5	49	0.2	0	0	-	0	0	-	Italy
17	528	1.6	0	0	-	0	0	-	Japan
0	0	-	0	0	-	0	0	-	Kuwait
0	0	-	0	0	-	0	0	-	Malaysia
43	471	1.5	0	0	-	3	22	0.1	Netherlands
31	237	0.7	2	4	0.0	0	0	-	Norway
0	0	-	0	0	-	0	0	-	Qatar
0	0	-	0	0	-	0	0	-	Republic of Korea
48	2 164	6.7	0	0	-	0	0	-	Russian Federation
0	0	-	0	0	-	0	0	-	Saudi Arabia
2	26	0.1	0	0	-	0	0	-	Singapore
8	247	0.8	0	0	-	0	0	-	Spain
5	19	0.1	12	127	0.9	0	0	-	Sweden
0	0	-	0	0	-	0	0	-	Thailand
0	0	-	0	0	-	0	0	-	Turkey
14	278	0.9	0	0	-	0	0	-	United Arab Emirates
7	518	1.6	0	0	-	0	0	-	United Kingdom
12	78	0.2	0	0	-	0	0	-	United States
0	0	-	0	0	-	0	0	-	Viet Nam
773	29 136	90.8	385	14 253	99.9	447	17 254	98.6	Total 35
46	736	2.3	0	0	-	4	96	0.5	Other owners
84	2 230	6.9	8	12	0.1	14	148	0.8	Unknown owners
903	32 101	100.0	393	14 265	100.0	465	17 498	100.0	TOTAL

Annex IV. True nationality of the 20 largest fleets by flag of registration, as at 1 January 2011[a]

Country or territory of ownership	Greece			China, Hong Kong SAR			India		
	Number of vessels	1 000 dwt	%	Number of vessels	1 000 dwt	%	Number of vessels	1 000 dwt	%
Belgium	16	2 480	3.5	21	850	0.9	1	14	0.1
Bermuda	3	138	0.2	17	3 111	3.4	0	0	-
Brazil	0	0	-	0	0	-	0	0	-
Canada	0	0	-	71	4 000	4.4	0	0	-
China	1	69	0.1	476	29 812	32.6	1	27	0.2
China, Hong Kong SAR	1	31	0.0	399	24 102	26.3	1	19	0.1
China, Taiwan Province of	0	0	-	26	1 602	1.8	0	0	-
Cyprus	3	12	0.0	3	240	0.3	0	0	-
Denmark	0	0	-	41	1 662	1.8	0	0	-
France	0	0	-	5	510	0.6	0	0	-
Germany	0	0	-	10	563	0.6	0	0	-
Greece	758	64 659	90.7	23	1 247	1.4	0	0	-
India	0	0	-	0	0	-	460	14 680	97.5
Indonesia	1	74	0.1	9	84	0.1	0	0	-
Iran (Islamic Republic of)	0	0	-	3	248	0.3	0	0	-
Isle of Man	0	0	-	0	0	-	0	0	-
Italy	5	31	0.0	0	0	-	0	0	-
Japan	0	0	-	83	3 991	4.4	0	0	-
Kuwait	0	0	-	0	0	-	0	0	-
Malaysia	0	0	-	0	0	-	2	32	0.2
Netherlands	0	0	-	0	0	-	2	10	0.1
Norway	0	0	-	51	3 609	3.9	0	0	-
Qatar	0	0	-	0	0	-	0	0	-
Republic of Korea	0	0	-	3	77	0.1	0	0	-
Russian Federation	0	0	-	1	8	0.0	0	0	-
Saudi Arabia	0	0	-	0	0	-	0	0	-
Singapore	0	0	-	13	461	0.5	0	0	-
Spain	0	0	-	0	0	-	0	0	-
Sweden	0	0	-	0	0	-	0	0	-
Thailand	0	0	-	0	0	-	0	0	-
Turkey	0	0	-	0	0	-	0	0	-
United Arab Emirates	0	0	-	1	299	0.3	5	76	0.5
United Kingdom	5	732	1.0	29	1 219	1.3	0	0	-
United States	8	389	0.5	35	2 406	2.6	0	0	-
Viet Nam	0	0	-	0	0	-	0	0	-
Total 35	801	68 614	96.3	1 320	80 102	87.5	472	14 858	98.7
Other owners	3	459	0.6	2	133	0.1	2	102	0.7
Unknown owners	82	2 185	3.1	194	11 282	12.3	19	94	0.6
TOTAL	886	71 258	100.0	1 516	91 518	100.0	493	15 054	100.0

Annex IV. True nationality of the 20 largest fleets by flag of registration, as at 1 January 2011[a]

Isle of Man			Italy			Japan			Country or territory of ownership
Number of vessels	1 000 dwt	%	Number of vessels	1 000 dwt	%	Number of vessels	1 000 dwt	%	
0	0	-	0	0	-	0	0	-	Belgium
7	2 067	10.6	0	0	-	0	0	-	Bermuda
0	0	-	0	0	-	0	0	-	Brazil
1	21	0.1	0	0	-	0	0	-	Canada
0	0	-	0	0	-	1	7	0.0	China
0	0	-	0	0	-	0	0	-	China, Hong Kong SAR
0	0	-	10	532	2.8	0	0	-	China, Taiwan Province of
0	0	-	0	0	-	0	0	-	Cyprus
44	501	2.6	4	44	0.2	0	0	-	Denmark
0	0	-	2	15	0.1	0	0	-	France
58	1 011	5.2	1	3	0.0	0	0	-	Germany
59	5 626	29.0	8	365	1.9	0	0	-	Greece
0	0	-	0	0	-	0	0	-	India
0	0	-	0	0	-	1	0	0.0	Indonesia
0	0	-	0	0	-	0	0	-	Iran (Islamic Republic of)
0	0	-	0	0	-	0	0	-	Isle of Man
0	0	-	616	16 557	85.9	0	0	-	Italy
16	1 574	8.1	0	0	-	724	18 943	98.5	Japan
0	0	-	0	0	-	0	0	-	Kuwait
5	572	2.9	0	0	-	0	0	-	Malaysia
2	2	0.0	7	9	0.0	0	0	-	Netherlands
60	2 040	10.5	6	54	0.3	1	78	0.4	Norway
0	0	-	0	0	-	0	0	-	Qatar
0	0	-	0	0	-	0	0	-	Republic of Korea
0	0	-	0	0	-	0	0	-	Russian Federation
0	0	-	0	0	-	0	0	-	Saudi Arabia
2	55	0.3	1	40	0.2	0	0	-	Singapore
0	0	-	0	0	-	0	0	-	Spain
0	0	-	1	7	0.0	0	0	-	Sweden
0	0	-	0	0	-	1	5	0.0	Thailand
0	0	-	4	27	0.1	0	0	-	Turkey
0	0	-	0	0	-	0	0	-	United Arab Emirates
93	5 232	26.9	3	15	0.1	0	0	-	United Kingdom
2	21	0.1	21	162	0.8	0	0	-	United States
0	0	-	0	0	-	0	0	-	Viet Nam
349	18 721	96.4	684	17 833	92.6	728	19 033	98.9	Total 35
10	55	0.3	28	1 156	6.0	0	0	-	Other owners
13	636	3.3	30	279	1.4	53	208	1.1	Unknown owners
372	19 412	100.0	742	19 268	100.0	781	19 240	100.0	TOTAL

Annex IV. True nationality of the 20 largest fleets by flag of registration, as at 1 January 2011[a]

Country or territory of ownership	Liberia			Malta			Marshall Islands		
	Number of vessels	1 000 dwt	%	Number of vessels	1 000 dwt	%	Number of vessels	1 000 dwt	%
Belgium	1	14	0.0	8	403	0.7	1	35	0.0
Bermuda	4	915	0.6	13	397	0.7	45	7 209	7.3
Brazil	25	6 185	3.7	0	0	-	2	342	0.3
Canada	5	353	0.2	2	31	0.1	5	298	0.3
China	14	735	0.4	6	106	0.2	15	1 425	1.4
China, Hong Kong SAR	64	4 612	2.8	3	111	0.2	4	50	0.1
China, Taiwan Province of	87	8 543	5.2	0	0	-	2	640	0.6
Cyprus	10	924	0.6	32	889	1.5	39	1 077	1.1
Denmark	4	167	0.1	39	504	0.8	7	376	0.4
France	1	145	0.1	7	438	0.7	2	12	0.0
Germany	1 120	51 875	31.3	131	3 280	5.4	241	10 939	11.1
Greece	481	30 417	18.4	468	27 702	45.4	380	25 198	25.5
India	4	334	0.2	3	249	0.4	6	568	0.6
Indonesia	4	291	0.2	0	0	-	1	48	0.0
Iran (Islamic Republic of)	0	0	-	52	7 567	12.4	0	0	-
Isle of Man	19	3 986	2.4	0	0	-	6	649	0.7
Italy	48	2 942	1.8	44	919	1.5	1	27	0.0
Japan	110	7 889	4.8	5	200	0.3	42	4 180	4.2
Kuwait	0	0	-	2	147	0.2	1	85	0.1
Malaysia	0	0	-	1	3	0.0	18	269	0.3
Netherlands	35	351	0.2	2	18	0.0	22	490	0.5
Norway	44	964	0.6	93	990	1.6	92	4 357	4.4
Qatar	5	51	0.0	0	0	-	29	3 609	3.7
Republic of Korea	4	513	0.3	2	8	0.0	35	1 682	1.7
Russian Federation	109	10 014	6.0	42	377	0.6	4	81	0.1
Saudi Arabia	20	5 055	3.1	0	0	-	0	0	-
Singapore	24	2 658	1.6	4	291	0.5	29	2 726	2.8
Spain	0	0	-	11	156	0.3	0	0	-
Sweden	11	469	0.3	1	28	0.0	0	0	-
Thailand	0	0	-	0	0	-	1	3	0.0
Turkey	17	551	0.3	209	5 651	9.3	69	3 094	3.1
United Arab Emirates	29	1 744	1.1	1	30	0.0	19	814	0.8
United Kingdom	36	1 583	1.0	23	417	0.7	4	158	0.2
United States	61	2 728	1.6	33	655	1.1	214	16 033	16.2
Viet Nam	0	0	-	0	0	-	0	0	-
Total 35	2 396	147 011	88.7	1 237	51 566	84.4	1 336	86 473	87.6
Other owners	126	5 979	3.6	192	4 223	6.9	106	5 509	5.6
Unknown owners	163	12 667	7.6	197	5 294	8.7	133	6 761	6.8
TOTAL	2 685	165 657	100.0	1 626	61 084	100.0	1 575	98 743	100.0

Annex IV. True nationality of the 20 largest fleets by flag of registration, as at 1 January 2011[a]									
NIS			**Panama**			**Republic of Korea**			**Country or territory of ownership**
Number of vessels	1 000 dwt	%	Number of vessels	1 000 dwt	%	Number of vessels	1 000 dwt	%	
0	0	-	2	20	0.0	0	0	-	Belgium
23	1 770	9.8	28	4 346	1.4	0	0	-	Bermuda
0	0	-	8	1 270	0.4	0	0	-	Brazil
1	21	0.1	9	331	0.1	0	0	-	Canada
0	0	-	548	23 978	7.9	8	103	0.5	China
0	0	-	129	6 351	2.1	0	0	-	China. Hong Kong SAR
0	0	-	327	13 167	4.3	1	9	0.0	China, Taiwan Province of
1	4	0.0	9	1 009	0.3	0	0	-	Cyprus
8	288	1.6	37	1 323	0.4	0	0	-	Denmark
3	76	0.4	11	292	0.1	2	19	0.1	France
0	0	-	23	3 370	1.1	0	0	-	Germany
0	0	-	389	15 947	5.2	1	29	0.2	Greece
0	0	-	21	919	0.3	0	0	-	India
0	0	-	11	145	0.0	0	0	-	Indonesia
0	0	-	6	32	0.0	0	0	-	Iran (Islamic Republic of)
0	0	-	5	816	0.3	0	0	-	Isle of Man
2	76	0.4	27	932	0.3	0	0	-	Italy
0	0	-	2 304	136 889	45.1	13	474	2.4	Japan
0	0	-	12	658	0.2	0	0	-	Kuwait
0	0	-	18	327	0.1	0	0	-	Malaysia
1	5	0.0	22	166	0.1	0	0	-	Netherlands
410	13 713	76.1	99	3 009	1.0	0	0	-	Norway
0	0	-	1	77	0.0	0	0	-	Qatar
0	0	-	359	26 292	8.7	736	18 135	93.0	Republic of Korea
0	0	-	52	249	0.1	0	0	-	Russian Federation
3	112	0.6	7	153	0.1	0	0	-	Saudi Arabia
0	0	-	103	3 422	1.1	0	0	-	Singapore
0	0	-	42	225	0.1	0	0	-	Spain
28	866	4.8	4	147	0.0	0	0	-	Sweden
0	0	-	11	63	0.0	1	27	0.1	Thailand
0	0	-	64	710	0.2	0	0	-	Turkey
0	0	-	100	2 581	0.8	0	0	-	United Arab Emirates
1	68	0.4	40	675	0.2	0	0	-	United Kingdom
11	840	4.7	159	5 178	1.7	8	135	0.7	United States
0	0	-	44	1 328	0.4	0	0	-	Viet Nam
492	17 839	99.1	5 031	256 396	84.4	770	18 932	97.1	Total 35
6	55	0.3	285	6 761	2.2	0	0	-	Other owners
11	116	0.6	1 246	40 622	13.4	84	560	2.9	Unknown owners
509	18 010	100.0	6 562	303 778	100.0	854	19 492	100.0	TOTAL

Annex IV. True nationality of the 20 largest fleets by flag of registration, as at 1 January 2011[a]

Country or territory of ownership	Singapore			United Kingdom			Total, top 20 registries		
	Number of vessels	1 000 dwt	%	Number of vessels	1 000 dwt	%	Number of vessels	1 000 dwt	%
Belgium	1	6	0.0	0	0	-	63	4 016	0.4
Bermuda	35	2 450	3.7	8	214	1.3	208	24 891	2.4
Brazil	2	330	0.5	0	0	-	40	8 763	0.8
Canada	0	0	-	0	0	-	198	16 020	1.5
China	21	1 194	1.8	11	505	3.0	3 157	104 607	10.0
China, Hong Kong SAR	35	1 474	2.2	10	95	0.6	667	37 092	3.5
China, Taiwan Province of	78	3 789	5.7	11	733	4.4	543	29 017	2.8
Cyprus	5	117	0.2	0	0	-	254	9 219	0.9
Denmark	127	8 962	13.4	44	2 279	13.5	811	31 606	3.0
France	13	397	0.6	36	2 349	13.9	120	5 664	0.5
Germany	30	1 107	1.7	60	1 516	9.0	3 440	110 430	10.5
Greece	18	336	0.5	6	49	0.3	3 025	195 818	18.6
India	24	1 339	2.0	0	0	-	522	18 207	1.7
Indonesia	53	1 131	1.7	0	0	-	87	2 010	0.2
Iran (Islamic Republic of)	0	0	-	0	0	-	71	11 027	1.0
Isle of Man	0	0	-	1	1	0.0	31	5 452	0.5
Italy	4	55	0.1	10	59	0.4	769	22 091	2.1
Japan	142	9 293	13.9	5	91	0.5	3 566	190 640	18.1
Republic of Korea	10	686	1.0	0	0	-	1 150	47 399	4.5
Kuwait	0	0	-	0	0	-	17	976	0.1
Malaysia	27	2 500	3.7	0	0	-	86	3 889	0.4
Netherlands	20	35	0.1	23	27	0.2	240	4 477	0.4
Norway	150	4 562	6.8	44	890	5.3	1 317	39 253	3.7
Qatar	0	0	-	0	0	-	35	3 737	0.4
Republic of Korea	10	686	1.0	0	0	-	1 150	47 399	4.5
Russian Federation	2	170	0.3	0	0	-	263	13 076	1.2
Saudi Arabia	0	0	-	1	2	0.0	50	10 270	1.0
Singapore	659	18 694	27.9	0	0	-	846	28 428	2.7
Spain	0	0	-	1	1	0.0	69	1 299	0.1
Sweden	10	200	0.3	28	576	3.4	110	2 943	0.3
Thailand	32	697	1.0	0	0	-	50	894	0.1
Turkey	0	0	-	0	0	-	373	10 226	1.0
United Arab Emirates	16	184	0.3	7	43	0.3	222	7 419	0.7
United Kingdom	62	483	0.7	234	2 096	12.4	571	13 692	1.3
United States	35	2 018	3.0	49	177	1.0	771	35 403	3.4
Viet Nam	1	28	0.0	0	0	-	45	1 356	0.1
Total 35	1 612	62 237	92.9	589	11 702	69.5	23 787	1 051 308	88.9
Other owners	44	751	1.1	14	136	0.8	1 017	30 936	2.6
Unknown owners	108	3 975	5.9	104	5 002	29.7	2 984	100 452	8.5
TOTAL	1 764	66 963	100.0	707	16 840	100.0	27 788	1 182 695	100.0

Source: Compiled by the UNCTAD secretariat on the basis of data provided by IHS Fairplay.

[a]   Cargo-carrying vessels of 1,000 GT and above.

Annex V. Container port throughput for maritime economies, 2008 and 2009 *(in TEU)*

Country or territory of ownership	2008	2009	Rank (2009)
Albania	46 798	68 780	114
Algeria	225 140	247 986	88
Antigua and Barbuda	32 562	29 150	123
Argentina	1 997 146	1 626 351	42
Aruba	140 000	125 000	107
Australia	6 098 405	6 196 745	20
Austria	335 173	290 466	82
Bahamas	1 702 000	1 297 000	43
Bahrain	269 331	239 705	91
Bangladesh	1 091 200	1 182 121	50
Barbados	87 255	75 015	113
Belgium	10 937 134	9 701 494	13
Belize	38 211	31 344	122
Benin	300 000	267 000	85
Brazil	7 238 976	6 574 617	18
Brunei Darussalam	90 366	85 577	111
Bulgaria	203 253	136 444	101
Cambodia	258 775	207 577	93
Cameroon	270 000	240 300	90
Canada	4 720 663	4 190 157	28
Cayman Islands	36 644	44 215	120
Chile	3 164 137	2 795 989	33
China	115 060 978	107 492 861	1
China, Hong Kong SAR	24 494 229	21 040 096	4
China, Taiwan Province of	12 971 224	11 352 097	11
Colombia	1 969 316	2 056 747	39
Costa Rica	1 004 971	875 687	56
Côte d'Ivoire	713 625	677 029	60
Croatia	168 761	130 740	105
Cuba	319 000	283 910	84
Cyprus	416 970	353 913	78
Congo	321 000	285 690	83
Denmark	740 682	621 546	63
Djibouti	356 462	519 500	69
Dominican Republic	1 138 471	1 263 456	44
Ecuador	670 831	1 000 895	52
Egypt	6 099 218	6 250 443	19
El Salvador	156 323	126 369	106
Estonia	180 927	130 939	103
Finland	1 605 442	1 113 253	51
France	4 671 989	4 490 583	25
French Guiana	45 000	40 050	121
French Polynesia	70 336	63 807	115
Gabon	158 884	130 758	104
Georgia	253 811	181 613	96
Germany	17 178 075	13 280 552	9

Annex V. Container port throughput for maritime economies, 2008 and 2009 *(in TEU)*

Country or territory of ownership	2008	2009	Rank (2009)
Ghana	555 009	493 958	71
Greece	672 522	935 076	54
Guadeloupe	170 729	142 692	100
Guam	167 784	157 096	98
Guatemala	937 642	906 326	55
Honduras	669 802	571 720	67
Iceland	267 151	193 816	94
India	7 672 457	8 011 810	15
Indonesia	7 404 831	7 243 557	16
Iran (Islamic Republic of)	2 000 230	2 206 476	37
Ireland	1 043 744	817 305	58
Israel	2 089 900	2 033 000	40
Italy	10 530 214	9 532 462	14
Jamaica	1 915 943	1 689 670	41
Japan	18 943 606	16 285 918	5
Jordan	582 515	674 525	61
Kenya	615 733	618 816	64
Kuwait	961 684	854 044	57
Latvia	225 467	184 399	95
Lebanon	861 931	994 601	53
Libyan Arab Jamahiriya	174 827	155 596	99
Lithuania	373 263	247 982	89
Madagascar	143 371	132 278	102
Malaysia	16 024 829	15 671 296	7
Maldives	53 650	56 000	118
Malta	2 407 332	2 323 941	35
Mauritania	57 478	62 269	116
Mauritius	454 433	406 862	75
Mexico	3 312 713	2 874 287	32
Morocco	919 360	1 222 000	49
Mozambique	241 237	214 701	92
Myanmar	180 000	160 200	97
Namibia	183 605	265 663	86
Netherlands	11 362 089	10 066 374	12
Netherlands Antilles	102 082	97 913	109
New Caledonia	119 661	119 147	108
New Zealand	2 295 575	2 302 894	36
Nicaragua	63 030	59 471	117
Nigeria	72 500	87 000	110
Norway	331 054	318 924	81
Oman	3 427 990	3 768 045	29
Pakistan	1 938 001	2 058 056	38
Panama	5 129 499	4 597 112	23
Papua New Guinea	250 252	257 740	87
Paraguay	9 317	7 045	125
Peru	1 235 326	1 232 849	48

Annex V. Container port throughput for maritime economies, 2008 and 2009 *(concluded)*

Country or territory of ownership	2008	2009	Rank (2009)
Philippines	4 471 428	4 306 723	27
Poland	859 341	671 552	62
Portugal	1 297 402	1 233 482	47
Qatar	400 000	410 000	74
Republic of Korea	17 417 723	15 699 161	6
Romania	1 380 935	594 299	65
Russian Federation	3 307 075	2 337 634	34
Saint Helena	700	623	126
Saint Lucia	70 202	51 942	119
Saint Vincent and the Grenadines	16 570	16 238	124
Saudi Arabia	4 652 022	4 430 676	26
Senegal	347 483	331 076	80
Singapore	30 891 200	26 592 800	3
Slovenia	353 880	343 165	79
South Africa	3 875 952	3 726 313	30
Spain	13 461 302	11 803 192	10
Sri Lanka	3 687 465	3 464 297	31
Sudan	391 139	431 232	72
Sweden	1 298 778	1 251 424	45
Switzerland	92 464	78 285	112
Syrian Arab Republic	610 607	685 299	59
Thailand	6 726 237	5 897 935	21
Trinidad and Tobago	554 093	567 183	68
Tunisia	424 780	418 880	73
Turkey	5 218 316	4 521 713	24
Ukraine	1 123 268	516 698	70
United Arab Emirates	14 756 127	14 425 039	8
United Kingdom	7 185 963	6 700 362	17
United Republic of Tanzania	363 310	370 401	77
United States	42 411 640	37 347 064	2
Uruguay	675 273	588 410	66
Venezuela (Bolivarian Republic of)	1 325 194	1 238 717	46
Viet Nam	4 393 699	4 840 598	22
Yemen	492 313	382 445	76
Total	514 858 737	469 414 358	

Source: UNCTAD secretariat, derived from information contained in Containerisation International Online (May 2011), from various Dynamar B.V. publications, and from information obtained by the UNCTAD secretariat directly from terminal operators and port authorities.

Note: Some figures are estimates. Port throughput figures tend not to be disclosed by ports until a considerable time after the end of the calendar year. Country totals may conceal the fact that minor ports may not be included; therefore, in some cases, the actual figures may be higher than those given.

Annex VI. UNCTAD Liner Shipping Connectivity Index, as at 1 January 2011

Country or territory	Index points					Rank 2004	Rank 2011
	2004	2010	2011	Average annual change 2004–2011	Change 2011/2010		
China	100.00	143.57	152.06	7.44	8.49	1	1
China, Hong Kong	94.42	113.60	115.27	2.98	1.67	2	2
Singapore	81.87	103.76	105.02	3.31	1.26	4	3
Germany	76.59	90.88	93.32	2.39	2.44	7	4
Netherlands	78.81	89.96	92.10	1.90	2.14	6	5
Republic of Korea	68.68	82.61	92.02	3.33	9.41	10	6
Malaysia	62.83	88.14	90.96	4.02	2.82	12	7
Belgium	73.16	84.00	88.47	2.19	4.47	8	8
United Kingdom	81.69	87.53	87.46	0.82	-0.07	5	9
United States	83.30	83.80	81.63	-0.24	-2.17	3	10
Spain	54.44	74.32	76.58	3.16	2.26	15	11
France	67.34	74.94	71.84	0.64	-3.10	11	12
Italy	58.13	59.57	70.18	1.72	10.61	14	13
Japan	69.15	67.43	67.81	-0.19	0.38	9	14
China, Taiwan Province of	59.56	64.37	66.69	1.02	2.32	13	15
United Arab Emirates	38.06	63.37	62.50	3.49	-0.87	18	16
Saudi Arabia	35.83	50.43	59.97	3.45	9.54	19	17
Morocco	9.39	49.36	55.13	6.53	5.77	78	18
Egypt	42.86	47.55	51.15	1.18	3.60	16	19
Viet Nam	12.86	31.36	49.71	5.26	18.35	55	20
Oman	23.33	48.52	49.33	3.71	0.81	31	21
India	34.14	41.40	41.52	1.05	0.12	21	22
Sri Lanka	34.68	40.23	41.13	0.92	0.90	20	23
Malta	27.53	37.53	40.95	1.92	3.42	25	24
Turkey	25.60	36.10	39.40	1.97	3.30	29	25
Canada	39.67	42.39	38.41	-0.18	-3.98	17	26
Panama	32.05	41.09	37.51	0.78	-3.58	22	27
Thailand	31.01	43.76	36.70	0.81	-7.06	23	28
Mexico	25.29	36.35	36.09	1.54	-0.26	30	29
South Africa	23.13	32.49	35.67	1.79	3.18	32	30
Lebanon	10.57	30.29	35.09	3.50	4.80	67	31
Brazil	25.83	31.65	34.62	1.26	2.97	28	32
Greece	30.22	34.25	32.15	0.28	-2.10	24	33
Algeria	10.00	31.45	31.06	3.01	-0.39	74	34
Argentina	20.09	27.61	30.62	1.50	3.01	37	35
Pakistan	20.18	29.48	30.54	1.48	1.06	36	36
Iran (Islamic Republic of)	13.69	30.73	30.27	2.37	-0.46	52	37

Annex VI. UNCTAD Liner Shipping Connectivity Index, as at 1 January 2011 *(continued)*

Country or territory	Index points					Rank 2004	Rank 2011
	2004	2010	2011	Average annual change 2004–2011	Change 2011/2010		
Sweden	14.76	30.58	30.02	2.18	-0.56	48	38
Israel	20.37	33.20	28.49	1.16	-4.71	35	39
Australia	26.58	28.11	28.34	0.25	0.23	26	40
Jamaica	21.32	33.09	28.16	0.98	-4.93	33	41
Colombia	18.61	26.13	27.25	1.23	1.12	39	42
Poland	7.28	26.18	26.54	2.75	0.36	92	43
Denmark	11.56	26.76	26.41	2.12	-0.35	64	44
Indonesia	25.88	25.60	25.91	0.00	0.31	27	45
Bahamas	17.49	25.71	25.18	1.10	-0.53	42	46
Uruguay	16.44	24.46	24.38	1.13	-0.08	43	47
Dominican Republic	12.45	22.25	22.87	1.49	0.62	59	48
Chile	15.48	22.05	22.76	1.04	0.71	44	49
Ecuador	11.84	18.73	22.48	1.52	3.75	63	50
Slovenia	13.91	20.61	21.93	1.15	1.32	51	51
Croatia	8.58	8.97	21.75	1.88	12.78	85	52
Romania	12.02	15.48	21.37	1.34	5.89	61	53
Ukraine	11.18	21.06	21.35	1.45	0.29	65	54
Peru	14.79	21.79	21.18	0.91	-0.61	47	55
Portugal	17.54	38.06	21.08	0.51	-16.98	41	56
Djibouti	6.76	19.55	21.02	2.04	1.47	98	57
Guatemala	12.28	13.33	20.88	1.23	7.55	60	58
Russian Federation	11.90	20.88	20.64	1.25	-0.24	62	59
Venezuela (Bolivarian Republic of)	18.22	18.61	19.97	0.25	1.36	40	60
Nigeria	12.83	18.28	19.85	1.00	1.57	56	61
Philippines	15.45	15.19	18.56	0.44	3.37	45	62
New Zealand	20.88	18.38	18.50	-0.34	0.12	34	63
Ghana	12.48	17.28	18.01	0.79	0.73	58	64
Trinidad and Tobago	13.18	15.76	17.89	0.67	2.13	53	65
Côte d'Ivoire	14.39	17.48	17.38	0.43	-0.10	50	66
Cyprus	14.39	16.20	17.12	0.39	0.92	49	67
Syrian Arab Republic	8.54	15.17	16.77	1.18	1.60	86	68
Jordan	11.00	17.79	16.65	0.81	-1.14	66	69
Mauritius	13.13	16.68	15.37	0.32	-1.31	54	70
Togo	10.19	14.24	14.08	0.56	-0.16	71	71
Benin	10.13	11.51	12.69	0.37	1.18	73	72
Senegal	10.15	12.98	12.27	0.30	-0.71	72	73
El Salvador	6.30	9.64	12.02	0.82	2.38	101	74

Annex VI. UNCTAD Liner Shipping Connectivity Index, as at 1 January 2011 (continued)

Country or territory	Index points					Rank 2004	Rank 2011
	2004	2010	2011	Average annual change 2004–2011	Change 2011/2010		
Namibia	6.28	14.45	12.02	0.82	-2.43	102	75
Kenya	8.59	13.09	12.00	0.49	-1.09	84	76
Yemen	19.21	12.49	11.89	-1.05	-0.60	38	77
United Republic of Tanzania	8.10	10.61	11.49	0.48	0.88	90	78
Cameroon	10.46	11.34	11.40	0.13	0.06	69	79
Finland	9.45	8.36	11.27	0.26	2.92	77	80
Angola	9.67	10.71	11.27	0.23	0.56	76	81
Congo	8.29	10.45	10.78	0.36	0.33	87	82
Puerto Rico	14.82	10.65	10.70	-0.59	0.05	46	83
Costa Rica	12.59	12.77	10.69	-0.27	-2.08	57	84
Mozambique	6.64	8.16	10.12	0.50	1.96	99	85
Lithuania	5.22	9.55	9.77	0.65	0.22	115	86
Bahrain	5.39	7.83	9.77	0.63	1.94	111	86
Honduras	9.11	9.09	9.42	0.04	0.33	80	88
Sudan	6.95	10.05	9.33	0.34	-0.72	95	89
Fiji	8.26	9.44	9.23	0.14	-0.21	88	90
New Caledonia	9.83	9.37	9.17	-0.09	-0.20	75	91
Papua New Guinea	6.97	6.38	8.83	0.27	2.45	94	92
Guam	10.50	8.78	8.76	-0.25	-0.02	68	93
French Polynesia	10.46	8.88	8.59	-0.27	-0.29	70	94
Nicaragua	4.75	8.68	8.41	0.52	-0.27	122	95
Bangladesh	5.20	7.55	8.15	0.42	0.60	116	96
Netherlands Antilles	8.16	7.97	8.14	-0.00	0.17	89	97
Gabon	8.78	8.55	7.97	-0.12	-0.58	81	98
Madagascar	6.90	7.38	7.72	0.12	0.34	96	99
Norway	9.23	7.93	7.32	-0.27	-0.61	79	100
Comoros	6.07	5.74	7.14	0.15	1.40	105	101
Libya	5.25	5.38	6.59	0.19	1.21	114	102
Cuba	6.78	6.57	6.55	-0.03	-0.02	97	103
Seychelles	4.88	5.16	6.45	0.22	1.29	120	104
Tunisia	8.76	6.46	6.33	-0.35	-0.13	83	105
Guinea	6.13	6.28	6.21	0.01	-0.07	104	106
Aruba	7.37	5.34	6.21	-0.17	0.87	91	107
Liberia	5.29	5.95	6.17	0.13	0.22	113	108
Ireland	8.78	8.53	5.94	-0.41	-2.59	82	109
Solomon Islands	3.62	5.57	5.87	0.32	0.30	133	110

Country or territory	Index points					Rank 2004	Rank 2011
	2004	2010	2011	Average annual change 2004–2011	Change 2011/2010		
Barbados	5.47	4.20	5.85	0.05	1.65	109	111
Estonia	7.05	5.73	5.84	-0.17	0.11	93	112
Mauritania	5.36	5.61	5.62	0.04	0.01	112	113
Kuwait	5.87	8.31	5.60	-0.04	-2.71	106	114
Latvia	6.37	5.98	5.51	-0.12	-0.47	100	115
Sierra Leone	5.84	5.80	5.41	-0.06	-0.39	107	116
Bulgaria	6.17	5.46	5.37	-0.11	-0.09	103	117
Cambodia	3.89	4.52	5.36	0.21	0.84	130	118
Gambia	4.91	5.38	5.24	0.05	-0.14	119	119
Haiti	4.91	7.58	4.75	-0.02	-2.83	118	120
Brunei Darussalam	3.91	5.12	4.68	0.11	-0.44	129	121
Iceland	4.72	4.70	4.68	-0.01	-0.02	123	121
American Samoa	5.17	4.85	4.56	-0.09	-0.29	117	123
Samoa	5.44	5.18	4.56	-0.13	-0.62	110	123
Albania	0.40	4.34	4.54	0.59	0.20	162	125
Cape Verde	1.90	3.69	4.24	0.33	0.55	153	126
Faroe Islands	4.22	4.21	4.20	-0.00	-0.00	125	127
Somalia	3.09	4.20	4.20	0.16	0.00	140	128
Iraq	1.40	4.19	4.19	0.40	-0.00	157	129
Suriname	4.77	4.12	4.16	-0.09	0.04	121	130
Saint Lucia	3.70	3.77	4.08	0.05	0.31	132	131
Guinea-Bissau	2.12	3.50	4.07	0.28	0.57	152	132
Montenegro	2.92	4.48	4.04	0.16	-0.44	143	133
Cayman Islands	1.90	2.51	4.03	0.30	1.52	154	134
Eritrea	3.36	0.02	4.02	0.09	4.00	138	135
Guyana	4.54	3.95	3.96	-0.08	0.01	124	136
Saint Vincent and the Grenadines	3.56	3.72	3.95	0.06	0.23	134	137
Grenada	2.30	3.71	3.93	0.23	0.22	149	138
Belize	2.19	3.95	3.85	0.24	-0.10	150	139
Georgia	3.46	4.02	3.79	0.05	-0.23	137	140
Democratic Republic of the Congo	3.05	5.24	3.73	0.10	-1.51	142	141
Tonga	3.81	3.73	3.72	-0.01	-0.01	131	142
Vanuatu	3.92	3.75	3.70	-0.03	-0.05	128	143
Equatorial Guinea	4.04	4.37	3.68	-0.05	-0.69	127	144
Northern Mariana Islands	2.17	3.43	w3.65	0.21	0.22	151	145
Palau	1.04	3.43	3.62	0.37	0.20	158	146
Micronesia (Federated States of)	2.80	3.43	3.62	0.12	0.19	144	147

Annex VI. UNCTAD Liner Shipping Connectivity Index, as at 1 January 2011 *(conluded)*

Country or territory	Index points					Rank 2004	Rank 2011
	2004	2010	2011	Average annual change 2004–2011	Change 2011/2010		
Qatar	2.64	7.67	3.60	0.14	-4.07	145	148
United States Virgin Islands	1.77	3.32	3.39	0.23	0.07	155	149
Myanmar	3.12	3.68	3.22	0.01	-0.46	139	150
Kiribati	3.06	2.86	3.11	0.01	0.25	141	151
Marshall Islands	3.49	2.83	3.08	-0.06	0.25	136	152
Saint Kitts and Nevis	5.49	2.84	2.66	-0.40	-0.18	108	153
Antigua and Barbuda	2.33	2.40	2.40	0.01	-0.00	146	154
Greenland	2.32	2.27	2.30	-0.00	0.03	148	155
Sao Tome and Principe	0.91	3.33	2.13	0.17	-1.20	159	156
Dominica	2.33	1.88	2.08	-0.04	0.20	147	157
Switzerland	3.53	2.58	1.85	-0.24	-0.73	135	158
Maldives	4.15	1.65	1.62	-0.36	-0.03	126	159
Bermuda	1.54	1.57	1.57	0.00	-0.00	156	160
Czech Republic	0.44	0.44	0.44	-0.00	-0.00	161	161
Paraguay	0.53	0.00	0.00	-0.08	0.00	160	162

Source: UNCTAD, based on data provided by Containerisation International Online, www.ci-online.co.uk.

Note: The Liner Shipping Connectivity Index is generated from five components: (a) the number of ships; (b) the total container-carrying capacity of those ships; (c) the maximum vessel size; (d) the number of services; and (e) the number of companies that deploy container ships on services to and from a country's ports. The data are derived from Containerisation International Online. The index is generated as follows: For each of the five components, a country's value is divided by the maximum value of that component in 2004, and for each country, the average of the five components is calculated. This average is then divided by the maximum average for 2004 and multiplied by 100. In this way, the index generates the value 100 for the country with the highest average index of the five components in 2004.

Annex VII. Countries' market share in selected maritime businesses, per cent of world total

COUNTRY OR TERRITORY	Countries' market share, with displayed numbers as percentages of the world total									
	2011 Population	2009 Port traffic, TEU	2009 Trade value, $	2009 GDP, $	2010 Ship building, GT	2010 Ship regitration, dwt	2010 Container ship operation, TEU	2010 Ship scrapping, dwt	2010 Officers, headcount	2010 Ratings, headcount
Albania	0.04	0.00	0.04	0.02	0.00	0.01	0.00	0.01	0.07	0.10
Algeria	0.51	0.05	0.31	0.24	0.00	0.06	0.01	0.00	0.27	0.24
Angola	0.19	0.00	0.12	0.05	0.00	0.00	0.00	0.00	0.02	0.10
Antigua and Barbuda	0.00	0.01	0.01	0.00	0.00	1.03	0.00	0.00	0.00	0.00
Argentina	0.60	0.35	0.31	0.54	0.00	0.08	0.06	0.02	0.18	0.49
Australia	0.31	1.19	1.31	1.65	0.02	0.17	0.21	0.00	0.76	0.51
Austria	0.12	0.07	1.13	0.65	0.00	0.00	0.00	0.00	0.00	0.00
Azerbaijan	0.12	0.00	0.05	0.07	0.00	0.05	0.00	0.00	0.11	0.04
Bahamas	0.00	0.29	0.02	0.01	0.00	5.05	0.00	0.00	0.02	0.00
Bahrain	0.02	0.06	0.08	0.04	0.00	0.05	0.00	0.00	0.00	0.00
Bangladesh	2.29	0.25	0.17	0.15	0.01	0.08	0.06	23.88	0.89	0.62
Barbados	0.00	0.00	0.01	0.01	0.00	0.09	0.00	0.00	0.00	0.00
Belgium	0.15	2.09	2.78	0.81	0.00	0.52	0.95	0.04	0.08	0.01
Belize	0.00	0.01	0.01	0.00	0.00	0.11	0.00	0.00	0.00	0.00
Bermuda	0.00	0.00	0.01	0.01	0.00	0.80	0.07	0.00	0.00	0.00
Bolivia (Plurinational State of)	0.15	0.00	0.03	0.03	0.00	0.01	0.00	0.00	0.06	0.06
Brazil	2.94	1.35	1.06	2.63	0.05	0.27	0.47	0.00	0.72	0.88
Brunei Darussalam	0.01	0.00	0.02	0.02	0.00	0.04	0.00	0.00	0.00	0.00
Bulgaria	0.10	0.04	0.18	0.08	0.05	0.05	0.00	0.00	1.75	3.23
Cambodia	0.21	0.05	0.04	0.02	0.00	0.20	0.00	0.00	1.29	1.73
Cameroon	0.28	0.05	0.03	0.04	0.00	0.00	0.00	0.00	0.02	0.02
Canada	0.49	0.90	2.62	2.30	0.00	0.27	0.04	0.00	2.24	0.45
Cape Verde	0.01	0.00	0.01	0.00	0.00	0.00	0.00	0.00	0.01	0.11
Cayman Islands	0.00	0.01	0.01	0.00	0.00	0.31	0.00	0.00	0.00	0.00
Chile	0.24	0.60	0.33	0.28	0.01	0.09	3.12	0.02	1.18	1.12
China	19.29	23.49	7.98	8.07	37.78	3.55	7.92	20.15	8.25	13.04
China, Hong Kong SAR	0.10	4.52	2.76	0.36	0.00	5.86	4.59	0.00	0.28	0.18
China, Macao SAR	0.01	0.00	0.04	0.04	0.00	0.00	0.00	0.00	0.00	0.00
China, Taiwan Province of	0.33	2.45	1.39	0.63	0.60	0.31	7.73	0.00	0.69	0.63
Colombia	0.65	0.44	0.26	0.39	0.00	0.01	0.00	0.00	0.10	0.41
Comoros	0.01	0.00	0.00	0.00	0.00	0.10	0.00	0.00	0.48	0.66
Cook Islands	0.00	0.00	0.00	0.00	0.00	0.00	0.00	0.00	0.10	0.12
Costa Rica	0.07	0.19	0.09	0.05	0.00	0.00	0.00	0.00	0.01	0.01
Côte d'Ivoire	0.31	0.15	0.06	0.04	0.00	0.00	0.00	0.00	0.00	0.00
Croatia	0.06	0.03	0.17	0.11	0.40	0.18	0.00	0.00	1.88	1.00
Cuba	0.16	0.06	0.08	0.00	0.00	0.00	0.00	0.00	0.36	0.45
Cyprus	0.02	0.08	0.06	0.04	0.00	2.46	0.16	0.00	0.47	0.07
Czech Republic	0.15	0.00	0.83	0.34	0.00	0.00	0.00	0.00	0.00	0.00
Democratic People's Republic of Korea	0.35	0.00	0.02	0.00	0.00	0.10	0.00	0.00	0.18	0.37

Annex VII. Countries' market share in selected maritime businesses, per cent of world total *(continued)*

COUNTRY OR TERRITORY	Countries' market share, with displayed numbers as percentages of the world total									
	2011 Population	2009 Port traffic, TEU	2009 Trade value, $	2009 GDP, $	2010 Ship building, GT	2010 Ship regitration, dwt	2010 Container ship operation, TEU	2010 Ship scrapping, dwt	2010 Officers, headcount	2010 Ratings, headcount
Democratic Republic of the Congo	1.04	0.00	0.03	0.00	0.00	0.00	0.00	0.00	0.00	0.01
Denmark	0.08	0.14	0.66	0.53	0.45	1.09	13.12	0.06	0.44	0.17
Djibouti	0.01	0.11	0.00	0.00	0.00	0.00	0.00	0.00	0.00	0.00
Dominica	0.00	0.00	0.00	0.00	0.00	0.13	0.00	0.00	0.00	0.00
Ecuador	0.22	0.22	0.12	0.09	0.00	0.03	0.00	0.00	0.15	0.77
Egypt	1.18	1.34	0.36	0.32	0.00	0.12	0.03	0.00	0.64	1.30
Equatorial Guinea	0.01	0.00	0.04	0.02	0.00	0.00	0.00	0.00	0.02	0.03
Eritrea	0.09	0.00	0.00	0.00	0.00	0.00	0.00	0.00	0.01	0.01
Estonia	0.02	0.03	0.08	0.03	0.00	0.01	0.01	0.03	0.43	0.91
Ethiopia	1.31	0.00	0.06	0.05	0.00	0.01	0.04	0.00	0.02	0.04
Faroe Islands	0.00	0.00	0.01	0.00	0.00	0.00	0.00	0.00	0.25	0.03
Falkland Islands (Malvinas)	0.00	0.00	0.00	0.00	0.00	0.00	0.00	0.00	0.00	0.00
Fiji	0.01	0.00	0.01	0.01	0.00	0.00	0.02	0.00	0.10	0.03
Finland	0.08	0.24	0.48	0.41	0.23	0.09	0.17	0.00	0.48	0.17
France	0.94	0.94	4.37	4.59	0.27	0.69	8.26	0.00	0.75	1.35
French Polynesia	0.00	0.01	0.01	0.00	0.00	0.00	0.00	0.00	0.04	0.05
Gabon	0.02	0.00	0.02	0.02	0.00	0.00	0.00	0.00	0.05	0.08
Gambia	0.03	0.00	0.00	0.00	0.00	0.00	0.00	0.00	0.01	0.02
Georgia	0.07	0.04	0.03	0.02	0.00	0.07	0.00	0.00	0.22	0.60
Germany	1.18	2.86	7.37	5.73	0.97	1.38	7.11	0.00	0.64	0.90
Ghana	0.36	0.12	0.06	0.03	0.00	0.01	0.00	0.00	0.30	1.01
Gibraltar	0.00	0.00	0.01	0.00	0.00	0.00	0.00	0.00	0.00	0.00
Greece	0.16	0.14	0.47	0.58	0.00	5.32	0.00	0.01	1.60	0.43
Greenland	0.00	0.00	0.01	0.00	0.00	0.00	0.01	0.00	0.00	0.00
Grenada	0.00	0.00	0.00	0.00	0.00	0.00	0.00	0.00	0.02	0.02
Guatemala	0.20	0.20	0.09	0.06	0.00	0.00	0.00	0.00	0.00	0.00
Guinea	0.15	0.00	0.01	0.00	0.00	0.00	0.00	0.00	0.01	0.01
Guinea-Bissau	0.02	0.00	0.00	0.00	0.00	0.00	0.00	0.00	0.01	0.02
Guyana	0.01	0.00	0.01	0.00	0.00	0.00	0.00	0.00	0.14	0.15
Haiti	0.14	0.00	0.02	0.01	0.00	0.00	0.00	0.00	0.01	0.01
Honduras	0.12	0.12	0.05	0.03	0.00	0.06	0.01	0.00	0.68	2.22
Hungary	0.14	0.00	0.62	0.22	0.00	0.00	0.00	0.00	0.13	0.18
Iceland	0.00	0.05	0.03	0.02	0.00	0.01	0.05	0.00	0.04	0.04
India	17.16	1.70	1.98	2.11	0.11	1.18	0.32	32.43	7.45	2.34
Indonesia	3.55	1.42	0.74	0.93	0.19	0.82	0.30	0.00	2.55	8.93
Iran (Islamic Republic of)	1.12	0.48	0.45	0.58	0.03	0.10	0.63	0.00	0.42	0.90
Iraq	0.44	0.00	0.27	0.03	0.00	0.01	0.00	0.00	0.05	0.05
Ireland	0.07	0.19	0.49	0.40	0.00	0.02	0.02	0.00	0.24	0.23
Israel	0.11	0.44	0.39	0.33	0.01	0.04	1.95	0.00	0.09	0.18
Italy	0.88	1.99	3.25	3.63	0.66	1.36	0.56	0.00	1.53	1.64

Annex VII. Countries' market share in selected maritime businesses, per cent of world total (continued)

COUNTRY OR TERRITORY	Countries' market share, with displayed numbers as percentages of the world total									
	2011 Population	2009 Port traffic, TEU	2009 Trade value, $	2009 GDP, $	2010 Ship building, GT	2010 Ship regitration, dwt	2010 Container ship operation, TEU	2010 Ship scrapping, dwt	2010 Officers, headcount	2010 Ratings, headcount
Jamaica	0.04	0.36	0.04	0.02	0.00	0.03	0.00	0.00	0.04	0.05
Japan	1.83	3.46	4.37	8.74	20.97	1.39	7.53	0.05	3.41	1.06
Jordan	0.09	0.15	0.12	0.04	0.00	0.03	0.00	0.00	0.06	0.02
Kazakhstan	0.22	0.00	0.23	0.18	0.00	0.01	0.00	0.00	0.00	0.00
Kenya	0.59	0.13	0.08	0.05	0.00	0.00	0.00	0.00	0.00	0.30
Kiribati	0.00	0.00	0.00	0.00	0.00	0.07	0.00	0.00	0.00	0.28
Kuwait	0.04	0.00	0.14	0.19	0.00	0.30	1.24	0.00	0.01	0.00
Latvia	0.03	0.04	0.08	0.04	0.00	0.01	0.00	0.00	0.88	0.34
Lebanon	0.06	0.21	0.13	0.06	0.00	0.01	0.00	0.00	0.04	0.11
Liberia	0.05	0.00	0.00	0.00	0.00	11.19	0.00	0.00	0.00	0.06
Libya	0.10	0.03	0.19	0.11	0.00	0.11	0.00	0.00	0.08	0.09
Lithuania	0.05	0.05	0.14	0.06	0.03	0.03	0.02	0.00	0.47	0.36
Luxembourg	0.01	0.00	0.19	0.08	0.00	0.09	0.00	0.00	0.36	0.31
Madagascar	0.32	0.03	0.03	0.01	0.00	0.00	0.00	0.00	0.03	0.15
Malaysia	0.41	3.33	0.98	0.33	0.09	0.80	0.60	0.00	1.01	4.14
Maldives	0.01	0.00	0.01	0.00	0.00	0.01	0.02	0.00	0.04	0.31
Malta	0.01	0.50	0.03	0.01	0.00	4.42	0.01	0.00	0.00	0.00
Marshall Islands	0.00	0.00	0.00	0.00	0.00	6.13	0.00	0.00	0.00	0.01
Mauritania	0.05	0.00	0.01	0.00	0.00	0.00	0.00	0.00	0.01	0.01
Mauritius	0.02	0.09	0.03	0.02	0.00	0.01	0.05	0.00	0.02	0.10
Mexico	1.64	0.62	1.95	1.49	0.00	0.14	0.00	0.00	0.05	0.05
Micronesia (Federated States of)	0.00	0.00	0.00	0.00	0.00	0.00	0.00	0.00	0.04	0.06
Mongolia	0.05	0.00	0.02	0.01	0.00	0.09	0.00	0.00	0.20	0.26
Montenegro	0.01	0.00	0.01	0.01	0.00	0.00	0.00	0.00	0.03	0.04
Morocco	0.46	0.00	0.26	0.15	0.00	0.03	0.04	0.00	0.14	0.46
Mozambique	0.33	0.02	0.03	0.02	0.00	0.00	0.00	0.00	0.02	0.02
Myanmar	0.00	0.00	0.03	0.05	0.00	0.02	0.02	0.00	1.75	2.91
Namibia	0.03	0.04	0.04	0.02	0.00	0.01	0.00	0.00	0.01	0.01
Netherlands	0.24	2.17	3.52	1.36	0.14	0.57	0.92	0.01	0.48	0.08
Netherlands Antilles	0.00	0.02	0.02	0.01	0.00	0.14	0.00	0.00	0.00	0.00
New Caledonia	0.00	0.02	0.02	0.00	0.00	0.00	0.00	0.00	0.01	0.01
New Zealand	0.06	0.39	0.20	0.20	0.00	0.03	0.12	0.00	0.10	0.13
Nicaragua	0.08	0.01	0.03	0.01	0.00	0.00	0.00	0.00	0.00	0.00
Nigeria	2.24	0.00	0.27	0.31	0.00	0.08	0.00	0.00	0.09	0.11
Norway	0.07	0.05	0.54	0.66	0.02	1.64	0.09	0.00	2.58	1.05
Oman	0.04	0.82	0.14	0.08	0.00	0.00	0.00	0.00	0.04	0.06
Pakistan	2.70	0.41	0.25	0.34	0.00	0.04	0.01	17.81	0.46	1.35
Panama	0.05	0.99	0.06	0.04	0.00	22.73	0.06	0.03	0.91	0.97
Papua New Guinea	0.09	0.06	0.03	0.01	0.00	0.01	0.00	0.00	0.07	0.08

Annex VII. Countries' market share in selected maritime businesses, per cent of world total *(continued)*

COUNTRY OR TERRITORY	Countries' market share, with displayed numbers as percentages of the world total									
	2011 Population	2009 Port traffic, TEU	2009 Trade value, $	2009 GDP, $	2010 Ship building, GT	2010 Ship regitration, dwt	2010 Container ship operation, TEU	2010 Ship scrapping, dwt	2010 Officers, headcount	2010 Ratings, headcount
Paraguay	0.09	0.00	0.06	0.02	0.00	0.00	0.00	0.00	0.08	0.09
Peru	0.42	0.28	0.17	0.22	0.00	0.03	0.00	0.00	0.20	0.12
Philippines	1.47	0.91	0.36	0.28	1.20	0.55	0.03	0.01	9.24	3.39
Poland	0.55	0.15	1.16	0.74	0.17	0.01	0.18	0.00	2.87	0.69
Portugal	0.16	0.31	0.55	0.39	0.01	0.10	0.13	0.01	0.07	0.26
Qatar	0.01	0.00	0.18	0.16	0.00	0.11	0.05	0.00	0.00	0.00
Republic of Korea	0.70	3.40	2.56	1.43	32.87	1.64	6.29	0.00	1.58	0.42
Republic of Moldova	0.06	0.00	0.03	0.01	0.00	0.04	0.00	0.00	0.15	0.20
Romania	0.32	0.13	0.43	0.28	0.64	0.02	0.00	0.06	2.98	0.83
Russian Federation	2.00	0.54	1.68	2.13	0.19	0.57	0.26	0.00	4.01	5.78
Saint Kitts and Nevis	0.00	0.00	0.00	0.00	0.00	0.10	0.00	0.00	0.27	0.35
Saint Vincent and the Grenadines	0.00	0.00	0.00	0.00	0.00	0.58	0.00	0.00	0.00	0.00
Samoa	0.00	0.00	0.00	0.00	0.00	0.00	0.00	0.00	0.02	0.03
Sao Tome and Principe	0.00	0.00	0.00	0.00	0.00	0.00	0.00	0.00	0.04	0.05
Saudi Arabia	0.38	0.95	0.69	0.62	0.01	0.18	0.07	0.00	0.00	0.00
Senegal	0.18	0.07	0.04	0.02	0.00	0.00	0.00	0.00	0.03	0.04
Serbia	0.11	0.00	0.13	0.08	0.01	0.00	0.00	0.00	0.00	0.00
Seychelles	0.00	0.00	0.01	0.00	0.00	0.02	0.00	0.00	0.01	0.05
Sierra Leone	0.08	0.00	0.00	0.00	0.00	0.06	0.00	0.00	0.00	0.00
Singapore	0.07	5.73	1.95	0.29	0.12	4.85	7.75	0.00	1.21	0.17
Slovakia	0.08	0.01	0.44	0.15	0.03	0.02	0.00	0.00	0.04	0.05
Slovenia	0.03	0.07	0.21	0.08	0.00	0.00	0.00	0.00	0.09	0.01
Solomon Islands	0.01	0.00	0.00	0.00	0.00	0.00	0.00	0.00	0.05	0.06
Somalia	0.14	0.00	0.01	0.00	0.00	0.00	0.00	0.00	0.01	0.01
South Africa	0.71	0.76	0.59	0.49	0.00	0.01	0.06	0.00	0.29	0.18
Spain	0.67	2.80	2.27	2.52	0.30	0.20	0.11	0.02	0.51	0.56
Sri Lanka	0.31	0.75	0.08	0.07	0.01	0.02	0.00	0.00	0.37	2.82
Sudan	0.65	0.09	0.07	0.11	0.00	0.00	0.00	0.00	0.01	0.01
Suriname	0.01	0.00	0.01	0.00	0.00	0.00	0.00	0.00	0.02	0.02
Sweden	0.13	0.27	0.94	0.69	0.01	0.17	0.11	0.00	0.95	0.72
Switzerland	0.11	0.02	1.23	0.84	0.00	0.08	12.29	0.00	0.00	0.00
Syrian Arab Republic	0.33	0.13	0.12	0.09	0.00	0.03	0.00	0.00	0.09	0.11
Thailand	0.96	1.29	1.07	0.47	0.01	0.29	0.45	0.00	0.98	0.72
Timor-Leste	0.02	0.00	0.00	0.00	0.00	0.00	0.00	0.00	0.00	0.01
Togo	0.10	0.00	0.01	0.00	0.00	0.02	0.00	0.00	0.06	0.07
Tonga	0.00	0.00	0.00	0.00	0.00	0.01	0.00	0.00	0.01	0.02
Trinidad and Tobago	0.02	0.12	0.06	0.03	0.00	0.00	0.00	0.00	0.02	0.02
Tunisia	0.15	0.05	0.15	0.07	0.00	0.01	0.01	0.00	0.08	0.16
Turkey	1.14	0.97	1.12	1.08	0.38	0.62	0.35	3.78	5.89	7.37

Annex VII. Countries' market share in selected maritime businesses, per cent of world total *(concluded)*

COUNTRY OR TERRITORY	Countries' market share, with displayed numbers as percentages of the world total									
	2011 Population	2009 Port traffic, TEU	2009 Trade value, $	2009 GDP, $	2010 Ship building, GT	2010 Ship regitration, dwt	2010 Container ship operation, TEU	2010 Ship scrapping, dwt	2010 Officers, headcount	2010 Ratings, headcount
Turkmenistan	0.07	0.00	0.03	0.00	0.00	0.00	0.00	0.00	0.00	0.00
Turks and Caicos Islands	0.00	0.00	0.00	0.00	0.00	0.00	0.00	0.00	0.01	0.01
Tuvalu	0.00	0.00	0.00	0.00	0.00	0.15	0.00	0.00	0.01	0.09
Uganda	0.50	0.00	0.03	0.00	0.00	0.00	0.00	0.00	0.00	0.00
Ukraine	0.65	0.11	0.36	0.20	0.07	0.07	0.00	0.02	4.35	1.59
United Arab Emirates	0.07	3.11	1.30	0.43	0.03	0.11	0.48	0.00	0.00	0.00
United Kingdom	0.90	1.71	3.81	3.74	0.00	2.90	0.28	0.00	2.43	1.30
United Republic of Tanzania	0.62	0.07	0.05	0.04	0.00	0.01	0.00	0.00	0.04	0.05
United States	4.52	7.93	12.75	23.69	0.25	1.01	2.24	0.76	3.49	2.40
Uruguay	0.05	0.13	0.05	0.06	0.00	0.01	0.00	0.00	0.01	0.14
Vanuatu	0.00	0.00	0.00	0.00	0.00	0.21	0.01	0.00	0.04	0.08
Venezuela Bolivarian Republic of)	0.40	0.27	0.31	0.58	0.00	0.12	0.00	0.00	0.24	0.49
Viet Nam	1.31	0.98	0.53	0.16	0.58	0.43	0.09	0.00	1.72	1.65
Yemen	0.35	0.14	0.06	0.05	0.00	0.00	0.00	0.00	0.02	0.02
Others	5.12	0.24	1.05	2.43	0.00	0.00	0.00	0.76	0.00	0.00
Others	5.12	0.24	1.05	2.43	0.00	0.00	0.31	0.00	0.00	0.76

Source: UNCTAD.

QUESTIONNAIRE

Review of Maritime Transport 2011

In order to improve the quality and relevance of the Review of Maritime Transport, the UNCTAD secretariat would greatly appreciate your views on this publication. Please complete the following questionnaire and return it to:

Readership Survey
Division on Technology and Logistics
UNCTAD
Palais des Nations, Room E.7041
CH-1211 Geneva 10, Switzerland
Fax: +41 22 917 0050
E-mail: transport.section@unctad.org

Thank you very much for your kind cooperation.

1. What is your assessment of this publication?

	Excellent	Good	Adequate	Poor
Presentation and readability	❏	❏	❏	❏
Comprehensiveness of coverage	❏	❏	❏	❏
Quality of analysis	❏	❏	❏	❏
Overall quality	❏	❏	❏	❏

2. What do you consider the strong points of this publication?

_____

_____

3. What do you consider the weak points of this publication?

_____

_____

4. For what main purposes do you use this publication?

Analysis and research	❏	Education and training	❏
Policy formulation and management	❏	Other(specify)	❏

_____

_____

5. How many people do you share/disseminate the *Review of Maritime Transport* with?

Less than 10 ❏   Between 10 and 20 ❏   More than 20 ❏

6. Which of the following best describes your area of work?

Government	❑	Public enterprise	❑
Non-governmental organization	❑	Academic or research	❑
International organization	❑	Media	❑
Private enterprise institution	❑	Other (specify)	❑

_____

_____

7. Personal information

Name (optional): _____

E-mail: (optional): _____

Country of residence: _____

8. Do you have any further comments?

_____

_____

_____

_____

***

HOW TO OBTAIN THIS PUBLICATION

Sales publications may be purchased from distributors of United Nations publications throughout the world. They may also be obtained by writing to:

UN Publications Sales and Marketing Office
300 E 42nd Street, 9th Floor, IN-919J
New York, NY, 10017 USA

Tel: +1-212-963-8302
Fax: +1-212-963-3489
Email:publications@un.org

https://unp.un.org/